THE BATTLE OF PETERSBURG

KRAUS REPRINT CO.
Millwood, N.Y.
1977

Extracted from:
U.S. Congress. Joint Committee on the Conduct of the
War. Report of the Joint Committee on the Conduct of
the War. 1863-1866.

ISBN 0-527-17558-7
LC 76-42075

KRAUS REPRINT CO.
A U.S. Division of Kraus-Thomson Organization Limited
Printed in U.S.A.

INTRODUCTION

In the summer of 1861 the cry heard in Washington was, "On to Richmond." The citizens of the north, as well as the Congress itself, believed that a single decisive battle would end the new-born Confederacy once and for all.

On July 21, President Lincoln, under pressure from Congress and his War Department, allowed General McDowell to advance against General Beauregard's forces at Manasas Junction—about thirty miles south of the capital—in the hope of claiming "one decisive battle." Under the horrified watch of spectators who had driven out to enjoy a picnic lunch and watch their boys "whip the rebels," a fierce and bloody battle ensued along a little creek called Bull Run. The resulting fight appeared at first to be a Union victory, but the tide quickly turned. Inexperienced federal troops first retreated and then panicked into a desperate race for the safety of Washington, leaving thousands of their dead and wounded behind.

Within three months federal troops again faced a Confederate force, this time on Harrison's Island—a day's march northwest of Washington—and again met bloody defeat in the Battle of Ball's Bluff. Killed during the battle was a United States Senator from Oregon, Colonel Edward E. Baker.

Congress, now under intense pressure to investigate the military disasters, attempted to develop a uniform war policy. On December 5, 1861, Senator Zachariah Chandler, a leader of western radicalism, presented a motion to create a joint Senate and House committee to determine the causes of the Union defeats at Bull Run and Ball's Bluff.

The Joint Committee on the Conduct of the War, under the chairmanship of Senator Benjamen F. Wade, held hearings and meetings from December 20, 1861, through the final days of the conflict some four years later. Although political infighting, personal prejudices, and regional differences often prevented a common understanding of military strategy, the detailed testimony and reports from the military officers and personnel directly involved with the day-to-day conduct of the war provide a unique picture of the Union's action during each critical phase of the conflict.

This monograph, extracted unedited and unabridged from the eight-volume *Report of the Joint Committee on the Conduct of the War, 1863-1866*, published by the U.S. Congress, makes available the individual reports, testimony, individual communiques, maps, and accompanying correspondence that resulted from the Committee's work. This unique monograph provides scholars and Civil War buffs with an opportunity to study and evaluate one individual segment of the Civil War.

Benedict A. Leerburger
Kraus Reprint Company

February 1977

CONTENTS

BATTLE OF PETERSBURG.

	Page.
Report	i
Testimony of Burnside, Major General A. E	13
Duane, Brevet Colonel James C	99
Ferrero, Brevet Major General Edward	105
Grant, Lieutenant General U. S	109
Hunt, Major General H. J	97
Loring, Lieutenant Colonel Charles G	91
Meade, Major General George G	30
Ord, Major General E. O. C	101
Potter, Brevet Major General Robert B	84
Pleasants, Lieutenant Colonel Henry	112
Turner, Brigadier General J. W	118
Van Buren, Brevet Lieutenant Colonel J. L	95
Warren, Major General G. K	80
Wilcox, Brevet Major General O. B	77
Appendix	122

BATTLE OF PETERSBURG.

In the Senate of the United States,
December 15, 1864.

On motion by Mr. ANTHONY,
Resolved, That the Joint Committee on the Conduct of the War be directed to inquire into and report the facts concerning the attack on Petersburg, on the 30th day of July, 1864.
Attest: J. W. FORNEY, *Secretary.*

Mr. WADE submitted the following

REPORT.

The Committee on the Conduct of the War, in pursuance of the foregoing resolution, submit the following report, with accompanying testimony:

In the attack upon the enemy's lines before Petersburg, the 16th, 17th, and 18th of June, 1864, the ninth corps gained an advanced position beyond a deep cut in the railroad, within about one hundred and twenty-five yards of the enemy's lines. Just in rear of that advanced position was a deep hollow, where work could be carried on entirely out of sight of the enemy.

Within a few days after that position had been gained, Lieutenant Colonel Henry Pleasants, 48th Pennsylvania volunteers, made the suggestion to General Potter, commanding the division, that a mine could be run under one of the enemy's batteries, by means of which it could be blown up, and an opening made in the enemy's lines. The suggestion having been submitted to General Burnside, it was approved by him, and work was commenced upon the mine on the 25th of June.

It will be seen from the testimony of Lieutenant Colonel Pleasants that he labored under disadvantages in the successful accomplishment of this important work, which would have deterred a man of less energy and determination. It was not merely the evident lack of faith in the success of the enterprise shown by all the officers of high rank but his division and corps commanders, but that lack of faith was accompanied by an entire failure to furnish the assistance and implements necessary to the success of the undertaking within a reasonable time. And your committee take pleasure in commending the zeal, energy, and persistence displayed on that occasion by Lieutenant Colonel Pleasants and the men of the 48th Pennsylvania regiment, under his command. And the failure of the attack, resulting from causes with which Colonel Pleasants could have no connexion, should not be allowed to detract from the meed of praise due to that officer.

The testimony of Colonel Pleasants, on that point, is as follows :

"Question. Can you fix the time when you mentioned the matter to General Burnside, when you commenced the work, &c.?

"Answer. The work was commenced at 12 o'clock, noon, on the 25th of June, 1864. I saw General Burnside the night previous, and commenced the mine right off—the next day.

"Question. Did you have any communication with any other commanders on the subject?

"Answer. No, sir.

"Question. About how many men did you employ in the work?

"Answer. My regiment was only about four hundred strong. At first I employed but a few men at a time, but the number was increased as the work progressed, until at last I had to use the whole regiment, non-commissioned officers and all. The great difficulty I had was to dispose of the material got out of the mine. I found it impossible to get any assistance from anybody; I had to do all the work myself. I had to remove all the earth in old cracker boxes. I got pieces of hickory and nailed on the boxes in which we received our crackers, and then iron-cladded them with hoops of iron taken from old beef and pork barrels.

"Question. Why were you not able to get better instruments with which to construct so important a work?

"Answer. I do not know. Whenever I made application I could not get anything, although General Burnside was very favorable to it. The most important thing was to ascertain how far I had to mine, because if I fell short of or went beyond the proper place the explosion would have no practical effect. Therefore, I wanted an accurate instrument with which to make the necessary triangulations. I had to make them on the furthest front line, where the enemy's sharpshooters could reach me. I could not get the instrument I wanted, although there was one at army headquarters; and General Burnside had to send to Washington and get an old-fashioned theodolite, which was given to me.

"Question. Do you know any reason why you could not have had the better instrument which was at army headquarters?

"Answer. I do not. I know this: that General Burnside told me that General Meade and Major Duane, chief engineer of the army of the Potomac, said the thing could not be done; that it was all clap-trap and nonsense; that such a length of mine had never been excavated in military operations, and could not be; that I should either get the men smothered for want of air or crushed by the falling of the earth, or the enemy would find it out, and it would amount to nothing. I could get no boards and lumber supplied to me for my operations. I had to get a pass, and send two companies of my own regiment with wagons outside of our lines to rebel saw-mills and get lumber in that way, after having previously got what lumber I could by tearing down an old bridge. I had no mining picks furnished me, but had to take common picks and have them straightened for my mining picks.

"Question. Was General Burnside the only officer who seemed to favor the mine?

"Answer. The only officer of high rank, so far as I learned. General Burnside, the corps commander, and General Potter, the division commander, seemed to be the only high officers who believed in it.

"Question. How long from the time you commenced the mine did it take you to finish it?

"Answer. I finished the whole thing, lateral galleries and all, ready to put the powder in, on the 23d of July.

"Question. How long would it have taken you had you been supplied with the proper tools and instruments?

"Answer. I could have done it in one-third or one-fourth of the time. The greatest cause of the delay was taking the material out.

"Question. How far did you have to carry it?

"Answer. The whole length of the mine, and to where it could be deposited, and every night I had to get the pioneers of my regiment to cut bushes and cover it up where it had been deposited; otherwise the enemy could have climbed up the trees in their lines and seen the pile of newly excavated earth.

"Question. What was the length of the mine?

"Answer. The main gallery was $510\frac{8}{10}$ feet in length; the left lateral gallery was 37 feet in length, and the right lateral gallery was 38 feet. The magazines were to be placed in the lateral galleries.

"Question. What were the dimensions of the galleries?

"Answer. They varied at different places; I suppose the average was $4\frac{1}{2}$ by $4\frac{1}{2}$ feet."

On the 26th of July, at the request of General Meade, the following plan of attack was submitted to him by General Burnside:

"HEADQUARTERS 9TH ARMY CORPS,
"*July* 26, 1864.

"I have the honor to acknowledge the receipt of your notes this morning by Captains Jay and Bache; also of a telegram from the commanding general, relating to the same subject.

"It is altogether probable that the enemy are cognizant of the fact that we are mining, because it is mentioned in their papers, and they have been heard to work on what are supposed to be the shafts in close proximity to our galleries. But the rain of night before last has no doubt much retarded their work; we have heard no sounds of work in them, either yesterday or to-day; and nothing is heard by us in the mine but the ordinary sounds of work on the surface above. This morning we had some apprehension that the left lateral gallery was in danger of caving in from the weight of the batteries above it, and the shock of their firing. But all possible precautions have been taken to strengthen it, and we hope to preserve it intact.

"The placing of the charges in the mine will not involve the necessity of making a noise. It is therefore probable that we will escape discovery if the mine is to be used within two or three days. It is nevertheless highly important, in my opinion, that the mine should be exploded at the earliest possible moment consistent with the general interests of the campaign. I state to you the facts as nearly as I can, and, in the absence of any knowledge as to the meditated movements of the army, I must leave you to judge the proper time to make use of the mine. But it may not be improper for me to say that the advantages reaped from the work would be but small if it were exploded without any co-operative movement.

"My plan would be to explode the mine just before daylight in the morning, or at about five o'clock in the afternoon. Mass the two brigades of the colored division in rear of my first line, in columns of division—"double columns closed in mass," the head of each brigade resting on the front line; and as soon as the explosion has taken place, move them forward with instructions for the division to take half distance, as soon as the leading regiments of the two brigades pass through the gap in the enemy's line, the leading regiment of the right brigade to come into line perpendicular to the enemy's line by the right companies 'on the right into line wheel,' the left companies 'on the right into line,' and proceed at once down the line of the enemy's works as rapidly as possible; and the leading regiment of the left brigade to execute the reverse movement to the left, running up the enemy's line. The remainder of the columns to move directly towards the crest in front as rapidly as possible, diverging in such a way as to enable them to deploy into column of regiments, the right column making as nearly as possible for Cemetery hill. These columns to be followed by the other divisions of the corps, as soon as they can be thrown in.

"This would involve the necessity of relieving these divisions by other troops before the movement, and of holding columns of other troops in readiness to take our place on the crest, in case we gain it, and sweep down it. It would, in my opinion, be advisable, if we succeed in gaining the crest, to throw the colored division right into the town. There is a necessity for the co-operation, at least in the way of artillery, of the troops on our right and left. Of the extent of this you will necessarily be the judge. I think our chances of success in a plan of this kind are more than even.

"The main gallery of the mine is 522 feet in length; the side galleries about forty feet each. My suggestion is, that eight magazines be placed in the lateral galleries, two at each end, say a few feet apart, in branches at right angles to the side gallery, and two more in each of the side galleries, similarly placed by pairs, situated equidistant from each other and the end of the galleries; tamp, beginning at the termination of the main gallery, say one hundred feet, leaving all the air space in the side galleries. Run out some five or six fuzes and two wires, to render the ignition of the charges certain. I propose to put in each of the eight magazines from twelve to fourteen hundred pounds of powder; the magazines to be connected by a trough of powder instead of a fuze.

"I beg to enclose a copy of a statement from General Potter on the subject:

"I would suggest that the powder train be parked in a woods near our ammunition train, about a mile in rear of this place. Lieutenant Colonel Pierce, chief quartermaster, will furnish Captain Strang with a guide to the place. I beg also to request that General Benham be instructed to send us, at once, eight thousand sand-bags, to be used for tamping and other purposes.

"A. E. BURNSIDE, *Major General.*

"Major General HUMPHREYS,
"*Chief of Staff.*"

General Burnside testifies that, under his orders, the division of colored troops, under General Ferrero, had been drilling for some weeks with the view of making the attack in the manner set forth in the plan submitted to General Meade. His reasons for selecting that division for the advance, and which were stated to General Meade in an interview with him on the 28th of July, were, that, in his opinion, they were in a better condition to make a charge than either of the white divisions. The colored troops had not been in any very active service, had not been exposed much, were not broken down by hard work, and had, besides, been drilled for some weeks with special reference to this charge. The white divisions, on the contrary, had performed very arduous duties since the commencement of the campaign, and since they had occupied the position before Petersburg had been in such close proximity to the enemy, that no man could raise his head above the parapets without danger of being fired at. They had been in the habit, during the whole of that time, of approaching the main line by covered ways, and of using every possible means of covering themselves from the fire of the enemy. In the opinion of General Burnside, in which he was sustained by the opinion of his inspector general, the white divisions were not then in a condition to make a vigorous charge.

General Meade objected to the colored troops being placed in the advance. His testimony upon that subject is as follows:

"Prior to issuing the orders for the assault, General Burnside told me it was his intention to place his colored division in the advance of the assaulting column. I objected to his doing so, on the ground, not that I had any reason to believe that the colored troops would not do their duty as well as the white troops, but that, as they were a new division and had never been under fire, had never been tried, and as this was an operation which I knew beforehand was one requiring the very best troops, I thought it impolitic to trust it to a division of whose reliability we had no evidence. Therefore I thought that he ought to take one of his white divisions that he knew from long service could be relied upon. General Burnside objected. I told him, then, that in view of his wishes upon the subject I would report the matter to the lieutenant general, state to him my reasons, and those of General Burnside, and let him decide. If he should decide that General Burnside's arguments were sound and mine were wrong, then I would yield. The matter was referred to General Grant, and he confirmed my view that it would be impolitic in a critical operation of that kind to take troops that were untried and place them in the advance, and it was upon that ground that General Burnside's opinion was overruled."

General Grant's testimony upon this point is as follows:

"General Burnside wanted to put his colored division in front, and I believe if he had done so it would have been a success. Still I agreed with General Meade in his objection to that plan. General Meade said that if we put the colored troops in front, (we had only that one division,) and it should prove a failure, it would then be said, and very properly, that we were shoving those people ahead to get killed because we did not care anything about them. But that could not be said if we put white troops in front. That is the only point he (General Meade) changed after he had given his orders to General Burnside."

Instructions were accordingly given to General Burnside to select one of his divisions of white troops to lead the assault; and the order of assault was also changed in respect to the sweeping down the enemy's lines to the right and left of the crater by the leading regiments of the assaulting column. General Burnside testifies that he received the instructions to select a division of white troops to lead the assault, in the afternoon of the day preceding the morning for the assault. As there were reasons for assigning each one of the three white divisions to that duty, he determined to decide the question by lot, which was done. General Ledlie drew the lot to lead the advance, with his division.

The mine was charged, and preparations made to spring it on the morning of the 30th of July.

The following orders were issued by General Meade:

ORDERS.

"HEADQUARTERS ARMY OF THE POTOMAC,
"*July* 29, 1864.

"The following instructions are issued for the guidance of all concerned:

"1. As soon as it is dark, Major General Burnside, commanding 9th corps, will withdraw his two brigades under General White, occupying the intrenchments between the Plank and Norfolk roads, and bring them to his front. Care will be taken not to interfere with the troops of the 18th corps moving into their position in rear of the 9th corps. General Burnside will form his troops for assaulting the enemy's works at daylight on the 30th, prepare his parapets and abatis for the passage of the columns, and have the pioneers equipped for work in opening passages for artillery, destroying enemy's abatis, and the intrenching tools distributed for effecting lodgement, &c., &c.

"2. Major General Warren, commanding 5th corps, will reduce the number of his troops holding the intrenchments of his front to the minimum, and concentrate all his available force on his right and hold them prepared to support the assault of Major General Burnside. The preparations in respect to pioneers, intrenching tools, &c., &c., enjoined upon the 9th corps, will also be made by the 5th corps.

"3. As soon as it is dark, Major General Ord, commanding 18th corps, will relieve his troops in the trenches by General Mott's division of the 2d corps, and form his corps in rear of the 9th corps, and be prepared to support the assault of Major General Burnside.

"4. Every preparation will be made for moving forward the field artillery of each corps.

"5. At dark, Major General Hancock, commanding 2d corps, will move from Deep Bottom to the rear of the intrenchments now held by the 18th corps, resume the command of Mott's division, and be prepared at daylight to follow up the assaulting and supporting columns, or for such other operations as may be found necessary.

"6. Major General Sheridan, commanding cavalry corps, will proceed at dark from the vicinity of Deep Bottom to Lee's mill, and at daylight will move with his whole corps, including Wilson's division, against the enemy's troops defending Petersburg on their right by the roads leading to that town from the southward and westward.

"7. Major Duane, acting chief engineer, will have the pontoon trains parked at convenient points in the rear, prepared to move. He will see that supplies of sand-bags, gabions, facines, &c., &c., are in depot near the lines, ready for use.

"He will detail engineer officers for each corps.

"8. At half past three ($3\frac{1}{2}$) in the morning of the 30th Major General Burnside will spring his mine, and his assaulting columns will immediately move rapidly upon the breach, seize the crest in the rear and effect a lodgement there. He will be followed by Major General Ord, who will support him on the right, directing his movement to the crest indicated, and by Major General Warren, who will support him on the left.

"Upon the explosion of the mine the artillery of all kinds in battery will open upon those points of the enemy's works whose fire covers the ground over which our columns must move, care being taken to avoid impeding the progress of our troops. Special instructions respecting the direction of fire will be issued through the chief of artillery.

"9. Corps commanders will report to the commanding general when their preparations are complete, and will advise him of every step in the progress of the operation and of everything important that occurs.

"10. Promptitude, rapidity of execution, and cordial co-operation are essential to success, and the commanding general is confident that this indication of his expectations will insure the hearty efforts of the commanders and troops.

"11. Headquarters during the operations will be at the headquarters of the 9th corps.

"By command of Major General Meade.

"S. WILLIAMS, *Ass't Adj't General.*

General Grant had shortly previous executed a movement on the north side of the James river, and to some extent turned the enemy's attention in that direction.

On the morning of the 30th of July the match was applied to the mine at the time designated, but it failed to explode in consequence of the defective fuze employed. The fuze supplied had been in pieces, requiring that it should be spliced. It ceased to burn at one of the points of junction. The additional precaution had been taken to lay the fuze in a train of powder, but the powder had become damp from being so long laid, some thirty or more hours, and that also failed to ignite. After waiting some time Lieutenant Jacob Douty, first lieutenant company K, and Sergeant Henry Rees, now second lieutenant company F, 48th Pennsylvania regiment, volunteered and went in the mine, ascertained the cause of the failure to explode, and relighted the fuze. The mine exploded at 4.42 a. m.

None of the witnesses seemed to be of the opinion that the delay in the explosion of the mine had any effect upon the result of the operation. The enemy, so far as could be ascertained, did not discover any of the preparations made for a movement. No opinion was expressed as to the effect upon our troops by their being obliged to wait an hour under arms before they had an opportunity to move forward.

In the course of from five to ten minutes after the explosion of the mine the division of General Ledlie charged from our lines and entered the enemy's line at the breach made by the explosion. The explosion had made a crater from 150 to 200 feet in length, about 60 feet in width, and from 25 to 30 feet in depth, presenting a serious obstacle to the passage of troops. The organization of the division was broken, and the troops crowded into the crater and sought shelter there and for a short distance in the adjoining lines of the enemy.

The first division met with but little resistance from the enemy before they reached the mine. Soon, however, fire was opened upon them from a battery of the enemy upon the right, and one upon the left, and, before long, from a battery in their front upon Cemetery hill.

Another division was thrown in with about the same result as with the first, the troops immediately seeking shelter in the crater of the mine and the lines of the enemy adjacent thereto. The third division was thrown in with a similar result. From 150 to 200 yards of the enemy's lines on either side of the crater were occupied by our troops in that manner. By that time the enemy had recovered from the confusion into which it had been thrown by the explosion of the mine, and a heavy fire of artillery and musketry was opened upon our troops from the right, left, and front.

Several efforts were made to reorganize our troops and charge the crest of Cemetery hill, but none of them were successful.

The fourth (colored) division was also ordered to advance, and did so under a heavy fire. They succeeded in passing the white troops, already in, but in a disorganized condition. They reformed to some extent and attempted to charge the hill in front, but without success, and broke in disorder to the rear. This was about 8.45 a. m., about four hours after the explosion of the mine.

At 9.45 a. m. General Burnside received a peremptory order from General Meade to withdraw his troops. General Burnside testifies that, "Upon the reception of the order to withdraw our troops from the enemy's lines, I went to General Meade's headquarters and requested that that order might be rescinded, stating that I did not think we had fought long enough on that day, and that I thought we could succeed in carrying the crest if we persevered in the attack. He said that the order to withdraw was final, and that he had ordered all offensive operations on the right and left to cease."

General Meade testifies, "He (General Burnside) was directed about ten or eleven o'clock to withdraw. The first order sent to him was a distinct order to withdraw. General Burnside came to the position where I was with General Grant, at the headquarters on the field, and stated that, in his judgment, it would be injudicious to withdraw at that moment—that it would cause great sacrifice of life. I immediately authorized him, in writing, to exercise his judgment in the withdrawal—to remain there as long as he deemed it necessary for the secure withdrawal of his command—stating that he could remain there, if he chose, until night."

The troops were withdrawn between one and two o'clock in considerable confusion, caused by an assault of the enemy, and returned to the lines they had occupied in the morning.

The details of the charge and of the several movements of the different bodies of troops are given in the testimony. The loss sustained by our troops was between four and five thousand in killed, wounded, and missing. No troops took part in the assault except those of the 9th corps and a brigade of the 18th corps. The only part taken in the operation by the 2d corps, on the right, and the 5th corps, on the left, was to employ their artillery, which had the effect of silencing the most of the enemy's batteries, but not all.

Your committee cannot, from all the testimony, avoid the conclusion that the first and great cause of disaster was the change made on the afternoon preceding the attack, in the arrangement of General Burnside to place the division of colored troops in the advance. The reasons assigned by General Burnside for not taking one of his divisions of white troops for that purpose are fully justified by the result of the attack. Their previous arduous labors, and peculiar position, exposed continually to the enemy's fire, had, as it were, trained them in the habit of seeking shelter; and, true to that training, they sought shelter the first opportunity that presented itself after leaving our lines. And it is but reasonable to suppose that the immediate commander of a corps is better acquainted with the condition and efficiency of particular divisions of his corps than a general further removed from them.

The conduct of the colored troops, when they were put into action, would seem to fully justify the confidence that General Burnside reposed in them. And General Grant himself, in his testimony, expresses his belief that if they had been placed in the advance, as General Burnside desired, the assault would have been successful, although at the time the colored troops were ordered in the white troops already in were in confusion and had failed in the assault upon the crest beyond the crater, and the fire of the enemy had become exceedingly destructive. The colored troops advanced in good order, passed through the enemy's lines and beyond our disorganized troops there, and, stopping but a short time to reform, made the charge as directed. But the fire of the enemy was too strong, and some other of our troops hurrying back through their lines, they were thrown into confusion and forced to retire.

The same reasons which, in the opinion of your committee, can be urged in favor of the selection for the advance which General Burnside made in his first plan, viz., his opportunity, from more intimate connexion with the troops of his corps, judging correctly which division was best fitted for that purpose, can also be urged against the mode of selection resorted to by him when compelled by the order of his commanding general to select another division to lead the assault. It may have been that, from the same causes, each of the three divisions of white troops had become, from the training of the previous forty days, unfitted for that duty. But the practice of leaving the selection of troops for an important undertaking to be determined by chance is one that does not commend itself to the judgment of your committee. It, however, is but just to General Burnside that the reasons which led him to resort to that mode of selection should be stated. His testimony is as follows:

"These three commanders (Generals Potter, Wilcox, and Ledlie) of the white divisions were then informed of the change in the plan, and also that one of their divisions must lead the assault. Considerable conversation occurred as to the condition of the different divisions. I said to them, 'There is a reason why either General Wilcox's or General Potter's division should lead the assault, and that is, that they are nearer to the point of assault, and it would require less time to get them into position for the work. But there is also a reason why General Ledlie's division should lead, which is, that his men have not been in such close proximity to the enemy as those of the other two divisions, and in fact have not had to do quite as hard work for the last thirty or forty days.' Each of the division commanders, as well as every officer in the command, who had given his attention to the subject in the least degree, was fully aware of the condition of the white troops, as I had previously stated it to General Meade, and was firmly impressed with the conviction that the colored troops were in much better condition to lead the attack, and of the wisdom of using the white troops as supports. There was no time to be lost, however, as the hour for springing the mine had been fixed for half past three o'clock the next morning, and it was now after noon. I finally decided that I would allow the leading division to be designated by lot, which was done. General Ledlie drew the lot to lead the advance, and the necessary orders were given for the movement of his division to the point from which the attack was to be made."

The order of attack as proposed by General Burnside was also changed by direction of General Meade, with the approval of General Grant. Instead of moving down to the right and left of the crater of the mine for the purpose of driving the enemy from their lines in those directions, and thus removing to that extent the danger of flank attacks by the enemy upon our advancing columns, General Meade directed that the troops should push at once for the crest of Cemetery hill. General Burnside also contemplated co-operative movements by troops on the right and left of his corps. Orders were given to General Warren to make a movement from his position if he deemed it advisable, but he reported that the enemy were in too strong force, and no movement was made. On the right, occupied by a portion of General Hancock's force, the same condition of things existed, and also a smaller force of our troops than were on the left. The enemy not being driven from their lines on either side of the mine, except for a short distance in consequence of the explosion of the mine, and the efforts of our troops to obtain shelter from the fire of the enemy, they organized attacking columns which finally succeeded in driving our forces from the position they had gained.

It will be seen from the testimony that when the order to withdraw was given by General Meade, against the representations made by General Burnside, orders were also given by General Meade for offensive operations to cease on the right and left of General Burnside's position, and General Ord's troops were at the same time withdrawn from the position where they had been placed in support of the 9th corps. The enemy were thus left entirely free to make such dispositions as they chose against the force of General Burnside within their lines. General Burnside's testimony upon this point is as follows:

"Upon the reception of the order to withdraw our troops from the enemy's lines, I went to General Meade's headquarters and requested that the order might be rescinded, stating that I did not think we had fought long enough, and that I thought we could succeed in carrying the crest if we persevered in the attack, and the other troops were put in. He said that the order to withdraw was final, and that he had ordered all offensive operations on the right and left to cease. This order, I consider, materially affected the result of our withdrawal, inasmuch as the enemy's forces upon our right and left were entirely unoccupied, and thereby had an opportunity of concentrating upon us during the withdrawal. It could hardly have been expected that the withdrawal could have been made without disaster after all offensive operations had ceased on the right and left, and the supporting force withdrawn from the rear. My only hope was that the force in the crater would be able to hold the position until a covered way could be dug from our advanced line out to the crater, a distance of a little over a hundred yards. This covered way had been commenced both in the crater and on our advanced line, and I instructed General Ferrero to push it forward as rapidly as possible, with such of his troops as had been driven back and collected in the advanced line. The communication between the advanced line and the crater was almost entirely cut off; and although the distance was so short, only about a hundred yards, it was next to an impossibility for messengers to reach the crater, much less to send in ammunition and water. The men had become very much exhausted with the heat and labors of the day.

"After I was informed by General Meade that the order was final to withdraw, and that there was no object in holding the crater by connecting its flanks with our old advanced lines, as I had suggested, I telegraphed to General White, my chief of staff, whom I had left at my field headquarters, that the orders to withdraw were peremptory; and I at once sent for the division commanders in order to consult as to the most favorable method and time for withdrawal. In the mean time my despatch to General White had been sent to the division commanders, and by them sent in to the crater for report from the brigade commanders. Previous to and during this time the enemy made several assaults upon our position, which were repulsed. Soon after this a heavy attack was made upon the left of our forces, driving us back, and causing a hasty evacuation of the crater by all who could get back to the main line."

It will also be seen from the testimony that General Meade claims that his orders in relation to levelling the parapets and removing the abatis of our line, so as to afford a sufficient *debouche* for our assaulting forces, were not carried out so fully as they should have been. General Burnside claims that those orders were carried out as fully as he could do so, without affording the enemy an opportunity to discover, prematurely, the movement in which he was engaged. As it appears, beyond all question, that more troops passed from our lines into those of the enemy than, under the circumstances, could be profitably managed or employed there, your committee do not regard that matter as having any important bearing upon the subject of their inquiry.

Your committee would also call attention to the fact that General Grant attributes the disastrous result of that assault, to a greater or less extent, to the troops being sent in unaccompanied by any of the division commanders. How far the division commanders would have been able, by their presence, to overcome the confusion and disorganization into which the troops were thrown, from the causes heretofore referred to, your committee are unable to say. None of the witnesses examined previous to General Grant made any reference to that fact. It was first brought to the notice of the committee near the close of their investigation, when they were unable to direct their attention to that particular point. They refer to it here, however, as the opinion of the highest officer in our service, and also because they deem everything relating to this most disastrous affair worthy of consideration.

Your committee desire to say that, in the statement of facts and conclusions which they present in their report, they wish to be distinctly understood as in no degree censuring the conduct of the troops engaged in this assault. While they confidently believe that the selection of the division of colored troops by General Burnside to lead the assault was, under the circumstances, the best that could have been made, they do not intend thereby to have it inferred that the white troops of the 9th corps are behind any troops in the service in those qualities which have placed our volunteer troops before the world as equal, if not superior, to any known to modern warfare. The services performed by the 9th corps on many a well-fought battle-field, not only in this campaign but in others, have been such as to prove that they are second to none in the service. Your committee believe that any other troops exposed to the same influences, under the same circumstances, and for the same length of time, would have been similarly affected. No one, upon a careful consideration of all the circumstances, can be surprised that those influences should have produced the effects they did upon them.

In conclusion they, your committee, must say that, in their opinion, the cause of the disastrous result of the assault of the 30th of July last is mainly attributable to the fact that the plans and suggestions of the general who had devoted his attention for so long a time to the subject, who had carried out to a successful completion the project of mining the enemy's works, and who had carefully selected and drilled his troops for the purpose of securing whatever advantages might be attainable from the explosion of the mine, should have been so entirely disregarded by a general who had evinced no faith in the successful prosecution of that work, had aided it by no countenance or open approval, and had assumed the entire direction and control only when it was completed, and the time had come for reaping any advantages that might be derived from it.

Respectfully submitted:

B. F. WADE, *Chairman.*

TESTIMONY.

WASHINGTON, *December* 17, 1864.

Major General A. E. BURNSIDE sworn and examined.

By the chairman:

Question. What is your rank and position in the army at the present time?
Answer. I am a major general of volunteers. At present I am waiting orders.

Question. Were you in the army of the Potomac on 30th of July, 1864, at the time a mine was sprung before Petersburg?
Answer. Yes, sir; I was in command of the 9th army corps, which made the assault on that occasion.

Question. Will you please give us, in your own way, a statement of such facts in connexion with that attack as you may consider important?
Answer. In the attack upon the enemy's lines, on the 16th, 17th, and 18th of June, the 9th corps gained an advanced position beyond a deep cut in the railroad, which was but a little more than a hundred yards from the enemy's lines. Just in rear of this advanced position was a deep hollow where work could be carried on, entirely out of the sight of the enemy. On the 26th of June I received a letter from General Potter, stating that he was of the opinion that a mine could be run from this hollow to a point under a battery of the enemy immediately opposite our position. I understood from him that the suggestion was first made by some of the non-commissioned officers and privates of the 48th Pennsylvania regiment, which was composed almost entirely of miners from Schuylkill county, Pennsylvania. It was then communicated by the commanding officer of the regiment, Lieutenant Colonel Pleasants, to General Potter.

I wrote to General Potter, requesting him to come to my headquarters with Colonel Pleasants, or to reduce his plan to writing. That evening he and Colonel Pleasants came to my headquarters, and the matter was fully talked over. I authorized them to commence the work, and stated that I would report what had passed between us to the commanding general of the army of the Potomac, and would inform them of the result; that no harm could occur from beginning the work, as it could be suspended if it should not be approved. I did communicate the substance of this conversation to the commanding general of the army of the Potomac, and received from him his assent, rather than his approval of the work. Other conversations were had, from time to time, with General Meade on the subject.

On the 3d day of July General Meade sent me a letter requesting an opinion as to the probability of success of an attack upon the enemy from our front. That letter, and the correspondence resulting from it, are as follows:

"HEADQUARTERS ARMY OF THE POTOMAC,
"12 m., *July* 3, 1864.

"The lieutenant general commanding has inquired of me whether an assult on the enemy's works is practicable and feasible at any part of the line held by this army. In order to enable me to reply to this inquiry, I desire, at your earliest convenience, your views as to the practicability of an assault at any point in your front, to be made by the 2d and 6th corps in conjunction with yours.

"Respectfully,

"GEO. G. MEADE,
"*Major General.*

"Major General BURNSIDE."

"HEADQUARTERS NINTH ARMY CORPS,
"July 3, 1864.

"I have delayed answering your despatch until I could get the opinion of my division commanders, and have another reconnoissance of the lines made by one of my staff. If my opinion is required as to whether now is the best time to make an assault, it being understood that if not made the siege is to continue, I should unhesitatingly say, wait until the mine is finished.

"If the question is between making the assault now and a change of plan looking to operations in other quarters, I should unhesitatingly say, assault now. If the assault be delayed until the completion of the mine, I think we should have a more than even chance of success. If the assault be made now, I think we have a fair chance of success, provided my corps can make the attack, and it is left to me to say when and how the other two corps shall come in to my support.

"I have the honor to be, general, very respectfully, your obedient servant,

"A. E. BURNSIDE,
"Major General, Commanding 9th Corps.

"Major General MEADE,
"Commanding Army of the Potomac."

It would seem that the language I employed in my letter was unfortunate, for it was entirely misunderstood, as will appear from the reply of General Meade, of the same date as follows:

"HEADQUARTERS ARMY OF THE POTOMAC,
"July 3, 1864.

"GENERAL: Your note by Major Lydig has been received. As you are of the opinion there is a reasonable degree of probability of success from an assault on your front, I shall so report to the lieutenant general commanding, and await his instructions.

"The recent operations in your front, as you are aware, though sanctioned by me, did not originate in any orders from these headquarters. Should it, however, be determined to employ the army under my command in offensive operations on your front, I shall exercise the prerogative of my position to control and direct the same, receiving gladly at all times suggestions as you may think proper to make. I consider these remarks necessary in consequence of certain conditions which you have thought proper to attach to your opinion, acceding to which in advance would not, in my judgment, be consistent with my position as commanding general of this army. I have accordingly directed Major Duane, chief engineer, and Brigadier General Hunt, chief of artillery, to make an examination of your lines, and to confer with you as to the operations to be carried on, the running of the mine now in progress, and the posting of artillery. It is advisable as many guns as possible, bearing on the point to be assaulted, should be placed in position.

"I agree with you in opinion that the assault should be deferred till the mine is completed, provided that can be done within a reasonably short period—say a week. Roads should be opened to the rear to facilitate the movements of the other corps sent to take part in the action, and all the preliminary arrangements possible should be made. Upon the reports of my engineer and artillery officers the necessary orders will be given.

"Respectfully, yours,

"GEO. G. MEADE,
"Major General, Commanding.

"Major General BURNSIDE,
"Commanding 9th Corps."

The next day I replied as follows:

"HEADQUARTERS 9TH ARMY CORPS, July 4, 1864.

"GENERAL: I have the honor to acknowledge the receipt of your letter of last evening, and am very sorry that I should have been so unfortunate in expressing myself in my letter. It was written in haste, just after receiving the necessary data upon which to strengthen an opinion already pretty well formed. I assure you, in all candor, that I never dreamed of implying any lack of confidence in your ability to do all that is necessary in any grand movement which may be undertaken by your army. Were you to personally direct an attack from my front I would feel the utmost confidence; and were I called upon to support an attack from the front of the 2d or 6th corps, directed by yourself, or by either of the commanders of those corps, I would do it with confidence and cheerfulness.

"It is hardly necessary for me to say that I have had the utmost faith in your ability to handle troops ever since my acquaintance with you in the army of the Potomac, and certainly accord to you a much higher position in the art of war than I possess; and I at the same time entertain the greatest respect for the skill of the two gentlemen commanding the 2d and 6th corps; so that my duty to my country, to you, and to myself, forbids that I should for a moment assume to embarrass you, or them, by an assumption of position or authority.

I simply desired to ask the privilege of calling upon them for support at such times, and at such points, as I thought advisable. I would gladly accord to either of them the same support, and would be glad to have either of them lead the attack; but it would have been obviously improper for me to have suggested that any other corps than my own should make the attack in my front. What I asked, in reference to calling upon the other corps for support, is only what I have been called upon to do, and have cheerfully done myself, in regard to other corps commanders.

"If a copy of my letter has been forwarded to the general-in-chief, which I take for granted has been done, that he may possess my full opinion, it may make the same impression upon him as upon yourself, and I beg that you will correct it; in fact, I beg that such impression may be, as far as possible, removed wherever it has made a lodgement. My desire is to support you, and in doing that I am serving the country.

"With ordinary good fortune we can pretty safely promise to finish the mine in a week; I hope in less time.

"I have the honor to be, general, very respectfully, your obedient servant,
"A. E. BURNSIDE,
"*Major General, Commanding 9th Army Corps.*

"Major General MEADE,
"*Commanding Army of the Potomac.*"

To which General Meade replied as follows:

"HEADQUARTERS ARMY OF THE POTOMAC, *July* 4, 1864.

"GENERAL: Your letter of this date is received. I am glad to find that there was no intention on your part to ask for any more authority and command than you have a perfect right to expect under existing circumstances. I did not infer from your letter that you had any want of confidence in me. I rather thought you were anticipating interference from others, and thought it best to reply as I did.

"Your letter has not been shown to any one, nor forwarded to the general-in-chief, and my answer has only been seen by the confidential clerk who copied it. I am very grateful to you for your good opinion, as expressed, and shall earnestly try to merit its continuance. In the trying position I am placed in, hardly to be appreciated by any one not in my place, it is my great desire to be on terms of harmony and good feeling with all, superiors and subordinates; and I try to adjust the little jars that will always exist in large bodies to the satisfaction of each one. I have no doubt, by frankness and full explanations, such as have now taken place between us, all misapprehensions will be removed. You may rest assured, all the respect due to your rank and position will be paid you while under my command.

"Truly yours,
"GEORGE G. MEADE, *Major General.*"

This correspondence is presented for the purpose of showing the views of General Meade in reference to putting into action the support on the flanks and in the rear, and also to show that I had no authority whatever to order in any of the supports.

Nothing of importance occurred in reference to the contemplated attack for several days after this correspondence took place. I had frequent conversations with General Meade in reference to the condition of the command, its position on the line, &c.

The 4th division of the 9th corps, under command of General Ferrero, composed entirely of colored troops, had been detached, at the beginning of the campaign, from my immediate command, and had received orders directly from General Grant's and General Meade's headquarters, up to the crossing of the James river.

During the month of July it was at intervals under my command, and I had made up my mind, in case an assault was to be made by the 9th corps, to put this division in the advance. I had so informed General Ferrero, and, at my suggestion, he submitted to me an opinion as to the formation which would be the most effective in passing over the ground in our front; which formation, after some consideration, I approved, and directed him to drill his troops with a view of making the attack in that way.

This first conversation must have been some three weeks before the attack was made, on the 30th of July.

The work on the mine was prosecuted with as much rapidity as possible, but it took a longer time to complete it than was at first supposed. Many obstacles were encountered, all of which, however, were finally overcome. There was, besides these natural obstacles, a considerable degree of personal discouragement during the prosecution of the work. Prominent officers expressed their fears that a mine of that length could not be successfully run, and particularly by the plan which Colonel Pleasants had adopted, that of simply relying upon the tenacity of the earth to keep the gallery intact, instead of putting up continuous supports along its whole length. His plan, however, succeeded, and the mine was finished not far from the 20th of July. I have not the means in my possession at this time of determining the exact date of its completion.

When completed, the fact was reported to General Meade, after which considerable discussion took place in reference to the charge that was necessary to explode the mine. In my opinion it should have been a charge of 12,000 pounds of powder, and I so expressed myself. It was finally decided that the charge should be 8,000 pounds. I do not mention this as anything material, but it happens to be a fact.

The enemy's works were blown up with the 8,000 pounds, but the declivity of the crater would not have been so great had it been done with 12,000.

On the 26th of July, I think, General Meade called upon me, through his chief of staff, for a detailed statement of my plan of attack from my front. I sent him the following communication :

"HEADQUARTERS 9TH ARMY CORPS, *July* 26, 1864.

"I have the honor to acknowledge the receipt of your notes of this morning by Captains Jay and Bache; also a telegram from the commanding general, relating to the same subject.

"It is altogether probable that the enemy are cognizant of the fact that we are mining, because it is mentioned in their papers, and they have been heard at work on what are supposed to be shafts in close proximity to our galleries.

"But the rain of night before last has no doubt much retarded their work. We have heard no sound of workmen in them either yesterday or to-day, and nothing is heard by us in the mine but the ordinary sounds of work on the surface above. This morning we had some apprehension that the left lateral gallery was in danger of caving in from the weight of the batteries above it, and the shock of their firing. But all possible precautions have been taken to strengthen it, and we hope to preserve it intact.

"The placing of the charges in the mine will not involve the necessity of making a noise. It is therefore probable that we will escape discovery if the mine is to be used within two or three days. It is nevertheless highly important, in my opinion, that the mine should be exploded at the earliest possible moment consistent with the general interests of the campaign. I state to you the facts as nearly as I can, and, in the absence of any knowledge as to the meditated movements of the army, I must leave you to judge of the proper time to make use of the mine. But it may not be improper for me to say that the advantages reaped from the work would be but small if it were exploded without any co-operative movement.

"My plan would be to explode the mine just before daylight in the morning, or at about five o'clock in the afternoon; mass the two brigades of the colored division in rear of my first line in columns of division 'double columns closed in mass,' 'the head of each brigade resting on the front line,' and, as soon as the explosion has taken place, move them forward with instructions for the division to take half distance, and as soon as the leading regiments of the two brigades pass through the gap in the enemy's line, the leading regiment of the right brigade to come into line perpendicular to the enemy's line by the 'right companies on the right into line, wheel,' the 'left companies on the right into line,' and proceed at once down the line of the enemy's works as rapidly as possible; and the leading regiment of the left brigade to execute the reverse movement to the left, moving up the enemy's line. The remainder of the columns to move directly towards the crest in front as rapidly as possible, diverging in such a way as to enable them to deploy into columns of regiment, the right column making as nearly as possible for Cemetery hill. These columns to be followed by the other divisions of the other corps as soon as they can be thrown in.

"This would involve the necessity of relieving these divisions by other troops before the movement, and of holding columns of other troops in readiness to take our place on the crest in case we gain it, and sweep down it. It would, in my opinion, be advisable, if we succeed in gaining the crest, to throw the colored division right into the town. There is a necessity for the co-operation, at least in the way of artillery, by the troops on our right and left. Of the extent of this you will necessarily be the judge. I think our chances of success in a plan of this kind are more than even.

"The main gallery of the mine is 522 feet in length; the side galleries about forty feet each. My suggestion is that eight magazines be placed in the lateral galleries, two at each end, say a few feet apart in branches at right angles to the side gallery, and two more in each of the side galleries, similarly placed by pairs situated equidistant from each other and the end of the galleries, thus:

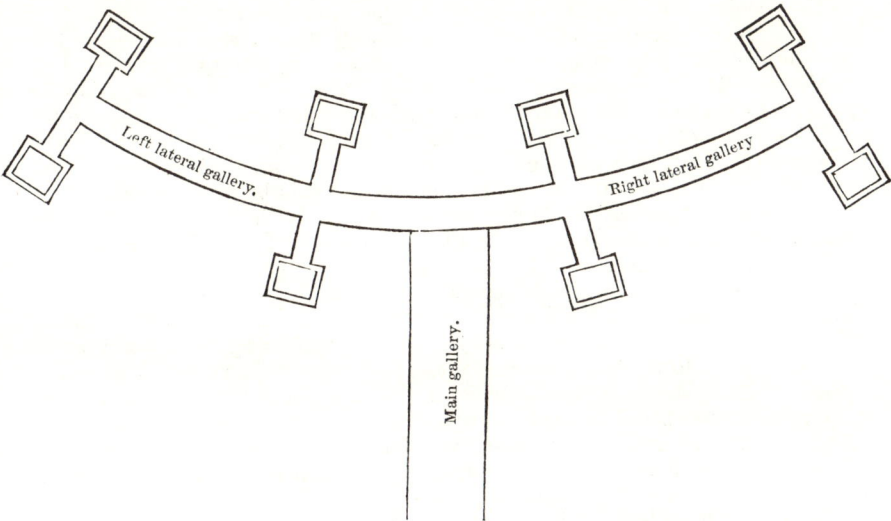

tamp, beginning at the termination of the main gallery, say one hundred feet, leaving all the air space in the side galleries. Run out some five or six fuzes and two wires, to render the ignition of the charge certain.

"I propose to put in each of the eight magazines from 1,200 to 1,400 pounds of powder the magazines to be connected by a trough of powder, instead of a fuze.

"I beg to enclose a copy of a statement from General Potter on the subject.

"I would suggest that the powder train be parked in a woods near our ammunition train, about a mile in rear of this place. Lieutenant Colonel Pierce, chief quartermaster, will furnish Captain Strang with a guide to the place. I beg also to request that General Benham be instructed to send us at once eight thousand sand-bags, to be used for tamping and other purposes.

"A. E. BURNSIDE, *Major General.*

"Major General HUMPHREYS, *Chief of Staff.*"

On Thursday, the 28th, when I called upon General Meade, at his headquarters, he informed me that that portion of my plan which contemplated putting the colored troops in the advance did not meet with his approval; and also, that he did not approve of the formation proposed, because he was satisfied that we would not be able, in the face of the enemy, to make the movements which I contemplated, to the right and left; and that he was of the opinion that the troops should move directly to the crest without attempting these side movements.

A long conversation ensued, in which I pointed out to General Meade the condition of the three white divisions, and urged upon him the importance, in my opinion, of placing the colored division in the advance, because I thought it would make a better charge at that time than either of the white divisions. I reminded him of the fact that the three white divisions had for forty days been in the trenches in the immediate presence of the enemy, and at no point of the line could a man raise his head above the parapet without being fired at by the enemy. That they had been in the habit, during the whole of that time, of approaching the main line by covered ways, and using every possible means of protecting themselves from the fire of the enemy. That their losses had been continuous during that time, amounting to from thirty to sixty men daily. That the men had had no opportunity of cooking upon the main line—everything having been cooked in the rear, and carried up to them. That they had had very few, if any, opportunities of washing; and that, in my opinion, they were not in condition to make a vigorous charge. I also stated that I was fortified in this opinion, which had been formed from personal observation, by the report of my inspector general, who had taken occasion to look at the troops with a view to making up his mind as to their effectiveness for a work of that kind.

General Meade still insisted that the black troops should not lead; that he could not trust them, because they were untried, and probably gave other reasons which do not occur to me at this moment. But he said that, inasmuch as I was so urgent in the matter, he would refer it to General Grant, whom he expected to visit that afternoon, and his decision of course would be final. I said to him that I would cheerfully abide by any decision that either one of them would make, but I must still urge upon him that I thought it of the utmost importance that the colored troops should lead.

General Meade did go to see General Grant that day, and I think returned the same afternoon, but I did not hear from him. During the next forenoon, Friday, General Wilcox and General Potter, commanding two of my white divisions, came to my headquarters to talk over the attack, which it was understood would be made the next morning. I told them I had been very much exercised the day before lest that portion of my plan which contemplated putting the colored division in advance should be changed by General Meade, but that I was pretty well satisfied he had given it up, because I had heard nothing further from him about it.

While in the midst of this conversation, or very soon after, General Meade came to my headquarters, and there told me that General Grant agreed with him as to the disposition of the troops, and that I would not be allowed to put the colored division in the advance. I asked him if that decision could not be reconsidered; he replied, "No, general, the order is final; you must detail one of your white divisions to take the advance." I said, "Very well, general, I will carry out this plan to the best of my ability."

I at once sent for my other division commander, General Ledlie. These three commanders of the white divisions were then informed of the changes in the plan, and also that one of their divisions must lead the assault. Considerable conversation occurred as to the condition of the different divisions; I said to them, "There is a reason why either General Wilcox's or General Potter's division should lead the assault, and that is, that they are nearer to the point of assault, and it would require less time to get them into position for the work. But there is also a reason why General Ledlie's division should lead, which is, that his men have not been in such close proximity to the enemy as those of the other two divisions, and in fact have not had to do quite as hard work for the last thirty or forty days." Each of the division commanders, as well as every officer in the command, who had given his attention to the subject in the least degree, was fully aware of the condition of the white troops, as I had previously stated it to General Meade, and were firmly impressed with the conviction that the colored troops were in much better condition to lead the attack, and of the wisdom of using the white troops as supports. There was no time to be lost, however, as the hour for springing the mine had been fixed for half past three o'clock the next morning, and it was now afternoon. I finally decided that I would allow the leading division to be designated by lot, which was done; General Ledlie drew the lot to lead the advance, and the necessary orders were given for the movement of his division to the point from which the attack was to be made.

General Ferrero, who commanded the colored division, had, with his officers, already examined the ground upon which he was to form, and had made a reconnoissance of the ground over which he was to pass at the time he expected to lead the attack. I sent General Ledlie with his brigade officers to make similar reconnoissances, which they did. At about four o'clock in the afternoon they reported to me that the examination had been made, and they only waited for darkness, and troops to relieve them, in order to get the division in position for the attack.

General Meade issued his battle order, a copy of which I have not with me, but which can no doubt be obtained very easily by the committee, either from the headquarters of the army of the Potomac or from the Adjutant General's office.

General Ord was to send troops to relieve my troops from their position on the line, in order that we might make the concentration for the assault. Much delay occurred that night in making these changes, in consequence of the difficulty of moving large bodies of troops at night, and from the fact that the officers of General Ord's command were not acquainted with the positions of our different divisions, although they had by personal reconnoissances informed themselves as well as possible, with the short notice they had.

The mine was charged as was designated by the plan, except in amount of powder. The fuze material was not furnished in sufficient quantity to run three or four separate fuzes, as was contemplated by the plan. In fact, we had but material enough to run one line of fuze, and that material came to us in small pieces of from ten to fifteen feet in length, and had to be spliced before it was laid.

The troops were in position in time for the assault. I issued orders to govern the different division commanders in the attack, and also sent them copies of the battle order of General Meade. One of the directions in the order of General Meade was "to level the breastworks and to remove the abatis before the explosion, so the troops could pass quickly to the front." This part of the order was necessarily inoperative, because of lack of time and the close proximity to the enemy, the latter of which rendered it impossible to remove the abatis from the front of our line without attracting, not only a heavy fire of the enemy, but also his attention to that point, and letting him know exactly what we were doing. But as far as was possible that portion of the order was carried out. It was afterwards found that the abatis which had to be removed when our troops did advance did not delay them more than five minutes.

General Meade made his headquarters for the day at my permanent headquarters, and I moved mine to what is called the "fourteen-gun battery," now known as Fort Morton, on the crest, just in rear of our main line some forty or fifty yards. A telegraph was run to my new headquarters from my old headquarters, where General Meade was stationed.

Directions were given to fire the mine at the time designated by General Meade. There was considerable delay in the explosion, which caused great uneasiness to all of us. General Meade sent several despatches to me during this delay to know the cause of it. I could give him no information on the subject, was quite as anxious about the delay as he was, and sent staff officers to ascertain the cause of it. I am of the opinion that to some of the messages which General Meade sent me during that time no answers were returned, because no satisfactory answers could be given.

It will be readily understood that the cause of the delay was not easy to be ascertained, because the fuze had been lighted, and a man going into the gallery to ascertain whether or not it was still burning would, in case of explosion, necessarily lose his life.

However, a commissioned and a non-commissioned officer of the 48th Pennsylvania regiment volunteered to go into the gallery. They ascertained that the fuze had died out about a hundred feet from the mouth of the main gallery. This was a thing that would not have occurred had we had material enough to have laid four or five fuzes; and I do not think it would have occurred had the fuze been continuous, or in but two or three pieces, instead of being, as it was, in so many pieces. It died out at one of the points of contact, where two of the pieces had been spliced together, either by the failure to put in powder, or by the powder becoming damp, or for some other reason which I do not myself know.

The fuze was relighted by those men, and Colonel Pleasants, who was in charge of the mine, informed me that the explosion would take place in eleven minutes from the time the information was given to Major Van Buren, my aide-de-camp. I immediately directed the major to give the information to General Meade's aid, Captain Jay, but I suppose before it reached him (General Meade) the mine exploded.

The leading division moved forward, passed over our own lines, and passed into the crater which was made by the explosion of the mine.

I will here submit a copy of the report which I made to General Meade of the operations of the 30th of July, as it will probably give a more accurate statement of what occurred on that day than I can now give from memory. The report is as follows:

"HEADQUARTERS NINTH ARMY CORPS,
"*Before Petersburg, Va., August* 13, 1864.

"GENERAL: I have the honor to submit the following report of the operations of this corps in the engagement of July 30th last.

"It will be necessary to advert to the preliminary operation of running a mine under the enemy's works. This project was proposed by Lieutenant Colonel Henry Pleasants, of the 48th Pennsylvania volunteers, to General Potter, who submitted the proposal to me soon after our sitting down before that place. It met my hearty consent and support. It was commenced June 25th, (twenty-fifth,) prosecuted with great zeal through a difficult soil, sometimes of the nature of quicksand, at others a heavy marl, and with no tools but the ordinary intrenching spade and pick. The main gallery was finished July 17th, 522 feet in length. It was then found that the enemy were at work in immediate proximity, and its further prosecution was conducted with great caution. Lateral galleries 37–38 feet in length, running under and nearly parallel to the enemy's works, were completed July 23d, and the mine was ready for the charge. This, by order from the general commanding, was put in on the 27th. It consisted of about 8,000 pounds of powder. Great praise is due to Colonel Pleasants and the officers and men of his regiment for the patient labor cheerfully bestowed on a work which deserved and met complete success.

"On the 26th of July, at the request of the commanding general, I submitted a plan of assault, which contemplated the placing of the colored division of this corps in the advance, that division not being wearied by long and arduous duties in the trenches, as were the other divisions. A certain formation of troops was also suggested. This plan was not adopted as to these two points, and the troops were put in in accordance with the orders of the commanding general.

"I received orders from the general commanding to spring the mine at 3.30 a. m. The troops were in position at that hour, massed behind the portion of our line nearest the point to be reached. The fuze, however, failed to ignite at a point where it had been spliced, and delay occurred. It was reignited, and the mine sprung at 4.45 a. m. Immediately the leading brigade of the first division, (the 2d,) under Colonel Marshall, started for the charge. There was a delay of perhaps five minutes in removing the abatis. Clearing that, the brigade advanced rapidly to the fort that had been mined, now a crater of large proportions, and an obstacle of great formidableness. Mounting a crest of at least 12 feet above the level of the ground, our men found before them a huge aperture of 150 feet in length by 60 in width, and 25 to 30 in depth, the sides of loose pulverized sand piled up precipitately, from which projected huge blocks of clay. To cross such an obstacle and preserve regimental organization was a sheer impossibility. The lines of the enemy on either side were not single, but involuted and complex, filled with pits, traverses, and bomb-proofs, forming a labyrinth as difficult of passage as the crater itself.

"After the training of the previous six weeks, it is not to be wondered at that the men should have sought shelter in these defences. Their regimental organizations were broken, and the officers undertook to reform before advancing. One regiment, the 2d Pennsylvania heavy artillery, advanced some 100 yards beyond the crater, but, not supported, fell back.

"It is reported that the enemy on my left opposite the 5th corps, on the explosion of the mine, left their lines and ran to the rear. But few shots were fired from that direction on the head of my column.

"An infantry fire was opened at once from the enemy's line up to within two hundred feet of the crater; and as soon as the guns could be brought to bear, artillery was opened upon our columns from across the ravine on our immediate right, and from several works at a distance in front of the extreme right of the old line of the 9th corps

"The 1st brigade of the 1st division immediately followed the 2d. The two filled the crater

BATTLE OF PETERSBURG.

seized part of the line of pits to the right, and began to cover themselves from the fire of the enemy's artillery, now opening from the crest in their immediate front.

"Before all of the regiments of the last brigade of the 1st division had left our line, at about 5 a. m., the 2d division commenced its advance on the right, the 2d brigade, General Griffin, leading. The distance to be traversed to reach the line of rebel works was 130 yards. The head of the column was somewhat deflected by the enemy's fire, and borne to the left, so that it struck the line near the crater, and the men of the two divisions became, in some degree, intermingled.

"Several attempts were made to advance, which resulted only in the gain of a little ground to the right. General Wilcox had, meanwhile, thrown in part of a brigade to the left of the crater, the remainder halting till the 1st division should advance. Part of the 2d brigade, Colonel Bliss, (2d division,) was also thrown forward into the enemy's line. The other regiments were held until the line should be partially cleared.

"At about 6.30 a. m. orders were again sent to the division commander not to halt at the works, but to advance at once to the crest, without waiting for mutual support.

"General Potter's division (the 2d) was at that time forming for an attack on the right, but under these orders its direction was changed to the front. Its formation in front of the lines was exceedingly difficult, owing to the heavy fire from the crest and from the troops the enemy had now brought up and placed behind the covered way in the ravine. The division charged, and almost reached the summit of the hill, but, unsupported, it fell back, taking shelter behind another covered way on the right.

"Meanwhile the few regiments of that division that had not previously left our lines advanced, seizing for a considerable distance the enemy's lines on the right.

"General Wilcox, on the left, found an advance impossible; his men dug from the mine two guns and held the left flank.

"Peremptory orders from the commanding general directed me to throw in all my troops and direct them against the crest. Under these orders I directed the 4th (colored) division to advance, which division I had hitherto held back, under the belief that those new troops could not be used to advantage in the crowded condition of the portion of the enemy's line held by us.

"The column was thrown forward and advanced gallantly over the slope of the crater, though by this time the ground was swept by a steady fire of artillery and infantry. A part of the column was deflected to the right and charged and captured a portion of the enemy's line with a stand of colors and some prisoners. The division, disorganized by passing the pit, crowded with men of the other divisions, then reformed as well as was possible beyond the crater, and attempted to take the hill; were met at the outset by a counter charge of the enemy, broke in disorder to the rear, passed through the crater and lines on the right, throwing into confusion and drawing off with them many of the white troops, and ran to our own lines. The enemy regained a portion of his line on the right. This was about 8.45 a. m.

"But not all of the colored troops retired; some held the pits behind which they had advanced, severely checking the enemy till they were nearly all killed.

"I believe that no raw troops could have been expected to have behaved better. Before reaching the point from which they had formed to charge, they had been shattered by the enemy's fire, broken by the exceedingly difficult passage of the enemy's lines, and disheartened by the inability of the other divisions to advance.

"At the time of the assault of the 4th division, General Wilcox threw out his 2d brigade, Colonel Humphreys's, and took an additional portion of the line on the left.

"Soon after the repulse, an assault from the front was made on the crater; it was gallantly repulsed with great loss to the enemy, none of them advancing to our lines except those who surrendered themselves.

"At this time the enemy had planted artillery at several points on the hill, and had gained the range of the crater and lines with great accuracy, his mortar firing being especially destructive.

"At 9.15 a. m. I received with regret a peremptory order from the general commanding to withdraw my troops from the enemy's line. The order was sent into the crater at 12.20 p. m. with instructions to brigade commanders on the spot to consult and determine the hour and manner of retiring. I directed General Ferrero to immediately commence a covered way to the crater, to meet one already begun from there.

"The men in the crater and lines adjoining had become exhausted with the severity of the day's work. They had made several and repulsed three distinct assaults, and had fought hand to hand with the enemy for the possession of his pits. They were suffering severely under a hot sun from want of water.

"Finding that their position was not to be held, the general determined, in order to save further loss of life, upon an evacuation of the lines. A message to that effect, requesting a heavy fire of infantry and artillery to right and left should be opened from the old lines, to distract the attention of the enemy, was on its way to me when another assault of the enemy was made. Seeing its preparation, and knowing their men to be discouraged by the proposed relinquishment of all the advantages gained at such cost, and disheartened that they were to expect no further support, Generals Hartranft and Griffin directed their troops to withdraw. It is feared the order was not clearly understood in the crater, as most of the troops, and all of the wounded then lying there in great numbers, were captured.

"During the engagement the batteries of the corps did efficient service, especially in keeping down the fire of the rebel fort on the left and in annoyance of the enemy's guns on the right. Twenty-three commanders of regiments were lost on that day, four killed, fifteen wounded, and four missing; two commanders of brigades—General W. F. Bartlett and Colonel E. G. Marshall—were taken prisoners.

"In a report so hurriedly made up, it will be impossible for me to mention the many acts of heroism which characterized the action; and I will only say that my entire command, officers and men, did all that gallant men could do under the circumstances.

"To my staff—Brigadier General Julius White, chief of staff; Lieutenant Colonel Lewis Richmond, assistant adjutant general; Lieutenant Colonel C. G. Loring, jr., assistant inspector general; Surgeon John E. McDonald, medical director; Surgeon James Harris, medical inspector; Major Edward M. Neill, assistant adjutant general; Major Philip M. Lydig, assistant adjutant general; Major J. L. Van Buren, aide-de-camp; Major William Cutting, aide-de-camp; Captain W. H. Harris, U. S. A., chief of ordnance; Captain H. A. Rathbone, commissary of musters; Captain Duncan A. Pell, aide-de-camp; Captain J. C. Paine, signal officer; Lieutenant D. S. Remmington, acting assistant quartermaster—I must express my thanks for their activity and gallantry during the action.

"Colonel Loring, Major Cutting, and Major Van Buren were detailed to accompany divisions, and discharged their duties in the most faithful and gallant manner.

"I must again express my thanks to Colonel Pleasants and the men of his regiment for their skilful and meritorious services.

"I have the honor to be, general, very respectfully, your obedient servant,

"A. E. BURNSIDE, *Major General, Commanding.*

"Brig. Gen. S. WILLIAMS,
"*Ass't Adj't General Army of the Potomac.*"

Question. How long after the explosion of the mine before your troops advanced to the first assault?

Answer. There was probably a delay of five minutes in removing the abatis, but no other delay occurred. They commenced the movement forward to the assault at once.

Question. Could you tell whether, on the explosion of the mine, the enemy abandoned any of their intrenchments to the rear of it?

Answer. There was no formidable line in rear of that one held by them at that time.

Question. What was the first effect of the explosion on the enemy, as far as you could see?

Answer. As was stated in my report, it was understood that a considerable portion, if not all of the enemy in their line in front of the fifth corps, abandoned their line temporarily.

Question. Did you deem it very essential that the troops who were to lead the advance should be trained for it somewhat before the springing of the mine?

Answer. Yes, sir; I deemed that essential. It is always better that officers commanding troops should know the work they have to do; and if the men can be drilled with a view to a specific work, they can always do that work better. I felt at the time that my reasons for putting in the colored troops first were good, and I have had no cause to change that opinion. Although it is necessarily a matter of opinion, and no one can ever tell what the result would have been had my plan been strictly adhered to, still I am clearly of the opinion that the colored troops would have made a better charge on that day than almost any other division of the army, in consequence of the peculiar circumstances by which the army had been surrounded. They had been fighting and marching up to the time that they crossed the James river, and my corps particularly had been constantly under fire after crossing the James, for forty days, so that a man could not raise his head above the breastworks without being shot at.

Question. And they were compelled to lie very much quiescent durnig that time?

Answer. Yes, sir; they had very little exercise, and that little in this constant state of suspense caused by the continuous musketry and artillery fire of the enemy.

Question. From your experience with colored troops, how would you say they compared in reliability as soldiers with the white troops, provided they have had the same training?

Answer. So far as I am myself concerned, I have the greatest faith in colored soldiers. I do not say they are fully equal to our white soldiers, because they have not the same intelligence; but they are quite as easily disciplined, and, as far as my experience goes, they stand fire quite as well as any troops we have had. And, with the exception of the intelligence which prevails to a considerable extent among our white soldiers, and which makes each man a pretty good judge of what he ought to do in a fight, I think the colored soldiers are as good soldiers as we have.

Question. To what do you attribute the failure of the 30th of July? The enterprise did fail, and I suppose you have some idea why it failed.

Answer. Well, sir, it is my opinion that the change that was made the day before the battle in the troops which were to lead the advance, and the directions which were given modifying the mode of putting the troops in, had a very serious effect upon the result. But I am not prepared to say that it would not have been a success even with those changes, had our troops on the right and left of the point assaulted attacked the enemy, and taken advantage of the weak condition of their lines. This is simply an opinion, given without reference to the action of the generals who commanded those troops, because I know nothing of their orders; and my opinion may be entirely erroneous.

By Mr. Loan:

Question. Was your assault sustained by the second corps on your right, or the fifth corps on your left?

Answer. No, sir, not to my knowledge. I do not think they attempted an attack. The 18th corps, under General Ord, had relieved my troops on that line, and a portion of that corps was held in reserve to assist us, and a brigade, or possibly a division, did make an attempt to charge the enemy's works.

By the chairman:

Question. In your judgment, was the failure of the fuze to ignite the mine on the first attempt attended with any disastrous effects?

Answer. I think not. I do not think the delay in the explosion of the mine resulted in giving the enemy any information of our movements. Therefore I do not think it resulted in any harm.

Question. Who is responsible for the deficiency in the supply of fuzes necessary to explode the mine?

Answer. I was directed to make my requisitions for fuze and powder upon the chief of artillery. I did so at the proper time. A despatch from one of his assistants came to me inquiring how much I desired, and I informed him of the distinct number of feet. I think, at any rate, I stated to him in substance that I wanted enough to run three or four fuzes in to the charge.

Question. Of course you were compelled to make use of such as he sent you?

Answer. Yes, sir.

By Mr. Loan:

Question. And the quantity supplied was sufficient for only one fuze?

Answer. Yes, sir.

By the chairman:

Question. Did you have any interviews with General Meade during the battle or afterwards on that day? If so, what took place during those interviews?

Answer. I had but one personal interview with General Meade that day, and that was after the battle. Upon the reception of the order to withdraw our troops from the enemy's lines, I went to General Meade's headquarters and requested that the order might be rescinded, stating that I did not think we had fought long enough, and that I thought we could succeed in carrying the crest if we persevered in the attack, and the other troops were put in. He said that the order to withdraw was final, and that he had ordered all offensive operations on the right and left to cease. This order, I consider, materially affected the result of our withdrawal, inasmuch as the enemy's forces upon our right and left were entirely unoccupied, and thereby had an opportunity of concentrating upon us during the withdrawal. It could hardly have been expected that the withdrawal could have been made without disaster, after all offensive operations had ceased on the right and left, and the supporting force withdrawn from the rear. My only hope was that the force in the crater would be able to hold the position until a covered way could be dug from our advanced line out to the crater, a distance of a little over a hundred yards. This covered way had been commenced both in the crater and on our advanced lines, and I instructed General Ferrero to push it forward as rapidly as possible, with such of his troops as had been driven back and collected in the advanced line. The communication between the advanced line and the crater was almost entirely cut off; and although the distance was so short—only about one hundred yards—it was next to an impossibility for messengers to reach the crater, much less to send in ammunition and water. The men had become very much exhausted with the heat and labors of the day.

After I was informed by General Meade that the order was final to withdraw, and that there was no object in holding the crater by connecting its flanks with our old advanced line, as I had suggested, I telegraphed to General White, my chief of staff, whom I had left at my field headquarters, that the orders to withdraw were peremptory, and I at once sent for the division commanders, in order to consult as to the most favorable method and time for withdrawal. In the mean time my despatch to General White had been sent to the division commanders, and by them sent into the crater for report from the brigade commanders. Previous to and during this time the enemy made several assaults upon our position, which were repulsed. Soon after this a heavy attack was made upon the left of our forces, driving us back, and causing a hasty evacuation of the crater by all who could get back to the main lines.

In the evening of that day General Meade sent me a message stating that he had understood that our troops had been driven from the crater, and he desired to know if such was the fact. I very improperly threw the message one side, and said to my staff officer, who was with me, that I would not answer such a message; that if General Meade felt disposed to cease offensive operations on the right and fetl, and leave us to get out of the crater as best we could, and had taken so little interest in the matter as not to know late in the evening that we had been driven from the crater before two o'clock, I certainly would not give him the information, and that I believed he knew all about it. He sent me, I think, two more messages during the evening, which I treated in the same way.

I refer to this as a piece of insubordination on my part for which no excuse can be offered; but it had no effect upon the result, as it occurred after the fight.

An unfortunate correspondence took place between General Meade and myself during the day, which reads as follows:

"JULY 30.

"General MEADE:

"I am doing all in my power to push the troops forward, and, if possible, we will carry the crest. It is hard work, but we hope to accomplish it. I am fully alive to the importance of it.

"A. E. BURNSIDE, *Major General.*"

"HEADQUARTERS ARMY OF THE POTOMAC,
"7.30 *a. m.*, 1864.
" Major General BURNSIDE :

"What do you mean by hard work to take the crest? I understand not a man has advanced beyond the enemy's line which you occupied immediately after exploding the mine.

"Do you mean to say your officers and men will not obey your orders to advance? If not, what is the obstacle? I wish to know the truth, and desire an immediate answer.

"GEO. G. MEADE, *Major General.*"

"HEADQUARTERS NINTH ARMY CORPS,
"Battery Morton, July 30, 1864.
"General MEADE :

"Your despatch, by Captain Jay, received. The main body of General Potter's division is beyond the crater. I do not mean to say that my officers and men will not obey my orders to advance. I mean to say that it is very hard work to advance to the crest.

"I have never, in any report, said anything different from what I conceived to be the truth. Were it not insubordinate, I would say that the latter remark of your note was unofficerlike and ungentlemanly.

"Respectfully, yours,

"A. E. BURNSIDE, *Major General.*"

I refer to this correspondence because it has been made the subject of charges against me upon which I was not tried. I felt, at the time I wrote the offensive despatch, that General Meade intended to imply that I had not made truthful reports, but I am now satisfied that he did not so intend.

General Meade ordered a court to investigate the operations of the 30th. This court was composed of General Hancock, who commanded the troops on my right, General Ayres, who commanded a division of troops on my left, (which division was selected for the purpose of making an attack from our left, but did not attack,) and General Miles, who commanded a brigade in General Hancock's corps, which was on my right. The judge advocate of the court was the inspector general at General Meade's headquarters.

I at once telegraphed to Mr. Stanton as follows :

"HEADQUARTERS 9TH ARMY CORPS, *August* 6, 1864.
"*To the Secretary of War of the United States, Washington :*

"While I have the greatest respect for the officers composing the court ordered by Special Order W. D. No. 258 to examine into the affair of the 30th instant, I beg to submit' that it should be composed of officers who do not belong to this army.

"While I am most willing, and feel it to be my due to have the fullest investigation, I should not, under the circumstances, demand one, nor seek to press the matter to an issue in any degree adverse to the general commanding the army of the Potomac. I am ready to await the verdict of time. But if an investigation is to be had, I feel that I have a right to ask that it be made by officers not in this army, and not selected by General Meade. All of the officers constituting the court held command in the supporting columns which were not brought into action on that day. The judge advocate is a member of General Meade's staff.

"General Meade has also preferred charges against me, upon which I desire to be tried.

"As the court convenes on Monday, the 8th instant, I respectfully request an answer may be returned as soon as possible.

"A. E. BURNSIDE, *Major General.*"

To this telegram I received the following reply :

"UNITED STATES MILITARY TELEGRAPH.

"[By telegraph from Washington, dated August 8, 1864—11 a. m.]

"Major General BURNSIDE :

"Your telegram of the sixth (6th) has been laid before the President, who directs me to say, that, while he would like to conform to your wishes, the detail for the court of inquiry having already been ordered, he does not see that any evil can result to you. The action of the board of inquiry will be merely to collect facts for his information. No charges or even imputations have reached him or the department in respect to you. It is not known here, except by your telegram, that General Meade has made against you any charges. He directs me further to assure you that you may feel entire confidence in his fairness and justice.

"EDWIN M. STANTON, *Secretary of War.*"

I stated in my evidence a few moments ago that General Meade ordered the court, which is the fact. It assembled under his order, and decided that such a court could not proceed without the authority of the President of the United States. The matter was then referred to Washington, and the existence of the court was legalized by the President. This court assembled and took its evidence, which I understand is now in the hands of the President.

There is also a point which will come up in this investigation, I suppose, inasmuch as it came up in the investigation before this military board; that is, as to the information which was furnished by me to General Meade during the action. I have simply to say, that I reported to him all important movements, and that I did not feel at any time that any information was withheld from him which was necessary to the making up of a correct opinion as to the state of affairs in my front. I will leave with the committee a copy of all messages received from General Meade by me during the action, and of all messages sent by me to General Meade, and by some of General Meade's officers, who were with me at intervals during the day, and who reported to General Meade the progress of affairs, which I considered the same as if reported myself.

Question. What reason did General Meade give for not having the attack made on the right and left, as you had suggested?

Answer. He never gave me any reasons. We never conversed upon the subject.

Question. An attack by the corps on your right and left was contemplated in the plan that you first submitted to him?

Answer. Yes, sir; and in the despatches, just referred to, will be found one from me to General Meade, requesting that General Warren's corps should be put in. I first sent him a despatch, taking as much responsibility as I thought I could, in view of his letter of the 3d of July, stating that if Warren's men could be concentrated, and I could designate the time when they could go in, I would let him know, making it a half request. Afterwards, becoming anxious, I sent him a despatch embracing these words: "Now is the time for Warren to go in." Notwithstanding the fact of his letter of the 3d of July, I thought I would take the responsibility of sending this despatch to him, and I did so.

By Mr. Chandler:

Question. As I understand it, the enemy's lines were very much weakened on their right and left at the time of the explosion of the mine?

Answer. Yes, sir. As I was informed by my signal officer, they took troops from in front of General Warren's corps, formed them in columns, and marched them around and assaulted our men who were trying to take the crest; but he did not report having seen any troops taken from their left opposite General Hancock's corps.

By the chairman:

Question. In your opinion were there any other of our troops engaged that day excepting those who were trying to advance through the crater?

Answer. No, sir.

Question. Did not that fact enable the enemy to concentrate a greater force upon those who were advancing than they could have done had they been vigorously attacked at other points of their lines?

Answer. There is scarcely a doubt of it.

Question. Do you know any reason why those other troops along our lines were not ordered to engage the enemy at the time you were endeavoring to penetrate beyond the crater?

Answer. No, sir; I do not know of any reason, and I do not know of any orders issued on that day, except those concerning my own command.

BATTLE OF PETERSBURG. 27

The following are the despatches from General Meade:

"No. 1.]   UNITED STATES MILITARY TELEGRAPH,
"*Headquarters Army of the Potomac, July* 30, 1864—3.20 a. m.

"Major General BURNSIDE: As it is still so dark, the commanding general says you can postpone firing the mine if you think it proper.
"A. A. HUMPHREYS,
"*Major General, Chief of Staff.*"

This despatch was answered either by a written or verbal message from me, stating that the mine would be exploded at the hour designated—3.30 a. m.

"No. 2.]   UNITED STATES MILITARY TELEGRAPH,
"*Headquarters Ninth Army Corps, July* 30, 1864—4.30 a. m.

"Major General BURNSIDE. Is there any difficulty in exploding the mine? It is three-fourths of an hour later than that fixed upon for exploding.
"A. A. HUMPHREYS,
"*Major General and Chief of Staff.*"

It is possible I did not answer this despatch, as I was at the time anxiously endeavoring to ascertain the cause of the delay in the explosion.

"No. 3.]   UNITED STATES MILITARY TELEGRAPH,
"*Headquarters Ninth Army Corps, July* 30, 1864—4.30 a. m.

"Major General BURNSIDE: If the mine cannot be exploded something else must be done, and at once. The commanding general is awaiting to hear from you before determining.
"A. A. HUMPHREYS,
"*Major General and Chief of Staff.*"

The cause of the delay had not been ascertained when I received this despatch:

"No. 4.]   UNITED STATES MILITARY TELEGRAPH,
"*Headquarters Ninth Army Corps, July* 30, 1864—4.35 a. m.

"General BURNSIDE: The commanding general directs, if your mine has failed, that you make an assault at once, opening your batteries.
"A. A. HUMPHREYS,
"*Major General and Chief of Staff.*"

Just as I received this despatch Major Van Buren reported the cause of the delay, and I directed him to inform General Meade's aid (who was waiting) of the cause. Very soon after the mine exploded.

"No. 5.]   UNITED STATES MILITARY TELEGRAPH,
"*Headquarters Army of the Potomac, July* 30, 1864—5.40 a. m.

"General BURNSIDE: The general commanding learns that your troops are halting at the works where the mine exploded, and he directs that all your troops be pushed forward to the crest at once. Call on General Ord to move forward his troops at once.
"A. A. HUMPHREYS,
"*Major General and Chief of Staff.*"

This was simply an order, and required no answer.

"No. 6.]   UNITED STATES MILITARY TELEGRAPH,
"*Headquarters Army of the Potomac, July* 30, 1864—5.40 a. m.

"General BURNSIDE: What news from your assaulting column? Please report frequently.
"GEO. G. MEADE, *Major General.*"

To this despatch I replied as follows:

"HEADQUARTERS NINTH ARMY CORPS,
"*Battery Morton, July* 30, 1864.

"General MEADE: We have the enemy's first line and occupy the breach. I shall endeavor to push forward to the crest as rapidly as possible.
"A. E. BURNSIDE, *Major General.*

"P. S.—There is a large fire in Petersburg.
"W. W. SANDERS, *Captain Sixth Infantry.*"

"UNITED STATES MILITARY TELEGRAPH,
"*Headquarters Army Potomac,* 6 *a. m., July* 30, 1864.
"Major General BURNSIDE, *Commanding* 9*th Corps:*
"The commanding general wishes to know what is going on on your left, and whether it would be an advantage for Warren's supporting force to go in at once.
"A. A. HUMPHREYS,
"*Major General and Chief of Staff.*"

This was answered as follows:

"6.20 *a. m.*
"General MEADE:
"If General Warren's supporting force can be concentrated just now, ready to go in at the proper time, it would be well. I will designate to you when it ought to move; there is scarcely room for it now on our immediate front.
"A. E. BURNSIDE, *Major General.*"

"UNITED STATES MILITARY TELEGRAPH,
"*Headquarters Army Potomac, July* 30, 1864—5.30 a. m.
"Major General BURNSIDE:
"Warren's force has been concentrated, and ready to move since 3.30 a. m. My object in inquiring was to ascertain if you could judge of the practicability of advancing without waiting for your column. What is the delay in your column moving? Every minute is most precious, as the enemy are undoubtedly concentrating to meet you on the crest; and if you give them time enough, you cannot expect to succeed. There will be no object to be gained in occupying the enemy's line; it cannot be held under their artillery fire, without much labor in turning it. The great point is to secure the crest at once and at all hazards.
"GEO. G. MEADE, *Major General.*"

I replied to this as follows:

"JULY 30, 1864.
"General MEADE:
"I am doing all in my power to push the troops forward, and, if possible, we will carry the crest. It is hard work, but we hope to accomplish it. I am fully alive to the importance of it.
"A. E. BURNSIDE, *Major General.*"

"HEADQUARTERS ARMY POTOMAC, 7.30 *a. m., July* 30, 1864.
"Major General BURNSIDE:
"What do you mean by hard work to take the crest? I understand not a man has advanced beyond the enemy's line which you occupied immediately after exploding the mine. Do you mean to say your officers and men will not obey your orders to advance? If not, what is the obstacle? I wish to know the truth, and desire an immediate answer.
"GEO. G. MEADE, *Major General.*"

"HEADQUARTERS NINTH ARMY CORPS,
"*Battery Morton, July* 30, 1864.
"General MEADE:
"Your despatch per Captain Jay received. The main body of General Potter's division is beyond the crater. I do not mean to say that my officers and men will not obey my orders to advance. I mean to say that it is very hard to advance to the crest.
"I have never in any report said anything different from what I conceived to be the truth. Were it not insubordinate, I should say that the latter remark of your note was unofficerlike and ungentlemanly.
"Respectfully yours,
"A. E. BURNSIDE, *Major General.*"

"HEADQUARTERS ARMY POTOMAC, 7.30 *a. m.,* 1864.
"Major General BURNSIDE:
"GENERAL: Will you do me the favor to send me a copy of my note to you per Captain Jay. I did not keep any copy, intending it to be confidential. Your reply requires I should have a copy.
"Respectfully yours,
"GEO. G. MEADE, *Major General.*"

This was answered by sending either a copy or the original note by the aid who brought the above despatch.

"UNITED STATES MILITARY TELEGRAPH,
"*Headquarters Army Potomac,* 8 *a. m., July* 30, 1864."

"General BURNSIDE:

"Since writing by Captain Jay, Captain Sanders has come in, and reported condition of affairs. He says Griffin has advanced and was checked. This modifies my despatch. Still I would like to know the exact morale of your corps. Ord reports that he cannot move until you get out of the way. Can't you let him pass out on your right, and let him try what he can do?

"GEO. G. MEADE, *Major General.*"

"U. S. MILITARY TELEGRAPH, BEFORE PETERSBURG,
"*Covered Way, Fourteen-Gun Battery, July* 30, 1864."

"General MEADE:

"Many of the ninth and eighteenth corps are retiring before the enemy. I think now is the time to put in the 5th corps promptly.

"A. E. BURNSIDE, *Major General.*"

"UNITED STATES MILITARY TELEGRAPH,
"*Headquarters Army Potomac,* 9.30 *a. m., July* 30, 1864."

"Major General BURNSIDE:

"The major general commanding has heard that the result of your attack has been a repulse, and directs that if in your judgment nothing further can be effected, that you withdraw to your own line, taking precaution to get your men back safely. General Ord will do the same.

"A. A. HUMPHREYS,
"*Major General and Chief of Staff.*"

"UNITED STATES MILITARY TELEGRAPH,
"*Headquarters Army Potomac, July* 30, 1864."

"General BURNSIDE:

"The major general commanding directs that you withdraw to your own intrenchments.

"A. A. HUMPHREYS, *Major General.*"

After the receipt of these despatches I went to General Meade's headquarters, as I before stated, to request that the orders might be rescinded.

"UNITED STATES MILITARY TELEGRAPH,
"*Headquarters Army Potomac, July* 30, 1864."

"General BURNSIDE and General ORD:

"You can exercise your own discretion in withdrawing your troops now, or at a later period—say to-night. It is not intended to hold the enemy's line which you now occupy any longer than is required to withdraw safely your men.

"GEORGE G. MEADE, *Major General.*"

The despatch, I think, passed me while I was on the way to General Meade's headquarters.

Besides the despatches from me, the following were sent from my headquarters by an aide of General Meade, who was with me during the day:

"HEADQUARTERS ARMY OF THE POTOMAC,
"5.50 *a. m., July* 30, 1864."

"General MEADE:

"The eighteenth corps have just been ordered to push forward to the crest. The loss does not appear to be heavy; some prisoners coming in.

"W. W. SANDERS, *Captain 6th Infantry.*"

"HEADQUARTERS ARMY OF THE POTOMAC,
"6.10 *a. m., July* 30, 1864."

"Major General MEADE, *Commanding:*

"General Burnside says he has given orders to all his division commanders to put everything in at once.

"W. W. SANDERS, *Captain 6th Infantry.*"

"HEADQUARTERS ARMY OF THE POTOMAC,
"8.45 *a. m., July* 30, 1864."

"General MEADE:

"One gun has just been taken out of the mine, and is now being put in position. Have not heard anything from the attack made from the left of the mine. One set of colors just sent in, captured by the negroes.

"W. W. SANDERS, *Captain 6th Infantry.*"

"HEADQUARTERS ARMY OF THE POTOMAC,
"9 a. m., July 30, 1864.
"General MEADE:
"The attack made on the right of mine has been repulsed. A great many men are coming to the rear.
"W. W. SANDERS, *Captain 6th Infantry.*"

In addition to these, General Meade received a despatch from Lieutenant Colonel Loring, my inspector general, which was intended for me, and was forwarded to me by him, (General Meade,) which assured me that he had the information contained in the despatch.

Testimony of Major General George G. Meade.

HEADQUARTERS ARMY OF THE POTOMAC,
Before Petersburg, Va., December 20, 1864.

Major General GEORGE G. MEADE sworn and examined.

By Mr. Chandler:

Question. What is your rank and position in the army?

Answer. I am a major general of the United States army, commanding the army of the Potomac.

Question. Will you state to the committee, in your own way, whatever you may deem important in relation to the battle before Petersburg, of July 30, 1864?

Answer. Immediately after that action took place, I felt that it was due to the public, to the army, and to myself, that the matter should be thoroughly investigated. I therefore applied to the President of the United States, the only power having authority to order such an investigation, to order a court of inquiry, which he immediately did. The court was composed of four of the most distinguished officers of this army. Major General Hancock was the president of it, and Brigadier General Ayres, and Brigadier General Miles, and some other officer, whose name I do not now recollect, were the other members of it.

That court was in session in this army within a few days after the battle. I appeared before it and submitted a full and complete statement and explanation of all the facts connected with the matter, and directed their attention to the proper persons to be called before them. They had before them all the officers who were then upon the ground, and thoroughly investigated the whole subject. Their proceedings were transmitted to the War Department, where, so far as my knowledge extends, they have been from that time to this. Of the result of those proceedings, the opinion of the court, or anything that occurred before them, excepting my own testimony, I am perfectly ignorant.

I would suggest to the committee that they call upon the War Department for a copy of those proceedings, as they will find there all the information which can possibly be obtained. And if, after an examination of those proceedings—which might be made a part of the testimony before you—any further information should be desired, it could easily be obtained by calling upon such officers as the committee might deem it advisable to examine.

At present the only documents I have with me are my official report, which I made to Lieutenant General Grant immediately after the affair, and some papers referred to in that report. Those, with the permission of the committee, I will now read and make part of my testimony. They give a general history of the transaction, but do not enter into details so much as I could do if I had all my despatches and official papers here.

BATTLE OF PETERSBURG.

"HEADQUARTERS ARMY OF THE POTOMAC,
"*August* 16, 1864.

"I have the honor to submit herewith a report of the operations on the 30th ultimo, when an unsuccessful assault was made on the enemy's works in front of Petersburg. Soon after occupying our present lines, Major General Burnside, commanding 9th corps, at the suggestion of Lieutenant Colonel Pleasants, 48th Pennsylvania volunteers, commenced the running of a gallery from his line to a battery occupied by the enemy, with a view of placing a mine under this battery. When my attention was called to this work, I sanctioned its prosecution, though at the time, from the reports of the engineers and my own examination, I was satisfied the location of the mine was such that its explosion would not be likely to be followed by any important result, as the battery to be destroyed was in a re-entering part of the enemy's line, exposed to an enfilading fire, and reverse fire from points both on the right and left. The mine being completed, and the movement of the 2d corps to the north side of the James having drawn off the greater portion of the confederate army, the lieutenant general commanding directed the explosion of the mine, and the assaulting the enemy's works. For this purpose the 18th corps was placed under my command, in addition to the army of the Potomac. On the 29th ultimo, a general order of battle was issued, a copy of which is herewith annexed, (marked A,) which will serve to show the plan of the proposed attack. On the 30th, owing to a defect in the fuze, the explosion of the mine was delayed from 3.30 to 4.45 a. m., an unfortunate delay, because it was designed to assault the crest of the ridge occupied by the enemy just before daylight, when the movement would in a measure be obscured. As soon as the mine was sprung, the 1st division 9th corps, Brigadier General Ledlie commanding, moved forward and occupied the crater without opposition. No advance, however, was made from the crater to the ridge, some 400 yards beyond; Brigadier General Ledlie giving as a reason for not pushing forward, that the enemy could occupy the crater in his rear, he seeming to forget that the rest of his corps and all of the 18th corps were waiting to occupy the crater and follow him. Brigadier Generals Potter and Wilcox, commanding 2d and 3d divisions, 9th corps, advanced simultaneously with Ledlie, and endeavored to occupy parts of the enemy's line on Ledlie's right and left, so as to cover those flanks, respectively, but on reaching the enemy's line Ledlie's men were found occupying the vacated parts, both to the right and left of the crater, in consequence of which the men of the several divisions got mixed up, and a scene of disorder and confusion commenced, which seems to have continued to the end of the operations. In the mean time the enemy, rallying from the confusion incident to the explosion, began forming his infantry in a ravine to the right, and planting his artillery both on the right and left of the crater. Seeing this, Potter was enabled to get his men out of the crater and enemy's line, and had formed them for an attack on the right, when he received an order to attack the crest of the ridge. Notwithstanding he had to change front in the presence of the enemy, he succeeded not only in doing so, but, as he reports, advancing to within a few yards of the crest, which he would have taken if he had been supported. This was after 7 a. m., more than two hours after Ledlie had occupied the crater, and yet he had made no advance. He, however, states that he was forming to advance when the 4th division, (colored troops,) General Ferrero commanding, came rushing into the crater, and threw his men into confusion. The 4th division passed beyond the crater, and made an assault, when they encountered a heavy fire of artillery and infantry, which threw them into inextricable confusion, and they retired in disorder through the troops in the crater, and back into our lines. In the mean time, in ignorance of what was occurring, I sent orders to Major General Ord, commanding 18th corps, who was expected to follow the 9th, to advance at once on the right of the 9th, and independently of the latter. To this General Ord replied, the only debouches were choked up with the 9th corps, which had not all advanced at this time. He, however, pushed on a brigade of Turner's division over the 9th corps parapets, and directed it to charge the enemy's line on the right, where it was still occupied. While it was about executing this order, the disorganized 4th division (colored) of the 9th corps came rushing back and carrying everything with them, including Turner's brigade. By this time—between 8 and 9 a. m.—the enemy, seeing the hesitation and confusion on our part, having planted batteries on both flanks in ravines where our artillery could not reach them, opened a heavy fire, not only on the ground in front of the crater, but between it and our lines, their mortars at the same time throwing shells into the dense mass of our men in the crater and adjacent works. In addition to this artillery fire, the enemy massed his infantry and assaulted the position. Although the assault was repulsed and some heroic fighting was done, particularly on the part of Potter's division and some regiments of the 18th corps, yet the exhaustion incident to the crowding of the men and the intense heat of the weather, added to the destructive artillery fire of the enemy, produced its effect, and report was brought to me that our men were retiring into our old lines. Being satisfied the moment for success had passed, and that any further attempt would only result in useless sacrifice of life, with the concurrence of the lieutenant general commanding, who was present, I directed the suspension of further offensive movements, and the withdrawal of the troops in the crater when it could be done with security, retaining the position till night if necessary. It appears that when this order reached the crater, 12.20, the greater portion of those that had been in were out; the balance remained for an hour and a half repulsing an attack of the enemy, but, on the enemy threatening a second attack, retreating in disorder, losing many prisoners. This terminated this most unfortunate and not very creditable operation. I forbear to comment in the manner I might otherwise deem myself justified in doing, because the whole subject, at my request, has been submitted for investigation by the President of the United States to a court of inquiry, with directions to report upon whom, if any one, censure is to be laid. I transmit herewith the reports of corps, division, and brigade commanders, giving the details of the operations of each corps. There are two remarks in the report of Major General Burnside which justice to myself requires I should notice. General Burnside has thought proper to state: "A plan of attack was submitted, involving the putting the colored division in advance, and a certain formation of troops, and that the plan was disapproved in these two particulars." This statement is not accurate. The proposition to place the colored division at the head of the assaulting column was disapproved, but no control was exercised over General Burnside in the tactical formation of his column. This will be seen by reference to the correspondence that passed upon the subject, marked B and C. Again, Major General Burnside says: "Peremptory orders from the commanding general directed me to throw in all my troops and direct them against the crest. Under these orders, I directed the 4th division, colored, to advance, which division I had hitherto held back, under the belief that these new troops could not be used to advantage in the crowded condition of the portion of the enemy's line held by us." I presume Major General Burnside here refers to the despatch addressed to him as follows. (See despatch of July 30, 6 a. m.)

"It was not intended by that order, nor was any such construction justified by its terms, to push forward the colored division into the overcrowded crater, there to add to the disorganization and confusion already existing, and of the existence of which I was utterly ignorant, but of which it is to be presumed, from the extract from his report, General Burnside was aware. The order required that the men in the crater should be pushed forward at all hazards to the crest beyond, and when they moved the colored division advanced after them. It will be seen to be the concurrent testimony of all parties that the failure of success was in a great measure due to the injudicious advance of the colored division into the overcrowded crater and adjacent parts of the enemy's line, and to the confusion produced by their retiring a disordered and disorganized mass, after attempting an assault. From the reports transmitted, I cannot perceive that the colored troops are open to any more censure for their conduct than the other troops engaged. I enclose herewith a list of casualties, amounting in all in the army of the Potomac and 18th corps to 4,400 killed, wounded, and missing; 246 prisoners, two (2) colors and two (2) guns were captured, but the latter were abandoned on retiring from the crater.

"In closing this report, I cannot forbear from expressing the poignant regret I experienced at the failure of an operation promising such brilliant results had it been successful. Had the mine been sprung at 3.30 a. m., and the crest promptly seized, as it is believed it could have been done in thirty minutes after the explosion, such a force could have been poured into the crest as to have rendered its repossession by the enemy impossible, and thus have rendered untenable all his lines around Petersburg. But the operation was essentially a *coup-de-main*, depending for success upon the utmost promptitude of movement, and the taking advantage of the shock produced on the enemy by the explosion of the mine. The causes of the failure justice to all parties requires I should leave to the court of inquiry to ascertain.

"Very respectfully, &c.,

"GEO. G. MEADE,
"*Major General, Commanding.*"

"Lieut. Col. T. S. BOWERS, *Assist. Adjt. General.*
"Official:

"S. WILLIAMS, *Assistant Adjutant General.*"

A.

"HEADQUARTERS ARMY OF THE POTOMAC, *July* 29, 1864.
"ORDERS.

"The following instructions are issued for the guidance of all concerned:

"1. As soon as it is dark, Major General Burnside, commanding ninth corps, will withdraw his two brigades under General White, occupying the intrenchments between the plank and Norfolk roads, and bring them to his front. Care will be taken not to interfere with the troops of the eighteenth corps, moving into their position in rear of the ninth corps. General Burnside will form his troops for assaulting the enemy's works at daylight of the 30th, prepare his parapets and abatis for the passage of the columns, and have the pioneers equipped for work in opening passages for artillery, destroying enemy's abatis, and the intrenching tools distributed for effecting lodgement, &c.

"2. Major General Warren, commanding fifth corps, will reduce the number of his troops holding the intrenchments of his front to the minimum, and concentrate all his available force on his right, and hold them prepared to support the assault of Major General Burnside. The preparations in respect to pioneers, intrenching tools, &c., enjoined upon the ninth corps will also be made by the fifth corps.

"3. As soon as it is dark, Major General Ord, commanding eighteenth corps, will relieve his troops in the trenches by General Mott's division of the second corps, and form his corps in rear of the ninth corps, and be prepared to support the assault of Major General Burnside.

"4. Every preparation will be made for moving forward the field artillery of each corps.

"5. At dark Major General Hancock, commanding second corps, will move from Deep Bottom to the rear of the intrenchments now held by the eighteenth corps, resume the command of Mott's division, and be prepared at daylight to follow up the assaulting and supporting columns, or for such other operations as may be found necessary.

"6. Major General Sheridan, commanding cavalry corps, will proceed at dark from the vicinity of Deep Bottom to Lee's mill, and at daylight will move with his whole corps, including Wilson's division, against the enemy's troops defending Petersburg on the right, by the roads leading to that town from the southward and westward.

"Major Duane, acting chief engineer, will have the pontoon train parked at convenient points in the rear, prepared to move. He will see that supplies of sand-bags, gabions, fascines, &c., are in depot near the lines, ready for use. He will detail engineer officers for each corps.

"8. At half past three in the morning of the 30th, Major General Burnside will spring his mine, and his assaulting columns will immediately move rapidly upon the breach, seize the crest in the rear, and effect a lodgment there. He will be followed by Major General Ord, who will support him on the right, directing his movement to the crest indicated, and by Major General Warren, who will support him on the left.

"Upon the explosion of the mine the artillery of all kinds in battery will open upon those points of the enemy's works whose fire covers the ground over which our columns must move, care being taken to avoid impeding the progress of our troops. Special instructions respecting the direction of fire will be issued through the chief of artillery.

"9. Corps commanders will report to the commanding general when their preparations are complete, and will advise him of every step in the progress of the operation, and of everything important that occurs.

"10. Promptitude, rapidity of execution, and cordial co-operation are essential to success, and the commanding general is confident that this indication of his expectations will insure the hearty efforts of the commanders and troops.

"11. Headquarters during the operation will be at the headquarters of the ninth corps.

"By command of Major General Meade.

"S. WILLIAMS,
"*Assistant Adjutant General.*

"Official:

"S. WILLIAMS, *A. A. G.*"

B.

"HEADQUARTERS NINTH ARMY CORPS, *July* 26, 1864.

"GENERAL: I have the honor to acknowledge the receipt of your notes of this morning by Captains Jay and Bache, also of a telegram from the commanding general relating to the same subject. It is altogether probable that the enemy are cognizant of the fact that we are mining, because it has been mentioned in their newspapers, and they have been heard to work on what are supposed to be shafts in close proximity to our galleries. But the rain of night before last no doubt filled their shafts and much retarded their work. We have heard no sounds of work in them either yesterday or to-day, and nothing is heard by us in the mine but the usual sounds of work on the surface above.

"This morning we had some apprehensions that the left lateral gallery was in danger of caving in from the weight of the batteries above it and the shock of their firing. But all possible precautions have been taken to strengthen it, and we hope to preserve it intact.

"The placing of the charges in the mine will not involve the necessity of making a noise. It is therefore probable that we will escape discovery if the mine is to be used within two or three days. It is nevertheless highly important, in my opinion, that the mine should be exploded at the earliest possible moment consistent with the general interests of the campaign. I state to you the facts as nearly as I can, and, in the absence of any knowledge as to the meditated movements of the army, I must leave you to judge the proper time to make use of the mine. But it may not be improper for me to say, that the advantages reaped from the work would be but small if it were exploded without any co-operative movement. My plan would be to explode the mine just before daylight in the morning, or about 5 o'clock in the afternoon, mass the two brigades of the colored division in rear of my first line, in column of divisions, 'double columns closed in mass'—the head of each brigade resting on the front line, and as soon as the explosion has taken place move them forward with instructions for the divisions to take half distance; and as soon as the leading regiments of the two brigades pass through the gap in the enemy's line, the leading regiments of the right brigade to come into line perpendicular to the enemy's line by the right companies 'on the right into line, wheel,' the left companies 'on the right into line,' and proceed at once down the line of the enemy's works as rapidly as possible; the leading regiments of the left brigade to execute the reverse movement to the left, moving up the enemy's line. The remainders of the two columns to move directly towards the crest in front as rapidly as possible, diverging in such a way as to enable them to deploy into columns of regiments, the right column making as nearly as may be for Cemetery hill. These columns to be followed by the other divisions of this corps as soon as they can be thrown in. This would involve the necessity of relieving these divisions by other troops before the movement, and of holding columns of other troops in readiness to take our place on the crest, in case we gain it, and sweep down it.

"It would be advisable, in my opinion, if we succeed in gaining the crest, to throw the colored division right into the town. There is a necessity for the co-operation, at least in the way of artillery, of the troops on my right and left; of the extent of this you will necessarily be the judge. I think our chances of success in a plan of this kind are more than even.

"The main gallery of the mine is five hundred and twenty-two (522) feet in length, the side galleries about forty (40) feet each. My suggestion is that eight magazines be placed in the lateral galleries—two at each end, say a few feet apart, in branches at right angles to the side galleries, and two more in each of the side galleries, similarly placed, situated by pairs equidistant from each other and the ends of the galleries, thus:

[See diagram, page 17.]

Tamping beginning at the termination of the main gallery, for, say, one hundred feet, leaving all the air space in the side galleries. Run out some five or six fuzes and two wires, to render the ignition of the charge certain.

"I propose to put in each of the eight magazines from twelve to fourteen hundred pounds of powder, the magazines to be connected by a trough of powder instead of a fuze.

"I beg to enclose a copy of a statement from General Potter on the subject. I would suggest that the powder train be parked in a wood near our ammunition train, about a mile in rear of this place; Lieutenant Colonel Pierce, chief quartermaster, will furnish Captain Strang with a guide to the place.

"I beg also to request that General Benham be instructed to send us at once eight thousand (8,000) sand-bags, to be used for tamping and other purposes.

"I have the honor to be, general, very respectfully, your obedient servant,

"A. E. BURNSIDE,
"*Major General, Commanding.*

" Major General HUMPHREYS, *Chief of Staff.*

" Official:

"CHARLES E. PEASE,
"*Assistant Adjutant General.*"

C.

"HEADQUARTERS ARMY OF THE POTOMAC,
"*July* 29, 1864—10.15 a. m.

"COMMANDING OFFICER 9*th Corps:*

"I am instructed to say that the major general commanding submitted to the lieutenant general commanding the armies your proposition to form the leading columns of assault of the black troops, and that he, as well as the major general commanding, does not approve the proposition, but directs that those columns be formed of the white troops.

"A. A. HUMPHREYS,
"*Major General and Chief of Staff.*

"Official copy:

"S. WILLIAMS, *A. A. G.*"

"HEADQUARTERS ARMY OF THE POTOMAC,
"*July* 30, 1864—6 a. m.
"Major General BURNSIDE, *Commanding 9th Corps.*

"Prisoners taken say there is no line in their rear, and that their men were falling back when ours advanced; that none of the troops have returned from the James. Our chance is now; push your men forward at all hazards, white and black, and don't lose time in making formations, but rush for the crest.

"G. G. MEADE,
"*Major General, Commanding.*

"Official copy:

"S. WILLIAMS, *A. A. G.*"

This report, which I made to Lieutenant General Grant immediately after the affair occurred, was accompanied by the official reports of the subordinate commanders. I subsequently appeared before the court of inquiry and made a very long and detailed statement, accompanied by all my despatches, illustrating all the events of the day, which it is not now in my power to make to this committee from want of material and the absence of those papers. I propose, therefore, with the sanction of the committee, to content myself with the submitting of those papers, provided that, if the suggestion I have made, that the committee call for the proceedings of this court of inquiry, is not acceded to, I shall then be permitted, upon some further occasion, when I can get my papers, to again appear before the committee and make such statement as I may desire to make.

Question. Can you state what was the cause of the delay in the explosion of the mine?

Answer. Yes, sir; that was caused by a defect in the fuze. That was an accident for which nobody was responsible. That was corrected by the gallantry of some soldiers, whose names I do not now remember, who went into the mine, found that the fuze had ceased to burn, and relighted it.

Question. Was there any delay in making the assault after the mine was exploded?

Answer. Yes, sir; not so much dely in making the assault as delay in taking advantage of the occupation of the crater of the mine within the enemy's line. There was some delay in making the charge. Arrangements which should have been made preparatory to that charge were not made so far as I can ascertain. There was not a sufficient *debouche* from our line of works. There was a high parapet in front of our lines, an abatis and other obstacles to keep the enemy from us. Those obstacles should have been removed to enable our troops to move out promptly. There was but a small opening made, by which the 9th corps, 15,000 men, moved out by the flank; whereas there should have been an opening sufficiently large to have allowed the whole corps to move out and to have gone to the crest in not more than thirty minutes.

I will furnish the committee with a map which will show exactly the relative position of the mine with the enemy's lines and to our own, and which will show the position which it was desirous to take after the explosion of the mine. The explosion of the mine was simply a preliminary operation for the purpose of making an opening in the enemy's line through which we might pour our troops and get in rear and occupy a hill behind their line which commanded all their works. But, after getting into the crater of the mine, the troops never advanced beyond. No effort was made to gain possession of the hill beyond until the enemy had collected such a force that our troops were repulsed.

Question. Could this abatis have been cleared away prior to the springing of the mine?

Answer. Certainly; and it ought to have been done, and it was ordered to be done during the night previous.

Question. Can you state about how much delay there was, after the springing of the mine, before the charge was made?

Answer. The charge never was properly made. I think that in the course of twenty or twenty-five minutes the troops advanced and occupied the crater of the mine. But the charge was to have been made from the mine. There was no firing upon our troops until they got to the mine—nothing but marching ahead for the first half hour. During that time anybody could walk across and get to the mine. The charge was to have been made from the mine to the hill beyond. That charge never was made. But the troops kept crowding into this crater, which was a large hole some 150 feet in length by 50 feet in width and 25 feet in depth. The troops just crowded into that hole and the adjacent parts of the enemy's lines which had been abandoned for about a hundred yards on each side of the crater. That was immediately filled up by our troops. There they remained, and the more men there were there the worse it was. Their commanders could not keep order among them. The difficulty was to get the men out of this crater and to the hill beyond.

I probably ought to add that the condition of the army, from the long campaign in which it had been engaged, the number of battles it had fought, and the frequent attempts it had made to take the enemy's works, which had resulted unsuccessfully, the heat of midsummer—from all these causes the condition of the army was in some measure unfavorable for all operations of this kind. The men did not fight at that time with the vim with which they fought when we first crossed the Rapidan.

I am probably as ignorant as the committee in regard to many of these details. I did not hear the testimony before the court of inquiry; I was not present when it was taken. But undoubtedly the solution of all these questions will be found in their proceedings. If I had them before me I could better answer your questions. I never could ascertain, and I do not know, why that charge was not made from the crater of the mine upon the crest of the hill beyond at the time when it might have been made.

I do not know who to censure, whether General Burnside or the soldiers of that command. I involved myself in a difficulty with General Burnside by surmising, during the course of the operations, that it was owing to some indisposition on the part of the men; that the men would not go forward; that their officers could not get them forward; and, in my anxiety to know the correct state of the case, in order that I might base my orders upon it—because I had made up my mind that if any such obstacle existed the men should be withdrawn and not uselessly slaughtered—I addressed a despatch between eight and nine o'clock in the morning to General Burnside, in reply to one which he had sent to me, in which he stated to me that he was trying to take the crest, but it was very hard. I asked what was the difficulty, and said that his men, so far as I could ascertain from such information as I could gather, had not advanced beyond the crater, and had made no attempt to take the crest; therefore I could not understand what the difficulty was. Then I asked him, "Is it that you cannot get your orders obeyed, and that your men will not advance? I want to know the truth."

I did not mean to impugn General Burnside's veracity, or to suppose for an instant that he would tell me what was not true. All I meant to say was, "If you know this, you are naturally reluctant to acknowledge it; and in order to give you an opportunity to do so, I will make my request as urgent and emphatic as possible." General Burnside considered it a personal reflection upon himself and his veracity, and became very indignant. But it was not that. I wanted to know the exact state of the case. I had received a despatch which was intended for General Burnside, about six o'clock in the morning, or a little after six. The mine had been sprung at 4.45. The despatch was brought to me by an orderly. I was then at General Burnside's former headquarters, where I had established my headquarters during the day. The despatch was written by Colonel Long, of General Burnside's staff, and was dated from the crater. It stated, "Ledlie's division has occupied the crater without opposition. But his men are crowding down in it, and he cannot get them forward." That was the first cause of difficulty in getting the men to go forward. I sent the despatch to General Burnside, informing him that I had read it, and asked him to use every measure to push the men forward. For if we did not immediately take advantage of the opening for us made by the explosion of the mine, the time would soon go by in which we could do so. I made no further allusion to that.

When it came to eight and nine o'clock, and no advance was made, and I got this despatch from General Burnside, that it was very hard to get the men forward, I asked him, " What is the difficulty? Is it that your men will not go forward?" I drew the attention of the court of inquiry particularly to that, and requested that they would investigate and ascertain whether there was any difficulty on the part of the men, because the thing has occurred before, and it may occur again, that men will not do what they are wanted to do; and if that is the case, no officer should be held responsible.

Question. Were the supporting corps, on the right and left, engaged at the time of the attack?

Answer. No, sir; they could not be engaged, because they could not get out of our lines. The theory of the attack was this: The explosion of the mine would make an opening in the enemy's lines. General Burnside's corps, of 15,000 men, was to immediately take advantage of that and rush through and get on the crest beyond. The moment that was done, they were to be followed by General Ord and his corps, and then by about 10,000 men of General Warren's corps, which was massed and held in readiness immediately on General Burnside's left; and then eventually to be followed by General Hancock's forces. I prepared a force of from 40,000 to 50,000 men, to take advantage of our success gained by General Burnside's corps. Their movements were essentially dependent upon General Burnside: if he failed, all the rest were to be kept quiet; when he did not get through, but was withdrawn, all the rest of the command was not called into action.

By Mr. Loan:

Question. If I understand your statement correctly, the theory of the operation was that after breaking their line by the explosion of the mine, General Burnside was to advance and seize the crest of the hill beyond. Then he was to be followed by General Ord and the 19th corps, and you had troops massed and all ready to support them if necessary?

Answer. Yes, sir.

Question. From where did the assault upon the troops in the crater come?

Answer. It came from the enemy.

Question. From what direction—from the right or left of the crater?

Answer. It came principally from the right of the crater—from a ravine to the right of the crater. There the enemy brought guns from all points, and threw their shells into the crater.

Question. It was expected, I suppose, that the shock of the explosion would distract the attention of the enemy. Was there any arrangement made to attack the enemy in front of the corps to the right and left of the position of General Burnside, so as to keep them engaged, and prevent their attacking General Burnside?

Answer. General Hancock was ordered, and so was General Warren, to hold themselves in readiness, and if there was the slightest disposition shown by the enemy to weaken their lines, to assault the enemy. They sent me reports that the enemy's lines in their front were strongly held, and that they could do nothing; that the enemy had sent away none of their troops in their front, and it was impossible to do anything there. All that matter is in my testimony for the court of inquiry. After reading that testimony before that court, which I hope you will do, if any question then arises I will very readily answer it. My despatches are away from here now.

Question. I understand that the plan was for General Burnside to throw in his troops as soon as the mine was sprung, and to occupy the crest of the hill beyond?

Answer. Yes, sir.

Question. What co-operating assistance did you direct to be given to General Burnside in that matter?

Answer. General Ord was directed to immediately follow General Burnside; to report to him, and to hold his command in readiness, which he did. General Warren was directed to mass all his available reservs, so as to prevent the enemy from making an attack, and to co-operate with General Burnside as soon as his (Burnside's) movements would justify his doing so. General Hancock was directed to hold his command in readiness, to watch the enemy's movements and keep them engaged in his front, and if he saw any abandonment of their lines, any opportunity to co-operate with General Burnside, to move forward and assault the enemy. Those orders were all given the morning of the attack

Question. Did the enemy in front of Generals Hancock and Warren evacuate any portion of their lines?

Answer. They held them so firmly that both of those officers reported to me on the field that it would be useless to make any assault upon them.

Question. Do you know whether any portion of the enemy opposed to Generals Hancock and Warren were directed against the forces of General Burnside in the crater?

Answer. I do not; my impression is, that the troops who operated against General Burnside's forces came from the enemy's extreme right, and did not embrace any that had been immediately in presence of our forces.

Question. Will you, as briefly as you can conveniently do so, tell us why it was that white troops, instead of colored troops, were placed in the advance to carry that work, as I understand the case?

Answer. Prior to issuing the orders for the assault General Burnside told me it was his intention to place his colored division in the advance of the assaulting column. I objected to his doing so on the ground, not that I had any reason to believe that the colored troops would not do their duty as well as the white troops, but that, as they were a new division, and had never been under fire— had never been tried—and as this was an operation which I knew beforehand was one requiring the very best troops, I thought it impolitic to trust it to a division of whose reliability we had no evidence; therefore, I thought he ought to take one of his white divisions that he knew, from long experience, could be relied upon. General Burnside objected. I told him, then, that in view of his wishes upon the subject, I would report the matter to the lieutenant general; state to him my reasons, and those of General Burnside's, and let him decide. If he should decide that General Burnside's arguments were sound, and mine were wrong, then I would yield. The matter was referred to General Grant, and he confirmed my view that it would be impolitic, in a critical operation of that kind, to take troops that were untried and place them in the advance, and it was upon that ground that General Burnside's opinion was overruled.

Question. What was the condition of General Burnside's white troops? Had they been exposed to any fatiguing duty for any great length of time previous to that assault?

Answer. They had been engaged in holding this line ever since we had arrived before Petersburg—just such duty as they are now performing, for that corps has got back into its old line.

Question. Was that duty calculated to exhaust the men and render them less efficient than under other circumstances?

Answer. I cannot say that I thought it was; as I have already told you, the general services performed by the army I thought had undoubtedly affected its morale. The whole army was not in the condition it was when it crossed the Rapidan. I do not think there was anything in the special services of the 9th corps to render that corps less efficient.

Question. Was there anything calculated to exhaust the white troops more than the colored troops?

Answer. I think not.

Question. The white troops were up to the same standard with the colored troops?

Answer. The colored troops had not been in the front. Up to that time they had not been engaged at all. The white troops had been engaged ever since they had crossed the Rapidan.

Question. Had the colored troops been drilled with especial view to making that charge?

Answer. I believe they had. By referring to my orders, a copy of which I have submitted to the committee, with my report, I think it will be apparent that so far as events could be anticipated in the movements of such large bodies of men, for there were nearly 50,000 men prepared to move, every contingency that could be thought of was had in view.

Question. Were the enemy in the habit of firing day and night upon our lines wherever any of our men showed themselves?

Answer. Yes, sir.

Question. Would it have been possible, without great loss of life, to have removed the abatis in front of the 9th corps?

Answer. Yes, sir, it could have been done at night, without great loss of life—at least, that is my impression. But whatever might have been the loss of life, it was absolutely necessary for our further operations. I am of the opinion that it would not have been accompanied by any great loss of life.

By Mr. Chandler:

Question. Would it not have called the attention of the enemy to the proposed movement?

Answer. If they had seen it, it would undoubtedly have drawn their attention to it. However, it was one of the risks which we had to run.

Question. Can you give the distance our assaulting column had to move to reach the crater of the mine?

Answer. As near as we could tell, it was about one hundred yards; that was the estimated distance; I should say the distance between the two lines was about a hundred yards.

By Mr. Loan:

Question. You think there was a failure to prepare the necessary *debouchement* for our troops?

Answer. I think that was one of the difficulties, that sufficient arrangements had not been made in advance.

Question. Can you tell what time elapsed between the springing the mine and the occupation of the crater by our troops?

Answer. I do not think it was more than ten or fifteen minutes before the head of the column got in. But at nine o'clock in the day the whole of General Burnside's troops had not got out; I do not think he ever got all his men out of our lines.

Question. Was there an attack upon the right when the order was given to attack and seize the crest of the hill directly?

Answer. So far as I understand the circumstances, they were as follows: When I found that there was delay in the movement of this column up to the crest, I sent a despatch to General Burnside, urging him to push forward all his troops, without distinction of color, and to gain the crest as soon as possible; that despatch he sent to General Potter, directing him to immediately advance to the crest. He sent him a peremptory order, which order General Potter received about the time he was becoming engaged with the enemy, who were threatening him from the right. The order being peremptory, without reference to the condition of affairs, which General Burnside did not know, and which I did not know. General Potter being a good soldier, began his movement toward the crest, and was met by another force of the enemy, and compelled to fall back; that is the way I understand it. But in regard to that you can obtain the testimony of General Potter and others, who may give a different view of the matter.

Question. You have stated that you consulted the lieutenant general in regard to placing the colored troops in advance; was any further plan of General Burnside in regard to that assault submitted to General Grant at the same time?

Answer. I think he was informed of everything that General Burnside had informed me of.

Question. As I understand the matter, General Burnside had submitted to you in a communication a plan of attack for your consideration?

Answer. Yes, sir, and which I never disapproved of. The only question of difference was in regard to the troops to be employed. I never objected to his plan of handling his troops; I only objected to the colored troops being placed in the advance. General Burnside seemed afterwards to be under the impression that I objected to all his plan;

Question. Was there anything in that plan which referred to the commanders of the corps on the right and left of General Burnside—any suggestions in regard to them?

Answer. No, sir, I do not think there was in that plan of his; but previous to that there had been a question between General Burnside and myself in reference to the corps commanders on his right and left, which I will explain to you, because I suppose that is what you refer to, and I want to make my way smooth as well as your own.

Question. I may be mistaken, but I asked the question so that if I am not mistaken you can explain it. If I understand the matter rightly, General Burnside suggested to you a plan of operations. The question I wanted to get at was whether that whole plan had been submitted to Lieutenant General Grant, and whether it met his approval, and your approval—whether it was adopted or not.

Answer. So far as my recollection serves me, I think there was no general plan, involving the movements of the whole army, submitted to me by General Burnside. There was a plan involving the movements of his own corps, which he submitted to me; but that referred simply to the movements of his advance division. The only objection I intended to make to that plan was to the use of the colored troops in the advance. As to his tactical formation, and what he was to do with his troops, I made no objection. Therefore I think it extremely probable that I did not submit to General Grant anything but the question in regard to the colored troops.

Question. I understand you to say that the delay in the explosion of the mine arose from the failure of the fuze to burn?

Answer. Yes, sir.

Question. How many lines of fuze were used to explode that mine?

Answer. I am under the impression that there were three lines of fuze; at least I think General Burnside so reported. Whether the fact was that there were three fuzes or not, I never inquired.

Question. There must have been a failure to burn of all three, if three were ignited. I want to ascertain whether there were three fuzes or not.

Answer. That is more than I can tell; I can only tell that the fuze failed to burn.

Question. If there was but one line of fuze, I wanted to learn whether ordinary prudence was exercised in a case of that importance. If there were three lines of fuze, there can be no question about the prudence exercised.

Answer. That would bring up a question which I never asked, whether there were three fuzes, and if so, whether they were all fired. I recollect very well that General Burnside said there were three fuzes; and my recollection is that when the delay was explained, General Burnside said the fault had been found in a fuze about fifty feet from the mouth of the gallery, and that the fuze had been reignited and had then gone off. But why it was that he did not ignite one of the other fuzes I do not know.

Question. Would not ordinary prudence in an affair of that magnitude have required the three fuzes to have been ignited, so as to have secured three chances for the explosion of the mine, instead of one?

Answer. Yes, sir.

Question. Were any orders sent to General Burnside to retreat, or to withdraw his troops from the crater?

Answer. Yes, sir; he was directed about ten or eleven o'clock to withdraw. The first order sent to him was a distinct order to withdraw. General Burnside came to the position where I was with General Grant, at the headquarters on the field, and stated that in his judgment it would be injudicious to withdraw at that moment—that it would cause great sacrifice of life. I immediately authorized him, in writing, to exercise his judgment in the withdrawal—to remain there as long as he deemed it necessary for the secure withdrawal of his command—stating that he could remain there, if he chose, until night.

Question. As I understand you, General Potter, who was moving to the right to attack, upon the reception of his orders changed his movement towards the crest of the hill, where he was met by the enemy and repulsed?

Answer. Yes, sir, so I understand.

Question. Were there any other troops of the 9th corps, or any troops of any corps that got beyond the crater during the engagement?

Answer. I think the colored troops got beyond the crater; were forming beyond the crater when they received the artillery fire which caused them to break and go to the rear.

Question. About what hour in the morning was that?

Answer. I cannot exactly say, but I should think it was about 8 o'clock; perhaps between 8 and 9 o'clock.

"HEADQUARTERS ARMY OF THE POTOMAC, *January* 16, 1865.

"SIR: I herewith transmit by the hands of my aid, Major Bache, additional testimony, which I desire placed on record in relation to the affair of July 30, 1864. It includes the statement made by me to the court of inquiry, and is forwarded in accordance with the privilege accorded me by the committee authorizing me to add anything I chose to my deposition of the 20th ultimo.

"Very respectfully, your obedient servant,

"GEORGE G. MEADE,
"*Major General United States Army.*

"Hon. B. F. WADE,
"*Chairman Com. on Conduct of War, Washington, D. C.*"

Major General Meade's testimony before Court of Inquiry.

Major General Meade, United States volunteers, being duly sworn, says:

I propose in the statement that I shall make to the court—I presume the court want me to make a statement of facts in connexion with this case—to give a slight preliminary history of certain events and operations which culminated in the assault on July 30, and which, in my judgment, are necessary to show to this court that I had a full appreciation of the difficulties that were to be encountered, and that I had endeavored, so far as my capacity and judgment would enable me, not only to anticipate, but to take measures to overcome those difficulties.

The mine constructed in front of General Burnside was commenced by that officer soon after the occupation of our present lines, upon the intercession of Lieutenant Colonel Pleasants, I think, of a Pennsylvania regiment, without any reference to, or any sanction obtained from, the general headquarters of the army of the Potomac. When the subject was brought to my knowledge I authorized the continuance of the operations, sanctioned them, and trusted that the work would at some time result in forming an important part in our operations. But from the first I never considered that the location of General Burnside's mine was a proper one, because, from what I could ascertain, the position of the enemy's works and lines erected at that time, the position against which he operated, was not a suitable one in which to assault the enemy's lines, as it was commanded on both flanks, and taken in reverse by their position on the Jerusalem plank road, and their works opposite the Hare House.

I will now read to the court the despatches which passed between Lieutenant General Grant, commanding the armies of the United States, and myself, which will bear in themselves a sort of history of the preliminary operations, a correspondence which resulted, as I said before, in the final arrangements for the assault on July 30th.

On the 24th of July I received a letter from the lieutenant general commanding, which I will now read. I had been previously informed by the lieutenant general commanding that he desired some operations to take place offensive against the enemy, and he had instructed the engineer officer at his headquarters, the engineer officer at General Butler's headquarters, and the engineer officer at the headquarters army of Potomac, to make an examination of the enemy's position, and give an opinion as to the probable result of an attack. Their opinion is contained in the following letter:

"HEADQUARTERS ARMIES OF THE UNITED STATES,
"City Point, Virginia, July 24, 1864.
'Maj. Gen. GEORGE G. MEADE, *Commanding Army of the Potomac:*

"The engineer officers who made a survey of the front from Bermuda Hundred report against the probability of success from an attack there; the chances they think will be better on Burnside's front. If this is attempted, it will be necessary to concentrate all the force possible at the point in the enemy's line we expect to penetrate. All officers should be fully impressed of the absolute necessity of pushing entirely beyond the enemy's present line, if they should succeed in penetrating it, and of getting back to their present line promptly if they should not succeed in breaking through.

"To the right and left of the point of assault all the artillery possible should be brought, to play upon the enemy in front during the assault. Thin lines would be sufficient for the support of the artillery, and all the reserves could be brought on the flank of their commands nearest to the point of assault, ready to follow in if successful. The field artillery and infantry, held in the lines during the first assault, should be in readiness to move at a moment's notice, either to their front or to follow the main assault, as they should receive orders. One thing, however, should be impressed on corps commanders; if they see the enemy giving way in their front, or moving from it to re-enforce a heavily assaulted position of their line, they should take advantage of such knowledge, and act promptly without waiting for orders from their army commander.

"General Ord can co-operate with his corps in this movement, and about five thousand troops from Bermuda Hundred can be sent to re-enforce you, or can be used to threaten an assault between the Appomattox and James river, as may be deemed best.

"This should be done by Tuesday morning, if done at all. If not attempted we will then start at the date indicated to destroy the railroad as far as Hicksford, at least, and to Weldon if possible.

"Please give me your views on this matter, and I will order at once. In this I have said nothing of the part to be taken by the cavalry, in case the enemy's lines are assaulted. The best disposition to be made of them probably would be to place them on the extreme left, with instructions to skirmish with the enemy, and drive him back, if possible, following up any success gained in that way according to the judgment of the commander, or orders he may receive.

"Whether we send an expedition on the railroad, or assault at Petersburg, Burnside's mine will be blown up.

"As it is impossible to hide preparations from our own officers and men, and consequently from the enemy, it will be well to have it understood as far as possible that just the reverse of what we intend is in contemplation.

"I am, general, very respectfully, &c.,

"U. S. GRANT, *Lieutenant General.*

"Official copy:

"S. F. BARSTOW, *A. A. G.*"

I desire to call the particular attention of the court to that communication, because it contains the views of the lieutenant general commanding with reference to the assault which should be made on Petersburg, and I wish them to compare this communication with the orders and arrangements that I gave and made, so that they may see that to the best of my ability I ordered everything which he indicated to be done.

At the time that this communication was made to me, however, I was under the impression that the obstacles to be overcome were more formidable than the subsequent operations made me to believe, and also that subsequent to that time there had been no movement of the army to produce that great weakening of the enemy's front which afterwards occurred. Therefore my reply was to the effect that I was opposed to our making the assault.

The following is my reply, sent on the 24th:

"HEADQUARTERS ARMY OF THE POTOMAC,
"*July* 24, 1864.

"GENERAL: I have received your letter per Lieutenant Colonel Comstock. In reply thereto I have to state that yesterday I made in person a close and careful reconnoissance of the enemy's position in my front. Although I could not detect any positive indication of a second line, yet, from certain appearances at various points, I became satisfied that a second line does exist on the crest of the ridge, just in rear of the position of Burnside's mine. I have no doubt of the successful explosion of the mine, and of our ability to crown the crater, effect a lodgement, and compel the evacuation of the enemy's present occupied line, but from their redoubt on the Jerusalem plank road, and from their position in front of the Hare House, their artillery fire would render our lodgement untenable, and compel our advance or withdrawal.

"The advance, of course, should be made, but its success would depend on the question whether the enemy have a line on the crest of the ridge. If they have, with the artillery fire they can bring to bear on the approaches to this second hill, I do not deem it practicable to carry the line by assault, and from my examination, together with the evident necessity of their having such a line, I am forced to believe we shall find one there.

"I cannot, therefore, advise the attempt being made, but should it be deemed expedient to take the risks, and there is certainly room for doubt, I would like a little more time than is given in your note in order to place in position the maximum amount of artillery to bear upon the lines not assaulted. In reference to the assaulting force, it will be composed of the 9th and 2d corps.

"The 5th corps will have to remain in their present position, and be prepared to meet any attempt of the enemy to turn our left flank, which is not altogether unlikely, particularly if we should fail in our assault, and be compelled to withdraw.

"I am fully impressed with the importance of taking some immediate action, and am satisfied that, excepting regular approaches, the springing of Burnside's mine and subsequent assault is the most practicable, and I am not prepared to say the attempt would be *hopeless.* I am, however, of the opinion, so far as I can judge, that the chances of its success are not such as to make it expedient to attempt it.

"Very respectfully, yours,

"GEORGE G. MEADE,
"*Major General, Commanding.*

"Lieutenant General U. S. GRANT.

"Official:

"S. F. BARSTOW, *A. A. G.*"

"P. S.—I enclose you a report of Major Duane, which confirms my views; if Wright is soon to return, and we can extend our lines to the Weldon railroad, we could then advance against the salient on the Jerusalem plank road, and make an attempt to carry them at the same time we assaulted in Burnside's front.

"This was my view some time ago, and we have been preparing the necessary siege works for this purpose. Under your instructions, however, none of the heavy guns and material have been brought to the front, and it would take, perhaps, two days to get them up.

"GEORGE G. MEADE.

"Official copy:

"S. F. BARSTOW, *A. A. G.*"

"HEADQUARTERS ARMY OF THE POTOMAC,
"*Office of Chief Engineer, July* 24, 1864.

"Major General MEADE, *Commanding Army of the Potomac:*

"In reply to your communication of this date, I have the honor to state that the line of the enemy's works in front of General Burnside is not situated on the crest of the ridge separating us from Petersburg. That the enemy have undoubtedly occupied this ridge as a second line.

"Should General Burnside succeed in exploding his mine, he would probably be able to take the enemy's first line, which is about one hundred yards in advance of his approach. Beyond this I do not think he could advance until the works in front of the 5th corps are carried, as the 9th corps column would be taken in flank by a heavy artillery fire from works in front of the centre of the 5th corps, and in front by fire from the works on the crest near the Cemetery hill. I do not believe that the works in front of the 5th corps can be carried until our lines can be extended so as to envelope the enemy's line.

"Very respectfully, your obedient servant,

"J. C. DUANE,
"*Major Engineers, United States Army.*

"Official copy:

"S. F. BARSTOW, *A. A. G.*"

In reply to that I received a communication or report from General Grant, the result of which was a suspension of the proposed attack:

"HEADQUARTERS ARMIES OF THE UNITED STATES,
"*City Point, July* 24, 1864.

"GENERAL: Your note, brought by Colonel Comstock, is received. It will be necessary to act without expecting Wright. He is now in Washington; but it is not fully assured yet that Early has left the valley, and if Wright was to start back no doubt the Maryland raid would be repeated. I am not willing to attempt a movement so hazardous as the one against entrenched lines, against the judgment of yourself and your engineer officers, and arrived at after a more careful survey of the grounds than I have given it. I will let you know, however, in the morning what determination I come to.

"Very respectfully, your obedient servant,

"U. S. GRANT, *Lieutenant General.*

"Major General MEADE,
  Commanding Army of the Potomac.

"Official copy:

"S. F. BARSTOW,
"*Assistant Adjutant General.*"

Next day I made a closer examination; and in the mean time a signal station was erected in a pine tree in front of General Burnside, which gave us a more complete view than we had previously had of the enemy's line. My observations modified my views, because I could not detect a second line, although I detected isolated batteries on the crest. I therefore wrote the following communication to General Grant, dated 12 m., July 26:

"HEADQUARTERS ARMY OF THE POTOMAC,
"*July* 26, 1864—12 m.

"Lieutenant General GRANT:

"More critical examinations from a new signal station would lead to the conclusion that the enemy have detached works on the ridge in front of Burnside, but they have no connected line. This fact increases the chances of a successful assault, taken in connexion with the fact that General Burnside does not now think the enemy have discovered his mine; on the contrary, believes they are laying the platform for a battery right over it.

"I have suspended the orders to load and discharge it to-morrow, as it may yet be useful in connexion with further operations.

"I am afraid the appearance of McLaws's division, together with Willcox's, previously reported, will prevent any chance of a surprise on the part of our people to-morrow. Yesterday's Richmond Examiner also says your strategic movements are known, and preparations made to meet them, referring, I presume, to Foster's operations.

"There was considerable shelling by the enemy yesterday afternoon all along our lines, brought on, I think, by Burnside discovering a camp he had not before seen and ordering it shelled. No serious casualties were produced on our side, but the 5th corps working parties were very much annoyed and interrupted. With this exception, all was quiet.
"GEO. G. MEADE, *Major General.*

"Official copy:
"S. F. BARSTOW, *A. A. G.*"

To which I received the following reply:

"UNITED STATES MILITARY TELEGRAPH,
"*By telegraph from City Point, 3 p. m., dated July* 26, 1864.

"Major General MEADE:

"The information you have just sent, and all information received on the subject, indicates a probability that the enemy are looking for a formidable attack either from General Burnside or north of the James river, and that they will detach from Petersburg heavily to prevent its success. This will make your remaining two corps, with the 18th, relatively stronger against the enemy at Petersburg than we have been since the first day. It will be well, therefore, to prepare for an assault in General Burnside's front, only to be made if further development justifies it. If made it would be necessary to abandon most of the front now held by the 5th corps.
"U. S. GRANT, *Lieutenant General.*

"Official copy:
"S. F. BARSTOW, *A. A. G.*"

There you perceive that the lieutenant general commanding ordered that whilst the 2d corps was across the James river I should immediately make an assault with the 9th and 5th, abandoning the line of the 5th corps. In answer to that I wrote him the following despatch:

"HEADQUARTERS ARMY OF THE POTOMAC,
"5.30 *p. m., July* 26, 1864.

"Lieutenant General U. S. GRANT:

"Telegram 3 p. m. received. The only preparation that can be made is the loading of Burnside's mine. I cannot advise an assault with the 2d corps absent, for some force must be left to hold our lines and protect our batteries.

"The withdrawal of the 5th corps would prevent any attempt on our part to silence the fire of the enemy's guns in front of the 5th corps, and unless these guns are silenced no advance can be made across the open ground in front of the 9th corps.

"It is not the numbers of the enemy which oppose our taking Petersburg; it is their artillery and their works, which can be held by reduced numbers against direct assault.

"I have just sent you a despatch indicating an attack on my left flank by the enemy. This is my weak point, and a formidable attack turning my flank would require all my force to meet successfully.
"GEO. G. MEADE, *Major General.*

"Official:
"S. F. BARSTOW, *A. A. G.*"

That produced a suspension of the order to attack until the return of General Hancock. The next despatch I received from General Grant was as follows:

"UNITED STATES MILITARY TELEGRAPH,
"BY TELEGRAPH FROM CITY POINT,
"12.20 *p. m., dated July* 28, 1864.

"Major General MEADE:

"Your despatch of 12 m. received. Unless something turns up north of the James between this and night that I do not expect, you may withdraw Hancock, to be followed by Sheridan, and make arrangements for assault as soon as it can be made. We can determine by the movements of the enemy before the time comes whether it will be advisable to go on with the assault. I will put in the 18th corps, or not, as you deem best.
"U. S. GRANT, *Lieutenant General.*"

"S. F. BARSTOW, *A. A. G.*"

"Official:

Which I answered at 1 p. m., July 28, as follows:

"HEADQUARTERS ARMY POTOMAC, 1 *p. m., July* 28, 1864.
"Lieutenant General GRANT:

"Your despatch of 12.20 received. On reflection, I think daylight of the 30th is the earliest time it would be advisable to make the assault. Besides the time required to get up heavy guns and mortars, we require the night to make certain preliminary arrangements, such as massing troops, removing abatis from the debouche of the assaulting column, &c. I shall make the assault with the 9th corps, supported by the 2d. The reserves of the 18th should be held in readiness to take part, and if developments justify it, all of Ord's and Warren's commands can be put in.

"Official:
"GEO. G. MEADE, *Major General.*
"S. F. BARSTOW, *A. A. G.*"

I will here observe that Lieutenant General Grant, in consequence of the service which the 2d corps had performed across the river, desired, and gave me directions verbally to that effect, to use the 18th corps in the assault, and to let the 2d corps take the place of the 18th in the line.

The next despatch I received was the following, dated City Point, July 29:

"HEADQUARTERS ARMIES OF THE UNITED STATES,
"*City Point, Va., July* 29, 1864.

"GENERAL: I have directed General Butler to order General Ord to report to you for the attack on Petersburg. The details for the assault I leave to you to make out.

"I directed General Sheridan, whilst we were at Deep Bottom last evening, to move his command immediately to the left of Warren from Deep Bottom. It will be well to direct the cavalry to endeavor to get round the enemy's right flank; whilst they will not probably succeed in turning the enemy, they will detain a large force to prevent it. I will go out this evening to see you; will be at your headquarters about 4 p. m.

"Very respectfully, your obedient servant,

"Official:
"U. S. GRANT, *Lieutenant General.*
"S. F. BARSTOW, *A. A. G.*"

"Major General GEO. G. MEADE,
"*Commanding Army of the Potomac.*

"P. S.—If you want to be at any place on the line at the hour indicated, inform me by telegraph, and I will meet you wherever you may be.
"U. S. G."

General Grant came to my headquarters at 4 p. m., July 29, and at that time I showed him the order for the assault next day, which I had just then prepared, and which order met with his perfect approbation; he read the order and expressed his satisfaction with it. No other despatches passed between the lieutenant general and myself.

Next morning, between half past three and four o'clock—before four o'clock, he arrived on the ground, at General Burnside's headquarters, and all further communications between us were verbal, until August 1, at 11.40 a. m., when I received the following despatch:

["Cipher, received 11.40 a. m.]
By *telegraph from City Point,* 9.30 *a. m., dated August* 1, 1864.

"Major General MEADE:

"Have you any estimate of our losses in the miserable failure of Saturday? I think there will have to be an investigation of the matter. So fair an opportunity will probably never occur again for carrying fortifications; preparations were good, orders ample, and everything, so far as I could see subsequent to the explosion of the mine, shows that almost without loss the crest beyond the mine could have been carried; this would have given us Petersburg with all its artillery, and a large part of the garrison beyond doubt. An intercepted despatch states that the enemy recaptured their line with General Bartlett and staff, seventy-five commissioned officers, and nine hundred rank and file, and recaptured five hundred of their men.

"Official:
"U. S. GRANT, *Lieutenant General.*
"S. F. BARSTOW, *A. A. G.*"

We had given our respective views concerning the assault, and particularly impressed my views with reference to the difficulty to be overcome. When it was ascertained that the movement of the 2d corps had drawn over to the north bank of the James five of the eight divisions composing General Lee's army, together with the information I had obtained that the enemy had no second line upon the ridge, but only one or two isolated batteries, I came to the conclusion that the explosion of the mine, and the subsequent assault on the crest I had every reason to believe would be successful, and would be followed by results which would have consisted in the capture of the whole of the enemy's artillery, and a greater part of his infantry.

The plan sketched out by Lieutenant General Grant in his despatch to me, which I endeavored to carry out, and for the execution of which I gave the necessary orders, was, that the mine should be exploded as early as possible in the morning, before daylight; that in the mean time the 9th corps should be massed and formed in assaulting columns; that every preparation should be made by removing the abatis so that the troops could debouche, and particularly the assaulting columns; that as soon as the mine was exploded, the assaulting columns should push forward; that a sufficient proportion should be left to guard the flanks of the main column, because they had to look for an attack on the flanks; that the main body should hold the lines during the attempt to gain the crest of the hill, and if it was successful then I intended to throw up the whole of the 18th corps, to be followed up by the 2d corps, and if necessary by the 5th corps, also. I do not suppose it is necessary to read the order. I will read it, however.

"ORDERS.

"HEADQUARTERS ARMY POTOMAC, *July* 29, 1864.

"The following instructions are issued for the guidance of all concerned:

"1. As soon as it is dark, Major General Burnside, commanding 9th corps, will withdraw his two brigades under General White, occupying the intrenchments between the Plank and Norfolk roads, and bring them to his front. Care will be taken not to interfere with the troops of the 18th corps moving into their position in rear of the 9th corps. General Burnside will form his troops for assaulting the enemy's works at daylight of the 30th, prepare his parapets and abatis for the passage of the columns, and have the pioneers equipped for work in opening passages for artillery, destroying enemy's abatis, &c., and the intrenching tools distributed for effecting lodgements, &c.

"2. Major General Warren, commanding 5th corps, will reduce the number of his troops holding the intrenchments of his front to the minimum, and concentrate all his available forces on his right, and hold them prepared to support the assault of Major General Burnside. The preparations in respect to pioneers, intrenching tools, &c., enjoined upon the 9th corps, will also be made by the 5th corps.

"3. As soon as it is dark Major General Ord, commanding 18th corps, will relieve his troops in the trenches by General Mott's division of the 2d corps, and form his corps in rear of the 9th corps, and be prepared to support the assault of Major General Burnside.

"4. Every preparation will be made for moving forward the field artillery of each corps.

"5. At dark Major General Hancock, commanding 2d corps, will move from Deep Bottom, to the rear of the intrenchments now held by the 18th corps, resume the command of Mott's division, and be prepared at daylight to follow up the assaulting and supporting columns, or for such other operations as may be found necessary.

"6. Major General Sheridan, commanding cavalry corps, will proceed at dark from the vicinity of Deep Bottom, to Lee's Mill, and at daylight will move with his whole corps, including Wilson's division, against the enemy's troops defending Petersburg on their right by the roads leading to that town from the southward and westward.

"7. Major Duane, acting chief engineer, will have the pontoon trains parked at convenient points in the rear, prepared to move. He will see that supplies of sand-bags, gabions, fascines, &c., are in depot near the lines, ready for use.

"He will detail engineer officers for each corps.

"8. At half past three in the morning of the 30th, Major General Burnside will spring his mine, and his assaulting columns will immediately move rapidly upon the breach, seize the crest in the rear, and effect a lodgement there. He will be followed by Major General Ord, who will support him on the right, directing his movement to the crest indicated, and by Major General Warren, who will support him on the left.

"Upon the explosion of the mine, the artillery of all kinds in battery will open upon those points of the enemy's works whose fire covers the ground over which our columns must move, care being taken to avoid impeding the progress of our troops.

"Special instructions respecting the direction of fire will be issued through the chief of artillery.

"9. Corps commanders will report to the commanding general when their preparations are complete, and will advise him of every step in the progress of the operations, and of everything of importance that occurs.

"10. Promptitude, rapidity of execution, and cordial co-operation are essential to success; and the commanding general is confident that this indication of his expectations will insure the hearty efforts of the commanders and troops.

"11. Headquarters during the operations will be at the headquarters of the 9th corps.

"By command of Major General Meade.

"S. WILLIAMS, *Assistant Adjutant General.*

"Official:

"S. F. BARSTOW, *A. A. G.*"

Having read to the court the correspondence which passed between the lieutenant general and myself preliminary to the operations, and having read the order for the operations, I now propose to read and accompany with some explanatory remarks the despatches and correspondence which passed between myself and Major General Burnside, who had the immediate active operations to perform; afterwards between myself and Major General Ord, between myself and Major General Warren, and between myself and Major General Hancock. These despatches, when compared with each other, and in connexion with the remarks which I shall make, will show the facts so far as they came to my knowledge; and I wish the court to bear in mind, and I desire to call their attention particularly to the paucity of information which was furnished me by Major General Burnside of the operations which were made, and to the difficulty that a major general commanding an army like the one I am commanding labors under to give direct orders in the ignorance of matters transpiring in the front at the immediate scene of operations.

Before the operations were concluded upon I called upon Major General Burnside to furnish me in writing what he proposed to do in case his mine was exploded. In response to which I received the following report:

"HEADQUARTERS NINTH ARMY CORPS, *July* 26, 1864.

"GENERAL: I have the honor to acknowledge the receipt of your notes of this morning by Captains Jay and Bache; also a telegram from the commanding general relating to the same subject.

"It is altogether probable that the enemy are cognizant of the fact that we are mining, because it has been mentioned in their newspapers, and they have been heard to work in what are supposed to be shafts in close proximity to our galleries; but the rain of night before last no doubt filled their shafts and much retarded their work. We have heard no sounds of work in them either yesterday or to-day, and nothing is heard by us in the mine but the usual sounds of work on the surface above. This morning we had some apprehensions that the left lateral gallery was in danger of caving in from the weight of the batteries above it and the shock of their firing; but all possible precautions have been taken to strengthen it and we hope to preserve it intact. The placing of the charges in the mine will not involve the necessity of making a noise. It is therefore probable that we will escape discovery, if the mine is to be used within two or three days. It is nevertheless highly important, in my opinion, that the mine should be exploded at the earliest possible moment consistent with the general interests of the campaign. I state to you the facts as nearly as I can; and, in the absence of any knowledge as to the meditated movement of the army, I must leave you to judge the proper time to make use of the mine; but it may not be improper for me to say, that the advantages to be reaped from the work would be but small if it were exploded without any co-operative movements.

"My plan would be to explode the mine just before daylight in the morning, or about five o'clock in the afternoon; mass the two brigades of the colored division in rear of my line in column of divisions—double column closed in mass; the head of each brigade resting on the front line, and as soon as the explosion has taken place move them forward, with instructions for the divisions to take half-distance; and as soon as the leading regiments of the two brigades pass through the gap in the enemy's line, the leading regiment of the right brigade to come into line perpendicular to the enemy's line by the right companies on the right into line, 'wheel the left companies on the left into line,' and proceed at once down the line of the enemy's work as rapidly as possible; the leading regiment of the left brigade to execute the reverse movement to the left, moving up the enemy's line; the remainder of the two columns to move directly towards the crest in front as rapidly as possible, diverging in such a way as to enable them to deploy into columns of regiments, the right column making as nearly as may be for Cemetery hill; these columns to be followed by the other divisions of this corps as soon as they can be thrown in; this would involve the necessity of relieving these divisions by other troops before the movement, and of holding columns of other troops in readiness to take our place on the crest, in case we gain it and sweep down it. It would be advisable, in my opinion, if we succeed in gaining the crest, to throw the colored division right into the town. There is a necessity for the co-operation, at least in the way of artillery, of the troops on my right and left; of the extent of this you will necessarily be the judge. I think our chances of success in a plan of this kind are more than even. The main gallery of the mine is five hundred and twenty-two (522) feet in length; the side galleries about forty feet each. My suggestion is, that eight magazines be placed in the lateral galleries—two at each end, say a few feet apart, in branches at right angles to the side galleries; and two more in each of the side galleries, similarly placed, situated by pairs, equidistant from each other and the end of the galleries, thus:

[See diagram, page 17.]

"Tamping beginning at the termination of the main gallery for, say, one hundred feet, leaving all the air space in the side galleries. Run out some five or six fuzes and two wires, to render the ignition of the charge certain. I propose to put in each of the eight magazines from twelve to fourteen hundred pounds of powder, the magazines to be connected by a trough of powder instead of a fuze.

"I beg to enclose a copy of a statement from General Potter on the subject. I would suggest that the powder train be parked in a wood near our ammunition train, about a mile in rear of this place. Lieutenant Colonel Pierce, chief quartermaster, will furnish Captain Strand with a guide to the place.

"I beg also to request that General Benham be instructed to send us, at once, eight thousand (8,000) sand-bags, to be used for tamping and other purposes.

"I have the honor to be, general, very respectfully, your obedient servant,

"A. E. BURNSIDE, *Major General, Commanding.*

"Major General HUMPHREYS, *Chief of Staff.*"

"Official:

"S. F. BARSTOW, *Assistant Adjutant General.*"

The request made in that letter by Major General Burnside was complied with—that is to say, sand-bags were furnished him; but the amount of powder asked for, which was twelve thousand pounds, was reduced to eight thousand pounds, upon the belief on my part, and on my engineers, that eight thousand pounds would be sufficient for the purpose.

Another matter in that despatch to which my attention was directed, and which was finally the subject of an order on my part, is the suggestion of Major General Burnside to place the colored troops at the head of the assaulting column. That I disapproved, and I informed him of my disapproval, which was based upon the ground, not that I had any reason to doubt, or any desire to doubt, the good qualities of the colored troops, but that I desired to impress upon Major General Burnside, which I did do in conversations, of which I have plenty of witnesses to evidence, and in every way I could, that the operation was to be a coup-de-main; that his assaulting column was to be as a forlorn hope, such as are put into breaches, and that he should assault with his best troops; not that I had any intention to insinuate that the colored troops were inferior to his best troops, but that I understood that they had never been under fire, nor that they should not be taken for such a critical operation as this, but that he should take such troops as from previous service could be depended upon as being perfectly reliable. Finding General Burnside very much disappointed—for he had made known to General Ferrero and his troops that they were to lead in the assault—and fearing that the effect might be injurious, and in order to show him that I was not governed by any motive other than such as I ought to be governed by, I told him I would submit the matter, with his reasons and my objections, to the lieutenant general commanding the armies, and I would abide by the decision of the lieutenant general as to whether it was expedient and right for the colored troops to lead the assault. Upon referring the question to the lieutenant general commanding, he fully concurred in my views, and I accordingly addressed to Major General Burnside, or had addressed to him, the following communication:

"HEADQUARTERS ARMY OF THE POTOMAC,
"10¼ a. m., July 29, 1864.

"Major General BURNSIDE, *Commanding 9th Corps:*

"I am instructed to say that the major general commanding submitted to the lieutenant general commanding the armies your proposition to form the leading columns of assault of the black troops, and that he, as well as the major general commanding, does not approve the proposition, but directs that these columns be formed of the white troops.

"A. A. HUMPHREYS, *Major General, Chief of Staff.*"

"Official:

"S. F. BARSTOW, *A. A. G.*"

The next despatches to Major General Burnside were addressed by me at 9.45 p. m., July 29, the evening before the action. I had received a despatch from General Ord, stating that it would take him till very late to relieve the troops in the trenches.

The following is my despatch to General Burnside:

"HEADQUARTERS ARMY OF THE POTOMAC,
"*July 29—9¾ p. m.*, 1864.

"Major General BURNSIDE, *Commanding 9th Corps:*

"A despatch from General Ord refers to the late hour at which his troops will relieve yours in the trenches. The commanding general has informed General Ord that it is not necessary for you to wait for your troops to be relieved in the trenches by General Ord before forming them for the assault. They should be formed for the assault at the hour you deem best, without any reference to General Ord's troops, who will enter the vacated trenches as soon as they can.

"A. A. HUMPHREYS,
"*Major General and Chief of Staff.*

"Official:

S. F. BARSTOW, *A. A. G.*"

My idea was that General Burnside should form his columns of assault, make all his preparations, take all his men out of the trenches, and move forward; and that then General Ord should occupy his trenches in case he should not find it necessary to return. No further despatches passed between General Burnside and myself. I think it proper to state, however, that on the day previous to the assault I was at General Burnside's headquarters, and had the good fortune to meet his three division commanders, and some conversation passed between us, and I would like the court to inquire into what transpired on that occasion, because I would like to impress upon the court, as I did impress upon General Burnside and his officers, that this operation which we had to perform was one purely of time; that if immediate advantage was not taken of the explosion of the mine, and the consequent confusion of the enemy, and the crest immediately gained, it would be impossible to remain there, for that as soon as the enemy should recover from their confusion, they would bring their troops and batteries to bear upon us and we would be driven out. That there were two things to be done, namely, that we should go up promptly and take the crest; for, in my judgment, the mere occupation of the crater and the holding on to that was of no possible use to us, because the enemy's line was not such a line as would be of advantage for us to hold, except to go from it to the crest; and that the troops were to be withdrawn when the assault proved unsuccessful.

I saw Potter, Ledlie, and Wilcox, and I referred in the presence of those gentlemen to the tactical manœuvres to be made between that crater and the crest—that the only thing to be done was to rush for the crest and take it immediately after the explosion had taken place; and that they might rest

BATTLE OF PETERSBURG.

assured that any attempt to take time to form their troops would result in a repulse.

These were all the despatches that transpired between General Burnside and myself before the day of the assault.

On the morning of the 30th, about a quarter past three o'clock, when I was about preparing to go forward to General Burnside's headquarters, I found that it was very dark, and suggestions being made by some of my officers that it was too dark to operate successfully, and that a postponement of the explosion of the mine might be advantageous, I accordingly addressed a despatch to General Burnside to the following effect:

"HEADQUARTERS ARMY OF THE POTOMAC,
"*July* 30, 1864—3.20 a. m.
"Major General BURNSIDE:
"As it is still so dark, the commanding general says you can postpone firing the mine if you think proper.
"A. A. HUMPHREYS,
"*Major General and Chief of Staff.*
"Official:
"S. F. BARSTOW, *A. A. G.*"

To that I received the following reply from General Burnside:

"BY TELEGRAPH FROM NINTH ARMY CORPS,
"*Dated July* 30, 1864—3.20 a. m.
"Major General HUMPHREYS:
"The mine will be fired at the time designated. My headquarters will be at the 14 gun battery.
"A. E. BURNSIDE, *Major General.*
"Official:
"S. F. BARSTOW, *A. A. G.*"

I then went over to General Burnside's headquarters, he, during these operations, being further to the front. The hour had arrived. I stood waiting. I heard no report from General Burnside and no explosion of the mine. In the mean time Lieutenant General Grant arrived. Finding that there was no explosion, I sent two staff officers, first Captain Jay, and then —— ——, I do not recollect the name of the other; but I sent two staff officers to General Burnside to ascertain what the difficulty was, if there was any difficulty; why his mine did not explode, if he knew; to which I received no answer. At 4.10 the following depatch was sent to him:

"HEADQUARTERS ARMY OF THE POTOMAC,
"*July* 30, 1864—4.15 a. m.
"Major General BURNSIDE:
"Is there any difficulty in exploding the mine? It is now three-quarters of an hour later than the time fixed upon for exploding it.
"A. A. HUMPHREYS,
"*Major General and Chief of Staff.*
"Official:
"S. F. BARSTOW, *A. A. G.*"

And to this I got no answer.

At 4.20 another despatch was sent to him, as follows:

"HEADQUARTERS ARMY OF THE POTOMAC, *July* 30, 1864.
"OPERATOR at General Burnside's field headquarters:
"Is General Burnside at his headquarters? The commanding general is anxious to learn what is the cause of delay.
"A. A. HUMPHREYS,
"*Major General and Chief of Staff.*
"Official:
"S. F. BARSTOW, *A. A. G.*"

I should have stated before this, that, in order to secure the speedy transmission of intelligence, I took the precaution to have a telegraph run from my headquarters, in General Burnside's camp, to where General Burnside had established his headquarters for the day, in the 14-gun battery.

The following is the next despatch I sent to General Burnside:

"HEADQUARTERS ARMY OF THE POTOMAC,
"*July* 30, 1864—4.35 a. m.

"Major General BURNSIDE:

"If the mine cannot be exploded, something else must be done, and at once. The commanding general is awaiting to hear from you before determining.

"A. A. HUMPHREYS,
"*Major General and Chief of Staff.*

"Official:

"S. F. BARSTOW, *A. A. G.*"

To this I received no reply. Finding that no replies were received, and the lieutenant general commanding desiring that an immediate assault should be made without reference to the mine, at 4.35 the following despatch was sent to General Burnside:

"HEADQUARTERS ARMY OF THE POTOMAC,
"*July* 30, 1864—4.35 a. m.

"Major General BURNSIDE, *Commanding 9th Corps:*

"The commanding general directs, that if your mine has failed, that you make an assault at once, opening your batteries.

"A. A. HUMPHREYS,
"*Major General and Chief of Staff.*

"Official:

"S. F. BARSTOW, *A. A. G.*"

The same orders you will find were sent to General Warren, to General Mott, and to General Hunt to open the artillery. About this time, however, about 4.40, the mine was exploded. In the mean time Captain Jay returned and informed me that the fuze had failed; that a defect was found, and the fuze had been overhauled about fifty feet or twenty-five feet, I forget the distance, from the entrance; that the defect had been ascertained and remedied, and that finally the mine had been exploded. So far as my recollection goes the mine was exploded about 4.40 or 4.45. At 5.45 a. m., one hour after the explosion of the mine, the following despatch was sent to General Burnside:

"HEADQUARTERS ARMY OF THE POTOMAC,
"*July* 30, 1864—5.40 a. m.

"Major General BURNSIDE:

"What news from your assaulting column? Please report frequently.

GEO. G. MEADE, *Major General.*

"Official:

"S. F. BARSTOW, *Assistant Adj. General.*"

The following despatch was received from him, apparently in answer to mine, although, through a difference in time, it is dated before it:

"BY TELEGRAPH FROM BATTERY MORTON,
"5.40 *a. m.,* dated *July* 30, 1864.

"General MEADE:

"We have the enemy's first line and occupy the breach. I shall endeavor to push forward to the crest as rapidly as possible.

"A. E. BURNSIDE, *Major General.*

"P. S.—There is a large fire in Petersburg.

"W. W. SANDERS, *Captain and A. D. C.*

"Official:

"S. F. BARSTOW, *Assistant Adj. General.*"

About this time, 5.45 or 5.50, (I see by reference to the despatch that it is 5.45,) an orderly came up to me and delivered me a despatch, which, upon opening, I found to be a despatch from Colonel Loring, inspector general of the 9th corps, written at the crater, and addressed to General Burnside, which despatch the orderly, not knowing where to find General Burnside, had brought to his old headquarters, where it found me. That despatch, so far as I recollect the purport of it, was to the effect that General Ledlie's troops occupied the crater, but, in his (Colonel Loring's) opinion, he feared the men could not be induced to advance beyond. That despatch was telegraphed to General Burnside, and sent to him by an officer, so that I have no copy of it. That was the substance of it, however. It was shown to General Grant and General Humphreys, both of whom can give their recollection of it in confirmation of mine. It is an important matter to be taken into consideration here that as early as 5.45 a. m. a despatch was placed in my hands stating that General Ledlie's troops could not be induced to advance.

In addition to that the following despatch was sent to him:

"HEADQUARTERS ARMY OF THE POTOMAC,
"*July* 30, 1864—5.40 a. m.

"Major General BURNSIDE, *Commanding 9th Corps*:

"The commanding general learns that your troops are halting at the works where the mine exploded. He directs that all your troops be pushed forward to the crest at once. Call on General Ord to move forward his troops at once.

"A. A. HUMPHREYS, *Major Gen. and Chief of Staff.*

"Official:
"S. F. BARSTOW, *Assistant Adj. General.*"

Fearing there might be some difficulty on the part of General Burnside's troops, I thought it possible that by another corps going in on his right encouragement might be given to his men, and a prompt assault might be made.

The next despatch I received was from an aide-de-camp, whom I had sent to General Burnside's headquarters to advise me of what was going on. It is dated 5.50, and is from Captain Sanders:

"BY TELEGRAPH FROM HEADQUARTERS, 14-GUN BATTERY,
"*July* 30, 1864—5.50 a. m.

"Major General MEADE:

"The 18th corps has just been ordered to push forward to the crest. The loss does not appear to be heavy. Prisoners coming in.

"W. W. SANDERS, *Captain and C. M.*

"Official:
"S. F. BARSTOW, *Assistant Adj. General.*"

The next despatch that I will read is one addressed to General Burnside, at 6 a. m.:

"HEADQUARTERS ARMY OF THE POTOMAC,
"*July* 30, 1864—6 a. m.

"Major General BURNSIDE:

"Prisoners taken say there is no line in their rear, and that their men were falling back when ours advanced; that none of their troops have returned from the James. Our chance is now. Push your men forward at all hazards—white and black—and don't lose time in making formations, but rush for the crest.

"GEO. G. MEADE, *Major Gen., Commanding.*

"Official:
"S. F. BARSTOW, *Assistant Adj. General.*"

Despatches were at this time also sent to Generals Ord and Warren. You can keep these dates in your mind.

The next despatch was received from Captain Sanders, at 6.10 a. m., as follows:

BATTLE OF PETERSBURG.

"BY TELEGRAPH FROM HEADQUARTERS 14-GUN BATTERY,
July 30, 1864—6.10 a. m.

"General MEADE:

"General Burnside says that he has given orders to all his division commanders to push everything in at once.

"W. W. SANDERS, *Captain and C. M.*

"Official:
"S. F. BARSTOW,
"*Assistant Adjutant General.*"

The following despatches are next in order:

"HEADQUARTERS ARMY OF THE POTOMAC,
"*July* 30—6.05 *a. m.*, 1864.

"Major General BURNSIDE, *Commanding 9th Corps:*

"The commanding general wishes to know what is going on on your left, and whether it would be an advantage for Warren's supporting force to go in at once.

A. A. HUMPHREYS,
" *Major General and Chief of Staff.*

"Official:
"S. F. BARSTOW,
"*Assistant Adjutant General.*"

"[Telegraph from headquarters 9th corps.]
"*Dated July* 30—6.20 *a. m.*, 1864.

"Major General MEADE:

"If General Warren's supporting force can be concentrated just now, ready to go in at the proper time, it would be well. I will designate to you when it ought to move. There is scarcely room for it now in our immediate front.

"A. E. BURNSIDE, *Major General.*

"Official:
"S. F. BARSTOW,
"*Assistant Adjutant General.*"

"HEADQUARTERS ARMY POTOMAC,
"*July* 30—6.50 *a. m.*, 1864.

"Major General BURNSIDE:

"Warren's force has been concentrated and ready to move since 3.30 a. m. My object in inquiring was to ascertain if you could judge of the practicability of his advancing without waiting for your column. What is the delay in your column moving? Every minute is most precious, as the enemy undoubtedly are concentrating to meet you on the crest, and, if you give them time enough, you cannot expect to succeed. There is no object to be gained in occupying the enemy's line. It cannot be held under their artillery fire without much labor in turning it. The great point is to secure the crest at once and at all hazards.

"GEO. G. MEADE, *Major General.*

"Official:
"S. F. BARSTOW,
"*Assistant Adjutant General.*"

At seven a. m. Lieutenant General Grant put into my hand a despatch from Colonel Comstock, an officer whom he had sent to see the progress of operations:

"[By telegraph from 5th army corps.]
"JULY 30—7 *a. m.*, 1864.

"Lieutenant General GRANT:

"Several regiments of Burnside's men are lying in front of the crater, apparently, of the mine. In their rear is to be seen a line of battle of a brigade or more, under cover, and I think between the enemy's line and ours. The volley firing half (½) hour ago was from the enemy's works in Warren's front.

"C. B. COMSTOCK, *Lieut. Colonel.*

"Official:
"S. F. BARSTOW,
Assistant Adjutant General.'

I read all these despatches over, that you may see how I was situated on the occasion, and what I knew of what was going on.

BATTLE OF PETERSBURG. 55

At 7.20—twenty minutes afterwards—I got the following despatch from General Burnside:

"[Telegraph from headquarters 9th corps.]"
"Received about 7.20 a. m., July 30, 1864.
"General MEADE:
"I am doing all in my power to push the troops forward, and, if possible, we will carry the crest. It is hard work, but we hope to accomplish it. I am fully alive to the importance of it.
"A. E. BURNSIDE, *Major General.*
"Official:
"S. F. BARSTOW,
"*Assistant Adjutant General.*"

Upon the receipt of this despatch from General Burnside, informing me that it was hard work to take the crest, at the same time he not having reported to me that anybody had attempted to take it, or that any part of his force had made any effort to take it; with the despatches from my officers, the despatch from Colonel Loring, and the despatch from Colonel Comstock, to the effect that the troops were lying there, I came to the conclusion that possibly there might be some difficulty in getting the men to move forward, either from the enemy's fire, or some imaginary obstacle the troops had to encounter; that, as it was now 7 o'clock, and that the place had been occupied at 5.30, I began to suppose that there was some reason for the delay which had not been officially reported. I considered it natural that General Burnside would be indisposed to make it known, so long as he had hopes of overcoming the difficulty. To me, in my position as major general commanding the army, it was a matter of the utmost importance, because it was my intention during the assault, and before it, that if we could not carry the crest promptly by a coup-de-main, to withdraw the troops as quickly and safely as possible. Impressed with this view, and in order to get at the exact condition of affairs, and to justify General Burnside, if there was any reason of that kind, I addressed him the following despatch:

"HEADQUARTERS ARMY OF THE POTOMAC,
"7.30 *a. m., July* 30, 1864.
"Major General BURNSIDE:
"What do you mean by hard work to take the crest? I understand not a man has advanced beyond the enemy's line which you occupied immediately after exploding the mine. Do you mean to say your officers and men will not obey your orders to advance; if not, what is the obstacle? I wish to know the truth, and desire an immediate answer.
"GEO. G. MEADE, *Major General.*
"Official:
"S. F. BARSTOW, *Assistant Adjutant General.*"

It is proper to say, that immediately after sending that despatch, and before receiving General Burnside's answer, I received a report verbally from Captain Sanders that an attempt had been made to make an attack on the right, I think by General Griffin, and that he had been repulsed. I immediately sent another despatch to General Burnside at 8 a. m., as follows:

"HEADQUARTERS ARMY OF THE POTOMAC,
"*July* 30—8 *a. m.,* 1864.
"To Major General BURNSIDE:
"Since writing by Captain Jay, Captain Sanders has come in and reported condition of affairs. He says Griffin has advanced and been checked; this modifies my despatch. Still I should like to know the exact morale of your corps. Ord reports he cannot move till you get out of the way. Can't you let him pass out on your right, and let him try what he can do?
"GEO. G. MEADE, *Major General.*
"Official:
"S. F. BARSTOW, *Assistant Adjutant General.*"

To the first of these two despatches, subsequent to sending the second, I received this reply:

"HEADQUARTERS 9TH CORPS, BATTERY MORTON,
"About 7.35 a. m., July 30, 1864.
"General MEADE:

"Your despatch by Captain Jay received. The main body of General Potter's division is beyond the crater. I do not mean to say that my officers and men will not obey my orders to advance; I mean to say that it is very hard to advance to the crest.

"I have never in any report said anything different from what I conceived to be the truth; were it not insubordinate, I would say that the latter remark of your note was unofficerlike and ungentlemanly.

"Respectfully, yours,

"A. E. BURNSIDE, *Major General.*
"Official:
"S. F. BARSTOW, *Assistant Adjutant General.*"

The next despatch that I received was one from Colonel Comstock, about the same time, 8 a. m.:

"[By telegraph from 5th army corps.]
"8 a. m., July 30, 1864.
"To Lieutenant General GRANT:

"About a brigade more of our men has moved up to the crater, and then filed off to the right along the enemy's line; they are still moving to the right.

"C. B. COMSTOCK,
"*Lieutenant Colonel and Aide-de-Camp.*
"Official:
"S. F. BARSTOW, *Assistant Adjutant General.*"

The next despatch I received was one dated 8.45 a. m., from Captain Sanders

"[By telegraph from headquarters 9th army corps.]
"8.45 a. m., July 30, 1864.
"To General MEADE:

"One gun has just been taken out of the mine, and is now being put in position. Have not heard anything from the attack made from the left of mine. One (1) set of colors just sent in, captured by the negroes.

"W. W. SANDERS, *Captain and Aide-de-Camp.*
"Official:
"S. F. BARSTOW, *Assistant Adjutant General.*"

At 9 a. m. I received the following despatch from General Burnside:

"[By telegraph from headquarters 9th army corps.]
"9 a. m., July 30, 1864.
"General MEADE:

"Many of the ninth (9th) and eighteenth (18th) corps are retiring before the enemy. I think now is the time to put in the fifth (5th) corps promptly.

"A. E. BURNSIDE, *Major General.*
"Official:
"S. F. BARSTOW, *Assistant Adjutant General.*"

That was the first information I had received that there was any collision with the enemy, or that there was any enemy present. At 9.30 a. m. the following despatch was sent to General Burnside:

"HEADQUARTERS ARMY OF THE POTOMAC,
"July 30, 1864—9.30 a. m.
"Major General BURNSIDE, *Commanding 9th Corps:*

"The major general commanding has heard that the result of your attack has been a repulse, and directs that if, in your judgment, nothing further can be effected, that you withdraw to your own line, taking every precaution to get the men back safely.

"A. A. HUMPHREYS,
"*Major General and Chief of Staff.*
"General Ord will do the same.

"A. A. HUMPHREYS,
"*Major General and Chief of Staff.*
"Official:
"S. F. BARSTOW, *Assistant Adjutant General.*"

Then I received the following despatch from Captain Sanders:

"[By telegraph from headquarters 9th army corps.]
"9 a. m. *July* 30, 1864.
"To Major General MEADE:
"The attack made on right of mine has been repulsed. A great many men are coming to the rear.
"W. W. SANDERS, *Captain and C. M.*
"Official: "S. F. BARSTOW,
"*Assistant Adjutant General.*"

The next despatch was this, from Colonel Comstock:

"[By telegraph.]
"HEADQUARTERS 5TH ARMY CORPS,
"*July* 30, 1864—9.35 a. m.
"To Lieutenant General GRANT:
"I cannot see that we have advanced beyond the enemy's line in the vicinity of the mine. From here, it looks as if the enemy were holding a line between that point and the crest.
"C. B. COMSTOCK,
"*Lieutenant Colonel and Aide-de-Camp.*
"Official: "S. F. BARSTOW,
"*Assistant Adjutant General.*"

The next despatch to General Burnside, at 9.45, was the peremptory order to withdraw:

"HEADQUARTERS ARMY OF THE POTOMAC,
"*July* 30, 9¾ a. m., 1864.
"To Major General BURNSIDE, *Commanding 9th Corps*:
"The major general commanding directs that you withdraw to your own intrenchments.
"A. A. HUMPHREYS,
"*Major General, Chief of Staff.*
"Official: "S. F. BARSTOW,
"*Assistant Adjutant General.*"

Receiving information from some person—I don't know who it was—that there was some difficulty about withdrawing at that time, that the safety of the column might be jeoparded by undertaking to withdraw it, the following despatch was sent to General Burnside, and also to General Ord, who had troops there at that time. None of my despatches to General Ord have been presented yet, because it would have confused matters. I will read them hereafter:

"HEADQUARTERS ARMY OF THE POTOMAC,
"*July* 30, 10 a. m., 1864.
"Major Generals BURNSIDE and ORD:
"You can exercise your discretion in withdrawing your troops now or at a later period; say to-night. It is not intended to hold the enemy's line which you now occupy any longer than is required to withdraw safely your men.
"GEO. G. MEADE, *Major General.*
"Official: "S. F. BARSTOW,
"*Assistant Adjutant General.*"

About that time, both Major General Burnside and Major General Ord came to the headquarters where General Grant and myself were temporarily located. General Burnside seemed to be very much displeased at the order of withdrawal, and expressed the opinion that if allowed to remain there, by nightfall he could carry that crest. As, however, he did not give any reason to show how he could take it, and as he had been from half past five in the morning till nearly ten, and not only had not taken it, but had his men driven out of the works he had been occupying, and as Major General Ord, whose troops were also there, upon being asked if the crest could be carried, answered very positively that it was entirely out of the question, it was determined by the lieutenant general commanding and myself, or rather I referred the matter to him, to know if he desired the orders changed—it was determined that no further attempt should be made to take the crest, but that the men should be withdrawn whenever that could be done with security.

There is now a very important point to which I will call the attention of the court, and which I want investigated very thoroughly, and that is the withdrawal from the crater.

At the time the order was given to withdraw the troops, the report of Major General Ord was, that the crater of the mine was so overcrowded with men that it would be nothing but murder to send any more men forward there. I do not recollect as to whether the report of Major General Burnside was so definite, but I believe the report of Colonel Loring was that there was at least one division of the troops in there. The impression left upon my mind was, that at that time there were as many men in the crater as would enable them to defend themselves if attacked, and in case no defence was necessary there was no occasion on my part to order troops to be sent there. I presumed that Major General Ord and Major General Burnside, having charge of that operation, would see that the men would be properly withdrawn.

This conclusion having been arrived at by the lieutenant general and myself, and it not appearing necessary that we should remain any longer at Major General Burnside's headquarters, the lieutenant general commanding withdrew to City Point, and I withdrew to my former headquarters, where I was in telegraphic communication with Major General Burnside, and where, under the common correspondence between a general officer commanding the army and his subordinates, not to say under a peculiar exigency, I expected to be informed of anything that should occur. I remained in total ignorance of any further transactions until about six or seven o'clock in the evening. About that hour a report, or a rumor, reached me that there were a number of our wounded men lying between the crater and our line, and I think an appeal was made to me by General Ord if something could not be done to remove these men. I was not aware that there was any difficulty in the way of removing them, and wondered why they had not been removed, presuming that our men were in the crater; and as no report had been made to me that they had been withdrawn, I directed a despatch to be sent to Major General Burnside, calling upon him for information. That despatch read as follows:

"HEADQUARTERS ARMY OF THE POTOMAC,
"*July* 30, 1864—7.40 p. m.
"Major GENERAL BURNSIDE, *Commanding 9th Corps:*

"The major general commanding desires to know whether you still hold the crater; and if so, whether you will be able to withdraw your troops from it safely to-night; and also to bring off the wounded. The commanding general wishes to know how many wounded are probably lying there. It will be recollected that on a former occasion General Beauregard declined to enter into any arrangement for the succor of the wounded and the burial of the dead lying under both fires; hence the necessity of immediate and active efforts for their removal in the present case.

"A. A. HUMPHREYS,
"*Major General and Chief of Staff.*

"Official:

"S. F. BARSTOW,
"*Assistant Adjutant General.*"

You will remember that I left General Burnside's headquarters about 10 o'clock, with the understanding that the troops were to be withdrawn when they could be withdrawn with security.

The following despatches were subsequently read by the witness:

BATTLE OF PETERSBURG.

"HEADQUARTERS ARMY OF THE POTOMAC,
"*July* 30, 1864—10.35 p. m.

"Major General BURNSIDE, *Commanding 9th Corps* :

"The major general commanding desires to know whether you have any wounded left on the field; and directs me to say that he is awaiting your reply to the despatch of 7.40 p. m.

"A. A. HUMPHREYS,
"*Major General and Chief of Staff.*

"Official:

"S. F. BARSTOW,
"*Assistant Adjutant General.*"

"HEADQUARTERS ARMY OF THE POTOMAC,
"*July* 31, 1864—8.40 a. m.

'To Major General BURNSIDE, *Commanding 9th Corps:*

"The major general commanding directs me to call your attention to the fact that you have made no report to him upon the condition of affairs in your front since he left your headquarters yesterday, and that you have made no reply to the two special communications upon the subject sent you last night at 7.40 p. m., and at 10.40 p. m.

"I am also directed to inquire into the cause of these omissions.

"A. A. HUMPHREYS,
"*Major General and Chief of Staff.*

"Official :

"S. F. BARSTOW,
"*Assistant Adjutant General.*"

"BY TELEGRAPH FROM HEADQUARTERS 9TH CORPS,
"*July* 31, 1864—9 a. m.

"Major General HUMPHREYS:

"Your despatch was received just as I was making out a report of our casualties. I have used every means to get something like accurate reports, but it has been difficult.

"The rumors are very numerous and exaggerated. I will send report by messenger. The order to retreat caused great confusion, and we have lost largely in prisoners.

"General Ord's men on our lines were not relieved.

"A. E. BURNSIDE, *Major General.*

"Official:

"S. F. BARSTOW,
"*Assistant Adjutant General.*"

"BY TELEGRAPH FROM HEADQUARTERS 9TH CORPS,
"*July* 31, 1864—6.40 p. m.

"Major General HUMPHREYS:

"The loss in this corps in the engagement of yesterday amounts to about 4,500; the great proportion of which was made after the brigade commanders in the crater were made aware of the order to withdraw.

"A. E. BURNSIDE, *Major General.*

"Official:

"S. F. BARSTOW,
"*Assistant Adjutant General.*"

"HEADQUARTERS ARMY OF THE POTOMAC,
"*July* 31, 1864—7.20 p. m.

"Major General BURNSIDE, *Commanding 9th Corps:*

"Your despatch relative to the loss in your corps yesterday is received.

"The commanding general requests that you explain the meaning of the latter part of your despatch, and again reminds you that he has received no report whatever from you of what occurred after 11 a. m. yesterday.

"A. A. HUMPHREYS,
"*Major General and Chief of Staff.*

"Official:

"S. F. BARSTOW,
"*Assistant Adjutant General.*"

"BY TELEGRAPH FROM 9TH CORPS,
"*July* 31, 1864—9.10 p. m.

"Major General HUMPHREYS, *Chief of Staff :*

"Your despatch of 7.20 p. m. received. Just before the order for withdrawal was sent in o the brigade commanders in the crater, the enemy made an attack upon our forces there nd were repulsed with very severe loss to the assaulting column. The order for withdrawal, leaving the time and manner of the execution thereof to the brigade commanders on the spot, was sent in, and while they were making arrangements to carry out the order the enemy advanced another column of attack. The officers, knowing they were not to be supported by other troops, and that a withdrawal was determined, ordered the men to retire at once to our old line. It was in this withdrawal, and consequent upon it, that our chief loss was made. In view of the want of confidence in their situation, and the certainty of no support, consequent upon the receipt of such an order, of which moral effect the general commanding cannot be ignorant, I am at a loss to know why the latter part of my despatch requires explanation.

"A. E. BURNSIDE, *Major General*.

"Official:

"S. F. BARSTOW,
"*Assistant Adjutant General*.

"HEADQUARTERS ARMY OF THE POTOMAC,
"*July* 31, 1864—9¼ p. m.

"Major General BURNSIDE, *Commanding 9th Corps:*

"Your despatch explanatory of that in relation to the loss in your corps yesterday is received.

"The major general commanding directs me to say that the order for withdrawal did not authorize or justify its being done in the manner in which, judging from your brief report, it appears to have been executed, and that the matter shall be investigated by a court.

"The major general commanding notices that the time and manner of withdrawal was left to the brigade commanders on the spot. He desires to know why there was not a division commander present where several brigades were engaged, and by whom the withdrawal could have been conducted.

"A. A. HUMPHREYS,
"*Major General and Chief of Staff*.

"Official:

"S. F. BARSTOW, *Assistant Adjutant General*."

So far as any information from General Burnside is concerned, I had to go to bed that night without knowing whether his troops were in the crater, or whether they were not. During the night despatches were received, referring to the relief of General Ord's troops next morning, July 31, at 8.40 and 9 a. m. The despatches 18¼ and 18½ were sent and received by General Humphreys. No despatch was received from General Burnside with reference to the withdrawal of these troops till 6 40 p. m., July 31, (marked 18¾,) to which was sent the one marked 19, at 9.10 p. m., July 31. The despatch was received from General Burnside, marked 19¼, and the reply, marked 20, was sent: Now, I beg leave to call the attention of the court to the fact that this despatch is dated 9.10 p. m., July 31, and although it does not give an official statement of the time of the withdrawal of the troops, I know, but only from other information, that the withdrawal was at about 2 p. m., July 30. And as I consider that my conduct is here the subject of investigation as much as that of any other officer or man engaged in this enterprise, I wish to repudiate, distinctly, any responsibility resting upon me for the manner of the withdrawal, beyond the orders I gave to the effect that the troops were to be withdrawn when they could be withdrawn with security; and if they had been able to repulse an attack of the enemy, it seems to me rather extraordinary that when another attack was threatened after the success, that they should be withdrawn simply because they were threatened with another attack. But that is the point to which I wish to call the attention of the court, and which I wish to have thoroughly investigated.

I believe these constitute the sum and substance of all the orders that passed between myself and Major General Burnside. But I respectfully submit to this court that so far as it was in my power as the commanding general of this army to give orders, I anticipated the difficulties that occurred, and endeavored to avoid them as much as I could do so, and that I cannot be held responsible for the failure which afterwards resulted.

Having finished my correspondence with and orders to General Burnside, I now propose to read the correspondence with and orders to General Ord, who was the officer commanding the force next to be employed after those of General Burnside, and whose movements it is important to know.

Major General Ord was directed to relieve his corps by General Mott's division of the 2d corps on the evening of the 29th. He was then to move and mass his troops in rear of the 9th corps, and it was intended that he should support the 9th corps whenever the 9th corps had effected a lodgement on the crest; that he was promptly to move up to them and support them on the crest. I had several interviews with General Ord on the 28th and 29th. I went with him and showed him the position; showed him exactly the ground; gave him all the information I had, and also caused him to send staff officers to select positions for the troops, so that when it became dark they might know the roads. On the morning of July 30, when it became evident to my mind that General Burnside's troops were not going to advance further than the crater, and when I had reason to suppose it was owing to some difficulty on the part of the troops themselves, and so far as any official report came to me, rather than obstacles presented by the enemy, I sent a despatch to General Ord changing his previous orders and directing him, instead of supporting General Burnside, to make an assault independent of General Burnside. That despatch and subsequent despatches are as follows:

"HEADQUARTERS ARMY OF THE POTOMAC,
"*July* 29, 9¾ *p. m.*, 1864.
"Major General ORD, *Commanding* 18*th Corps*:

"Your despatch of 9.25 p. m. is received. The commanding general does not consider it necessary for General Burnside to wait for your troops to relieve his in the trenches. General Burnside can form his troops for the assault without reference to yours, and your troops can file into the trenches at any time after they are vacated. General Burnside is telegraphed to that effect.

"A. A. HUMPHREYS,
"*Major General, Chief of Staff.*
"Official copy:
"S. F. BARSTOW, *Assistant Adjutant General.*"

"HEADQUARTERS ARMY OF THE POTOMAC,
"*July* 30, 4.50 *a. m.*, 1864.
"Major General ORD, *Commanding* 18*th Corps*:

"General Burnside is ordered, if his mine has failed, to open all his batteries and assault at once. You will consider the orders the same as if the mine had exploded and the assault made in consequence.

"A. A. HUMPHREYS,
"*Major General, Chief of Staff.*
("Just before this was finished the mine exploded and the batteries opened. It was not sent.—A. A. H.)
"Official copy:
"S. F. BARSTOW, *Assistant Adjutant General.*"

"HEADQUARTERS ARMY OF THE POTOMAC,
"*July* 30, 6 *a. m.*, 1864.
"Major General ORD, *Commanding* 18*th Corps*:

"The major general commanding directs that you at once move forward your corps rapidly to the crest of the hill, independently of General Burnside's troops, and make a lodgement there, reporting the result as soon as attained.

"A. A. HUMPHREYS,
"*Major General, Chief of Staff.*
"Official copy:
"S. F. BARSTOW, *Assistant Adjutant General.*"

"[By telegraph from headquarters 9th army corps.]
JULY 30, 8 *a. m.*, 1864.
'To General MEADE:

"General Turner in my front reports that the only place I can get out of the line is opposite the crater. It is already full of men who cannot develop. I shall put in my column as soon as I can. It is impossible, by reason of the topography, to charge in the manner you indicate. I must go in by head of column and develop to the right. This is reply to orders from General Meade to push for crest of hill regardless of General Burnside's troops. General Ames makes similar reports.

"E. O. C. ORD, *Major General.*

"Official copy:
"S. F. BARSTOW, *Assistant Adjutant General.*

"HEADQUARTERS ARMY OF THE POTOMAC,
"*July* 30, 9¾ *a. m.*, 1864.
"Major General ORD, *Commanding* 18*th Corps:*

"The major general commanding directs that you withdraw your corps to the rear of the 9th corps, in some secure place.

"A. A. HUMPHREYS,
"*Major General, Chief of Staff.*

"Official copy:
"S. F. BARSTOW, *Assistant Adjutant General.*

"HEADQUARTERS ARMY OF THE POTOMAC,
"*July* 30, 10 *a. m.*, 1864.
"Major Generals BURNSIDE and ORD:

"You can exercise your discretion in withdrawing your troops now or at a later period, say to-night.
"It is not intended to hold the enemy's line which you now occupy any longer than is required to withdraw safely your men.

"GEORGE G. MEADE, *Major General.*

"Official copy:
"S. F. BARSTOW, *Assistant Adjutant General.*"

There were some other despatches to General Ord of a similar character, (but I do not see them here,) to endeavor to get him forward, independent of the 9th corps, to make an isolated attack, an attack of his own, independent of the 9th corps. Owing to the obstacles presented—the fact that there was no proper *debouche* for our troops to that portion of the enemy's line, and the fact that the crater was overcrowded with men—General Ord, considering those obstacles insurmountable, confined his operations to sending forward, I think, only one brigade. But General Ord and his division commanders have made reports, which will be placed before you. I forgot to bring them with me to-day.

At about 9.45 a. m. the same orders were sent to General Ord as to General Burnside, with reference to the withdrawal of the troops. That finishes all that passed between General Ord and myself.

The other supporting column was under Major General Warren on the left.

In the original order General Warren was directed to mass his available troops on the right of the line, and to make all his preparations to support General Burnside in the assault wherever he should be ordered.

At 4.40 a. m. the following despatch was sent to him:

"HEADQUARTERS ARMY OF THE POTOMAC,
"*July* 30, 4.40 *a. m.*, 1864.
"Major General WARREN, *Commanding* 5*th Corps:*

"General Burnside is directed, if his mine has failed, to open all his batteries and assault. Upon hearing his batteries open you will open all in your front.

"A. A. HUMPHREYS,
"*Major General and Chief of Staff.*

"Official:
"S. F. BARSTOW, *Assistant Adjutant General.*

At 5.50, one hour afterwards, and immediately after my receiving the information that General Burnside's corps occupied the crater, the following despatch was sent to him:

BATTLE OF PETERSBURG.

"HEADQUARTERS ARMY OF THE POTOMAC,
"*July* 30, 5.50 *a. m.*, 1864.

'Major General WARREN, *Commanding 5th Corps:*

"General Burnside is occupying the crater with some of his troops. He reports that no enemy is seen in their line. How is it in your front? Are the enemy in force there or weak?

"If there is apparently an opportunity to carry their works, take advantage of it and push forward your troops.

"A. A. HUMPHREYS,
"*Major General and Chief of Staff.*

"Official:

"S. F. BARSTOW, *Assistant Adjutant General.*"

I wish to call the attention of the court to the fact that as early as 5.50 I authorized General Warren, if he saw any opportunity of doing anything with his corps, not only in support of General Burnside, but as an independent operation of his own, that he should take advantage of it and push forward his troops. His reply, dated 6 a. m., is as follows:

"[By telegraph from 5th army corps.]
"JULY 30, 6 *a. m.*, 1864.

"To Major General HUMPHREYS:

"Your despatch just received. It is difficult to say how strong the enemy may be in my front. He has batteries along the whole of it. I will watch for the first opportunity. I can see the whole line where I am. The enemy has been running from his first line in front of General Burnside's right for some minutes, but there seems to be a very heavy line of troops just behind it in high breastwork. There is a battery in front of General Burnside's left which fires towards the river, the same as it did on the 18th of June, and which our artillery fire has but very little effect on.

"G. K. WARREN, *Major General.*

"Official copy:

"S. F. BARSTOW, *Assistant Adjutant General.*"

At 6.15 a. m. another despatch was received from him, as follows:

"[By telegraph from headquarters 5th army corps.]
"JULY 30, 6.15 *a. m.*, 1864.

"To Major General HUMPHREYS:

"I have just received a report from my line on the centre and left. The enemy opened with musketry when our firing commenced, but our own fire kept it down, and also that of all their artillery except in the second line on the main ridge, from which they fire a little. Major Fitzhugh, of the artillery, is badly wounded by a musket ball in the thigh. None of the enemy have left my front, that we can see.

"G. K. WARREN, *Major General.*

"Official copy:

"S. F. BARSTOW, *Assistant Adjutant General.*"

Then at 6.20 another despatch, No. 29, came from General Warren, in which he states that what we thought was a heavy line of the enemy behind the line occupied by Burnside's troops, as the sunlight comes out and the smoke clears away, proves to be our own troops in the enemy's position.

"[By telegraph from 5th army corps.]
"JULY 30, 6.20 *a. m.*, 1864.

"To Major General HUMPHREYS:

"What we thought was the heavy line of the enemy behind the line occupied by General Burnside, proves, as the sunlight comes out and the smoke clears away, to be our own troops in the enemy's position.

"G. K. WARREN, *Major General.*

"Official copy:

"S. F. BARSTOW, *Assistant Adjutant General.*"

You will perceive that at 5.40 I authorized General Warren and directed him to make an attack without waiting for the support of General Burnside—that is, if circumstances would justify his making an attack; and that his replies here indicate that no such attack was practicable. Coming to that conclusion, and receiving information from the signal officers that the enemy had left their extreme right, which I presumed they would do, to mass on the centre to receive our attack, the following despatch was sent to General Warren at half past six o'clock:

"HEADQUARTERS ARMY OF THE POTOMAC, *July* 30, 6.30 *a. m.*, 1864.

"Major General WARREN, *Commanding 5th Corps:*

"The signal officer reports that none of the enemy's troops are visible in their works near the lead works. The commanding general wishes, if it is practicable, that you make an attack in that direction. Prisoners say there are but three divisions in the works, and but one line of intrenchments, thinly filled with their troops.

"A. A. HUMPHREYS, *Major General and Chief of Staff.*"

"A despatch just going to Wilson to make a lodgement on the Weldon railroad and move up along it to the enemy's right flank.

"Official copy:

"S. F. BARSTOW, *Assistant Adjutant General.*"

"HEADQUARTERS FIFTH ARMY CORPS, *July* 30, 6.40 *a. m.*, 1864.

"General HUMPHREYS:

"I have all my troops on my right except General Crawford. I have sent him your despatch, with directions to do whatever he can on the left with Baxter's brigade and half of Ledlie's.

"Do you mean for me to move Ayres in that direction? The enemy have a 30-pounder battery on the main ridge in my front, behind their first line. We cannot make out what his second line is.

"Respectfully,

"G. K. WARREN, *Major General.*

"Official copy:

"S. F. BARSTOW, *Assistant Adjutant General.*"

"HEADQUARTERS ARMY OF THE POTOMAC, *July* 30, 7 *a. m.*, 1864.

"Major General WARREN, *Commanding 5th Corps:*

"What about attacking the enemy's right flank near the lead works with that part of your force nearest to it?

"A. A. HUMPHREYS, *Major General, Chief of Staff.*"

"Official:

"S. F. BARSTOW, *Assistant Adjutant General.*"

The next despatch in order is the following, dated 7.30 a. m., to General Warren:

"HEADQUARTERS ARMY OF THE POTOMAC, *July* 30, 7½ *a. m.*, 1864.

"Major General WARREN, *Commanding 5th Corps:*

"Your despatch respecting attacking the enemy's extreme right received. The general commanding will await General Crawford's reconnoissance before determining whether you should send Ayres also in that direction.

"A. A. HUMPHREYS, *Major General, Chief of Staff.*

"Official:

"S. F. BARSTOW, *Assistant Adjutant General.*"

General Ayres still remained on the right, and the orders still existed to do anything with him that could be done to advantage. At 7.50 a. m. we have the next despatch from General Warren:

"HEADQUARTERS FIFTH ARMY CORPS, *July* 30—7.50 a. m.

"Major General HUMPHREYS:

"I have just returned from the scene of General Burnside's operations. In my opinion, the battery of one or two guns to the left of General Burnside should be taken before attempting to seize the crest. It seems to me it can be done, as we shall take the infantry fire quite obliquely. This done, the advance upon the main hill will not be difficult. I think it would pay you to go to General Burnside's position. You can see in a moment, and it is as easy to communicate with me as by telegraph.

"It will be some time before we can hear from Crawford.

"Respectfully.

"G. K. WARREN, *Major General.*

"Official copy:

"S. F. BARSTOW, *Assistant Adjutant General.*"

Nothing further was received while we awaited developments from General Crawford until 8 a. m., when the following despatch was received from General Warren :

"BY TELEGRAPH FROM HEADQUARTERS 5TH ARMY CORPS,
"July 30, 1864—8 a. m.
"Major General HUMPHREYS:
"I sent your despatch to General Crawford with directions to do what he could. He says the lead works are over a mile from the angle of my picket line. I do not think an attack upon the enemy's works at or near that point at all practicable. With the force I can spare, I can make a demonstration if it is desired; the cavalry are moving and I will have my left uncovered. He sent word he will await further orders. He is so far off that I do not think it well to wait for anything more he can do, and I renew my suggestion that you take a look at things from General Burnside's headquarters and direct me either to go in with Burnside or go around to my left with Ayres's division and I do the other thing.
"G. K. WARREN, *Major General.*
"Official copy:
"S. F. BARSTOW,
"*Assistant Adjutant General.*"

Notwithstanding that it was considered that General Warren's original order authorized him to take the batteries if it could be done, inasmuch as he was directed to move and attack with General Crawford, and as it was suggested that General Ayres might be required, it was thought proper to send him the following order at 8¾ a. m.:

"HEADQUARTERS ARMY OF THE POTOMAC,
"July 30, 1864—8¾ a. m.
"Major General WARREN, *Commanding 5th Corps:*
"Your despatch is received. The major general commanding directs that you go in with Burnside, taking the two-gun battery. The movement on the left need not be carried further than reconnoissance to see in what force the enemy is holding his right. The cavalry are ordered to move up on your left and to keep up connexion.
"A. A. HUMPHREYS,
"*Major General, Chief of Staff.*
"Official copy:
"S. F. BARSTOW,
"*Assistant Adjutant General.*"

At 9.15 a. m. the following despatch was received from General Warren:

"BY TELEGRAPH FROM HEADQUARTERS 5TH ARMY CORPS,
"July 30, 1864—9.15 a. m.
"Major General HUMPHREYS:
"Just before receiving your despatch to assault the battery on the left of the crater occupied by General Burnside, the enemy drove his troops out of the place and I think now hold it. I can find no one who knows for certainty or seems willing to admit, but I think I saw a rebel battle-flag in it just now and shots coming from it this way. I am therefore, if this is true, no more able to take the battery now than I was this time yesterday. All our advantages are lost. I await further instructions, and am trying to get at the condition of affairs for certainty.
"G. K. WARREN, *Major General.*
"Official copy:
"S. F. BARSTOW,
"*Assistant Adjutant General.*"

At this time the conclusion had been arrived at by the lieutenant general commanding and myself that the affair was over, and that nothing more could be done; and soon afterwards, orders similar to those which were sent to others were sent to General Warren, that he should not make any attempt to take the two-gun battery. The following despatches were sent to General Warren:

"HEADQUARTERS ARMY OF THE POTOMAC,
"*July* 30, 1864—9.25 a. m.
" Major General WARREN:
"The attack ordered on the two-gun battery is suspended.
"GEO. G. MEADE, *Major General.*
"Official copy:
"S. F. BARSTOW,
"*Assistant Adjutant General.*"

"BY TELEGRAPH FROM HEADQUARTERS 5TH CORPS,
"*July* 30, 1864—9.45 a. m.
" Major General HUMPHREYS, *Chief of Staff:*
"GENERAL: I find that the flag I saw was the enemy's, and that they have reoccupied all the line we drove them from, except a little around the crater which a small force of ours still hold.
"Respectfully,
"G. K. WARREN, *Major General.*
"Official copy:
"S. F. BARSTOW,
"*Assistant Adjutant General.*"

"HEADQUARTERS ARMY OF THE POTOMAC,
"*July* 30, 1864—9.45 a. m.
" General WARREN, *at 9th Corps Headquarters:*
"A despatch has been sent to your headquarters, rescinding order to attack; all offensive operations are suspended. You can resume your original position with your command.
"GEORGE G. MEADE.
"Official:
"S. F. BARSTOW,
"*Assistant Adjutant General.*"

"HEADQUARTERS ARMY OF THE POTOMAC,
"*July* 30, 1864—5 p. m.
" Major Generals WARREN and BURNSIDE:
"Signal officers report the enemy returning rapidly from the north side of the James. Every preparation should be made to strengthen the line of works where any obstacles have to-day been removed. The lines should be held strongly with infantry and artillery, posted wherever practicable—available reserves held in hand ready for movement in case it becomes necessary. I anticipate offensive movements on the part of the enemy, and expect it will be by a movable column, turning our left and threatening our rear.
"GEORGE G. MEADE,
"*Major General, Commanding.*
"Major General Hancock will, to-night, resume his former position and General Ord his also.
"Official copy:
"S. F. BARSTOW, *Assistant Adjutant General.*"

These are all the orders and communications that passed between General Warren and myself. He was authorized to attack, if he could see a good chance to attack; when he reported no chance to attack, and was asked what force he had available, he reported that he had no force available except he moved Ayres; he was directed not to move Ayres until information was received from Crawford; only, if he could attack the two-gun battery in his front, he was ordered to attack it, and then the operations were subsequently suspended.

Now I have read you the communications that passed between myself and General Grant, myself and General Burnside, myself and General Ord, and myself and General Warren. It now remains for me to read the communications that passed between myself and General Hancock, and myself and General Mott.

The first was a communication sent 4.40 a. m. to General Mott.

"HEADQUARTERS ARMY OF THE POTOMAC,
"*July* 30, 1864—4.40 a. m.
"'Brigadier General MOTT, *Commanding Division in intrenchments of* 18*th Corps, Old Headquarters of* 18*th Corps:*
"General Burnside is ordered, if his mine has failed, to open all the batteries on his front and assault at once.
"Upon hearing his batteries open, have all the batteries of the 18th corps opened.
"A. A. HUMPHREYS, *Major General, Chief of Staff.*
"Official:
"S. F. BARSTOW, *Assistant Adjutant General.*"

At 4.50 a. m. the following despatch was sent to the telegraph operator at the headquarters of the 18th corps:

"HEADQUARTERS ARMY OF THE POTOMAC, *July* 30—4.50 a. m.
"OPERATOR *at Headquarters* 18*th Corps:*
"Send the following message by orderly to General Hancock:
"Major General HANCOCK, *Commanding* 2*d Corps:*
"The commanding general wishes you to be about the headquarters of the 18th corps, so that he can communicate with you at any time.
"A. A. HUMPHREYS, *Major General, Chief of Staff.*
"Official:
"S. F. BARSTOW, *Assistant Adjutant General.*"

The following despatch dated July 30, 6 a. m., was sent to General Hancock, after the mine was occupied:

"HEADQUARTERS ARMY OF THE POTOMAC,
"*July* 30, 1864—6 a m.
"Major General HANCOCK, *Commanding* 2*d Corps:*
"The major general commanding directs me to say that General Burnside reports the enemy's line in his front abandoned, and the prisoners taken say that there is no second line. The commanding general may call on you to move forward at any moment, and wishes you to have your troops well up to the front prepared to move. Do the enemy's lines in front of Mott's division appear to be thinly occupied, and is there any chance to push forward there?
"A. A. HUMPHREYS, *Major General, Chief of Staff.*
"Official:
"S. F. BARSTOW, *Assistant Adjutant General.*"

The following despatches were sent and received:

"BY TELEGRAPH FROM HEADQUARTERS 2D ARMY CORPS,
"*July* 30, 1864—6 a. m.
"Major General HUMPHREYS:
"It is not possible to say about the line in front of General Mott, as both keep down firing whenever a head is shown. General Ord left word for me by General Mott that there was no place to assault here, as the line was not only protected by abatis, but by wire. This was the decision of himself and his division commanders, and he requested General Mott so to inform me. I know nothing more about it. I will be prepared for your orders.
"W. S. HANCOCK.
"Official copy:
"S. F. BARSTOW, *Assistant Adjutant General.*"

"BY TELEGRAPH FROM HEADQUARTERS 2D CORPS,
"*July* 30, 1864—6.20 a. m.
"Major General HUMPHREYS, *Chief of Staff:*
"I have sent out to have General Mott's line examined as far as practicable, to see how strong the enemy appear to hold their line in General Mott's front.
"W. S. HANCOCK.
"Official copy:
"S. F. BARSTOW, *Assistant Adjutant General.*"

"BY TELEGRAPH FROM HEADQUARTERS 2D CORPS,
"*July* 30, 1864—6.30 a. m.
"Major General HUMPHREYS:
"I have directed General Mott to advance a skirmish line to see whether the enemy hold a strong line in his front.
"W. S. HANCOCK, *Major General.*
"Official copy:
"S. F. BARSTOW, *Assistant Adjutant General.*"

"By Telegraph from Headquarterters 2d Corps,
" *July 30, 1864—6.50 a. m.*

" General Geo. G. Meade :

"The brigade next to General Burnside's attempted an advance of a skirmish line just now and lost the officer in command of the line and several men in getting over the parapet. The enemy's mortars are at work, but they cannot fire much artillery other than this. The other brigades have not yet been heard from. Your despatch is just received. I will continue to watch the enemy in my front.

"W. S. HANCOCK, *Major General.*

" Official copy :

"S. F. BARSTOW, *Asst. Adj't General.*"

" Headquarters Army of the Potomac,
" *July 30, 1864—7 a. m.*

" Major General Hancock :

" The report from prisoners would indicate weakness in the enemy's line—that a considerable portion has been vacated.

" If Burnside and Ord gain the crest, the enemy cannot hold in your front, for they will be open to attack from front and rear. It was to take advantage of this contingency that I wanted you to have your troops in hand.

" The orders to Mott are all right. If the enemy are in force and prepared, you will have to await developments; but if you have reason to believe their condition is such that an effort to dislodge them would be successful, I would like to have it made. Burnside now occupies their line, but has not pushed up to the crest, though he reports he is about doing so.

" GEO. G. MEADE.

" Official :

"S. F. BARSTOW, *Asst. Adj't General.*"

" By Telegraph from Headquarters 2d Corps,
" *July 30, 1864—7 a. m.*

"General Humphreys, *Chief of Staff :*

" Report from 2d brigade, General Mott's division, shows that the enemy are there in some strength, having two batteries which they fire seldom, owing to the close proximity of our riflemen. The commanding officer of the brigade says he can see every man who leaves his front to their right, and none have left since daylight. He is using mortars effectively. I will report any change of troops.

"W. S. HANCOCK, *Major General.*

" Official copy :

"S. F. BARSTOW, *Asst. Adj't General.*"

" By Telegraph from Headquarters 2d Army Corps,
". *July 30, 1864—9 a. m.*

" Major General Humphreys :

" General Mott's remaining brigade deceived the enemy in their front by putting their hats on rammers above the parapet, which elicited quite a spirited volley.

"W. S. HANCOCK, *Major General.*

" Official copy :

"S. F. BARSTOW, *Asst. Adj't General.*"

" Headquarters Army of the Potomac,
" *July 30, 1864—9.25 a. m.*

" Major General Hancock :

" Offensive operations have been suspended. You will for the present hold in force the lines held by the 18th corps. Make your dispositions accordingly.

" GEO. G. MEADE, *Major General, Commanding.*

" Official :

"S. F. BARSTOW, *Asst. Adj't General.*"

" Headquarters Army of the Potomac,
" *July 29, 1864—10 a. m.*

" Brigadier General Wilson, *Com'dg 3d Division Cavalry :*

" The major general commanding directs that you concentrate your division on the left, somewhere near the plank road, and hold its available force ready for prompt movement.

" The guard left with trains should be merely sufficient to protect them against any small irregular parties of the enemy. The dismounted enemy should form this guard. Please report your location as soon as established.

" Very respectfully, your obedient servant,

"A. A. HUMPHREYS,
" *Major General and Chief of Staff.*

"P. S.—The patrols and pickets on the north side of the Blackwater should be reduced to the minimum consistent with watching the main avenues of approach.
"Official copy:
"S. F. BARSTOW, *Asst. Adj't General.*"

"HEADQUARTERS OF THE ARMY OF THE POTOMAC,
"*July* 29, 1864—2¼ p. m.
"Brigadier General WILSON,
"*Com'dg Cavalry Division, Jordan's Point:*
"The commanding general considers that not more than one regiment should remain north of the Blackwater, and that he be so posted as to be brought in rapidly to-morrow morning.
"A. A. HUMPHREYS,
"*Major General and Chief of Staff.*
"Official copy:
"S. F. BARSTOW, *Asst. Adj't General.*"

"HEADQUARTERS ARMY OF THE POTOMAC,
"*July* 29, 1864—3¼ p. m.
"Brigadier General WILSON, *Commanding 3d Division Cavalry Corps:*
"GENERAL: Major General Sheridan is ordered to move at dark to Lee's mill, and at daylight against the enemy's troops defending Petersburg on their right, by the roads leading to that town from the southward and westward.
"Your division will accompany him, and the commanding general directs that you be prepared to call in your patrols and pickets early to-morrow morning and move with the cavalry corps. You will send a staff officer to meet General Sheridan and receive his instructions.
"A. A. HUMPHREYS,
"*Major General and Chief of Staff.*
"Official copy:
"S. F. BARSTOW,
"*Assistant Adjutant General.*"

"HEADQUARTERS ARMY OF THE POTOMAC,
"*July* 29, 1864—10 p. m.
"Major General SHERIDAN:
"The commanding general directs that you keep up connexion with our left, in the operations of to-morrow.
"A. A. HUMPHREYS,
"*Major General and Chief of Staff.*
"Official copy:
"S. F. BARSTOW,
"*Assistant Adjutant General.*"

These include the despatches sent to the cavalry. I would explain that the separate orders to General Wilson were issued because General Sheridan was across the James river, at Deep Bottom, with two divisions, and I had to issue separate orders to General Wilson, so that he might be ready for the movement next day.

Here are some despatches which are of no particular consequence, but I will introduce them here. They are despatches from the signal officers, indicating the movements of the enemy:

"HEADQUARTERS ARMY OF THE POTOMAC,
"*July* 29, 1864—3 p. m.
"Brigadier General WHITE,
"*Commanding (temporary) Division, 9th Corps:*
"The major general commanding directs that, as soon as it is dark, you withdraw your command from the intrenchments you are now holding, and move to the position of the 9th corps, and report to your corps commander. You will call in your pickets upon moving.
"You will at once report to Major General Burnside, and receive his instructions as to the route you will take.
"Very respectfully, &c.,
"A. A. HUMPHREYS,
"*Major General and Chief of Staff.*
"Official:
"S. F. BARSTOW,
"*Assistant Adjutant General.*"

"HEADQUARTERS ARMY OF THE POTOMAC,
"*July* 30, 1864—4.45 a. m.
"Colonel WAINWRIGHT, *Chief of Artillery, 5th Corps:*
"General Burnside is directed, if his mine has failed, to open all his batteries on his front and assault at once. Upon hearing his batteries open, those of the 5th corps will open also.
"A. A. HUMPHREYS,
"*Major General and Chief of Staff.*
"Official:
"S. F. BARSTOW,
"*Assistant Adjutant General.*"

"PLANK ROAD SIGNAL STATION,
"*July* 30, 1864—5 a. m.
"Major B. F. FISHER:
"There are no tents or the sign of any force on the right of the enemy's line near lead works.
"The two batteries directly in front of station, which opened heavily this morning, have ceased firing.
"A large building is burning in the city.
"I have seen no movement of the enemy's troops.
"J. B. DUFF,
"*Lieutenant, Signal Officer.*
"Official:
"S. F. BARSTOW,
"*Assistant Adjutant General.*"

"[By telegraph from Plank Road Signal Station.]
"HEADQUARTERS ARMY OF THE POTOMAC,
"*July* 30, 1864—6.20 a. m.
"Major FISHER:
"The enemy's infantry has been passing to our right for twenty minutes; first noticed them at a point due west of the station marching in rear of their line; they came out in plain view at a point northwest from station. The column was at least a strong brigade; all the camps, one-quarter mile of lead works, have been broken up; the largest visible from station has just been broken up and the troops moved to our right.
"J. B. DUFF, *Signal Officer.*
"Official:
"S. F. BARSTOW,
"*Assistant Adjutant General.*"

["By telegraph from 5th corps.]
"JULY 30, 1864.
"Major FISHER:
"The enemy are wholly concealed along the line in view of this station. Not one has been seen; only three guns, and those in redoubts, at Gregor House. Reply to us.
"Copy sent to General Warren.
"S. LYON, *Lieutenant.*
"Official:
"S. F. BARSTOW,
"*Assistant Adjutant General.*"

It was on these reports of the signal officers that General Warren's orders were predicated.
The following is the report of the chief of engineers :

"HEADQUARTERS ARMY OF THE POTOMAC,
"*Office of Engineers, August* 5, 1864.
"SIR : In compliance with directions received from you to-day, I have the honor to make the following report of the duty performed by the engineer officers during the assault of July 30.
"In compliance with directions from the chief of staff, I detailed an officer of engineers for duty with each corps that was ordered to take part in the attack on the 30th of July.
"Major Michler, who was charged with selecting the position of the column on the right, after having reconnoitred the position, reported to General Ord, and was informed that his subordinate generals had already examined the position, were thoroughly acquainted with the ground, and required no further assistance. They had already determined to take the same position indicated by Major Michler. Two engineer officers belonging to the 18th corps accompanied the movement.

"Lieutenant Benyaurd, engineer, who has been on duty on the 9th corps front, reported to General Burnside, and remained with him during the whole affair.

"After having consulted with the commanding general of the 5th corps as to the direction his column would take, I proceeded to the batteries in front of that corps and assisted Colonel Abbott in directing their fire so as to silence that of the enemy against the assaulting column. I then repaired to the right of his line. By this time, however, the attack had been abandoned and my services were no longer required.

"Very respectfully,

"J. C. DUANE, *Major Engineers.*

"Brigadier General S. WILLIAMS,
"*Assistant Adjutant General Army of the Potomac.*

"Official:

"S. F. BARSTOW, *A. A. G.*"

I believe I have now read every despatch that I have received, and the court are fully aware of all the information that I received on the ground.

I would state that in the general orders issued on the night previous to the assault the cavalry was ordered to make this attack on the left. Two divisions of the cavalry corps were over at Deep Bottom. They could not cross the river until after the second corps had crossed, so that it was late in the day before they came up. Indeed, the head of the column did not appear before the offensive operations were suspended. As General Wilson had been ordered to be in readiness, however, and in view of the unavoidable delay of Sheridan, orders were sent to General Wilson not to wait for General Sheridan, but to push on himself to the Weldon railroad and make an assault upon the enemy. No report was received from General Sheridan. General Sheridan was sick. General Gregg reported in the evening that he had advanced his cavalry, and that they had found the enemy in force at Ream's station, at Gurley's house, and at various other points along the railroad. There was no attack made by the cavalry except at Lee's mills, where General Gregg, encountering cavalry, drove them away to water his horses.

When it was known that our offensive operations were suspended, orders were sent to the cavalry that they should push on as far as possible and find out the enemy's position; but the original orders about going into town were modified, inasmuch as the operations in our immediate front were suspended.

I desire to say to the court that it has not been my disposition or intention to throw censure upon anybody for the unfortunate failure; that, indeed, I have not been furnished with the necessary information to enable me to do so. I have not yet received Major General Burnside's, or his subordinate commanders', official reports. I have very little knowledge of what actually transpired except from the despatches you have heard read here. I have been groping in the dark since the commencement of the attack. I did not wish to take any unpleasant measures, but I thought it my duty to suggest to the President of the United States that this matter should be investigated, and that the censure should be made to rest upon those who are entitled to it. What I have done has been to show that I tried to do all I could to insure success.

FOURTH DAY.

COURT ROOM, HEADQUARTERS 2D CORPS,
August 10, 1864.

The court met pursuant to adjournment.

Present: Major General Hancock, Brigadier Generals Ayres and Miles, and Colonel Schriver, judge advocate.

There were also present Generals Ferrero, Potter, and Wilcox, of the 9th corps, General Mott, of the 2d, and General Carr, of the 18th.

The proceedings of the third day were read and approved.

Testimony of General Meade continued.

Questions by General Burnside:

Question. Where were your headquarters during the action of the 30th?

Answer. From four o'clock until about eleven—I am not exactly confident as to the time of leaving it—my headquarters, as announced in the order of battle on the day previous, were established at the headquarters of the 9th corps. At eleven o'clock, or about that time, as near as I can remember, I removed to the headquarters of the army of the Potomac, which are situated about three-quarters of a mile to the eastward of the headquarters of the 9th corps, and are in telegraphic communication with the same headquarters where I remained during the rest of the day.

Question. How far was that from the scene of action?

Answer. If by the scene of action is meant the crater of the mine and that portion of the enemy's line in front of it, so far as I have knowledge of the ground, derived from maps, I should suppose that the headquarters of the 9th corps were possibly a mile to the eastward of the crater, and my headquarters are three-quarters of a mile, as I stated, beyond that, still further to the east.

Question. Could anything of the action be seen from there?

Answer. Nothing could be seen from any of the points that I occupied.

Question. Did you go further to the front during the action? If so, where?

Answer. I did not leave the headquarters of the 9th corps during the active operations.

Question. Did you not know that there were several positions on our line where you could see the action for yourself, and yet be in as proper a place for you as in General Burnside's permanent camp, and also have full personal communications with Generals Burnside and Ord, and be much nearer to General Warren, and likewise have telegraphic communication with the rest of the army?

Answer. I undoubtedly was aware that there were points of the line where I could see more of the action than I could see at the position I occupied, but I was not aware that there was any point where I could see anything particularly or on which I could base my orders. I adopted the position I did in consequence of its being a central one and in telegraphic communication with all parts of the line where officers were stationed with whom it was necessary to communicate; and having a large staff, and many communications to receive, and many persons to communicate with, and being there in telegraphic communication, I considered it more proper to remain where I announced to the army my headquarters would be, and where all information could be sent to me, than to make any change of position as intimated in the question. Besides which, I desire to say to this court that it has been a matter of policy with me to place myself in such position that my communications made, and the replies made thereto, should be made in such way as a record could be kept of them, and not be confined to verbal communications, which are often subject to misapprehension and to misconstruction. There undoubtedly was telegraphic communication from General Burnside's headquarters in the field—the fourteen-gun battery, as it was called—with the other headquarters in the army.

Question. Did you not have an aide-de camp with General Burnside during most of the action?

Answer. During a portion of the time I did have Captain Sanders, aide-de-camp, at the headquarters of General Burnside. I sent him there in consequence of not receiving any communication from General Burnside, in the hope that he would be enabled to send me some information.

Question. Was not Captain Sanders sent there before the mine exploded?

Answer. No, sir; he was sent there some considerable time after the mine exploded; that is, upon the duty that I now refer to. I have previously stated to the court that before the mine exploded I sent two officers to endeavor to explain the delay. One was Captain Jay, and one might have been Captain Sanders; but they returned before the explosion of the mine. After the explosion of the mine I sent Captain Sanders on the duty that I now refer to, which was to remain at General Burnside's headquarters and communicate to me anything which he could ascertain. I think it further proper to add to this answer to this question that, finding I did not get the information which I desired to have, or which I thought I could have, and fearing that my having sent an aide-de-camp—the object being to facilitate the transmission of information—might be used to deter responsible officers from communicating information to the commanding general, I withdrew Captain Sanders, before the action closed, by an order.

Question. For what purpose was he sent? Was it not to report to you the state and progress of affairs, and did he not so report?

Answer. I have already answered the first part of that question. As to his reports, all the despatches from him are on file in my evidence before the court. As to whether he reported all he should have reported, and all the information to be obtained, I presume the court will ascertain from him and from other evidence.

Question. Was there any information not furnished you by General Burnside, or through other sources, which, if received, would have influenced your conduct of the action? If so, what?

Answer. I have already informed the court that all the information I received has been placed before them in the shape of official documents. It is impossible for me to say what my action would have been if I had received any other information. I acted upon the information I received.

Question. What time did Captain Sanders leave General Burnside to return to you?

Answer. I should say it was about half past eight; between that and nine, as near as I can recollect. I have a copy of the order to him, which I can furnish if desired.

Question. You state that General Burnside's despatch of 9 a. m. was the first information you had received that any collision had taken place, or that there was any enemy in our front; had you not, before the receipt of this despatch, written to General Burnside in reference to General Griffin's attack and repulse; also, received a despatch from Captain Sanders speaking of captured colors; also, seen and examined rebel prisoners taken that morning?

Answer. In reply to that question, I would say that I am willing to assume that there is an apparent discrepancy in my testimony, which I am very glad to have an opportunity of explaining. I should suppose that any one cognizant of the circumstances that took place on that day, even of the most general nature, would know that I never meant to say that I did not know that there was no enemy anywhere. I was fully aware that when the crater was occupied a number of prisoners were taken. I was also aware that the enemy occupied their lines both on the right and on the left of the position occupied by General Burnside; and I did know that Captain Sanders had made a report of captured colors, and that an attack had been made in front of Griffin; but my whole attention was absorbed in the endeavor to have a charge made to the crest, and my thoughts were all upon that; and when I said this was the first intimation I had of there being any enemy in the front, I meant any enemy so situated as to prevent a direct assault upon the crest. Besides which, I must throw myself upon the consideration of the court, and say that the vast number of despatches, the frequency with which they were sent and received, was such that my memory may not serve me well, and the incidents may be, in a measure, not related in the exact order in which they occurred. I wish to call the attention of the court to a very important fact for the benefit of General Burnside, if it results to his benefit as well as to mine, and that is the difficulty of having the time of these despatches uniform. A despatch is sent to me marked with the time of the officer who sends it, but the time by his watch may be ten or fifteen minutes different from mine. But I do honestly and conscientiously say that that was the first positive information, when I received that despatch that the men of the 9th and 18th corps were returning, that I had that there was any such force or disposition of the enemy as to render it questionable that that assault could be made.

General Burnside here remarked, "I want the record in such a shape as to enable the casual reader and the revising officer to see that there was, before that time, an effort on my part, or on the part of some person near me, to give information, and not an effort to cast any imputation on General Meade, and I do not desire to invalidate his testimony, but simply to elaborate. I am confident that there is no disposition on the part of General Meade to make erroneous statements."

Question. Have you a note written me by you about two weeks before the assault as to the practicability of an assault in my front, my answer thereto, your second letter, and my reply, and will you be kind enough to furnish copies?

Answer. I presume that those documents, like all other official documents, are on file. I will have a search made for them, and as soon as they are discovered will very cheerfully furnish General Burnside or the court a copy of them.

[General Burnside explained that one of them was a semi-official letter, and General Meade, being reminded of the purport of it, answered that he did not think he had it.]

By the court:

Question. What knowledge had you of the movements of the different divisions of the enemy on July 30?

Answer. I had very positive information from deserters, not only those who came within my own lines here, but those who came into the lines of General Butler, and those who came into the lines of General Hancock, that there were but three divisions of the enemy in our front, consisting of Mahone's division of Hill's corps; and Johnson's and Hoke's divisions of Longstreet's corps; and that the other divisions of Lee's army were on the north side of the James river, confronting General Hancock and Sheridan, on the 29th. I also received the same information from prisoners taken that morning. During the operations I received information from the signal officers on the plank road that the enemy were moving troops from their right to their centre, which I anticipated, and upon receiving that information the orders were sent to General Warren to endeavor to turn the enemy's right by pushing forward General Crawford, and to General Wilson to push on without delay, without waiting for the arrival of General Sheridan, coming from Deep Bottom.

Question. Did the order to suspend operations (given about 9 a. m. July 30) originate with Lieutenant General Grant?

Answer. No, sir; the order, I think, originated with myself. Some time before the order was given, I informed Lieutenant General Grant that, as far as I could see, there was no prospect of our succeeding in the manner in which we had expected to do; that the time had passed for the coup-de-main to succeed; and I suggested to him that we should immediately withdraw the troops, to which he acceded. About that time a despatch was received from the signal officer of the 5th corps, stating that the colored troops had captured a brigade of the enemy, with four of their colors, to which, however, I did not attach much importance, not knowing how a signal officer could see an operation of that kind when it did not come to me from the officer in charge of the operations. We nevertheless suspended this order and held it in abeyance until the arrival of the despatch of General Burnside, informing me that some of the men of the 18th and 9th corps were retiring, and I think also that the Lieutenant General himself rode down to our trenches and made some personal examination, and had seen General Ord, and had some conversation with him. Upon his return, from what he had learned from General Ord, and subsequently an officer coming in and saying that the colored troops, instead of capturing a brigade and four colors, had themselves retired in great confusion, which information. I think, was given me by Major Fisher, the chief signal officer, I again referred the subject to the lieutenant general, and again gave him my opinion that, as it was then about 9.25, it was unnecessary to make any other efforts, and an unnecessary sacrifice of life; my idea being that they could be withdrawn without any difficulty then, as we should have difficulty later in the day in withdrawing them. To this he assented, and the order was given to withdraw them. Afterwards, when the information was received from General Burnside of the difficulty of retiring, then the order was modified.

Question. Were any instructions given for destroying the bridges in Petersburg in case the crest was gained?

Answer. There were not, for two reasons: and first, if we had succeeded, as I hoped we would, in overcoming the enemy, we should have driven them across the Appomattox, and should have wanted those bridges to follow them, but the contingency of their destroying those bridges was held in view, and it was to meet that contingency that the chief engineer was ordered to have a pontoon train brought up so that we could throw our own bridges. My expectation was, that if we had succeeded in the coup-de-main, these three divisions of the enemy would have gone out of our way, and we should be enabled to cross not only the Appomattox, but also Swift run, and open communication with General Butler at Bermuda Hundred before General Lee could send any re-enforcements from the five divisions that he was known to have north of the James river.

"HEADQUARTERS ARMY OF THE POTOMAC,
"*July* 26, 12 *m.*, 1864.

"Major General BURNSIDE:

I wish you would submit in writing your project for the explosion of your mine, with the amount of powder required, that the preliminary question may be definitely settled. You had better also look for some secure place in the woods, where the powder required can be brought in wagons, and kept under guard; thus saving the time it will take to unload it from the vessels and haul it to your camp. Whenever you report as above, and designate a point, I will order the powder brought up.

"GEORGE G. MEADE, *Major General.*

"Official:

"S. F. BARSTOW,
"*Assistant Adjutant General.*"

"HEADQUARTERS ARMY OF THE POTOMAC.,
"*July* 26, 1864.

"Major General BURNSIDE, *Commanding 9th Corps:*

"GENERAL: The major general commanding directs me to inquire whether anything has transpired connected with your mine that leads you to believe it is in danger from counter-mining. If it is your conviction that it is so endangered, then the commanding general authorizes you to make every preparation for springing it; but directs that you do not explode it earlier than to-morrow afternoon, Wednesday, the 27th, say at four o'clock, if not otherwise ordered. The commanding general further directs me to say that the charge of the mine should be determined by the usual rules governing such subjects. It is not intended by the commanding general to follow the explosion of the mine by an assault or other operations. If, therefore, the mine can be preserved for use at some early future day, when circumstances will admit of its being used in connexion with other operations, the commanding general desires that you take no steps for exploding it as herein prescribed.

"A. A. HUMPHREYS,
"*Major General and Chief of Staff.*

"Official:

"S. F. BARSTOW,
"*Assistant Adjutant General.*"

The foregoing is substantially the statement which I made to the court of inquiry.

It alludes to all the points which required any explanation on my part, so far as my own conduct was concerned.

There is one point, however, which I deem it proper to elaborate before this committee, because I have reason to believe it will be set forth prominently in the testimony of others, and that is the position I occupied on the field. The selection of this position was made the day previous, and was due to the fact that from it there were lines of telegraph running to the Avery and Jordan houses, which I presumed would be in the vicinity of the headquarters of the 5th and 2d corps, and instructions were given to run a line to the 14-gun battery, where General Burnside had informed me he should establish his headquarters. The object of its selection was to secure a central position, where I could be in prompt communication with the several corps commanders. During the operations I remained there, because, having announced it as the headquarters in the field, I feared if I left it some important communication might be sent, and time lost in hunting me up to deliver it. It was for this reason, stated at the time to the lieutenant general commanding, that when he went to the front I did not accompany him. It was for this reason, also, that when Major General Warren proposed I should go over to his position, I did not accede to his request, for it seemed to me then, as it does now, that any information General Warren had in any manner acquired could be transmitted to me by telegraph as well as if I went there to see for myself, and the objection to going was the danger that during my absence others might have information equally as important, which would not, owing to my absence, be promptly transmitted. I now refer to not going to General Warren's headquarters, because I am satisfied from the testimony of others that nothing was to be seen from there; and General Warren had himself transmitted me erroneous intelligence, which he subsequently corrected. Nor would going down to the front line of our works have produced any change, because the lieutenant general on returning from them acknowledged to me that nothing could be seen, and he left there under the impression that all was going on well, when he met Major General Ord, who reported to him our people were being driven back.

Furthermore, I have the testimony of Major General Ord and others, that owing to the smoke from the artillery, and a mist which prevailed part of the time, there was really nothing to be seen or known, unless you went to the crater itself.

Now, I am willing to admit that had I gone to the crater I should perhaps have known earlier the true condition of affairs and had I foreseen what subsequently occurred, I should undoubtedly have gone, but it would not have been because it was my place, but it would have been because I felt myself called upon to assume the duties of the corps, division, and perhaps brigade commanders. My failure to do so, in ignorance of any necessity for so doing, I respectfully submit should not be deemed a cause for censure. And it may be well for the committee to inquire who did go to the crater and give their personal superintendence to the movement of the troops, and if it is found that any corps or division commanders whose immediate commands were there did not go, and did not deem themselves called upon to go, I trust I shall have the benefit of the superior knowledge they were presumed to possess, being not only nearer to the scene of action, but having communication with the troops there.

The points, therefore, which I desire to call the attention of the committee to are:

1st. The position I selected was a proper one, had my orders been carried out to promptly transmit to me everything that occurred.

2d. That the testimony of others proves that it was a proper position, because those in other parts of the field, whose duty it was to transmit information to me, did not do so, and the inference therefore is that they could not, or did not, see or hear anything that would have influenced my action.

3d. I have the testimony of the lieutenant general commanding, and Major General Ord, Brigadier General Hunter, Major Duane, and others who were at various points in the front, that nothing positive could be seen or known of the actual state of affairs.

4th. I maintain it would have been wrong in me to have left my post without the strongest reason for so doing, and in confirmation of this I refer the committee to the fact on record, that between 5 and 10 o'clock I received and transmitted over one hundred despatches and orders, averaging one every three minutes, and that had I been absent it would have been impossible to have given the orders I did. If the committee will study what I did do on that day, they will see the impossibility of my having attended to all these points, and be at the same time riding round to see if my subordinates were doing their duty.

I feel satisfied that, on a deliberate review of what did occur, the committee will agree with me, that though possibly it might have been of advantage for me to have gone to the immediate front, it could only have been so in consequence of the failure of others to do what they should have done, and that under the circumstances, and with the knowledge I had, my course was the proper one.

Testimony of Brevet Major General O. B. Wilcox.

HEADQUARTERS ARMY OF THE POTOMAC,
Before Petersburg, Va., December 20, 1864.

Brevet Major General O. B. WILCOX sworn and examined.

By Mr. Chandler:

Question. What is your rank and position in the army?

Answer. I am a brevet major general of volunteers. At the time of the operations you are investigating I commanded the third division; and I now command the first division of the 9th corps.

Question. Will you state such facts as you may deem important, in relation to the operations of July 30, 1864?

Answer. The attack of the 30th of July was intended and expected to be a surprise. It was thought that the mine could be exploded before or at daylight; that it could be exploded at any minute desired. It was ordered to be exploded at half past three, and every preparation was made for a speedy assault. The mine failed to explode at the time fixed, in consequence of a defect in the fuze. It did not explode until a quarter to five o'clock, or some time after daybreak. This probably gave the enemy some warning of a movement, because they must have noticed an unusual number of troops massed in rear of the works near the mine, so that, in point of time, it was not wholly a surprise. The explosion was expected to throw up masses of earth and stones at such a distance that our own troops were a little apprehensive of the effects of the explosion. The mine was less than 140 yards from our works, behind which the assaulting column was massed. In consequence of the explosion, there was a little hesitation on the part of the leading troops—those of General Ledlie's division. But in a few minutes those troops went forward and filled the gap caused by the explosion of the mine. There was a mistake on the part of one of the brigades of the first division, in going into the mine instead of striking the works to the right of the mine. Thus, at the beginning of the movement, the whole of the first division found themselves in the very narrow gap, which was very much deepened by the explosion, so that it was some twenty-five feet in depth. In the mean time the enemy had begun to recover from their surprise, and a fire was brought to bear from nearly every direction upon the troops at the crater, so that it was very difficult to form the troops outside of the crater. I think the first mistake made was in not moving the troops to the right and left of the crater, instead of through the crater; whose mistake that was I do not know. The intention was that the first division should move first, and pass over the works and proceed to Cemetery hill; the next division, mine, was to cross the works as soon as the first division should leave them, and then move up to the left of Cemetery hill, so as to protect the left flank of the first division; and the next division, following mine, was to move in the same way to the right of Cemetery hill, so as to protect the right flank of the first division. The ninth corps being out of the way, it was intended that two other corps should pass through and be ready to follow up the result; but in consequence of this narrow gap being filled up with troops, all huddled together in the crater itself, and unable to move under the concentrated fire of the enemy, no other troops could be got in. When I came down to support the first division, I found that division, and three regiments of my division, together with the regiments of the second division which had gone in on my right, so completely filling up the crater that no more troops could be got in there. I therefore ordered an attack, with the rest of my division, on the works of the enemy, to the left of the crater. This attack was made, and was successful, and the works to the left of the crater, for some 150 yards of the intrenchments, were held for some time by my troops. I do not think that the tactical arrangements for the troops for that movement were such as I would have ordered. But it is always easier to judge of those things afterwards than before. I think that, in the first place, there should have been a storming party of picked troops, every man of whom should have known his business, and should have known that he was to go through the works of the enemy, and gain the top of Cemetery hill, without regard to rank or formation; and those should have been followed by troops in order, and ready to fight a battle. I think that the next division should have moved down the enemy's line to the left, and captured their men and guns, and the next division should have moved down on the other flank, inside the enemy's intrenchments. This, I think, would have opened the way for the whole army; but the order was for everything to move right on towards Cemetery hill, and the passage-way was so narrow that it proved to be impossible to do so.

By Mr. Julian:

Question. Whose order was that?

Answer. The general order of General Meade was that Cemetery hill should be crowned. The particulars of that order came from General Burnside; that is, the movements of the divisions. At the same time, I think that other points of attack should have been selected, and other demonstrations or series of attacks made.

By Mr. Loan:

Question. Will you name those other points?

Answer. Along the line to the right and left of the crater, in front of the 5th and 18th corps.

Question. Where was the 18th corps?

Answer. The line of the 18th corps was to the right of the 9th, and the troops, except a portion for the trenches, came up and formed to the right and rear of the 9th.

Question. Where was General Hancock's corps?

Answer. His corps was in rear of the centre, in reserve. The 18th corps was on our right, and the 5th corps on our left, in reserve, such of it as was brought out of the trenches, and the 2d corps, Hancock's, was in reserve, in rear of all. I would say here that operations by mining at a particular point have very seldom yielded any general results, so far as the history of war teaches.

Question. What we desire to learn is, if there were any errors committed, and if so, to ascertain those errors, and the cause of the failure.

Answer. Certainly.

By Mr. Chandler:

Question. Do you know what General Burnside's original plan of assault was?

Answer. Yes, sir; General Burnside originally intended to make his colored division the storming party. The colored troops were the freshest troops in the corps, the other troops having been under fire in the trenches some fifty days. The colored troops had been drilled with a view to this movement on Cemetery hill, and it was intended that they should lead the advance, and crown Cemetery hill. That movement was countermanded by higher authority.

Question. Do you know whether it was contemplated in the original plan of General Burnside that there should be a movement to the right and left of the assaulting column?

Answer. To a considerable extent it was.

Question. And the troops were drilled with a view to that movement?

Answer. Yes, sir.

Question. Can you state at what time you received your orders as to the part you were to take in the assault of the 30th?

Answer. About dusk of the afternoon before.

Question. Up to that time your part had not been assigned to you?

Answer. Not fully; I would say that the general plan of the movement was known to me about noon of the 29th.

Question. And the change in the troops to lead the assault?

Answer. That was known by me about noon of the day before, (29th.) My orders I received about dusk.

By Mr. Loan:

Question. How long was it after our troops first entered the crater before the enemy opened fire upon them from the right and left?

Answer. I do not think it was over ten minutes; it may have been fifteen minutes from the time we struck the crater.

By Mr. Chandler:

Question. How long was it, after the explosion of the mine, before the commencement of the assault?

Answer. I should judge that the troops commenced to move to the assault about five minutes after the explosion. The troops were sheltering themselves from the effects of the explosion, they were so close to the mine, so that it took five minutes, perhaps ten minutes, to form them in order to move forward. It was about fifteen minutes before the troops got to the crater after the explosion, and they had to pass over about 140 yards besides what they were staggered back by the explosion.

By Mr. Loan:

Question. Do you know from what points the troops of the enemy were drawn that opened this fire upon our troops on the right and left of the crater?

Answer. The first fire was opened from troops in the enemy's trenches, on the right and left. The fire which we next encountered was from the enemy's field artillery, which took position in the rear of the crater, and which fired into and over the crater, and even over our own works. The third movement of the enemy was made, as I supposed by re-enforcements which the enemy brought up. But in the mean time, as I judged, the enemy drew troops from their intrenchments in front of the 5th corps, and moved them around and attacked our troops in the crater.

Question. Do you know any reason why the 5th corps could not have attacked the enemy's troops in front of them, and held them in check during this assault by the 9th corps?

Answer. I thought the 5th corps was to make such an attack. But when I found there was no room for my division to go in where the other troops had gone, I supposed that an attack was to be made on the right and left.

Question. Do you know any reason why it was not done?

Answer. I do not, other than the ordinary obstacles of the intrenchments. I know of no reason why the order was not given. My opinion is that the attack should have been made.

Question. Now, the same question in regard to the enemy's troops on the right?

Answer. A vigorous attack should have been made on both sides.

Question. Do you know of any reason why an attack was not made?

Answer. The troops of the 18th corps were massed on the right, and their lines were thinned out; but still, I think there should have been a vigorous attack made on the right of the crater.

Question. Were there troops there that could have held the enemy's troops on the right?

Answer. I think there were, viz: 18th corps men.

Question. Do you know of any reason why that should not have been done?

Answer. I know of no reason why the attack should not have been made. The success of the thing would depend entirely upon other matters.

Question. I understand you to say that there was a mistake in the movements of one of the brigades of the 1st division in entering the crater, instead of passing over the works to the right?

Answer. Yes, sir.

Question. Do you know how that mistake occurred, and who was responsible for it?

Answer. I cannot state from personal knowledge, only from information derived from General Ledlie.

Question. About what hour of the day were our troops withdrawn?

Answer. It was between one and two o'clock.

Question. Did your command ever get beyond the crater?

Answer. My command got outside of the crater to the left, but not towards Cemetery hill, because they would have had to pass to the front of the first division to do that.

Question. Your orders were to pass through and take a position to the left upon Cemetery hill, so as to protect the left flank of the first division?

Answer. Yes, sir; subsequently, when it was found that the first division had not been able to move forward, my orders—the general order to all the 9th corps division commanders—were to press forward. But, in consequence of the way being blocked up by the advance, it was impossible to get the troops through, and that order was not carried out.

Testimony of Major General G. K. Warren.

HEADQUARTERS ARMY OF THE POTOMAC,
Before Petersburg, Va., December 20, 1864.

Major General G. K. WARREN sworn and examined.

By Mr. Loan:

Question. What is your rank and position in the army?

Answer. Major general of volunteers, commanding the fifth army corps.

Question. Please state concisely whatever you may deem important in regard to the springing of the mine and the assault upon the enemy's lines on the 30th of July last.

Answer. On that particular occasion I had very little to do. A mine was begun in front of General Burnside's lines, and when completed arrangements were made to explode it, and follow up the explosion with an assault. My duty was to support General Burnside's assault with two of my divisions, and hold the line that I occupied with my other division.

After the mine was sprung, and General Burnside's troops gained possession of the crater and the enemy's lines contiguous, they were nearly expelled from it by the enemy, without my troops being called into support, and the attack was abandoned.

I do not consider that I was in position to say, authoritatively, what was the exact fault, or who was to blame; whether the fault was in the conception of the plan or in its execution.

Question. Your command was on the left of the 9th army corps?
Answer. Yes, sir.
Question. In front of the enemy's works?
Answer. Yes, sir.
Question. Had you any orders to attack the enemy on your front at the time General Burnside made his assault?
Answer. No, sir, no more than that the batteries in my front and what infantry was there should keep down the fire of the enemy in my front, which was effectually done. The enemy did not use his guns in our front to any extent.
Question. Did the enemy in your front join in the attack upon the troops of the 9th corps while in the crater?
Answer. I think not; I think they took no part in that attack.
Question. Have you any knowledge of what troops of the enemy on the left of the ninth corps were used to oppose our troops in the crater?
Answer. I have no knowledge; but I have understood that they came from west of the lead works to the left of my corps. It was a part of the general order that our cavalry should go around and attack the enemy in that position, but they did not get there.
Question. That is a matter of which you had no especial charge?
Answer. No, sir. My place in the programme was rather insignificant, so far as any knowledge of the affair was concerned.
Question. How were you to support the assault of General Burnside?
Answer. To follow his column.
Question. Was any place assigned to you particularly?
Answer. I was to have followed on as soon as I could. My troops were closed up on General Burnside's left, and as soon as his troops had got out of the way I was to follow on. The kind of support I should have rendered would have depended upon circumstances, and what General Burnside called upon me to do; for his being in command at the time, and directing the attack, we were to receive instructions from him as to where he wanted support, and how and when.
Question. Did you receive any instructions to obey General Burnside's orders as to the time when you were to assist him, and how?
Answer. I did not get any instructions to obey his orders specially; I would have done that by virtue of his rank on the ground, without any special instructions.
Question. I understand your statement to be that no part of the troops of the enemy in your immediate front were used in assaulting our troops in the crater, but that you held them in that part of their lines.
Answer. I think none were.
Question. Had you means of ascertaining certainly in regard to that matter?

Answer. As much as anybody in our army had, unless the enemy could have moved right from under my eyes without my seeing them. We did not any of us know how much covered way they had. But I am quite well satisfied that they did not take part in the attack.

Question. Do you know how long it was after our troops entered the crater before the enemy opened fire on them from the left, or opposite your front? I understand that from the time of the explosion of the mine everything was quiet for a time, and that our troops crossed over from our lines to the crater without any guns being fired upon them at all, and that the troops of the enemy did not rally immediately after our troops entered the crater.

Answer. Judging from what I saw, I think the enemy opened fire on the left of General Burnside's line immediately after the troops started. I think that one or two guns there were fired upon the crater, and I do not know but they opened fire from the right; I do not know about that.

Question. Was there any fire opened from Cemetery hill?

Answer. There was a thirty-pounder battery there, or one or two $4\frac{1}{2}$-inch guns upon the ridge, that fired all around; they kept firing almost all day—at least I judge so from the shot lying around afterwards. It had not much influence on the affair, however.

Question. Was there any attack upon our troops from the left that amounted to anything, that you knew of?

Answer. No, sir; none at all from the left.

Question. Do you know where the enemy's troops came from that attacked our troops in the crater?

Answer. I should think they came nearly in a direct line from this church, [indicating on the map,] obliquely from General Burnside's right.

Question. At what time did you receive your orders to co-operate in this assault?

Answer. In the afternoon of the preceding day.

Question. Were there any reasons why you should not have attacked the enemy directly in your front? I have heard it suggested that the enemy might have been attacked on the right and left of General Burnside's column.

Answer. It was not a part of the programme.

Question. What I mean is, do you know any reason why it should not have been a part of the programme?

Answer. I should say myself that I had no better chance to attack there after the mine was sprung than I had the day before. I might just as well have attacked at any other time, and a great deal better a month before, because the enemy had not then so many abatis, or batteries, &c. I fought a battle there on the 18th of July with all my corps, and with as much vigor as I could, when the enemy had had but one day's preparation, and did not succeed. Then they had had forty-two days' preparation. There was no more reason why I should have attacked the lines on my front on that day than on any day of the preceding forty-two. I had, with more men, failed in my attack before.

Question. And that was a reason why you should not have attacked on the 30th?

Answer. Yes, sir; if I had been asked beforehand I should have said that I would not advise it. But if I had been ordered to do it I should have done it. We have had to do a great deal of attacking in this campaign which did not seem exactly right to those in front; but it had a bearing upon other parts of the field which we could not understand. One of the most difficult things in a campaign is to subordinate your own particular ideas to the general plan. We have learned that now.

Question. You know of no other reason than what you have assigned?

Answer. No, sir; no other.

Question. What did your corps do on that day?

Answer. I do not know that I could say we did anything more than I have already stated, except to retire to the camp.

By Mr. Chandler:

Question. Will you state what, in your opinion, should have been the manner in which that assault should have been made?

Answer. In my opinion there should have been two independent columns, perhaps as large as a division each, to have rushed in immediately after the explosion of the mine, and have swept down the enemy's lines right and left, clearing away all their artillery and infantry by attacking in the flank and rear. This would then have allowed the main column to follow on to the main crest rapidly and without molestation. I believe that insufficient preparation was made in not making wider covered ways, and in not more thoroughly levelling our own parapets and removing our own abatis. The consequence was, that the troops seemed to move very slowly, and went forward very stragglingly, like a skirmish line. Those that reached the crater apparently huddled into it, and made no attempt, that I know of, to take the enemy's lines to the right and left. The object of mining the enemy's lines at any one point was evidently to give the opportunity to take the rest of the enemy's lines in flank and reverse, and then the troops in front of those lines could move forward. Unless this part was properly carried out at the breach, all the rest of the forces would necessarily have to remain quiescent.

Question. If that had been done, what do you think would have been the result of the attack?

Answer. I think we would undoubtedly have gained the whole of the enemy's outer lines, and probably Petersburg.

By Mr. Loan:

Question. Could they have taken the line of Cemetery hill?

Answer. The main column should not have been bothered with the flank movement, but should have gone right on for the hill as soon as the road was clear; and it would not have been molested if the other had opened out for it. A similar programme to that was sketched in the order issued by General Hunt to the artillery, though I believe it was not in the general instructions. It was, probably, such an obvious matter that it was not thought worth while to specify it.

Question. In regard to the levelling of the parapets [and removing the abatis, preparatory to the assault, could that have been done with ordinary prudence, or would it have cost an unusual loss of life?

Answer. It should have been done at any hazard. If that could not be done the whole thing would be a failure.

Question. Did not the success of a movement of this kind depend upon its being a surprise, and the celerity with which the necessary operations were carried out?

Answer. Yes, sir.

Question. The lines of the two armies being so near each other, as they were, would not any attempt to remove the abatis and lower the parapets to any considerable extent have attracted the attention of the enemy, and put him on his guard?

Answer. The whole thing, except making the covered ways, could have been done in half an hour, and that time would not have benefited the enemy much. In fact, the more men he had got into the mine, the more would have been blown up.

Question. What delay actually occurred after the explosion of the mine in the movement of the assaulting column, in consequence of the insufficient preparations?

Answer. What I meant was that the whole thing seemed to move slowly, and the men to straggle along up.

Question. Did you understand the delay to be occasioned by the failure to remove the abatis and to lower the parapets?

Answer. That was a part of it. I also said that the covered ways should have been very much wider; that was a very important part of it; that was inside of our own lines. The rear of General Burnside's troops had not got done moving to the front, when the head of the column was repulsed. There was no lack of troops, for there was no space for them to go up. If I had been there myself, I should have charged the enemy's lines right down to the right and left at once. If I could not have carried the two batteries each side of me I should not have tried to do anything else.

Question. Yet you would have felt yourself under obligations to have obeyed any special orders to you in regard to your action there?

Answer. Yes, sir.

Question. Even if they had been at variance with your opinion as to what was judicious to have been done?

Answer. Yes, sir; but if I had been charged with conducting the assault, and those things I complain of had existed, I should consider myself personally blamable for it.

Question. If you had received positive orders to the contrary?

Answer. No, sir; but if I had been charged with assaulting that point, and I had not cleared away those obstacles, I should have considered myself at fault.

Question. Was there any failure in the movement on that account?

Answer. Yes, sir; enough, in my opinion, to have marred any plan.

Question. How long was it from the time of the explosion of the mine until the head of General Burnside's column was in the crater?

Answer. That I do not know. I have heard it variously estimated from a few minutes to an hour. It was in the gray of the morning, and in the smoke, and I saw nothing of it myself.

Question. What is your opinion based upon, when you say the troops were delayed?

Answer. As soon as I could see, I saw them going up in a straggling manner, and the rear of the column was not out of the trenches until the time I have mentioned. To express to you how it was, the bringing back of the wounded through the covered ways almost stopped the column going to the front.

Question. That was inside of our lines?

Answer. Yes, sir; they should not have been allowed to bring any wounded men into our lines at that time. Check the advancing column under the fire of the enemy, and in my opinion it is nearly whipped then.

Question. It is liable to be repulsed?

Answer. Yes, sir.

Testimony of Brevet Major General Robert B. Potter.

HEADQUARTERS ARMY OF THE POTOMAC,
Before Petersburg, Va., December 20, 1864.

Brevet Major General ROBERT B. POTTER sworn and examined.

By Mr. Chandler:

Question. What is your rank and position in the army?

Answer. I am a brigadier general and a brevet major general of volunteers, commanding the 2d division of the 9th army corps.

Question. Will you state to the committee, as concisely as possible, what you know in relation to the springing of the mine and assault upon the enemy's works on the 30th of July last?

Answer. About the 24th of June, I should think, the idea of mining under the enemy's works in my immediate front was suggested to me; in fact, I had thought of it before, and several others had thought of the same thing. Lieutenant Colonel Pleasants, commanding the 48th Pennsylvania volunteers, came to my quarters and suggested to me that he was familiar with mining, and that many of the men in his regiment were miners, and that they thought they could undermine one of the enemy's works in my immediate front. After some conversation with him, I wrote a communication to General Burnside, who was then my corps commander, suggesting this plan of mining the enemy's works, giving some of the details. The general subsequently sent for me to come to his headquarters and bring Colonel Pleasants with me, which I did, and we had an interview with him. Subsequently he notified us that he had submitted the plan to the general commanding the army of the Potomac, who had approved of the same, and that we were authorized to undertake the work. We then went to work and pushed the mine along as well as we could until, about the 17th of July, we were near the completion of the mine. We were then under the enemy's works, and were directed to hold up. We did nothing for several days, except to secure the work we had already performed. Afterwards we were ordered to go on and finish the work and put in the charge, which was completed about the 26th or 27th of July. On the 29th of July General Burnside sent me an order to report at his headquarters. Arriving there I found General Wilcox, who then commanded the 3d division of the 9th corps. We had some conversation about the explosion of the mine and the proposed attack; then General Ledlie, who commanded the 1st division, was sent for. The general plan of the attack, as proposed by General Burnside, was explained to us. While this interview was going on, General Meade, accompanied by General Ord and some staff officers, arrived there and had some conversation of a general nature. General Meade stated, to some extent, his ideas as to what ought to be done. They left, I think, to look at the position. It was understood that General Ord's troops were to come up to support the attack and to relieve a portion of our corps. Shortly afterwards, General Meade returned. At that time General Burnside, I presume, had made all the suggestions he wished in regard to the attack, and the only question was as to what troops should lead the attack. General Burnside suggested that, as we were all in the same position, the fairest way to decide the matter was by lot, which was accordingly done. By that decision General Ledlie was to lead the advance with his division, General Wilcox was to follow with his division, and I was to follow with my division after General Wilcox. The colored division of General Ferrero, who was not present at the time—General White was then temporarily in command of the division—was to come in last. The theory of the attack was, that after the explosion of the mine the leading division should advance immediately through the breach made in the enemy's works and attempt to seize the crest of the hill beyond, known as Cemetery hill; General Wilcox was then to follow through the breach and deploy on the left of the leading division and attempt to seize the line of the plank road; my division was to pass to the right of General Ledlie's division and form, so as to protect his right flank, on the line of a ravine which ran to the right, and which it was supposed it would be difficult to cross; then the division of General Ferrero, which was composed exclusively of colored troops, was to advance in case we secured a lodgement there, pass over the line of General Ledlie's division, and make an immediate assault on the town of Petersburg.

Some time in the course of the evening of the 29th of July, I think about nine o'clock, we received General Meade's written order, and an order from

General Burnside in conformity thereto. The general detail of those orders was in conformity with the plan that had been suggested.

During the afternoon previous I had sent for my brigade commanders and explained the plan of attack to them, and directed them where to mass their troops, so that they should be prepared. One of my brigades, which held the trenches immediately in front of the mine, and extending around to the Norfolk railroad, was to have been relieved by a division of General Ord's command, commanded by General Carr. Owing to the darkness of the night, or to some other cause, only two regiments of this division of General Carr had arrived by 12 o'clock at night. General Carr himself then came to my headquarters and told me that his division had got astray. I told him that as soon as it came up he should relieve me. He relieved a small portion of my line to the right. About two o'clock in the morning, finding that my division had not been relieved, I wrote to General Burnside, and suggested to him that, as my troops had not been relieved, it would, perhaps, not be safe to take all the troops out of the trenches; that I would relieve a portion of the brigade in the trenches, clear the trenches immediately in front of the mined work, leaving a strong picket line there, and mass that portion of the brigade relieved with the rest of the division.

About three o'clock in the morning, just as I was getting on my horse, General Carr came to me and said that he had found the rest of his troops, and that they would be up in half an hour. I told him I thought it would be too late then to change the programme. The time fixed for the explosion of the mine was, I think, half past three o'clock. I had my troops massed—those that were out of the trenches—on the right-hand side of the covered way that led from the rear of the line down to my line immediately in front of the mine.

The troops of General Wilcox were massed immediately on my left. General Ferrero's troops, I believe, were to General Wilcox's left and rear. General Ord's troops were massed mostly in a woods, some 500 or 600 yards in rear of where I had my troops massed. I had one regiment, which had been engaged in making the mine, which I had received orders not to put in the attack unless it was absolutely necessary. That regiment was in the rear, and I was using them as a provost guard. I had a small regiment as an engineer regiment, provided with levelling tools, &c.

The mine failed to explode at the time fixed. I waited for some time, and finally sent to inquire what was the matter. In the mean time I received a report from the officer in charge of the mine, Colonel Pleasants, that the fuze had gone out, and that an officer and a sergeant had volunteered to go in and light it again. At this time it had become daylight, but the enemy showed no indications of having discovered the dispositions we had made for the attack. I immediately reported the facts to my superior. I think it was about a quarter before five o'clock that the explosion took place. It was then broad daylight. Immediately all our batteries opened.

Finding that my column did not advance, as I had ordered, I sent to find out what was the difficulty. Before I got a report, however, Colonel Pleasants came back and told me that the first division had advanced across to the enemy's works, and had got into the crater of the mine and halted there, checking all the rest of the column. This report I sent to General Burnside. At the same time I sent an order to the commanding officer of my first brigade—the leading brigade—General Griffin, to advance to the right of the mine, if possible, and make an attack there on his own account; that it was important to press forward as quickly as possible before the enemy recovered.

About midnight of the night before, I had, on my own responsibility, given an order to General Griffin to deploy a line of skirmishers, who were to advance to the right of where we were expected to make an attack, and, if they found the enemy were stunned by the explosion, not to wait for the advance of the other troops, but he was to push ahead immediately with his brigade, and make a lodgement to the right. I impressed upon him the importance of time, for the success of this movement depended mainly upon its being a surprise.

In consequence of that order, as soon as General Griffin found that the division of General Ledlie was in the mine, he advanced his skirmishers, and followed with his brigade. The smoke which arose from the explosion, and the immense cloud of dust which hung over the place, made it almost impossible to see anything, and to some extent some of the leading regiments of his troops and those of General Ledlie's division got mixed up.

The confusion was increased to some extent by the colonel of one of the leading regiments being killed immediately after they struck the crater of the mine, or the lines of the enemy's works.

Colonel White, who led the advance, and who was taken prisoner on that occasion, advanced promptly through the line of the enemy's works, and turned to the right as he was ordered. Meeting with some opposition, and finding that the division of General Ledlie was not advancing, he halted, and sent back for orders. I was still urging General Griffin to press forward as rapidly as possible.

As soon, I suppose, as my report could have reached General Burnside that the troops of General Ledlie had halted at the crater, he sent me a verbal order by an aide-de-camp to the effect that I was to advance, instead of going where I had intended, and attempt to carry the hill in front of the mine. This order I immediately communicated to my subordinate commanders, and gave such orders as were necessary to alter the disposition of the troops, and endeavored to push my column forward. But the difficulty which I had apprehended immediately occurred, viz: that as soon as we advanced into the opening in the enemy's lines we found it filled with men. The troops were thrown into confusion, and it was impossible to do anything with them.

By this time, which was probably a half or three-quarters of an hour after the explosion of the mine, the enemy had recovered from the apparent panic into which they had been thrown, and had opened their batteries and concentrated their fire upon this point. There was a very severe fire. The worst fire I saw came from the right. There was a battery there behind some timber which it was very difficult for our batteries to reach. I ordered my own batteries to turn their whole attention to that one, but it apparently produced no effect at all.

The affair went on in this way for some time. We were endeavoring to press ahead. I got three or four of my regiments across and beyond this line of the enemy's works, and was getting them into pretty good shape. I was convinced that something must be done to create a diversion and distract the enemy's attention from this point. I accordingly gave orders to Colonel Bliss, who commanded my second brigade, to send two of his regiments to support General Griffin, and to take the remainder of his brigade and make an attack on the right. Subsequently it was arranged that the two regiments going to the support of General Griffin should pass into the crater, turn to the right, and sweep down the right of the enemy's works. This order was carried out. Colonel Bliss was partially successful, and we got possession of the line of the enemy's works to the right of the crater for the space of 200 or 300 yards, and one of my regiments got up within twenty or thirty yards of this battery which I was anxious to silence.

At this time I wrote a despatch to General Burnside, in which I stated that it was my opinion from what I had seen, and from the reports which I had received from my subordinate officers, that too many men were being forced in at this one point; that the troops there being in confusion, it was absolutely necessary that an attack should be made from some other point of the line, in order to divert the enemy's attention, and give us time to straighten out our line a little. To that despatch I never received any answer.

I kept receiving these orders to push our men forward as fast as I could

That in substance was about all the orders I received that day, up to the time of the withdrawal.

Some little time after this I received a copy of an order, which seemed to be a general order to division commanders, to the effect that we should attack at once with all our force, or press ahead with all our force at once, or something of that kind. I was at that time doing all I could to press my division forward, and consequently gave very little attention to this order, as I felt satisfied I was already doing my own duty in regard to it. It did not occur to me to reflect what effect that order would have upon the other divisions; but soon after this, as I was going back to report to General Burnside, I heard cheering, and turned around and saw the division of colored troops coming up to make an attack. They were advancing some distance to my left, moving obliquely to the right, and running parallel to the enemy's lines, who were firing on them. They then attempted to advance forward through the crater of the mine, and then to the right, where most of my men were; some of those troops halted when they found the other troops lying down; some of them advanced up to the ground where my men were, and formed in among them.

This added somewhat to the confusion. The colored troops made a very spirited attack, and behaved remarkably well while coming up. But the place they came into was a place where we could hardly hope for any success, because the troops were so much broken up. They got up, gained some little ground, and then some time elapsed in trying to straighten out the men who had got confused.

I went on immediately to try and find General Burnside, and ask him not to send any more men there. When I did find him General Ord was at the same place. Just as I commenced to speak to him some confusion arose, and I immediately turned back and found that this division of colored troops had given way and was coming back. I went then to look after my own division. No effort that I am aware of was made after that for the renewal of the attack at that point, more than the general order to press our troops forward.

I was in conversation with General Burnside, to whom I had again returned, for I wanted to withdraw one of my brigades, the one under Colonel Bliss, and make an attack still further to the right. I thought that by attacking on the other side of the ravine, I could burst through the line and get in rear of the battery which was annoying me, and relieve my troops in that way. General Burnside told me that he had received an order to prepare for the withdrawal of his troops, and that I should not take any steps until he had seen General Meade.

We did nothing more then except to hold our position until I received an order from General Burnside to report at his headquarters. General Ord's command was withdrawing at this time. I went there and had some conversation with him as to our position, &c., as to the practical difficulties in withdrawing our troops, and also the advantage of holding the position we had already gained.

We were then ordered to make arrangements for withdrawing our troops. Before I got back to my division—in fact, I think before I left General Burnside's headquarters—the enemy made an attack on us and forced our troops out of the position we had gained, and we then resumed our old position.

Question. Do you know the cause of the delay in the explosion of the mine?

Answer. Yes, sir; the fuzes went out where they were spliced.

Question. Do you know the cause of that?

Answer. I do not; I think there were three of the Gomez fuze; I subsequently inquired, but could not find out definitely what was the difficulty. The fuze, where it went out, did not seem to be wet, or anything like that, but had probably absorbed some of the dampness of the air. The charging of the mine, &c., was not strictly in accordance with the rules of engineering. The charge was larger than that laid down in the books, and the arrangement, in some respects, was different. My recollection is, that from where the charge was tamped there was about forty feet length of fuze. The mine was about one hundred and thirty yards long. Of course it required some time before a man would make up his mind that the explosion would fail, and before he would go in the mine to examine, and it took some little time to readjust it.

By Mr. Loan:

Question. You say you think there were three fuzes; have you any personal knowledge of the number of fuzes?

Answer. No, sir, I have not.

Question. At the commencement of your testimony you say it was determined by lot which division of General Burnside's corps should lead the advance; do you know any reason why the colored division should not have led that advance?

Answer. General Burnside was very anxious to have the colored division lead the advance on that occasion. We had been discussing this thing a long time. The reason why that division was not allowed to lead the advance was this: The morning that General Meade came with General Ord to General Burnside's headquarters we were discussing the plan of this attack under the theory that the colored division was going to take the lead. General Meade said, "I saw General Grant, and he agrees with me that it will not do to put the colored division in the lead." The reason why they were not put in was because General Meade would not permit it.

Question. Were those colored troops defective in any respect?

Answer. Not at all, that I know of, except that they had never been tried in action.

Question. Do you know whether they had been drilled with a view to making this assault?

Answer. Yes, sir, I had seen them drilling, and had discussed the matter with General Ferrero, and had seen the plan for the assault.

Question. I will ask you, as a military man, whether those colored troops were competent to make that assault at that time?

Answer. In my opinion they were the most fit troops in the corps, at that time, to make that assault.

Question. What kind of service had the white troops been rendering? Was it, or not, of an exhaustive nature, tending to reduce the morale and spirit of the troops in reference to making an assault at that time?

Answer. The white troops of the corps had been in the trenches from the 19th of June under the immediate fire of the enemy, which at that time was very severe. Our losses were very considerable indeed. The weather was very hot, and the labor of building works, &c., was very exhaustive. In fact, the troops were in very bad condition physically. The losses on the line around Petersburg at that time, from the heavy fire of the enemy, were principally confined, I think, to the ninth and eighteenth corps. Before taking up this position they had been very heavily engaged on the 17th and 18th of June, and had lost very heavily.

Question. What was the spirit of the troops, owing to this exhaustive labor—higher or lower than was usual with that command?

Answer. I think it was lower than usual with them.

Question. What had the colored troops been doing?

Answer. They had been in the rear. I do not think they had been doing anything in particular. They had principally been drilling with a view to making this assault. They slashed considerable timber and built some works on the left.

Question. Was their morale high or low, comparatively speaking?

Answer. As far as I could judge it was very good.

Question. What troops of the enemy were they who fired upon our troops as they entered the crater? And how long was it from the time our troops entered the crater of the mine until the enemy opened fire upon them?

Answer. The musketry fire opened immediately; the enemy's artillery did not reply for some time; I think it was fifteen or twenty minutes before I noticed any artillery firing.

Question. What troops of the enemy opened fire?

Answer. The troops occupying that line of works.

Question. Do you know of any reason why our troops upon the right of General Burnside's line did not attack the troops of the enemy opposite to them?

Answer. I do not know any reason, except from hearsay.

Question. Do you know of any military reason why they should not have been ordered to do so?

Answer. I do not.

Question. Was there any military obstruction or obstacle that would have rendered it injudicious to have given such an order?

Answer. Not that I could see. The enemy's works were very strong; I cannot say anything more than that.

Question. That you may understand the object I have in view in making these inquiries, I will say that I understand the lines of the two armies, where the mine was, were opposed to each other and about a hundred yards apart, and it was the business of those confronting each other to hold their respective lines?

Answer. Yes, sir.

Question. Now at the time that General Burnside made his assault, was it judicious for the commands on his right and left to have attacked the enemy's troops in their immediate front, and to have kept them engaged so as to prevent their firing upon General Burnside's advancing column?

Answer. In my opinion it was.

Question. Do you know of any military reason why such orders might not have been judiciously given?

Answer. I think it probable that our line to the right was rather weakly held.

Question. Who was in command on the right?

Answer. I think that General Mott's division of General Hancock's corps occupied the line to our right. The troops of General Ord which had been holding the line to our right had been massed to support this attack, and the position they had held had been taken by this division of General Mott, which I think had been drawn from the north side of the James for the purpose of relieving General Ord's troops. The explosion of the mine and the assault following it had been preceded by a diversion by General Hancock upon the north side of the James. General Hancock himself that day was on that part of our line, to the right.

Question. Were the troops under his command brought into action that day in any way?

Answer. Not that I am aware of.

Question. At what time did you receive orders to withdraw your command from that assault?

Answer. I think it must have been about mid-day.

Question. Do you, as a military man, think that any advantage could have been gained by continuing the contest longer on that day?

Answer. Not at that point.

Question. Would a longer continuance of the contest, with the troops capable of fighting, have been of any benefit in relieving those in the crater of the mine from the confusion into which they had been thrown?

Answer. A demonstration on our right and left I think would have relieved us.

Question. Was it possible to have made that demonstration with any troops that were available at that time?

Answer. I think so.

Testimony of Lieutenant Colonel Charles G. Loring.

HEADQUARTERS ARMY OF THE POTOMAC,
Before Petersburg, Va., December 20, 1864.

Lieutenant Colonel CHARLES G. LORING sworn and examined.

By Mr. Chandler:

Question. What is your rank and position in the army?

Answer. Lieutenant colonel and assistant inspector general of the 9th army corps.

Question. Did you hold that position on the 30th of July last?

Answer. I did.

Question. Will you state concisely the facts within your knowledge in relation to the assault made by the 9th corps on that day?

Answer. I had made, with Colonel Van Buren, the position of the enemy a subject of special study; and therefore, on that occasion, I volunteered to go in with the first division that was to go in. The plan of the attack was changed from that first decided upon by General Burnside. His plan had been to have the colored division, under General Ferrero, lead the assault, and to have the attack made with a certain formation of the troops engaged. Both of those points were countermanded on the day previous to the actual assault. The reason for selecting the colored troops to lead in the assault, I suppose, was in some slight measure due to an opinion I had expressed, as follows: Some time previous to the intended assault I officially informed General Burnside that, in my opinion, the white troops of his corps were not in a fit condition to make the assault; that many of them had been for six weeks in close proximity to the enemy's lines, within one hundred and thirty yards; that all of them had been very near the enemy's fire; and that when troops are exposed, as they were, day and night for six weeks to an incessant fire, it is impossible that they should have the same spirit as fresh troops. In addition to that, before sitting down before the enemy's lines, they had been very much worn by the long and arduous campaign, in which, as I considered, the 9th corps had performed more arduous services than the other corps. But even if they had been fresh when they had arrived before Petersburg, the experience of those six weeks—during which they had been under fire day and night without cessation, so that it was impossible to get to the rear even to attend to the calls of nature without being exposed to being killed on the spot; during which period their losses had averaged over thirty (30) per day, amounting in the whole to one man in eight—was enough at least to weaken the zeal of the men. For this reason, principally, General Burnside selected to lead the assault the colored division, which up to that time had never been under any serious fire. Parts of it had been engaged in one or two little skirmishes, but the division had never been under any serious fire. That division was, therefore, selected upon the principle that fresh troops are much better to make an assault than old but worn-out troops. This plan was changed at noon of the day previous to the assault, and the first division of white troops, under General Ledlie, was selected to lead the attack the next morning.

At about half past two o'clock of the morning of the 30th I went with General Ledlie down to the front line, and we took our position very near the line, close in rear of it, with his division, waiting for the mine to explode. There was a delay of perhaps three-quarters of an hour in the explosion of the mine. But I do not think the enemy discovered at all that we had made any unusual preparations. As soon as the explosion took place the division started to go in. But it was not with the formation that General Burnside had desired, nor with exactly the same object. General Burnside's plan had been to throw in a column, the two leading regiments of which were to wheel, the one to the right and the other to the left, and sweep down the enemy's lines on either side, while the main body were to press on to the top of the hill beyond the crater of the mine. This formation, as I understand, was altered by orders from headquarters. The first brigade that went in started from our lines in three lines, with instructions to the brigade commander, as also to the commander of the second brigade, to push on at once for the top of Cemetery hill. I crossed over myself while the brigade which started second (being the first brigade) was passing out of our lines, and went into the crater of the mine, where I found the brigade that first started (being the second brigade) crowded together. The crater presented an obstacle of fearful magnitude. I suppose it was a hole of about 200 feet in length, by perhaps 50 or 60 feet in width, and nearly 30 feet in depth. The sides of it were composed of jagged masses of clay projecting from loose sand. The upper surface had been of sand, with a lower stratum of clay. It was an obstacle which it was perfectly impossible for any military organization to pass over intact, even if not exposed to fire. The whole brigade was broken up in confusion, and had utterly lost its organization. The officers were endeavoring to reform their men, but it was an exceedingly difficult operation. I remained there for about ten minutes. By that time the rest of the division had come up, and the whole of the first division was in the crater or lines immediately adjoining. It was all in the same confused condition. I went back to report to General Ledlie the condition his division was in, and to see if he could not rectify it. I then went up and told General Burnside of the state of affairs. From that time forward my position was mostly near General Ledlie in our old front line. As to what occurred with General Potter's division I cannot say, as that was some distance from where we were placed. Nor did I have any particular connexion with any other transactions until the ordering in of the colored division, which I think took place about half past seven o'clock. I cannot be precise as to the time, for I have not my notes with me. The troops in the crater of the mine had remained in confusion. They had spread themselves for a short distance both on the right and left of the crater, though it was exceedingly difficult for them to do so. The lines of the enemy were found to be of the most intricate nature. There was one uniform front line; then in the rear there were various lines, traverses between them, and bomb-proofs. It was more like a honey-comb than anything that can be seen on our lines; so that it was exceedingly difficult for troops to spread themselves either way, either to the right or to the left. It had to be done, not by any movement of a mass of troops, but by hand-to-hand fighting. All that I know of what took place beyond those lines I know from hearsay only, as the lines were so high as to cut off the view. I know from reports brought to me by others that our troops made several attempts to get up the hill, but I did not see that myself.

Nothing especial occurred, so far as I saw, until about half past seven o'clock, when the colored division was ordered in. At that time I was standing in our front line. General Ferrero, who commanded the colored division, was standing near me when the order was brought to him, by one of General Burnside's staff, to lead his division also into the crater, and to push for the top of the hill. The order struck me as being so unfortunate that I took the liberty to countermand it on the spot. General Ferrero hesitated, as he said here was a positive order from General Burnside. I told him that I was the senior staff-officer present, and that, in General Burnside's name, I would countermand the order until I could go up and inform General Burnside of the state of affairs.

I went up and represented to General Burnside that this colored division could not be expected to pass the lines of the old troops; that it was impossible to expect green troops to succeed where old troops had failed before them; and furthermore that, instead of accomplishing any good result, they would only throw into confusion the white troops that were already in that line and holding it. General Burnside did not reply to me, as he usually does to his staff officers, by stating his reasons for disagreeing with them, but simply repeated his previous order.

That evening, after the affair was all over, General Burnside showed me a written order from General Meade, directing him to throw in all his troops and push for the top of Cemetery hill; and he added that under those instructions he felt that he could not have done otherwise than he did.

The colored division went in very gallantly indeed. The fire of the enemy, at that time, was exceedingly heavy, especially from some batteries in a ravine on the right, and also from some batteries on our left. There was consequently a cross-fire directed upon the ground over which the colored division had to pass. Besides that, they were exposed to a cross-fire of infantry.

They went in very gallantly. I think it was about half an hour after that that they came running back in confusion. I understood that not only were they driven back in confusion, but it entailed also a heavy loss upon the white troops then in the enemy's line of works, and who came out with the colored troops.

I remained at the front until towards noon, when General Burnside ordered all his division commanders to report at his headquarters, he having received a peremptory order to cease aggressive operations and withdraw his troops. He directed me to carry the order down to the front line, and to send it in to the troops that were in the crater. I think the officer who carried the order to the brigade commanders of General Potter's division was the only officer who succeeded in getting in. The order was sent in, and indorsements were put upon it by the various brigade commanders then in the crater. One only advised waiting until night; the others advised immediate evacuation when they found that it was intended by the general commanding that the line should be evacuated, and not permanently held.

After General Burnside had received the order that offensive movements should cease, and while his men were yet struggling in the crater, the troops of General Ord, stationed in rear of the mine as a support to the 9th corps, were the greater part withdrawn, and in such way as to disclose the movement to the enemy.

Soon after this order came in the enemy prepared another charge, and the brigade commanders decided to evacuate at once, which was done, leaving, I believe, many in the crater, who were taken prisoners.

By Mr. Loan:

Question. What troops went into the crater of the mine besides those of General Ledlie's division?

Answer. General Ledlie's division was to go in first; the whole of that division went into the crater, or lines immediately adjoining. General Potter's division was to go in next, but to go in on the right of the other. I did not see them, and I do not know how many of them went into the crater. I simply saw the head of the column going in. I understood that they all went into the enemy's lines, but I cannot say positively about that. General Wilcox's division also went in, at the same place where General Ledlie's division went in. I think four of his regiments—I am not sure of the number—failed to get in. In starting from our line, they bore off too much to the left and came back to our own line, and did not go in. I think that, with that exception, the whole of General Wilcox's division went into the enemy's lines. The regiments of his division went in at different times, not as a division, but disjointedly. And at half past seven, about two hours and a half after the mine exploded, the whole of the colored division went in at the same point.

Question. How many of those troops gained the high ground beyond the crater, within the enemy's lines—the ground outside of the crater?

Answer. I cannot say how many. They made a great many attempts to charge up the hill, but how far they reached I cannot say, because I was not with them. I was not in the crater at the time they made any of their charges; only those on the spot could answer that question.

Question. Are you able to state how many of our troops were in the crater at the time the order to retreat was given?

Answer. I am not.

Question. Can you tell what the men were doing in the crater from the time General Ledlie's division entered it until the order to withdraw was given?

Answer. They immediately prepared the ground in front to protect themselves, and those who had arms and ammunition prepared to defend themselves.

Question. That would only be one line at the lips of the crater?

Answer. Yes, sir; and they also held a long stretch of the enemy's lines, to the right and left of the crater.

Question. What troops?

Answer. General Potter's troops held the line on the right, and General Wilcox's troops that on the left.

Question. Were those lines held by troops that had originally gone into the crater of the mine?

Answer. No, sir; almost all of the first division were collected together in the crater; some few of them were on the right; the most of General Potter's command were on the right; almost all of General Wilcox's command were on the left; some few of them were also in the crater. Two guns of the enemy were dug out of the ruins and turned against the enemy. At one time we held at least 400 or 500 yards of the enemy's lines, the crater in about the centre.

Question. Do you know where the troops of the enemy opposed to our troops in the crater were brought from?

Answer. When the column first went into the crater there was very little opposition. But the enemy's infantry remained within their lines within 200 feet of the crater; I myself saw them within 200 feet of the crater. They remained there when we went in, until gradually driven out, man by man, and our line spread in that way. After we had been there some time the enemy brought some troops to the top of the hill. There were two slight earthworks there in which they had mounted field-pieces, which fired shrapnell and canister all the morning. They came to the top of the hill, and then down a covered way which was on the right, which covered way they used as a breastwork. It connected with their lines, and from that they fired the whole time.

Question. Was there any eminence which commanded the crater, or were our men in the crater protected?

Answer. The men in the crater could be protected from direct fire by standing down in the bottom of it, but those standing on the top of the crater were exposed to a steady fire of canister from the hill beyond, which was decidedly higher than the crater, and the enemy brought their mortars to bear upon the crater, so as to drop their shells right over it.

Question. If I understood you rightly, you stated that on the day before the assault the plan of attack, as well as the tactical arrangement of the troops, were changed?

Answer. Yes, sir.

Question. By what kind of an order, verbal or written; and by whom was the order given?

Answer. So far as I know it was only a verbal order. General Meade came to General Burnside's headquarters at about noon of the day previous to the assault, and there gave the order.

Question. Did you hear General Meade give the order?

Answer. I was not present.

Question. Then all you know about it is from information derived from others?
Answer. Yes, sir.

By Mr. Chandler:

Question. Do you know the cause of the delay in the explosion of the mine?
Answer. While we were waiting there I wrote to Colonel Pleasants, asking the cause of the delay. He replied to me that the fuze had gone out at a place where it had been spliced together; that he had sent some one in to rectify it— to rejoin it and relight it—and that it would go off at a certain time which he named, which time it did go off.
Question. Were there one or more fuzes?
Answer. I think there were two laid, but I am not certain.
Question. You have no personal knowledge of that?
Answer. No, sir. I wish to say a word in relation to the enemy's artillery fire. I understand an officer of high authority has said that the enemy's artillery fire was silenced during the latter part of that affair. I can only say that it is the opinion of one who could not have been in the front line that day. I was myself in our front line, except for the short time that I was in the crater, and the short time when I went to report to General Burnside on two or three occasions; with those exceptions, I was in the front line the whole of that morning, and I know that the enemy kept up a very steady and heavy fire of artillery from both the left and right, raking the whole of the ground from our line to the crater of the mine; and further, that from the hill in front of the crater they kept up a steady stream of shrapnell and canister, whenever any demonstration was made by our troops. I can testify to this very positively, as I was present on the spot.

Testimony of Brevet Lieutenant Colonel J. L. Van Buren.

HEADQUARTERS ARMY OF THE POTOMAC,
Before Petersburg, Va., December 20, 1864.

Brevet Lieutenant Colonel J. L. VAN BUREN sworn and examined.

By Mr. Chandler:

Question. What is your rank and position in the army?
Answer. I am a major and additional aide-de-camp, and brevet lieutenant colonel.
Question. What was your position on the 30th of July last?
Answer. Major, and aide de-camp on the staff of Major General Burnside, then commanding the 9th corps.
Question. Will you state, as concisely as possible, what you know in regard to the action of that day?
Answer. On the night before the assault I was detailed by General Burnside to be with General Potter, who commanded the second division of the 9th corps. There was a staff officer detailed to each division. I reported to General Potter about half past two o'clock on Saturday morning, the day of the assault, and went with him to the front line where the reserves were massed. On the way there we met an officer from Colonel Pleasants, who reported that the mine had been fired and would explode at 3.41 a. m. After waiting a certain time and hearing no explosion, General Potter sent down to inquire about it, and I went over and reported to General Burnside that General Potter had sent down. I then returned to General Potter. An officer from Colonel Pleasants reported that the fuze had gone out, but he had had it relighted, and the mine would explode in a certain number of minutes. I went back to General Burnside and reported

this to him, and to Captain Jay, of General Meade's staff, who had been sent by General Meade to ascertain the cause of the delay in the explosion; and while I was there, at 4.42 a. m., the mine exploded. I then returned to General Potter, and remained with him I should suppose for one hour, reporting to General Burnside by letter any information that came to me in regard to General Potter's troops. General Potter's division was the second in the order of attack in the assault that followed the explosion. About seven o'clock I told General Potter I thought I would go down myself and see what I could ascertain, and I went down to our front line. While I was there Captain Harris, of our staff, came and asked for General Ledlie, who commanded the division that led the assault; I told him I was just going over to the crater, and would take over any orders to him. Captain Harris had orders from General Burnside that General Ledlie must push forward his division at once. I went over to the crater, but did not find General Ledlie there; I saw his two brigade commanders, General Bartlett and Colonel Marshall, and communicated the orders to them; soon afterwards a staff officer came in from General Ledlie with the same orders. After some little delay Colonel Marshall said to me that he did not think he could advance from where he was; that the enemy were on his flank. I told him I would go down with him and look at his line. As you go out of the crater of the mine you come into a labyrinth of bomb-proofs and magazines with passages between. The enemy's rear line was about twenty-five yards in rear of their front line, and between them were these bomb-proofs, making a very bad place for troops to pass over. In that way for about three hundred yards our first division was crowded in some confusion; beyond this came the high rear line, and on the other side of that was the enemy's covered way, and in that the most of General Potter's division. I went down the line to the right, about three hundred yards, to where the line crooked, and just the other side of the line were the enemy, and quite sharp firing was going on. Colonel Marshall told me that he did not see how he could charge with those men on his flank; I told him that the orders were imperative, and the charge on the crest must be made. We formed a line of his brigade on the right, and General Bartlett's brigade on the left, so far as we could on the bad ground, and charged, but, meeting a very heavy fire, the line broke and fell back. I then assisted Colonel Marshall in reforming his men. While we were reforming Colonel Marshall's brigade along the enemy's line the head of the colored division came over the crest of the crater right down this line and knocked all to pieces the formation we had secured. Colonel Bates, in command of one of the colored regiments, was at the head of this colored column. Colonel Bates apparently did not know where he was going to strike for. I pointed out a white house on Cemetery hill as the objective point. It seemed to me that by detaching a force, and charging down the line at the same time that we charged in front, we should probably capture the enemy's men on the right who were annoying us. I started back towards the crater; when I got very near there I saw the movement of this colored column, jumping out from the enemy's line towards our line in the rear and striking off towards the right. They carried about two hundred yards of the enemy's lines, capturing a color and quite a number of prisoners. I went with them as far as they went, and then came back to the crater to see the officers there. Just as I got to the crater the second brigade of the colored division came across, going right through the crater and somewhat to the right, and right over the tops of the bomb-proofs and over the men of the first division. They came on in good style, under a sharp fire, but were much broken and disordered by the unfavorable ground and the crowded condition of the pits. All this time the fire of the enemy was very heavy. There were two guns in what was known as the fort on the left of the New Market road, and two guns just across a ravine to the right. They were throwing canister and shrapnell in there in a very lively way. There was some mortar firing also.

I then saw Colonel Sigfried, who commanded the right brigade of the colored division, and Colonel Thomas, who commanded the left brigade. General Ferrero was not there. I gave them their instructions for the final charge of the whole division. I instructed Colonel Thomas to form his brigade as far to the front as he possibly could; Colonel Sigfried to form on his right, and then to charge directly for Cemetery hill. I instructed Colonel Marshall and General Bartlett to form their brigades, as much as the nature of the ground would permit, in the rear of the colored division and support the charge.

I suppose this must have been about a quarter to nine o'clock. Having made these arrangements I started back to report to General Burnside. But the difficulties in the way of getting back were so great, the firing being very heavy, and the covered way being crowded with the troops of the eighteenth corps, that it took me a very long time to get up. Before I got up there the colored division had made their charge and been repulsed.

Then occurred the trouble that had been anticipated. When they fell back into the enemy's lines, which were already crowded with the troops of the white divisions, and with their own stragglers, their formation was utterly broken up. They lost coherence, and a great part of the colored division came surging back in confusion.

I saw General Burnside and reported to him all that I had done. In the course of twenty minutes after that came an order from General Meade for the withdrawal of the troops, which finished operations for the day.

We stayed around there long enough to attend to anything that had to be done, and then we went back.

Question. What was the cause of the delay in the explosion of the mine?

Answer. A failure to burn at a place where the fuze was spliced. The fuze came out, and of course it had to be spliced, and at one of the places of junction it had failed to burn.

Question. In how many pieces did you receive the fuze?

Answer. I knew at the time, but I would not pretend to state now.

Question. Do you know whether there was more than one fuze laid to fire the charge in the mine?

Answer. The fuze was laid in a trough of powder; if the one did not go off the other would. I would not be certain about the number of fuzes.

Testimony of Major General H. J. Hunt.

HEADQUARTERS ARMY OF THE POTOMAC,
Before Petersburg, Va., December 20, 1864.

Major General H. J. HUNT sworn and examined.

By Mr. Chandler:

Question. What is your position and rank in the army?

Answer. I am a major general, commanding the artillery of the army of the Potomac.

Question. Will you state what information you have in regard to the attack on the 30th of July last on the enemy's lines before Petersburg?

Answer. About the 3d of July I was ordered, in conjunction with Major Duane, of the engineers, to make an examination of the lines of the enemy facing east in front of Petersburg, and to ascertain whether an assault was practicable, especially in front of Generals Burnside and Warren. I made the examination with Major Duane, and reported, I think on the 6th of July, that an open assault would be very dangerous, and that it would be better to have our approaches partake rather of the nature of regular approaches. This was ordered to be executed, and proper measures were taken by Major Duane and myself to carry them on so far as the means would permit. There were not sufficient troops to extend our left sufficiently to embrace the angle of the enemy's works, where their lines turn and run towards the west. The work was consequently slow. About the 28th of July, after the principal batteries had been erected, orders were issued for an attack on the position of the enemy in front of General Burnside's line, as a mine which he had constructed, and which it was meant to work into the operation, had been completed. It was necessary, in order that the assault should be successful at the point indicated, that the angle of the enemy's lines, of which I have spoken, should be in our possession, or that such preparation should be made as should suppress his fire at that point, his principal batteries being those, and from that position the whole ground in front of our line could be swept. From the want of troops to envelope that position it was impracticable to carry forward approaches against that angle so as to get it in our possession. I therefore limited myself to bringing such a weight of artillery to bear upon it as would keep down its fire and also to keep down the fire along the whole of the enemy's lines, upon which was placed the battery which had been undermined. The plan of General Burnside, who was to make the assault, as given to me by him, was to send forward a heavy column of troops so arranged that as soon as the explosion should take place, or the mine was sprung, they would pass over the mine and form to the right and left perpendicularly, and sweep down the enemy's lines. The troops with which he intended to assault Petersburg were to advance immediately after the others, assault the battery behind the mine on the crest held by the enemy, and pass on from there into Petersburg. My preparations were all made on the 28th of July, and examined and verified on the 29th. On the morning of the 30th the mine was sprung a little over an hour after the time appointed. The artillery opened as directed, and succeeded remarkably in keeping down the enemy's fire, as he was evidently surprised. There was one battery upon the crest behind the mine, which opened at intervals, but which was always silenced after firing not more than two or three rounds. The battery next to the one undermined, on the left, as we looked at it, was silenced, with the exception of one or two guns in a hollow, near the left flank of the battery next the mine. From this gun, or perhaps two guns, a fire was kept up at intervals on the position of the crater of the mine. That battery was one, as I understood it, that was to have been in our possession within ten or fifteen minutes after the explosion of the mine; that is, as soon as troops could pass from the crater and sweep to the left and get possession of it. The position of the guns which, if any, would have commanded that hollow, was immediately behind the mine, and between that position and the enemy's battery there was a fringe of woods which was to have been cut away by General Burnside's troops, but which had not been cut away down to the 29th, when I sent down to see if all the preparations had been made. General Burnside declined cutting away that wood, as so doing would alarm the enemy. I could not see very clearly what took place about the mine, as I had to look after my own guns, which covered a very large extent of ground. But after some delay, an hour and a half I suppose, I saw portions of the troops that had formed close to the enemy's lines. I did not see them advance beyond the enemy's line. About 8 or half past 8 o'clock, or rather in the course of the morning, for I will not be positive about the time, an order was given for the troops to charge.

Question. You spoke about a delay in the explosion of the mine. Do you know the cause of that delay?

Answer. I understood at the time that it was owing to the fuze which led to the mine having become broken.

Question. Do you know whether there was one or more fuzes laid to the charge in the mine?

Answer. I do not know how many fuzes were placed in it. I furnished safety fuzes enough to make three or four lines. But I understood that it was determined, instead of using this safety fuze, to use a wooden pipe filled with powder. But I cannot speak positively as to that.

Question. Do you know the condition of the fuze that was furnished; was it in good condition, and in a few or many pieces?

Answer. I do not know in what pieces it was furnished. I know there were some hundred yards of it. I did not see it myself; I ordered it from City Point to General Burnside, and that order was handed over to the ordnance officer. It was sent by the ordnance officer at City Point to the ordnance officer of General Burnside's corps, Captain Harris, I believe.

Testimony of Brevet Colonel James C. Duane.

HEADQUARTERS ARMY OF THE POTOMAC,
Before Petersburg, Va., December 20, 1864.

Brevet Colonel JAMES C. DUANE sworn and examined.

By Mr. Chandler:

Question. What is your rank and position in the army?

Answer. I am a major of engineers, and brevet colonel, and acting chief engineer of the army of the Potomac.

Question. Will you state what you know about the attack upon the enemy's lines before Petersburg, on the 30th of July last?

Answer. Orders were given to concentrate all our fire in order to silence the enemy's fire while General Burnside's operations were going on after the explosion of the mine. The position I had at 3 o'clock on the morning of the 30th was on General Warren's line; I was assisting General Abbott in directing his fire. The 18th corps was massed in rear and a little to the right of the 9th corps. A portion of the 5th corps was massed along the line of the Norfolk railroad, in the cut, ready to support the attack of the 9th corps. As soon as the explosion took place all the guns on the line of the 5th corps opened fire and completely silenced the enemy's fire. I remained on the line of the 5th corps until nearly 8 o'clock, during which time we kept up a constant fire. I then proceeded to General Warren's headquarters. When I arrived there I found that the troops that had proceeded to the crater of the mine were falling back. With regard to the operations of the 9th corps I had very little to do. General Burnside took on himself the entire charge of the engineering operations there.

By Mr. Loan:

Question. What, in your opinion, was the cause of the failure of the attack?

Answer. I think the difficulty was that proper measures had not been taken to clear away the obstructions both in front of our own line and the enemy's line; and also in making the attack by the flank instead of in columns.

Question. What number of columns do you think the assaulting force should have been composed of?

Answer. I think they should have gone up in three columns.

Question. In what relation to each other do you think those columns should have been?

Answer. The leading or centre column should have gone to the crater of the mine and removed the obstructions, so as to have allowed a column on the right and one on the left to have followed immediately after.

Question. At what distance from each other?

Answer. The distance at that point could not have been greater probably than 150 yards on each side.

Question. Of what strength should those columns have been?

Answer. Each a division of a corps. I had supposed that the arrangement was that the whole of the 9th corps should have gone in, and the portion of the 5th corps that was massed for its support, and the whole of the 18th corps, to have gone in immediately after.

Question. Was there any other cause, in your judgment, that contributed to the disaster of that day?

Answer. I cannot state about that. I was not at the point where the mine was exploded. All I know about that is from hearsay.

Question. Did you receive any instructions to make an examination with General Hunt, chief of artillery, as to the front of the rebel line in regard to the placing of the artillery prior to the attack?

Answer. We had a general order to take charge of that line.

Question. At what time was that order given?

Answer. I forget the date; but it must have been some two or three weeks previously.

Question. Did you make an examination with a view to the springing of this mine and making this assault?

Answer. Towards the latter part of the time such examination was made. The first order in the beginning of July was to make an examination in reference to a general attack.

Question. Was there any special order given to you and General Hunt to examine the rebel line in front of the 5th corps, with a view of silencing the rebel batteries, while the assault was being made by the 9th corps?

Answer. Yes, sir; there was.

Question. Who issued that order, and at what time was it issued?

Answer. I think it was given to me verbally. I am not certain whether it was by General Meade himself or by his chief of staff.

Question. It was issued by General Meade's authority?

Answer. Yes, sir.

Question. About how long previous to the time when the assault was made?

Answer. I should think it was about ten days; I am not certain about the time. We had ample time, however, to establish our batteries and put in position all the guns that could be placed in that line.

Question. And if I understand you rightly, the batteries on the rebel right, in front of General Warren's corps, were effectually silenced at the time of the attack?

Answer. Yes, sir; I was enabled, in about half an hour, to stand on top of the parapet. The enemy's batteries were effectually silenced.

Question. What position did the enemy's batteries occupy that were firing upon our troops in the crater of the mine?

Answer. There were two guns which took a position in a ravine—two field-pieces which were run down there, and which commenced firing about an hour after we had taken possession of the crater; at least that was the first I saw of their firing; they may have fired previously to that time.

Question. Those were the only two guns upon our left which fired upon our troops in the crater?

Answer. Yes, sir.

Question. What other guns of the enemy were there that fired upon our troops in the crater?

Answer. There were some guns over on the right, but I could not see what they were from my position.

Testimony of Major General E. O. C. Ord.

CITY POINT, Va., *December* 20, 1864.

Major General E. O. C. ORD sworn and examined.

By Mr. Chandler:

Question. What is your rank and position in the army?
Answer. Major general, now in command of the 24th army corps.
Question. What was your command on the 30th of July last?
Answer. I was then in command of the 18th army corps, and of a part of the 10th army corps.
Question. Will you state such facts as may have come to your knowledge, and which you may deem important, in relation to the attack by the 9th corps on the enemy's lines before Petersburg, on the 30th of July last?
Answer. I will read the report which I made of that affair, and then I will answer such additional questions as you may think proper to ask.

"HEADQUARTERS EIGHTEENTH ARMY CORPS,
"*Near Petersburg, August* 3, 1864.

"GENERAL: In obedience to orders from General Meade (to whom I was ordered to report) the 1st and 3d divisions of the 18th corps were, on the night of the 29th of July, placed in the trenches of General Burnside's front, relieving portions of his command as trench guards, that the 9th corps might prepare to assault the enemy's line next a. m. The 2d division 10th corps, Brigadier General Turner commanding, and the 2d division 18th corps, Brigadier General Ames commanding, were placed in rear of General Burnside's corps as reserve supports, and in positions selected by him. Their orders were to await orders, to be sent as soon as the result of the assault next morning by the 9th corps could decide where supports might be needed.

"About 5 o'clock a. m., 30th of July, the mine in front of the 9th corps sprung, and I took my position near General Burnside awaiting the result of his assault, and with an understanding that as soon as his corps could get out, General Turner was to follow his (Burnside's) rear division and support it on the right, beyond our lines. About 6 o'clock General Burnside told me it was time for General Turner to move, and I directed General Turner accordingly; but the general got ahead of Potter's division, 9th corps, and was obliged to wait until it had passed. To understand the manner of the movement, I quote General Burnside's order, dated July 29, for the assault, which says:

"1. 'The mine will be exploded to-morrow morning at half past three. * * *

"2. 'General Ledlie will immediately, upon the explosion of the mine, move his troops forward. * * * * *

"3. 'General Wilcox will move his division forward after General Ledlie has passed through the first line of the enemy's works, bearing off to the east. * * *

"4. 'General Potter will move his division forward to the right of General Ledlie's as soon as it is apparent that he will not interfere with the movement of General Wilcox's division, and will, as near as possible, protect the right flank of General Ledlie's from any attack in that quarter, and establish a line on the crest of a hill which seems to run from the Cemetery hill, nearly at right angles to the enemy's main line, directly in our front. * * * *

"5. 'General Ferrero will move his division immediately after General Wilcox until he reaches our present advance line, where he will remain until the ground in his front is entirely cleared by the other three divisions, when he will move forward over the same ground that General Ledlie moved over, will pass through our lines, and, if possible, move down and occupy the village to our right.'

"Thus it will be seen that all three of his rear divisions had to follow each the action of those in its front; and I learned afterwards that the passage out and to our front line of breastworks was by a long trench or covered way and through a breach in our works. Hence the movements were slow, and there was delay especially after the enemy had massed his men, and our wounded coming from the front began to choke this covered way. About half past six a. m., having sent General Turner, commanding my advance division, an order to move forward on the crest of hill to right of Potter, (see the above order directing General Potter to establish a line on the crest of the hill,) near or on the Jerusalem plank road, in reply to this General Turner reported that General Burnside's troops filled the trenches in his front, occupying the crater and blocking up the way. About this time, or shortly after, I received an order directly from General Meade's headquarters, as follows:

"'You will at once move forward your corps rapidly to the crest of the hill, independently of General Burnside's troops, and make a lodgement there, reporting the result as soon as obtained.'

"This order I sent at once to Generals Turner and Ames. The latter was with his division closing up on Turner, and keeping his men massed for a movement in any direction. General Turner replied:

"'The only place I can get out of the lines is opposite the crater. It is already full of men who cannot develop. I shall put in my column as soon as I can. It is impossible, by reason of the topography, to charge in the manner you indicate. I must go in by head of column and develop to the right.'

"From General Ames I received the following:

"'I find that the covered way is the only way of getting to the front. General Turner occupies the road, and it is impossible for me to move until he gets out of my way.'

"Now I had not seen the ground, and supposed, all this time, that there were several places of exit, and the ground tolerably free from obstructions.

"I sent Generals Turner's and Ames's replies to General Meade, and went myself to the front, where I found our men were debouching *into* the crater, and in a short space of the enemy's trench on each side of it. I met General Turner just from the crater, (only 75 yards off,) and saw Burnside's white and black men needlessly filing into the crater, and into this short line of the enemy's works, under a destructive cross-fire. The enemy, just then, had brought up an additional six-gun battery, and was sweeping the 75 yards of bare up hill, where the 9th corps debouched, with a cross-fire of canister, grape, and musketry. I also saw that the crater and trench adjacent were in a sort of a re-entrant angle of the enemy's work, and that the men who had crowded in them were useless, and, in a measure, helpless. The crater was a *big hole*, some twenty feet deep, and was shortly afterwards rendered almost inaccessible by the cross-fire, and the trenches near it were crowded with men who were indisposed or unable to go forward; and I saw that the black troops were charging out *by the flank*, increasing this mass of men huddled under the enemy's fire. I directed General Turner not to put his men in the crater or the trench already filled with men, but to make a charge to the right where the enemy were massing. This he did, and I gave him all the aid in my power; the men climbing up and over our parapet, and dashing towards the enemy's trench in good style. (See Turner's report.) On my return to headquarters of General Burnside, I overtook General Grant, and he directed me to say to General Burnside that 'no more men should be sent into the crater or trenches of the enemy already filled, but he (General Burnside) should send forward intrenching tools, and hold all his men had gained.' I did so, and again ordered General Turner to push his whole division out, and to the right. Immediately thereafter—about 8 o'clock—I received from General Turner the following despatch:

"'Colonel Bell's brigade, in attempting to gain ground to the right on the enemy's line, was severely met by the enemy's fire, when a regiment of colored troops stampeded and broke through the brigade, carrying it all with them into our line.'

"This I communicated to General Meade, and repeated my orders to Turner to get his other brigade out to attack, but shortly afterwards (before my last order could be communicated) I received orders from General Meade to draw my men all inside our trenches to the rear, and afterwards an order was received to turn with my corps* to my own front.

"I may mention here, that when General Burnside had received the information that his men had occupied the crater, and a part of his command was in front of the crater—not advancing—I wrote the following despatch before I had any order from General Meade:

"'HEADQUARTERS EIGHTEENTH ARMY CORPS, 6½ *o'clock*, 30*th*.

"'GENERAL MEADE: Turner, in my front, reports that Burnside's troops fill our trenches in his front, occupying the crater, the enemy still holding their trenches to the right and left of the crater. Shall I order the divisions (two) of the 18th corps to try and charge the enemy's trenches over the heads of the men? Rifle firing has almost ceased in our front, and both parties covering.

"'E. O. C. ORD, *Major General of Volunteers.*'"

"The despatch I submitted to General Burnside, and he requested me to wait a few moments and he would have the way cleared. It was shortly after this I received the first order from General Meade to advance independently of General Burnside's troops. After receiving the order from General Meade to draw off my men and go back to my own front, I found that if I drew out the 1st and 3d divisions, 18th corps, which had been placed by General Burnside in his trenches, the trenches would be left too weak, and hence I directed General Carr, commanding these divisions, to remain where he was until night, when General Burnside promised to relieve him. The next day I asked General Burnside for the two (2) divisions left in his trenches, and finding that he could not send them all to me without inconvenience, I telegraphed General Meade that I could get along with the part which had been returned. The whole reported that night or the next morning.

"Enclosed you will find reports of division commanders and reports of casualties.

"I am, sir, respectfully, your obedient servant,

"E. O. C. ORD,

"*Major General of Volunteers, Commanding.*

"Major General A. A. HUMPHREYS,

"*Chief of Staff, Army of the Potomac.*"

---

* Should be *command*.

Question. To what do you attribute the failure of that enterprise?

Answer. In the first place, the crater of the mine was in a very bad place for a storming party to go in. It was swept by a flanking fire of the enemy; it was up hill; and, as it appeared to me, it was not covered by any of our batteries. The ground to the left and front of the mine was marshy, and covered by bushes and trees. No preparations had been made for our troops to pass out to our right or left. They could only get out by a single long trench or covered way; so that in the slow process of getting 10,000 or 12,000 men up through this narrow space and out through a single opening the enemy had an opportunity to make preparations to meet them. All this produced delay.

There should have been several openings made, and the troops should have attacked the enemy at several points at once. The mine was to have been sprung at half past three o'clock in the morning. But the last division of General Burnside's troops did not get out until nearly eight o'clock; some of the men were not out then. On account of the slow exit of these men, the enemy had an opportunity of pounding them as they came out in small force, by concentrating their fire upon them. That was one cause of failure. Another was that when the men did get out, from what I learn they were not sufficiently disciplined as soldiers to obey orders and advance as directed. The troops that first went out, as I was told, were dismounted cavalry—a very bad specimen of troops.

Question. If I understand you, this crater being too narrow a space through which to push an army successfully for a surprise, there should have been simultaneous attacks made at other points along the line?

Answer You do not get precisely my idea. The men had to go through a long narrow trench, about one-third of a mile in length, before they got into our extreme outwork, and then they went into this crater, and were piled into that hole, where they were perfectly useless. They were of about as much use there as so many men at the bottom of a well. Afterwards they filed into the trenches on either side of the crater for a small space, and covered themselves there as well as they could. If there had been several places of exit instead of but one, we could have tried the enemy elsewhere, and some of our parties might have been successful if others had been headed off.

Question. Of course this delay did not come under your observation, and the cause of it is not known to you?

Answer. When they had decided to follow in the order of General Burnside's march, one after the other through this one trench, and through one opening, that produced a delay which should have been anticipated. Better provision should have been made for the attack.

By Mr. Loan:

Question. What parts of the enemy's lines were open to attack with any chance of success?

Answer. I think it probable success might have been attained on the left and right of the crater, at the distance of half a mile, if our parapets had been opened during the night, and parties of men held there in readiness had dashed out upon the nearest works of the enemy, immediately after the explosion; for we learned afterwards that upon the explosion the enemy abandoned several of their batteries nearest our works, thinking they were also mined.

Question. What forces of ours were opposite those points where you think attacks might have been successfully made?

Answer. I had all of my available troops directly in rear of General Burnside's command, and reported to him and obeyed his directions by General Meade's orders. General Warren, I think, remained with his command on the left of General Burnside. There were no troops prepared on the right strong enough to make an attack. General Mott, who took my place there, had, I think, only one division, though quite a large one, to occupy the place of a much larger force while it was relieved for the attack. And it would not have been advisable to have had his troops attack.

Question. We then had no men on the right who could have made an attack there?

Answer. The answer I gave in regard to what might have been done referred to arrangements to have been made a day or so previous, by which troops could have been massed opposite the different places of exit, and then have gone out as soon as required. But the troops were massed all in this one place, along this covered way, a portion of them in front of this work, and the balance in rear by divisions, so that they were all in a column.

Question. That relates to the 9th corps, and to your corps in their rear?

Answer. Yes, sir.

Question. But your remark would not apply to General Warren's command?

Answer. I should not suppose it would apply to his command, if arrangements had been made beforehand.

Question. What I mean is the situation of General Warren's command as it was on the morning of the 30th of July. Were his troops in a situation where they could have attacked the enemy on our left?

Answer. I really do not know, because I am not aware how his troops were located. If they could have attacked by prearrangement, I think they were in a situation to have attacked.

Question. It would have been necessary to have arranged the troops, to have attacked on the right and left, in assaulting columns at half a mile distance from the crater, in connexion with the main assault through the crater?

Answer. Yes, sir; that suggested itself in answer to your question. We can never tell before an event takes place what might succeed half so well as we can afterwards, and a criticism that is advanced after the occurrence should, of course, be received with all this allowance.

Question. The cause of the failure was chiefly owing to the want of a proper outlet or *debouchment* for the troops?

Answer. Not entirely.

Question. No, not entirely, but chiefly?

Answer. My answer was intended to cover more than the fact of the *debouchment* not being a proper one. The massing the troops and sending them out by such a long, narrow covered way is what I particularly referred to, and which caused them to be very slow in their movements.

Question. Who decided upon the locality of your troops when they were ordered to be massed in the rear of General Burnside's corps?

Answer. I do not know positively, but my impression is that, the mine being General Burnside's idea, and he having been at work at it for some time, he made nearly all the arrangements for the explosion and the attack.

Question. Did he give directions for the location of your troops?

Answer. Yes, sir; he located them himself.

Question. Were they massed by his directions?

Answer. By his selection; for I sent my officers to report to him, and to get their situations from him.

Question. How long was it after the explosion of the mine before the head of General Ledlie's column entered the crater?

Answer. That I do not know; because I was not then near enough to the mine to see that; I was back with General Burnside.

Question. Have you any knowledge what troops of the enemy those were that opened this cross-fire upon our advancing columns? What I want to get at is, whether they were those troops that occupied the intrenchments, or whether they were drawn from some other parts of the enemy's line.

Answer. I cannot speak positively; but my impression is that they came in from other points. They almost always keep troops in reserve along their lines, so that when an attack is made, they can dash at once towards the threatened point.

Question. What was the effect of the explosion upon the enemy's troops in the trenches?

Answer. I think, from what I learned afterwards, that those batteries nearest the mine were partially abandoned, but that the trenches, under which it was not expected a mine could be easily built, were not abandoned except in the immediate vicinity of the crater.

Question. Do you know whether the troops in the enemy's trenches opened fire immediately upon our advancing column, or was there some delay?

Answer. I learned from others that there was some little delay; I do not know positively.

Question. Can you state whether our troops were enabled to pass across the space between our line and the crater before they were met by any fire from the enemy?

Answer. That I can only state from what others told me; I did not go to the front until I found that my divisions were impeded, and that difficulties were encountered in carrying out my orders.

Question. Were they impeded by the fire from the enemy's batteries on the right, or on the left, that were sweeping across the space between our lines and the crater?

Answer. The enemy's battery that I spoke of in my report took a position on the right of the crater as we faced the enemy's lines; there were other batteries a little more removed playing on the left also. The most destructive fire, however, was musketry and grape.

Question. From what locality?

Answer. From the right and left and front, apparently; but more particularly from the right.

Question. How was the enemy's infantry protected?

Answer. The nature of the ground to the right as we went out was such that our intrenchments fell off down into a swamp or bottom. There were bushes and tall trees in front of us, and we could not see anything in that direction thirty or forty yards off, and the enemy could form there, entirely screened, and in such position as to be in flank and in a measure in rear of those going from our works to the crater.

Testimony of Brevet Major General Edward Ferrero.

CITY POINT, VA., *December* 20, 1864.

Brevet Major General EDWARD FERRERO sworn and examined.

By Mr. Loan:

Question. What was your rank and position in the army on the 30th of July last?

Answer. I was then a brigadier general, commanding a division.

Question. What is your present rank?

Answer. Brevet major general.

Question. In what corps was your command last July?

Answer. It was the fourth division of the 9th army corps, and was composed of colored troops.

Question. We have been instructed to inquire into the operations of the 30th of July last, the springing of the mine, the attack by the 9th corps, &c. Will you state, in the first place, what you know in relation to the charging of the mine that was exploded on that day?

Answer. I know nothing about that; I had no connexion whatever with it.

Question. Had you, previously to the 30th of July, drilled your division with a view to making an assault after the springing of the mine?

Answer. I had, for over three weeks.

Question. What was the condition of your troops at that time, as to their spirit and morale?

Answer. They were in fine condition—better than any other troops in the army for that purpose. We were expecting to make this assault, and had drilled for weeks, and were in good trim for it.

Question. Had you made any examination of the ground and other preliminary arrangements with a view to the assault?

Answer. Before the commencement of the mine I had had a conversation with General Burnside, as it was intended I should make the assault, and submitted to him a plan, which is already in the report. I had surveyed the ground, made an examination, and given my plan of attack, which had been approved by General Burnside, and it was submitted to General Meade.

Question. Will you give the outlines of that plan—how the advance was to be made, and in what form?

Answer. The mine was under a considerable fort upon the right. There was a small fort a short distance, probably six hundred yards, to the left, with three or four guns. My idea was to make an assault at the moment of the explosion of the mine between those two points. I wanted to advance one brigade, which was to be the leading brigade, then divide it in two parts, one portion to go to the right and sweep the enemy's lines in that direction, and the other portion to go down the left and sweep the lines in that direction. The other two brigades of the division were to march forward in column, and carry the crest of Cemetery hill.

Question. Your object was to cross the enemy's works between the two forts?

Answer. Yes, sir, and not go over the point where the explosion was to take place, because the mass of earth that would be thrown up there would impede any troops. The object was to gain every moment at the explosion of the mine. My idea was to clear the enemy's line of works, and thus prevent a fire in our rear, as well as in our front.

Question. At what time was it decided not to use your division for that purpose?

Answer. The night before the assault I received the first intimation that they were not to be so used.

Question. What troops were used for that purpose?

Answer. The first division of the 9th army corps, under General Ledlie, was assigned the lead of the assault.

Question. What was the condition of those troops at that time? Had they been engaged in any exhaustive labors?

Answer. They were not the troops to put in at that time, from the very fact that they had been constantly under fire for a long period—so much so that it had become a second nature with them to dodge a bullet; from having been in such close contact with the enemy they had acquired that habit.

Question. Do you know anything about the arrangement for the *debouchment* of that command?

Answer. Every arrangement was made that it was possible to make under the circumstances, as it was necessary that we should do everything without giving information to the enemy. Nothing more could have been done without exposing our plans.

Question. Then one of the main elements of success in this enterprise consisted in the surprise of the thing?

Answer. Undoubtedly.

Question. Was it desirable in that connexion that our troops should move very rapidly after the explosion?

Answer. That was certainly very necessary.

Question. To what extent were the abatis removed, and the parapets levelled, in front of our own works, in order to enable the troops to *debouch* rapidly?

Answer. That point was probably the nearest point to the enemy upon our whole line, and it was utterly impossible to do anything more than was done. There was enough done to enable the troops to get over with all the necessary rapidity required at that moment.

Question. Did the troops move rapidly forward after the mine was sprung?

Answer. I was where I could witness the column movement. By my time they moved from five and a half to six minutes after the explosion. They could not move sooner on account of the concussion of the explosion, which would naturally prevent their going forward for a few moments.

Question. Have you any knowledge as to the effect produced by the explosion upon the enemy's troops in the vicinity of the mine?

Answer. I can state nothing further than that they seemed to be perfectly paralyzed for quite a long space of time.

Question. Was there any firing upon the part of the enemy upon our troops as they crossed over the space between our outer works and their lines?

Answer. The firing was very light on the first column that went up.

Question. Can you assign any reason for the confusion that ensued after the assault had been begun, and our troops had entered the crater?

Answer. Yes, sir. In the first place, the nature of the ground was such as to cause confusion among men who had been accustomed to seek shelter under fire for five or six weeks. The crater was a hole some twenty-five or thirty feet deep and fifty or sixty feet broad. When the men got into that hole they became confused, and it was utterly impossible to get them out. That was one of those things which will happen with the best of troops.

Question. Was there any remedy for that misfortune, when the troops refused to come out?

Answer. I am hardly at liberty to say. I was not in command of the army.

Question. What do you think could have been done?

Answer. We all differ in opinion.

Question. That is true; but we ask your opinion, as a military man.

Answer. I think myself that if the assault had been made a little to the left it would have been better. There would not have been so much impediment.

Question. I refer to the time when General Ledlie's division had been thrown into this inextricable confusion, in the bottom of this hole, and the men refused to come out from the shelter afforded them there; was there, after that occurrence, any chance to remedy the condition of affairs by any other movements which could have been made?

Answer. I cannot answer that question, because, not being in command of the army, I was not aware of the condition of the enemy, the number of troops on either side, their position, &c., all of which things it is supposed the general commanding is informed of.

Question. I had supposed you might have seen what force the enemy afterwards developed, and what his means of defence were.

Answer. I have since heard what his force was.

Question. You do not know what he actually did on the ground?

Answer. Yes, sir; I was there and saw it.

Question. Could we have used our forces at other points with any probability of gaining a success?

Answer. I think an attack made upon some other portions of the enemy's lines would probably have been successful.

Question. Upon what portions?

Answer. There were no other portions available except in front of the 5th corps.

Question. Have you any means of knowing from what points the enemy drew the troops that he concentrated upon our forces in the crater of the mine?

Answer. Nothing more than from the reports of the signal officers, who saw them moving their troops in the vicinity of the town after the assault was made, and from the heavy fire we sustained there.

Question. There is no doubt about there being a heavy concentration of troops there. What I want to ascertain is from what localities those troops of the enemy were drawn.

Answer. It is reported that they were drawn from in front of the 5th corps.

Question. If they were drawn from in front of the 5th corps, they must have weakened their lines there?

Answer. Yes, sir.

Question. And you think it probable that a vigorous attack there might have been successful?

Answer. Yes, sir, it might.

Question. It would have had the effect of relieving the troops in the crater from the severe cross-fire?

Answer. Yes, sir.

Question. Was it possible for General Ord to have made any judicious movement upon the right, if he had been so ordered, so as to have compelled the attention of the enemy to the right of the crater?

Answer. I do not think the nature of the ground would have admitted anything of the kind. I had surveyed the whole of that ground with a view to this assault, and I knew all about it.

Question. Will you state, as a military man, whether you think the dangers of the disaster were enhanced by the narrowness or insufficiency of the *debouchment* prepared for the troops of the 9th corps?

Answer. I do not think so. I think the great impediment was in front.

Question. The going into that hole, and being subjected to that cross-fire?

Answer. Yes, sir; the troops moved very handsomely up to that position.

Question. After the third division of the 9th corps had gone in, your division was then ordered to advance?

Answer. Yes, sir.

Question. What was the condition of the white troops at the crater and beyond, at the time you were ordered to make your advance?

Answer. They were without any organization; just one mass of human beings seeking shelter in the bomb-proofs of the enemy.

Question. About what number of men composed the three divisions that preceded yours?

Answer. I could not tell you at this time. I could give the strength of my own division.

Question. At what time in the day did you receive orders to advance?

Answer. About an hour and a half after the explosion of the mine.

Question. What was the strength of your division?

Answer. I had four thousand three hundred men for duty.

Question. Please narrate what occurred after your division began to move.

Answer. I received an order to advance my troops and pass the white troops which had halted, and move on and carry the crest of the hill at all hazards. I had but a few paces to move to our outer breastworks. Previous to that I had sent a staff officer to ascertain the condition of affairs at the front. From his report I did not think it advisable to move my division in, as there were three divisions of white troops already huddled together there. I reported to Colonel Loring, of General Burnside's staff, who requested me to halt until he could report to

General Burnside. I refused to do so, when he gave me an order in General Burnside's name to halt, and I did so. He then went off to report to General Burnside, and came back and reported that the order was peremptory for me to carry my division through at all hazards. I then started with my division; they went in magnificently under a most galling fire; they passed beyond the white troops, captured the only prisoners captured that day, some two hundred and fifty to three hundred, together with a rebel stand of colors, and recaptured a stand of our colors belonging to a regiment of white troops of the 9th army corps. They were a little broken by going through the mass of white troops there, and the colonel in command of the first brigade of the division proceeded to reform for the assault. There was a dismounted cavalry regiment, I think of the second division of the 9th corps, a little off to one side. As my troops started, the color guard of that regiment came back on the double-quick, broke through the ranks of my leading brigade, which of course caused my negroes to break. My troops came back in very bad order. Finding no shelter there, as the white troops had all the shelter, they came back to our main line, inside of which they were reformed, and there they remained the balance of the day. As my troops went in so gallantly under a most galling fire, I maintain that, had they led the assault when there was comparatively no fire, nothing could have stopped them until they got into Petersburg.

Question. Where were the batteries located which you found to be most effective against your troops?

Answer. There was a battery off to the right of the crater, beyond a ravine, which enfiladed the line; then there was a battery on the left which also enfiladed the line.

Question. What was the strength of the battery to the left?

Answer. Two pieces of field artillery.

Question. Did it move into position after the mine was sprung?

Answer. No, sir; the men abandoned it at the time of the springing of the mine, and then came back.

Question. Was that battery in front of General Warren's command?

Answer. No, sir; it was on what was still the old front of the 9th corps.

Question. Were those the only batteries that were effective?

Answer. Those two were the only batteries that enfiladed the line; we had a fire directly in front, and from a battery a little to the left of the centre.

Question. Were those field guns in front brought into position after the springing of the mine?

Answer. I think they were permanent batteries.

Question. What was the reason for changing the plan of allowing your division to lead the assault, as had been first contemplated?

Answer. I do not know the reason; I only know that General Meade opposed it, and that General Grant approved his decision.

Testimony of Lieutenant General U. S. Grant.

CITY POINT, VA., *December* 20, 1864.

Lieutenant General U. S. GRANT sworn and examined.

By Mr. Chandler:

Question. Will you give the committee such information as you may deem important in regard to the action before Petersburg, on the 30th of July last?

Answer. As you are aware, I made a feint on the north side of the James river, which I intended to convert into an attack if everything should prove favorable. By that movement the attention of the enemy was called to that side of the river, causing them to concentrate there. They were so well fortified there that an advance on that side could not be made without great sacrifice of life.

General Burnside had, prior to this, made a mine in front of the 9th corps, which I would not allow to be exploded until such time as it could be used advantageously. Finding that the principal part of the enemy's forces had been drawn to the north side of the James, I telegraphed to General Meade that then was the time to charge the mine and explode it, and directed him to make preparations to assault. My despatch gave no details at all how this was to be done. I left that to him, knowing him, as I did, to be fully capable of determining when and what ought to be done.

He prepared an order for assault, which was submitted to and approved by me. I think now it was all that we could have done; I think he could not have done better.

I was over on the north side of the river when these arrangements were made. I came back to the south side of the river before the explosion took place, and remained with General Meade until probably a half or three-quarters of an hour after the springing of the mine. I then rode down to the front; that is, I rode down as far as I could on horseback, and then went through to the front on foot. I there found that we had lost the opportunity which had been given us.

I am satisfied that if the troops had been properly commanded, and been led in accordance with General Meade's order, we would have captured Petersburg with all the artillery and a good portion of its support, without the loss of 500 men. There was a full half hour, I think, when there was no fire against our men, and they could have marched past the enemy's intrenchments just as they could in the open country.

But that opportunity was lost in consequence of the division commanders not going with their men, but allowing them to go into the enemy's intrenchments and spread themselves there, without going on further, thus giving the enemy time to collect and organize against them. I think I can say nothing more on that point.

I blame myself a little for one thing. General Meade, as I stated, on my telegraphic despatch from the north side of the James river, made his orders most perfectly. I do not think that now, knowing all the facts, I could improve upon his order.

But I was informed of this fact: that General Burnside, who was fully alive to the importance of this thing, trusted to the pulling of straws which division should lead. It happened to fall on what I thought was the worst commander in his corps. I knew that fact before the mine was exploded, but did nothing in regard to it. That is the only thing I blame myself for. I knew the man was the one that I considered the poorest division commander that General Burnside had—I mean General Ledlie.

By Mr. Loan:

Question. There has been a great deal of controversy in regard to the sufficiency of the *debouchment* prepared by General Burnside for the egress of his troops after the explosion of the mine?

Answer. That I could not swear to exactly. I went beyond his *debouchment*, but did not think to note it. But I am satisfied that he did not make the *debouchment* that he was ordered to make. I know that as well as I know anything that I cannot exactly swear to. I went beyond it myself, and on my return to the rear ordered the troops back.

Question. I suppose the success of this enterprise was dependent in a great measure upon the surprise of the enemy, caused by the explosion of the mine, and prompt movements afterwards to avail yourself of the distraction occasioned by it?

Answer. It all depended upon that.

Question. Was there not some danger of apprising the enemy of the contemplated movement by undertaking to level the parapets and remove the abatis and other obstructions in front of our line?

Answer. Not at all. That could be done entirely under cover of the night. After dark we could take down any of our parapets and remove our abatis without their noticing it.

Question. So far as you are advised in the matter, was not a part of the disaster owing to the slow movement of our troops in passing over the ground?

Answer. I think if I had been a corps commander, and had had that in charge, I would have been down there, and would have seen that it was done right; or, if I had been the commander of the division that had to take the lead, I think I would have gone in with my division. We have a great many officers here who would have done the same thing.

Question. Did the slowness of the movement tend to promote the disaster?

Answer. I do not think that that alone had any effect at all.

Question. What, then, do you think was the cause of the disaster?

Answer. I think the cause of the disaster was simply the leaving the passage of orders from one to another down to an inefficient man. I blame his seniors also for not seeing that he did his duty, all the way up to myself.

Question. You think that the opportunity for success passed by owing to the confusion of the troops in consequence of the inefficiency of that division commander?

Answer. Yes, sir. As I understand it, the troops marched right into the breach caused by the explosion without there being a single division commander there. They had no person to direct them to go further, although the division commanders were directed in the most positive terms to march to what is called Cemetery hill, which would have given us everything.

Question. Speaking of those orders, was it judicious to direct the main advancing column to proceed directly to Cemetery hill without any regard to the enemy on their right and left?

Answer. Cemetery hill commanded the rear of their intrenched line; it commanded everything.

Question. The troops had to pass over considerable ground to reach Cemetery hill?

Answer. Only 300 or 400 yards.

Question. Then to accomplish that object, you do not think it would have been necessary to have taken possession of the enemy's batteries and intrenchments on the right and left of the crater of the mine?

Answer. Not at all. If they had marched through to the crest of that ridge they would then have taken everything in rear. I do not think there would have been any opposition at all to our troops had that been done. I think we would have cut off entirely those of the enemy to our right, while those on the left would have tried to make their escape across the Appomattox.

Question. There has been something said in regard to the changing of General Burnside's plan of putting his division of colored troops in the advance.

Answer. General Burnside wanted to put his colored division in front, and I believe if he had done so it would have been a success. Still I agreed with General Meade in his objection to that plan. General Meade said that if we put the colored troops in front (we had only that one division) and it should prove a failure, it would then be said, and very properly, that we were shoving those people ahead to get killed because we did not care anything about them. But that could not be said if we put white troops in front. That is the only point he changed, to my knowledge, after he had given his orders to General Burnside. It was then that General Burnside left his three division commanders to toss coppers or draw straws which should and which should not go in front.

By Mr. Julian:

Question. That change was made the evening before the assault, was it not?

Answer. I cannot say whether it was the evening before the explosion or twenty-four hours earlier.

Question. Was General Burnside's plan submitted to you for consideration?

Answer. He had no plan; he had merely to execute an order.

Question. He desired to use his colored troops for the advance?

Answer. Yes, sir; and that part was changed, I thought then very properly, and I think so yet; for we had but one division of colored troops in the whole army about Petersburg at that time, and I do not think it would have been proper to put them in front, for nothing but success would have justified it.

Testimony of Lieutenant Colonel Henry Pleasants.

WASHINGTON, D. C., *January* 13, 1865.

Lieutenant Colonel HENRY PLEASANTS sworn and examined.

By the chairman:

Question. Were you in the army of the Potomac at the time the mine was sprung before Petersburg, on the 30th of July last; if so, in what capacity?

Answer. I was there at that time. I was then lieutenant colonel of the 48th Pennsylvania volunteers, and commanding the regiment at the time the explosion took place.

Question. What connexion did you have with the construction of the mine?

Answer. I proposed it and executed the work. I had the whole charge of everything connected with its construction.

Question. Will you state who originated the mine, and what was done in regard to it?

Answer. I was then commanding the first brigade of the second division of the 9th corps. That corps was then under the command of Major General Burnside. While commanding the brigade I frequently had occasion to go to the front line. I noticed a little cup of a ravine near to the enemy's works. I having been a mining and civil engineer many years before the war, it occurred to me that a mine could be excavated there. I examined the ground, and after I had satisfied myself that it could be done, I spoke to the officer next in rank above me, Brigadier General Potter, commanding the division, and explained to him what I proposed to do and how I proposed to do it, and what would be the effect of an explosion of that kind upon the enemy. He received the idea favorably, and wrote a note to General Burnside in relation to it. General Burnside sent for me, and I explained to him carefully the mode of ventilating the mine and everything about it. He seemed very much pleased with the proposition, and told me to go right on with the work.

Question. Can you fix the time when you mentioned the matter to General Burnside, when you commenced the work, &c.?

Answer. The work was commenced at 12 o'clock noon on the 25th of June, 1864. I saw General Burnside the night previous, and commenced the mine right off the next day.

Question. Did you have any communication with any other commanders on the subject?

Answer. No, sir.

Question. About how many men did you employ in the work?

Answer. My regiment was only about four hundred strong. At first I employed but a few men at a time, but the number was increased as the work progressed, until at last I had to use the whole regiment, non-commissioned officers and all. The great difficulty I had was to dispose of the material got out of the mine. I found it impossible to get any assistance from anybody; I had to do all the work myself. I had to remove all the earth in old cracker boxes. I got pieces of hickory and nailed on the boxes in which we received our crackers, and then iron-claded them with hoops of iron taken from old pork and beef barrels.

Question. Why were you not able to get better instruments with which to construct so important a work?

Answer. I do not know. Whenever I made application I could not get anything, although General Burnside was very favorable to it. The most important thing was to ascertain how far I had to mine, because if I fell short of or went beyond the proper place the explosion would have no practical effect; therefore I wanted an accurate instrument with which to make the necessary triangulations. I had to make them on the furthest front line, where the enemy's sharpshooters could reach me. I could not get the instrument I wanted, although there was one at army headquarters, and General Burnside had to send to Washington and get an old-fashioned theodolite, which was given to me.

Question. Do you know any reason why you could not have had the better instrument which was at army headquarters?

Answer. I do not. I know this: that General Burnside told me that General Meade and Major Duane, chief engineer of the army of the Potomac, said the thing could not be done; that it was all clap-trap and nonsense; that such a length of mine had never been excavated in military operations, and could not be; that I would either get the men smothered for want of air, or crushed by the falling of the earth; or the enemy would find it out, and it would amount to nothing. I could get no boards and lumber supplied to me for my operations. I had to get a pass and send two companies of my own regiment with wagons outside of our lines to rebel saw-mills and get lumber in that way, after having previously got what lumber I could by tearing down an old bridge. I had no mining picks furnished me, but had to take common army picks and have them straightened for my mining picks.

Question. Was General Burnside the only officer who seemed to favor the mine?

Answer. The only officer of high rank, so far as I learned. General Burnside, the corps commander, and General Potter, the division commander, seemed to be the only high officers who believed in it.

Question. How long from the time that you commenced the mine did it take you to finish it?

Answer. I finished the whole thing, lateral galleries and all, ready to put the powder in, on the 23d of July.

Question. How long would it have taken you had you been supplied with the proper tools and instruments?

Answer. I could have done it in one-third or one-fourth of the time. The greatest cause of the delay was taking the material out.

Question. How far did you have to carry it?

Answer. The whole length of the mine, and to where it could be deposited. And every night I had to get the pioneers of my regiment to cut bushes and cover it up where it had been deposited, otherwise the enemy could have climbed up the trees in their lines and seen the pile of newly excavated earth.

Question. What was the length of the mine?

Answer. The main gallery was $510\frac{8}{10}$ feet in length; the left lateral gallery was 37 feet in length, and the right lateral gallery was 38 feet. The magazines were to be placed in the lateral galleries.

Question. What were the dimensions of the galleries?

Answer. They varied at different places. I suppose the average was 4½ by 4½ feet.

Question. Did the enemy discover that you were mining there?

Answer. Deserters came into our lines from the enemy, who stated that they had found out where the mine was, and were trying to countermine. They said that some deserters from the 5th corps in our army had told them about it. General Burnside ordered me to stop all work on a certain day on that account, and to listen for one day; but not hearing anything of the enemy's working, we resumed our work. I did not hear them working until I got right under the fort. They did a great deal of hammering. While I was propping up the mine that we had dug, I made no noise. I had the timber all framed and notched outside of the mine, and it was put together by hand, without any blows.

Question. Was the mine placed directly under the fortification, or close by it?

Answer. It was exactly under it, except that the right lateral gallery made a little circular direction on account of avoiding a shaft which we supposed the enemy were making near by. It did not move out of line much, so that when the explosion took place it would tear up all around there, any how.

Question. What amount of powder was used?

Answer. I called for twelve thousand pounds; they gave me eight thousand.

Question. What means did you take to consume the powder, so that it would have the proper effect?

Answer. I had bags of sand interspersed with logs. There was no tamping between the magazines; it was left all open there, so that there might be oxygen enough for the combustion of the powder. Outside of the lateral galleries, in the main gallery, it was tamped.

Question. What means did you use to insure the explosion of the powder?

Answer. I used three lines of fuze, called the blasting fuze. I asked for fuze, and they sent me this common blasting fuze. There were troughs running from one magazine to the other, half filled with powder; and then from where the two lateral galleries joined there were two troughs with fuzes in them. The troughs were half filled with fine powder; then from a certain distance out there was nothing but three fuzes, without any powder. The fuze I received was cut in short pieces; some of them are only ten feet long.

Question. Why was that?

Answer. I do not know.

Question. Was not that an objection to it?

Answer. A great objection.

Question. Was there any danger that it would not communicate at those parts where it was joined?

Answer. It did not, and had to be relighted.

Question. Who had the courage to go down into the mine and relight it?

Answer. I had a lieutenant and a sergeant with me in the mine when I lighted it the first time.

Question. How far in did it go out?

Answer. I had a fuze about ninety feet long, and it burned about forty feet—the whole three fuzes.

Question. How long did you wait to find out whether it would explode?

Answer. I waited from quarter after three, the time it was first lighted, until quarter after four, when it was relighted, and exploded at sixteen minutes to five.

Question. Have you been accustomed to use these fuzes in your engineering work?

Answer. Not a great deal; I had seen it done; my province was to do the instrumental work and surveying.

Question. Is there generally much uncertainty about the ignition of powder by means of these fuzes?

Answer. No, sir, unless they are spliced, and then they are very uncertain.

Question. Could you not procure fuzes that were not spliced?

Answer. It was too late after the fuzes came. The mine was prepared and ready for the powder to be put in on the 23d of July, and the enemy was trying to find me out all this time; but I could not get powder to put in, or permission to put it in, until the 28th or 29th.

Question. What reason was given you for that?

Answer. No reason at all; they were not ready, that was all. General Burnside told me he had not permission yet to explode it. I was afraid the enemy would find me out that week.

Question. After you had commenced that mine, and before its completion, could you not have obtained fuzes of the proper quality from coal mines and other places?

Answer. These fuzes were sufficiently good if they had not been cut up.

Question. Was there any difficulty in obtaining fuze that was not spliced?

Answer. When it came it was too late. Besides, as it turned out, it was better that it went out then than if it had gone off at half past three.

Question. I am endeavoring to ascertain whether there was any carelessness in regard to this fuze; to ascertain what reason military men could give for spending so much time on a mine, and then not having their powder and fuze of the proper quality ready when the mine was ready. Whose fault was that?

Answer. I presume this fuze, like the powder, was stored at Fortress Monroe. They sent just whatever they had. It hardly ever happens that they require fuze for that distance.

Question. Then ought they not to have taken special pains to have obtained it, for they knew how long the mine was to be?

Answer. Well, it was not done.

Question. They could have brought other powder from Fortress Monroe in less than twenty-four hours?

Answer. Yes, sir, in a day at least. I do not know why they did as they did.

Question. You state that you prepared three fuzes and laid them?

Answer. Yes, sir.

Question. Why was that?

Answer. I wanted to make a certain thing of it; but all three of the lines were spliced, and all three went out. The whole of the tamping, putting in the powder and everything, was completed at 6 p. m. on the 28th of July, and remained there until it was exploded on the morning of the 30th of July; and the powder remaining there a day and a half in the mine of course became damp.

Question. Did it not require some nerve to go in there and relight those fuzes?

Answer. At first it did; but afterwards we felt certain that the reason the mine did not explode was that the fuzes had gone out.

Question. Who went in to relight them?

Answer. Lieutenant Jacob Douty, 1st Lieutenant company K, 48th Pennsylvania volunteers, (he has since been mustered out,) and Sergeant Henry Rees, now 2d lieutenant company F, 48th Pennsylvania volunteers.

Question. They volunteered to go in?

Answer. Yes, sir; but I would not let them go in at first, until I felt convinced of the cause of the failure to explode.

Question. Had you been furnished with all the facilities in the power of those in charge there to have completed and exploded the mine, how long would it have taken you from the commencement until the mine was completed?

Answer. I think about twelve days.

Question. Were you present when the mine was exploded?

Answer. Yes, sir; my regiment having been engaged in constructing the mine, was not in the battle, but I volunteered on General Potter's staff, and was through the engagement, and was there at the time of the explosion.

Question. What effect did the explosion seem to have on the enemy?

Answer. It completely paralyzed them.

Question. What did the enemy do?

Answer. Those that were not killed ran away.

Question. What effect did it have on the next tier of fortifications of the enemy?

Answer. There was no other tier—nothing beyond that. There was a partially completed little earthwork beyond, but nothing in it.

Question. What, in your judgment, was the cause of the failure of that enterprise?

Answer. I have thought of that a great deal. There were several causes for the failure. The first one, and immediate one, was the failure of the first division of the 9th corps to go beyond the enemy's works. The whole of them, or a great portion of them, went up very promptly and occupied the enemy's works. There was nothing to resist them; but they remained there and did not go beyond; and when the other divisions came up, having orders to go through the same gap, the second division to form on the right of the first, and the third division to form on the left of the first, and to go on to Cemetery hill—when the other divisions came into the crater and that portion of the enemy's works which the first division occupied, they got all mixed up; they were all in a medley. That was the immediate reason of the failure.

Question. Suppose they had gone promptly through and taken possession of the heights in force, what then would have been the effect?

Answer. The enemy must have evacuated their line, or else we would have cut their army in two. I stated in my report that there was no cannon shot fired, as I thought, for an hour—I think it was two hours, but I will say one—from the left, and from the right but very few scattered shots, and no infantry firing from the front for half an hour; from the left for twenty minutes, and a few far to the right.

Question. You have stated the immediate reason of the failure: what was the more remote reason?

Answer. Another reason was, that the troops were not massed sufficiently near to our breastworks. It was feared that the explosion would throw up a great deal of debris and boards and everything of that kind into the air, and injure our men when they come down; and although I urged it upon General Burnside to mass them nearer the breastworks, still he would not agree to it for fear the men would be injured. The consequence was, that when the second brigade of the second division of the ninth corps came up in the morning, they came up by the flank, just straggling along, and not together, as they would have done if they had been right close up to the line.

By Mr. Loan:

Question. Did you testify as a witness before the court of inquiry which was ordered to investigate this matter by the commander of the army of the Potomac?

Answer. No, sir; I was on leave of absence then, and was not called.

Question. Will you state the circumstances under which that leave of absence was obtained.

Answer. I made application for leave of absence to attend to private business, and it was granted me by General Meade.

Question. Had it in any way for its object to avoid your testimony being given there?

Answer. Well, I did not want to go before the board; I thought no good would come of it; it would only make me enemies, and I thought it better, as long as I remained in the army, that I should not go before the board. Therefore I made application for leave of absence.

Question. Who granted that leave of absence?

Answer. General Meade was the only person who had authority to grant it.

Question. Have you any reason to believe that General Burnside was aware of your disinclination to testify as a witness before that board?

Answer. General Burnside was not there.

Question. I should have said General Meade; had he any reason to know it?

Answer. I do not know.

Question. Why was it you did not wish to testify? Did you or not deem your knowledge of the facts material to the investigation of that affair?

Answer. No, sir, I did not. My only reason was, that I thought perhaps my testimony might be injurious to some of the general officers; and as the failure was a fact, and it could not be remedied, no good would come of it if I did testify, and it might have been the means of losing me some friends and making me some enemies. That was the reason I did not wish to testify. I have a copy of my report here, to which I have referred while giving my testimony, for the purpose of being correct in reference to dates, &c.

Question. Will you furnish the committee with a copy of that report?

Answer. I will, sir.

The following is a copy of the report referred to:

HEADQUARTERS 48TH PENN'A VETERAN VOLUNTEERS,
Near Petersburg, Va., August, 1864.

COLONEL: I have the honor to submit the following report, relating to the mine I excavated in front of the second division of the 9th corps.

It was commenced at 12 o'clock m., the 25th of June, 1864, without tools, lumber, or any of the materials requisite for such work. The mining picks were made out of those used by our pioneers; plank I obtained, at first, by tearing down a rebel bridge, and afterwards by sending to a saw-mill, five or six miles distant. The material excavated was carried out in hand-barrows made out of cracker boxes. The work progressed rapidly till the 2d of July, when it reached an extremely wet ground; the timbers gave way and the gallery nearly closed, the roof and floor of the mine nearly meeting. Retimbered it and started again. From this point had to excavate a stratum of marl, whose consistency was like putty, and which caused our progress to be necessarily slow. To avoid this, I started an inclined plane, and in about one hundred feet rose thirteen and a half feet perpendicularly.

On the 17th of July the main gallery was completed, being five hundred and ten and $\frac{8}{10}$ feet in length. The enemy having obtained some knowledge of the mine, and having commenced searching for it, I was ordered to stop mining, which was, however, resumed on the 18th of July by starting the left lateral gallery. At 6 p. m., July 18, commenced the right lateral gallery; but as the enemy could be heard very plainly working in the fort over us, I caused this gallery to be excavated a little beyond and in rear of their work, and gave to it a curved line of direction. The left gallery, being thirty-seven feet long, was stopped at midnight on Friday, July 22; the right gallery, being thirty-eight feet long, was stopped at 6 p. m., July 23. The mine could have been charged and exploded at this time. I employed the men, from that time, in draining, timbering, and placing in position eight magazines, four in each lateral gallery. Having received the order to charge the mine on the 27th of July, I commenced putting in the powder at 4 p. m., and finished at 10 p. m. The tamping was begun at 10 p. m., July 27, and completed at 6 p. m., July 28. Thirty-four feet of main gallery was tamped, and ten feet of the entrance of each of the side galleries; but the space between the magazines was left untamped.

I received orders from corps headquarters, on the 29th of July, to fire the mine at half past three a. m., July 30. I lighted the fuze at 3.15 a. m., and having waited till 4.15 a. m., an officer and sergeant of my regiment volunteered to go in and examine into the cause of the delay, and found that the fire had stopped where the fuzes were spliced. They relighted it, and at sixteen minutes of five the powder exploded.

The charge consisted of three hundred and twenty kegs of powder, each containing about twenty-five pounds. It was placed in eight magazines, connected with each other by troughs half filled with powder. These troughs from the lateral galleries met at the inner end of the main one, and from this point I had three lines of fuzes for a distance of ninety-eight feet. Not having fuzes as long as required, two pieces had to be spliced together to make the required length of each of the lines.

The mine was ventilated at first by having the fresh air go in along the main gallery as far as it was excavated, and to return charged with the gases generated by the breathing and exhalation of the workmen, by the burning of the candles, and by those liberated from the ground, along and in a square tube made of boards, and whose area was sixty inches. This tube led to a perpendicular shaft twenty-two feet high, out of which this vitiated air escaped. At the bottom of this shaft was placed a grating, in which a large fire was kept burning continually, which, by heating the air, rarefied it, and increased its current. Afterwards I caused the fresh air to be let in the above-mentioned wooden tube to the end of the work, and the vitiated air to return by the gallery and out of the shaft, placing a partition with a door in the main gallery a little out of the shaft, to prevent its exit by the entrance of the mine. The latter plan was more advantageous, because the gases had to travel a less distance in the mine than before.

As the excavation in the mine progressed, the number of men required to carry out the material increased, until at last it took nearly every enlisted man in my regiment, which consisted of nearly four hundred effective men. The whole amount of material excavated was 18,000 cubic feet.

The great difficulty to surmount was to ascertain the exact distance from the entrance of the mine to the enemy's works, and the course of these works. This was accomplished by making five separate triangulations, which differed but slightly in their result. These triangulations were made in our most advanced line, and within 133 yards of the enemy's line of sharpshooters.

The size of the crater formed by the explosion was at least two hundred feet long, fifty feet wide, and twenty-five feet deep.

I stood on top of our breastworks and witnessed the effect of the explosion on the enemy. It so completely paralyzed them that the breach was practically four or five hundred yards in breadth. The rebels in the forts, both on the right and left of the explosion, left their works, and for over an hour not a shot was fired by their artillery. There was no fire from infantry from the front for at least half an hour; none from the left for twenty minutes, and but few shots from the right. The accompanying drawings which I have made, and forward with this report, will explain whatever else has been omitted here.

I have the honor to be, colonel, very respectfully, your obedient servant,

HENRY PLEASANTS,
Lieutenant Colonel.

Testimony of Brigadier General John W. Turner.

WASHINGTON, D. C., *January* 17, 1865.

Brigadier General JOHN W. TURNER sworn and examined.

By Mr. Loan:

Question. What is your rank and position in the army?

Answer. I am a brigadier general of volunteers, and upon the staff of Major General Butler.

Question. What was your position on the 30th of July last?

Answer. I was in command of the second division of the 10th army corps. My division was detached from the 10th army corps and attached to the command of General Ord, commanding the 18th corps.

Question. What part did you take in the assault made upon the lines before Petersburg on the 30th of July last?

Answer. On the 29th of July I was ordered to hold myself, with my division, in readiness to participate in the assault that was to be made the next morning in General Burnside's front, with additional instructions from General Ord to report to General Burnside on the afternoon of the 29th for detailed instructions as to the position my division should occupy during the night, and the part I would have to take in the next day's work. I did so, and my instructions from General Burnside were that my division would follow immediately after the 9th corps. It was designed that the 9th corps should assault the enemy's line on the springing of the mine, and immediately push for Cemetery hill. My division would follow close after, move off to the right, and cover the movement of the 9th corps on Cemetery hill on its right flank. General Burnside further told me that, in case they did not succeed in gaining Cemetery hill, they would undoubtedly hold possession of the enemy's lines, which they would take in the vicinity of the mine, and then I probably would not be brought into the engagement at all.

I went over the ground carefully with a staff officer of General Burnside's staff, visited the gallery leading to the mine and the route over which I was to take my division, especially through the woods, arriving at the point where I was directed to mass my division. I returned to General Burnside and asked him if there were any other troops to pass over that road during the night. Knowing the confusion that was likely to occur in the movement of troops during the night, particularly a dark night, I wanted no mistake to be made, and that I should be in my position at the time the attack was to be made, which was at half past three o'clock, the hour at which the mine was to have been sprung.

Just after nightfall I withdrew my troops from the trenches they were occupying and moved them to a point just in rear of where I was to mass them, where the road led into the woods. I there halted and waited for General Ledlie's division to pass, which was the division that General Burnside informed me would pass over that road, and the only division that was to pass. I was told to wait for it, and that after it had passed there would be nothing in my way to prevent my taking up my position. I arrived at the point where this road led into the woods about twelve o'clock at night, there halted my division and remained waiting for General Ledlie. To make sure, I had despatched a staff officer to General Ledlie's headquarters to ascertain when his division moved, as it was quite dark and it was very difficult to distinguish troops in the night time, more particularly to what division they belonged. I remained there until about half past two o'clock, when General Ledlie's division commenced passing. I remarked that it was pretty late for that division to pass to get into its position to move out at the time designated (at half past three) to make the assault, knowing the difficulties of the road. It passed me, and I immediately moved my division to the point designated, which was at the commencement of the covered way which led to our immediate front, through which all the troops were obliged to pass. It was a narrow covered way. I reported to General Ord about daylight that my troops were in position. He ordered me to wait for further orders.

Some time after five o'clock, between five and half past five, the mine was exploded. I immediately moved my division down this covered way towards the front, the leading regiments of it. Feeling an anxiety to get my men as far forward in support of the assault as possible, I moved them down a hundred yards and there halted. I then mounted a small mound of earth to observe the fighting that was going on. I remained there, I should judge, about half an hour. I then went myself to the front in order to gather all the information I could, so that I might be well informed when I got my orders. I returned, and I should judge it was half past six when I got my first orders to move to the front. My orders from General Ord were, "Follow Potter's division and move out to the right." The last of the troops of Potter's division had just then passed me. I was obliged to take my division down this covered way, where I could have only a two-file front, and in some places only a single file, and followed close on to the rear of General Potter's column. When the head of my column reached the point at which our assaulting column had passed through our lines, it was, as near as I recollect, about 7 o'clock.

I jumped upon a parapet to observe what was going on. Immediately in front of me lay the crater, about seventy-five yards distant. The men were in it and around it in great confusion; they were lying down, seeking shelter from the fire of the enemy, which at that time had become exceedingly warm. The enemy had succeeded in getting a cross-fire of artillery and musketry over the ground lying between our line and the crater. My idea was that the 9th corps would penetrate the enemy's line and double them up to the right and to the left, and then I was to pass out and cover the right flank of the assaulting column; but the enemy still held possession of their lines up to within one hundred yards of the crater when I arrived, which surprised me. It left me no alternative of going out anywhere but directly opposite the crater, where the 9th corps went out. I could see no movement taking place beyond the crater towards Cemetery hill. The troops lay very thick in and around the crater, evidently more than could find cover from the enemy's fire. At that moment I received an order from General Ord again to move out rapidly to the right and cover General Potter on his right flank. It was evident to my mind that General Ord did not understand the topography of the country and the condition of affairs as they were at that moment. It was impossible to move out to the right. The idea was that we would dispossess the enemy of their lines, roll them up to the right, and allow me to go out to the right over any portion of our lines for four hundred yards. That state of affairs did not exist. To have gone out to the right I should have had to mount the parapet exposed to the enemy's fire directly opposite to me, (and they had their lines well manned at that time,) push through our own abatis, cross the morass through the enemy's abatis, and mount his line, which was a line that had been deemed impregnable for two months previous, and the only manner of getting at them was by breaking them, as was done by the crater, and then doubling them up. But the enemy held possession of their line, and to go out right in front of the crater was piling men on top of men already in and around there. I sent back word to General Ord that it was impossible to go out in the manner he had indicated. To make sure, I gave orders to my leading brigade (which was arriving very slowly in consequence of passing through this long, narrow covered way) to mass as it arrived, while I went over and examined the ground in and around the crater. I passed over there, and was confirmed in the judgment which I had held previously from mounting the parapet. The crater was full of men; they were lying all around, and every point that would give cover to a man was occupied. There was no movement towards Cemetery hill; the troops were all in confusion and lying down. I asked one or two officers there if an attempt had been made to move on Cemetery hill. They said the attempt had been made, but it had failed. I then said, "You ought to intrench your position here, and you have too many troops here already to intrench. There are so many troops here that they are in each other's way; they are only exposed to this terrific fire of the enemy," which was then growing warmer and warmer, and was a very severe fire. While I was talking to an officer—we had sought shelter in the crater—the head of the colored division appeared at the crest of the crater, and the division commenced piling over into the crater and passing across it on the other side as well as they could. I exclaimed, "What are these men sent in here for? it is only adding confusion to the confusion which already exists." The men literally came falling right over into this crater on their hands and knees; they were so thick in there that a man could not walk. Seeing that I was going to be covered up there, and be entirely useless, I thought I would go out. As I had no control over these troops, and supposing there were officers in command, I said, "If you can get these troops beyond this line so that I can get out, I will move my division right out and cover your right flank;" and I went back for the purpose of doing so. I met General Ord on our line at the head of my division. I said, "General, unless a movement is made out of the crater towards Cemetery hill, it is murder to send more men in there. That colored division should never have been sent in there; but there is a furor there, and perhaps they may move off sufficiently for me to pass my division out." "Well," said he, "do so if they move." A very few moments after I thought they had started to make a rush towards Cemetery hill, and I immediately ordered my leading brigade, which was massed by regiments, to charge to the right of the crater. The colored division by that time had nearly, if not quite, all got into the crater; had passed to the right of it perhaps fifty yards, and were all lying down, principally this side of the enemy's line and in it, and were trying to cover themselves the best way they could. My leading brigade charged over our line up to the enemy's works, and took possession of about one hundred yards of it; but there were no movements of the troops in and around the crater to advance on Cemetery hill. At the time my leading brigade charged I directed the head of my second brigade to move out through a break in our works where a creek passed through it, so as to join hands on the right of the first brigade and charge the enemy's lines beyond. They succeeded in getting only about half way between our lines and the lines of the enemy, when they were stopped by the enemy's fire. The first brigade, as I said, succeeded in reaching the enemy's works, and took possession of about one hundred yards of it, when they laid down. I immediately sent word to my first brigade commander, who was within hailing distance—within sight, probably seventy-five yards off—to take his leading regiment and charge by the right flank, so as to sweep down the enemy's lines, while I brought up the second brigade. I was in hopes to take possession of a still greater length of the enemy's line. I returned to the brigade commander of my third brigade, and ordered him to mass his troops behind our lines, and hold them in readiness for any exigency. I had but just given him his instructions when my first brigade charged by the right flank, in obedience to my orders. I immediately passed over the line to the second brigade to give the command "Forward!" I had got, probably, half way between our line and the enemy's lines—which were perhaps only a hundred yards apart at that point, and it was a very broken country, thick underbrush and morass—when, looking to the left, I saw the troops in vast numbers come rushing back, and immediately my whole first brigade came back, and then my second brigade on my right, and everything was swept back in and around the crater, and probably all but about one-third of the original number stampeded back right into our lines. After some exertion I rallied my men of the first and second brigades after they got into our lines, while my third brigade held the line. After rallying them I placed them in position in the line, and remained there until probably the middle of the afternoon, when I received orders to retire. I would state, further, that the peculiar topography of the ground had a great influence in determining the result. It was impossible to assault in mass; columns had to come up only two file front.

Question. Why was there any necessity for your coming up that covered way within our line, after the 9th corps had charged?

Answer. The fire of the enemy had not been reduced, and it swept all the ground from the position where our division was massed up to the front of our line.

Question. What was the distance?

Answer. I suppose that distance was four hundred yards. When I was down there the day before I did not intend to pass through that covered way, knowing the great delay it would cause in trying to get troops through there. My idea was, and it was the idea conveyed at General Burnside's headquarters, that the 9th corps breaking the enemy's line would double it up to the right, and then I expected to move my division right over hill and vale—it was very rough. But by the time I got orders to move my division, the enemy's fire covered the ground.

Question. And you were compelled to use the covered way because of the enemy's fire?

Answer. Yes, sir; it was so heavy that the troops could not come up otherwise without great loss.

Question. You spoke about your first brigade passing to the enemy's line; did they pass through the crater?

Answer. No, sir; to the right of the crater.

Question. Did they pass through the enemy's line, and charge his parapet?

Answer. Yes, sir.

Question. While you were in the crater, or at any other time, did you see any of the division commanders of the 9th corps in the crater, or immediately with their troops?

Answer. I did not. I did not know General Potter, but I recognized no division commander of the 9th corps there. When I was in the crater I tried to find a division commander, for I had supposed I would find one in there, and I wanted to impress upon him my idea of the necessity of moving forward, because then was the time to determine what to do. It was one of two things; if we failed to move towards Cemetery hill, there was but one other thing to do, to intrench ourselves in the position we had gained, and we should have turned our attention to it. There was already twice the number of troops in and around the crater necessary to intrench themselves. They were in each other's way; and it was necessary also to open a communication between the crater and our own line. I went over there to see the ground, and to see a general officer and converse with him on that point, as I had no command or control over any of the 9th corps.

APPENDIX.

WAR DEPARTMENT,
Washington City, February 8, 1865.

SIR: In compliance with your request I transmit herewith a copy of the testimony before the court of inquiry of which Major General W. S. Hancock was president, in relation to the explosion of a mine and attack upon the enemy's lines before Petersburg, Virginia, on the 30th July, 1864.

I am, sir, very respectfully, your obedient servant,

EDWIN M. STANTON, *Secretary of War.*

Hon. B. F. WADE,
U. S. Senate, Chairman Committee on Conduct of War.

RECORD OF THE COURT OF INQUIRY INSTITUTED BY SPECIAL ORDER No. 258, 1864, W. D.

NOTE.—The erasures and interlineations in this record were almost unavoidable under the circumstances, but they were not regarded sufficiently objectionable to warrant the delay which would have attended the preparation of a fairer copy. The corrections were all made with the knowledge of the court.

EDWARD SCHRIVER,
Inspector General, Judge Advocate.

Record of the proceedings of court of inquiry instituted by virtue of the following orders:

SPECIAL ORDERS, }   WAR DEPARTMENT,
No. 258.   }   *Adj't General's Office, Washington, D. C., Aug.* 3, 1864.

[Extract—Paragraph 43.]

By direction of the President a court of inquiry will convene in front of Petersburg at 10 o'clock a. m. on the 5th instant, or as soon thereafter as practicable, to examine into and report upon the facts and circumstances attending the unsuccessful assault on the enemy's position on the 30th of July, 1864.

The court will report their opinion whether any officer or officers are answerable for the want of success of said assault; and if so, the name or names of such officer or officers.

Detail for the court.

Major General W. S. Hancock, Brigadier General R. B. Ayres, Brigadier General N. A. Miles; and Colonel E. Schriver, inspector general, judge advocate, United States volunteers.

By order of the Secretary of War:

E. D. TOWNSEND,
Assistant Adjutant General.

FIRST DAY.

COURT ROOM, HEADQUARTERS SECOND CORPS,
August 6, 1864.

The court met pursuant to the foregoing orders.

Present: Major General Hancock, Brigadier Generals Ayres and Miles, and Colonel Schriver, judge advocate.

The order instituting the court was read, and the court and the judge advocate were sworn according to law.

The judge advocate then presented and read the orders issued from the headquarters of the army of the Potomac on the 29th of July, 1864, containing the "instructions for the guidance of all concerned" in the operations against the enemy's position before Petersburg, on the 30th of July, as follows:

HEADQUARTERS ARMY OF THE POTOMAC,
July 29, 1864.

Orders.—The following instructions are issued for the guidance of all concerned:

1. As soon as it is dark Major General Burnside, commanding 9th corps, will withdraw his two brigades under General White, occupying the intrenchments between the plank and Norfolk roads, and bring them to his front. Care will be taken not to interfere with the troops of the 18th corps moving into their position in rear of the 9th corps.

General Burnside will form his troops for assaulting the enemy's works at daylight of the 30th, prepare his parapets and abatis for the passage of the columns, and have the pioneers equipped for work in opening passages for artillery, destroying enemy's abatis, &c., and the intrenching tools distributed for effecting lodgement, &c.

2. Major General Warren, commanding 5th corps, will reduce the number of his troops holding the intrenchments of his front to the minimum, and concentrate all his available force on his right, and hold them prepared to support the assault of Major General Burnside. The preparations in respect to pioneers, intrenching tools, &c., enjoined upon the 9th corps, will also be made by the 5th corps.

3. As soon as it is dark, Major General Ord, commanding 18th corps, will relieve his troops in the trenches by General Mott's division of the 2d corps, and form his corps in rear of the 9th corps, and be prepared to support the assault of Major General Burnside.

4. Every preparation will be made for moving forward the field artillery of each corps.

5. At dark, Major General Hancock, commanding 2d corps, will move from Deep Bottom to the rear of the intrenchments now held by the 18th corps, resume the command of Mott's division, and be prepared at daylight to follow up the assaulting and supporting column, or for such other operations as may be found necessary.

6. Major General Sheridan, commanding cavalry corps, will proceed at dark from the vicinity of Deep Bottom to Lee's mill, and at daylight will move with his whole corps, including Wilson's division, against the enemy's troops defending Petersburg on their right, by the roads leading from the southward and westward.

7. Major Duane, acting chief engineer, will have the pontoon trains parked at convenient points in the rear prepared to move. He will see that supplies of sand-bags, gabions, facines, &c., are in depot near the lines ready for use. He will detail engineer officers for each corps.

8. At half past three in the morning of the 30th Major General Burnside will spring his mine, and his assaulting columns will immediately move rapidly upon the breach, seize the crest in the rear, and effect a lodgement there. He will be followed by Major General Ord, who will support him on the right, directing his movement to the crest indicated, and by Major General Warren, who will support him on the left. Upon the explosion of the mine the artillery of all kinds in battery will open upon those points of the enemy's works whose fire covers the ground over which our columns must move, care being taken to avoid impeding the progress of our troops. Special instructions respecting the direction of fire will be issued through the chief of artillery.

9. Corps commanders will report to the commanding general when their preparations are complete, and will advise him of every step in the progress of the operation, and of everything important that occurs.

10. Promptitude, rapidity of execution, and cordial co-operation are essential to success, and the commanding general is confident that this indication of his expectations will insure the hearty efforts of the commanders and troops.

11. Headquarters during the operation will be at the headquarters of the 9th corps.

By command of Major General Meade:

S. WILLIAMS,
Assistant Adjutant General.

Whereupon the court directed the judge advocate to notify all the officers named therein of the institution and design of the court, so as to enable them to be present during its sessions, which was done by addressing the following circular to each:

COURT ROOM, HEADQUARTERS SECOND CORPS,
August 6, 1864.

SIR: The court of inquiry instituted by the War Department, Special Orders No. 258, of August 3, 1864, for the investigation of the facts and circumstances which attended the unsuccessful assault on the enemy's lines before Petersburg on the 30th ultimo, will meet here on the 8th instant, and the days following, at ten o'clock a. m., and I am directed to acquaint you thereof, so that you may be present at the court's session, should you desire to do so. Please acknowledge the receipt of this communication to me at the headquarters of the army of the Potomac.

Very respectfully, sir, your obedient servant,

EDWARD SCHRIVER,
Inspector General, Judge Advocate.

Addressed to Major Generals Meade, Burnside, Warren, Sheridan, and Ord, and Brigadier Generals White, Hunt, and Mott, and Major Duane.

The court then adjourned, to meet at ten o'clock a. m. on the 8th instant.

SECOND DAY.

COURT ROOM, HEADQUARTERS SECOND CORPS,
10 *o'clock a. m , August* 8.

The court met pursuant to adjournment.

Present: Major General Hancock, Brigadier Generals Ayres and Miles, and Colonel Schriver, judge advocate.

The proceedings of the first day were read and approved.

The judge advocate stated that he had engaged Mr. Finley Anderson, a phonographer, to record the proceedings, so long as he should do so to the court's satisfaction, and Mr. Anderson was sworn according to law.

It is here recorded, also, that all officers of rank who it is supposed participated in the affair of the 30th ultimo have been informed that they could be present at the court's sessions, and make any statements they may regard important to themselves, should they see fit.

Major General G. G. Meade, United States volunteers, being duly sworn, says:

I propose in the statement that I shall make to the court—I presume the court want me to make a statement of facts in connexion with this case—to give a slight preliminary history of certain events and operations which culminated in the assault on July 30, and which, in my judgment, are necessary to show to this court that I had a full appreciation of the difficulties that were to be encountered, and that I had endeavored, so far as my capacity and judgment would enable me, not only to anticipate, but to take measures to overcome those difficulties.

The mine constructed in front of General Burnside was commenced by that officer soon after the occupation of our present lines, upon the intercession of Lieutenant Colonel Pleasants, I think, of a Pennsylvania regiment, without any reference to, or any sanction obtained from, the general headquarters of the army of the Potomac. When the subject was brought to my knowledge I authorized the continuance of the operations, sanctioned them, and trusted that the work would at some time result in forming an important part in our operations. But from the first I never considered that the location of General Burnside's mine was a proper one, because, from what I could ascertain, the position of the enemy's works and lines erected at that time, the position against which he operated, was not a suitable one in which to assault the enemy's lines, as it was commanded on both flanks, and taken in reverse by their position on the Jerusalem plank road, and their works opposite the Hare House.

I will now read to the court the despatches which passed between Lieutenant General Grant, commanding the armies of the United States, and myself, which will bear in themselves a sort of history of the preliminary operations, a correspondence which resulted, as I said before, in the final arrangements for the assault on July 30.

On the 24th of July I received a letter from the lieutenant general commanding, which I will now read. I had been previously informed by the lieutenant general commanding that he desired some operations to take place offensive against the enemy, and he had instructed the engineer officer at his headquarters, the engineer officer at General Butler's headquarters, and the engineer officer at the headquarters of the army of the Potomac, to make an examination of the enemy's position, and give an opinion as to the probable result of an attack. Their opinion is contained in the following letter.—(See document marked A, appendix.)

I desire to call the particular attention of the court to that communication, because it contains the views of the lieutenant general commanding with reference to the assault which should be made on Petersburg, and I wish them to compare this communication with the orders and arrangements that I gave and made, so that they may see that to the best of my ability I ordered everything which he indicated to be done.

At the time that this communication was made to me, however, I was under the impression that the obstacles to be overcome were more formidable than the subsequent operations made me to believe, and also that subsequent to that time there had been no movement of the army to produce that great weakening of the enemy's front which afterwards occurred. Therefore my reply was to the effect that I was opposed to our making the assault.

The following is my reply, sent on the 24th.—(See document B and B 2.)

In reply to that I received a communication or report from General Grant, the result of which was a suspension of the proposed attack.—(Document C.)

Next day I made a closer examination; and in the mean time a signal station was erected in a pine tree in front of General Burnside, which gave us a more complete view than we had previously had of the enemy's line. My observations modified my views, because I could not detect a second line, although I detected isolated batteries on the crest. I therefore wrote the following communication to General Grant, dated 12 m., July 26.—(Document D.)

To which I received the following reply.—(Document E.)

There you perceive that the lieutenant general commanding ordered that whilst the 2d corps was across the James river I should immediately make an assault with the 9th and 5th, abandoning the line of the 5th corps. In answer to that I wrote him the following despatch.—(Document F.)

That produced a suspension of the order to attack until the return of General Hancock. The next despatch I received from General Grant was the following.—(Document G.)

Which I answered at 1 p. m., July 28, as follows.—(Document H.)

I will here observe that Lieutenant General Grant, in consequence of the services which the 2d corps had performed across the river, desired, and gave me directions verbally to that effect, to use the 18th corps in the assault, and to let the 2d corps take the place of the 18th in the line.

The next despatch I received was the following, dated City Point, July 29.—(Document I.)

General Grant had come to my headquarters at 4 p. m., and at that time I showed him the order for the assault next day, which had just then been prepared, and which order met with his perfect approbation; he read the order and expressed his satisfaction with it. No other despatches passed between the lieutenant general and myself.

Next morning, between half past three and four o'clock—before four o'clock, he arrived on the ground, at General Burnside's headquarters, and all further communications between us were verbal, until August 1, at 11.40 a. m., when I received the following despatch.—(Document J.)

We had given our respective views concerning the assault, and I particularly impressed my views with reference to the difficulties to be overcome. When it was ascertained that the movement of the 2d corps had drawn over to the north bank of the James five of the eight divisions composing General Lee's army, together with the information I had obtained that the enemy had no second line upon the ridge, but only one or two isolated batteries, I came to the conclusion that the explosion of the mine, and the subsequent assault on the crest, I had every reason to believe would be successful, and would be followed by results which would have consisted in the capture of the whole of the enemy's artillery, and a greater part of his infantry.

The plan sketched out by Lieutenant General Grant in his despatch to me, which I endeavored to carry out, and for the execution of which I gave the necessary orders, was, that the mine should be exploded as early as possible in the morning, before daylight; that in the mean time the 9th corps should be massed and formed in assaulting columns; that every preparation should be made by removing the abatis so that the troops could debouch, and particularly the assaulting columns; that as soon as the mine was exploded, the assaulting columns should push forward; that a sufficient proportion should be left to guard the flanks of the main column, because they had to look for an attack on the flanks; that the main body should hold the lines during the attempt to gain the crest of the hill, and if it was successful then I intended to throw up the whole of the 18th corps, to be followed by the 2d corps, and if necessary by the 5th corps, also. I do not suppose it is necessary to read the order. I will read it, however.—(Document K.)

Having read to the court the correspondence which passed between the lieutenant general and myself preliminary to the operations, and having read the order for the operations, I now propose to read and to accompany with some explanatory remarks the despatches and correspondence which passed between myself and Major General Burnside, who had the immediate active operations to perform; afterwards between myself and Major General Ord, between myself and Major General Warren, and between myself and Major General Hancock. These despatches, when compared with each other, and in connexion with the remarks which I shall make, will show the facts so far as they came to my knowledge; and I wish the court to bear in mind, and I desire to call their attention particularly to the paucity of information which was furnished me by Major General Burnside of the operations which were made, and to the difficulty that a major general commanding an army like the one I am commanding labors under to give direct orders in the ignorance of matters transpiring in the front at the immediate scene of operations.

Before those operations were concluded upon I called on Major General Burnside to furnish me in writing what he proposed to do in case his mine was exploded. In response to which I received the following report.—(Document L.)

The request made in that communication by Major General Burnside was complied with—that is to say, sand-bags were furnished him; but the amount of powder asked for, which was twelve thousand pounds, was reduced to eight thousand, upon the belief on my part, and on that of my engineers, that eight thousand pounds would be sufficient for the purpose.

Another matter in that despatch to which my attention was directed, and which was finally the subject of an order on my part, is the suggestion of Major General Burnside to place the colored troops at the head of the assaulting column. That I disapproved, and I informed him of my disapproval, which was based upon the ground, not that I had any reason to doubt, or any desire to doubt, the good qualities of the colored troops, but that I desired to impress upon Major General Burnside, which I did do in conversations, of which I have plenty of witnesses to evidence, and in every way I could, that this operation was to be a coup-de-main; that his assaulting column was to be as a forlorn hope, such as are put into breaches, and that he should assault with his best troops; not that I had any intention to insinuate that the colored troops were inferior to his best troops, but that I understood that they had never been under fire, nor that they should not be taken for such a critical operation as this, but that he should take such troops as from previous service could be depended upon as being perfectly reliable. Finding General Burnside very much disappointed—for he had made known to General Ferrero and his troops that they were to lead in the assault—and fearing that the effect might be injurious, and in order to show him that I was not governed by any motive other than such as I ought to be governed by, I told him I would submit the matter, with his reasons and my objections, to the lieutenant general commanding the armies, and I would abide by the decision of the lieutenant general as to whether it was expedient and right for the colored troops to lead the assault. Upon referring the question to the lieutenant general commanding, he fully concurred in my views, and I accordingly addressed to Major General Burnside, or had addressed to him, the following communication.—(Document M.)

[The following despatches read near the end of the testimony are here inserted, as directed, in their proper places.]—(Documents M 1, and M 2.)

The next despatch to Major General Burnside was addressed by me at 9.45 p. m., July 29, the evening before the action. I had received a despatch from General Ord, stating that it would take him till very late to relieve the troops in the trenches.

The following is my despatch to General Burnside.—(Document N.)

My idea was that General Burnside should form his columns of assault, make all his preparations, take all his men out of the trenches, and move forward; and that then General Ord should occupy his trenches in case he should find it necessary to return. No further despatches passed between General Burnside and myself. I think it proper to state, however, that on the day previous to the assault I was at General Burnside's headquarters, and had the good fortune to meet his three division commanders, and some conversation passed between us, and I would like the court to inquire into what transpired on that occasion, because I would like to impress upon the court, as I did impress upon General Burnside and his officers, that this operation which we had to perform was one purely of time; that if immediate advantage was not taken of the explosion of the mine, and the consequent confusion of the enemy, and the crest immediately gained, it would be impossible to remain there, for that as soon as the enemy should recover from their confusion, they would bring their troops and batteries to bear upon us and we would be driven out. That there were two things to be done, namely, that we should go up promptly and take the crest; for, in my judgment, the mere occupation of the crater and the holding on to that was of no possible use to us, because the enemy's line was not such a line as would be of advantage to us to hold, except to go from it to the crest; and that the troops were to be withdrawn when the assault proved unsuccessful.

General HANCOCK, *president*. Do you not mean that you met four division commanders, instead of three, as you said, at the headquarters of General Burnside?

General MEADE. No; I mean three. I saw Potter, Ledlie, and Wilcox, and I mentioned in the presence of those gentlemen the tactical manœuvres to be made between that crater and the crest—that the only thing to be done was to rush for the crest and take it immediately after the explosion had taken place; and that they might rest assured that any attempt to take time to form their troops would result in a repulse.

Those were all the despatches that transpired between General Burnside and myself before the day of the assault.

On the morning of the 30th, about a quarter past three o'clock, when I was about preparing to go forward to General Burnside's headquarters, I found that it was very dark, and suggestions being made by some of my officers that it was too dark to operate successfully, and that a postponement of the explosion of the mine might be advantageous, I accordingly addressed a despatch to General Burnside to the following effect.—(Document O.)

To that I received the following reply from General Burnside.—(Document P.)

I then went over to General Burnside's headquarters, he, during these operations, being further to the front. The hour had arrived. I stood waiting. I heard no report from General Burnside and no explosion of the mine. In the mean time Lieutenant General Grant arrived. Finding that there was no explosion, I sent two staff officers, first Captain Jay, and then ——— ———, I do not recollect the name of the other; but I sent two staff officers to ascertain from General Burnside what the difficulty was, if there was any difficulty; why his mine did not explode, if he knew; to which I received no answer. At 4.10 the following depatch was sent to him.—(Document Q.)

And to this I got no answer.

At 4.20 another despatch was sent to him, as follows.—(Document R.)

I should have stated before this, that, in order to secure the speedy transmission of intelligence, I took the precaution to have a telegraph run from my headquarters, in General Burnside's camp, to where General Burnside had established his headquarters for the day, in the 14 gun battery.

The following is the next despatch I sent to General Burnside.—(Document S.)

To this I received no reply. Finding that no replies were received, and the lieutenant general commanding desiring that an immediate assault should be made without reference to the mine, at 4.35 the following despatch was sent to General Burnside.—(Document T.)

The same orders, you will find, were sent to General Warren, to General Mott, and to General Hunt to open the artillery. About this time, however, about 4.40, the mine was exploded. In the mean time Captain Jay returned and informed me that the fuze had failed; that a defect was found, and the fuze had been overhauled about fifty feet or twenty-five feet, I forget the distance, from the entrance; that the defect had been ascertained and had been remedied, and that finally the mine had been exploded. So far as my recollection goes, the mine was exploded about 4.40 or 4.45. At 5.45 a. m., one hour after the explosion of the mine, the following despatch was sent to General Burnside.—(Document U.)

The following despatch was received from him, apparently as an answer to mine, although through a difference in time, it is dated before it.—(Document V.)

About this time, 5.45 or 5.50, (I see by reference to the despatch that it is 5.45,) an orderly came up to me and delivered me a despatch, which, upon opening, I found to be a despatch from Colonel Loring, inspector general of the 9th corps, written at the crater, and addressed to General Burnside, which despatch the orderly, not knowing where to find General Burnside, had brought to his old headquarters, where it found me. That despatch, so far as I recollect the purport of it, was to the effect that General Ledlie's troops occupied the crater, but, in his (Colonel Loring's) opinion, he feared the men could not be induced to advance beyond. That despatch was telegraphed to General Burnside, and sent to him by an officer, so that I have no copy of it. That was the substance of it, however. It was shown to General Grant and General Humphreys, both of whom can give their recollection of it in confirmation of mine. It is an important matter to be taken into consideration here, that as early as 5.45 a. m. a despatch was placed in my hands stating that General Ledlie's troops could not be induced to advance.

In addition to that, the following despatch was sent to him.—(Document W.)

Fearing that there might be some difficulty on the part of General Burnside's troops, I thought it possible that by another corps going in on his right encouragement might be given to his men, and a prompt assault might be made.

The next despatch I received was from an aide-de-camp, whom I had sent to General Burnside's headquarters to advise me of what was going on. It is dated 5.50, and is from Captain Sanders.—(Document X.)

The next despatch that I will read is one addressed to General Burnside, at 6 a. m.—(Document Y.)

Despatches were at this time also sent to Generals Ord and Warren. You can keep these dates in your mind.

The next despatch was received from Captain Sanders, at 6.10 a. m., as follows.—(Document Z.)

The following despatches are next in order.—(Documents 1, 2, and 3.)

At 7 a. m. Lieutenant General Grant put into my hand a despatch from Colonel Comstock, an officer whom he had sent to see the progress of operations.—(Document 4.)

I read all these despatches over, that you may see how I was situated on the occasion, and what I knew of what was going on.

At 7.20—twenty minutes afterwards—I got the following despatch from General Burnside.—Document 5.)

Upon the receipt of this despatch from General Burnside, informing me that it was hard work to take the crest, at the same time he not having reported to me that anybody had attempted to take it, or that any part of his force had made any effort to take it; with the despatches from my officers, the despatch from Colonel Loring, and the despatch from Colonel Comstock, to the effect that the troops were lying there, I came to the conclusion that possibly there might be some difficulty in getting the men to move forward, either from the enemy's fire, or some imaginary obstacle the troops had to encounter; that, as it was now 7 o'clock, and that the place had been occupied at 5.30, I began to suppose that there was some reason for the delay which had not been officially reported. I considered it natural that General Burnside would be indisposed to make it known, so long as he had hopes of overcoming the difficulty. To me, in my position as major general commanding the army, it was a matter of the utmost importance, because it was my intention during the assault, and before it, that if we could not carry the crest promptly by a coup-de-main, to withdraw the troops as quickly and safely as possible. Impressed with this view, and in order to get at the exact condition of affairs, and to justify General Burnside, if there was any reason of that kind, I addressed him the following despatch.—(Document 6.)

It is proper to say, that immediately after sending that despatch, and before receiving General Burnside's answer, I received a report verbally from Captain Sanders that an attempt had been made to make an attack on the right, I think by General Griffin, and that he had been repulsed. I immediately sent another despatch to General Burnside at 8 a. m., as follows.—(Document 7.)

To the first of these two despatches, subsequent to sending the second, I received this reply.—(Document 8.)

The next despatch that I received was one from Colonel Comstock, about the same time, 8 a. m.—(Document 9.)

The next despatch I received was one dated 8.45 a. m., from Captain Sanders.—(Document 10.)

At 9 a. m. I received the following despatch from General Burnside.—(Document 11.)

That was the first information I had received that there was any collision with the enemy, or that there was any enemy present. At 9.30 a. m. the following despatch was sent to General Burnside.—(Document 12.)

Then I received the following despatch from Captain Sanders.—(Document 13.)

The next despatch was this, from Colonel Comstock.—(Document 14)·

The next despatch to General Burnside, at 9.45, was the peremptory order to withdraw.—(Document 15.)

Receiving information from some person—I don't know who it was—that there was some difficulty about withdrawing at that time, that the safety of the column might be jeopardized by undertaking to withdraw it, the following despatch was sent to General Burnside, and also to General Ord, who had troops there at that time. None of my despatches to General Ord have been presented yet, because it would have confused matters. I will read them hereafter.— (Document 16.)

About that time, both Major General Burnside and Major General Ord came to the headquarters where General Grant and myself were temporarily located. General Burnside seemed to be very much displeased at the order of withdrawal, and expressed the opinion that if allowed to remain there, by nightfall he could carry that crest. As, however, he did not give any reason to show how he could take it, and as he had been from half past five in the morning till nearly ten, and not only had not taken it, but had his men driven out of the works he had been occupying, and as Major General Ord, whose troops were also there, upon being asked if the crest could be carried, answered very positively that it was entirely out of the question, it was determined by the lieutenant general commanding and myself—or rather I referred the matter to him, to know if he desired the orders changed—it was determined that no further attempt should be made to take the crest, but that the men should be withdrawn whenever that could be done with security.

There is now a very important point to which I will call the attention of the court, and which I want investigated very thoroughly, and that is the withdrawal from the crater.

At the time the order was given to withdraw the troops, the report of Major General Ord was, that the crater of the mine was so overcrowded with men that it would be nothing but murder to send any more men forward there. I do not recollect as to whether the report of Major General Burnside was so definite, but I believe the report of Colonel Loring was that there was at least one division of the troops in there. The impression left upon my mind was, that at that time there were as many men in the crater as would enable them to defend themselves if attacked, and in case no defence was necessary there was no occasion on my part to order troops to be sent there. I presumed that Major General Ord and Major General Burnside, having charge of that operation, would see that the men would be properly withdrawn.

This conclusion having been arrived at by the lieutenant general and myself, and it not appearing necessary that we should remain any longer at Major General Burnside's headquarters, the lieutenant general commanding withdrew to City Point, and I withdrew to my former headquarters, where I was in telegraphic communication with Major General Burnside, and where, under the common correspondence between a general officer commanding the army and his subordinates, not to say under a peculiar exigency, I expected to be informed of anything that should occur. I remained in total ignorance of any further transactions until about six or seven o'clock in the evening. About that hour a report, or a rumor, reached me that there were a number of our wounded men lying between the crater and our line, and I think an appeal was made to me by General Ord if something could not be done to remove those men. I was not aware that there was any difficulty in the way of removing them, and wondered why they had not been removed, presuming that our men were in the crater; and as no report had been made to me that they had been withdrawn, I directed a despatch to be sent to Major General Burnside, calling upon him for information. That despatch read as follows.—(Document 17.)

You will remember that I left General Burnside's headquarters about 10 o'clock, with the understanding that the troops were to be withdrawn when they could be withdrawn with security.

[The following despatches were subsequently read by the witness :]—(Documents 18, 18¼, 18½, 18¾, 19, 19¼, 20.)

So far as any information from General Burnside is concerned, I had to go to bed that night without knowing whether his troops were in the crater, or whether they were not. During the night despatches were received, referring to the relief of General Ord's troops next morning, July 31, at 8.40 and 9 a. m. The despatches 18¼ and 18½ were sent and received by General Humphreys. No despatch was received from General Burnside with reference to the withdrawal of these troops till 6 40 p. m., July 31, (marked 18¾,) to which was sent the one marked 19, at 9.10 p. m., July 31. The despatch was received from General Burnside, marked 19¼, and the reply, marked 20, was sent. Now, I beg leave to call the attention of the court to the fact that this despatch is dated 9.10 p. m., July 31, and although it does not give an official statement of the time of the withdrawal of the troops, I know, but only from other information, that the withdrawal was at about 2 p. m., July 30. And as I consider that my conduct is here the subject of investigation as much as that of any other officer or man engaged in this enterprise, I wish to repudiate, distinctly, any responsibility resting upon me for the manner of the withdrawal, beyond the orders I gave to the effect that the troops were to be withdrawn when they could be withdrawn with security; and if they had been able to repulse an attack of the enemy, it seems to me rather extraordinary, when another attack was threatened after the success, that they should be withdrawn simply because they were threatened with another attack. But that is the point to which I wish to call the attention of the court, and which I wish to have thoroughly investigated.

I believe those constitute the sum and substance of all the orders that passed between myself and Major General Burnside. But I respectfully submit to this court that so far as it was in my power, as the commanding general of this army, to give orders, I anticipated the difficulties that occurred, and endeavored to avoid them as much as I could do so, and that I cannot be held responsible for the failure which afterwards resulted.

Having finished my correspondence with and orders to General Burnside, I now propose to read the correspondence with and orders to General Ord, who was the officer commanding the force next to be employed after those of General Burnside, and whose movements it is important to know.

Major General Ord was directed to relieve his corps by General Mott's division of the 2d corps on the evening of the 29th. He was then to move and mass his troops in rear of the 9th corps, and it was intended that he should support the 9th corps whenever the 9th corps had effected a lodgement on the crest; that he was promptly to move up to them and support them on the crest. I had several interviews with General Ord on the 28th and 29th. I went with him and showed him the position; showed him exactly the ground; gave him all the information I had, and also caused him to send staff officers to select positions for the troops, so that when it became dark they might know the roads. On the morning of July 30, when it became evident to my mind that General Burnside's troops were not going to advance further than the crater, and when I had reason to suppose it was owing to some difficulty on the part of the troops themselves, and so far as any official report came to me, rather than obstacles presented by the enemy, I sent a despatch to General Ord changing his previous orders and directing him, instead of supporting General Burnside, to make an assault independent of General Burnside. That despatch and subsequent despatches are as follows.—(Documents 21, 22, 23, 23¼, 23½, 24.)

There were some other despatches to General Ord of a similar character, (but I do not see them here,) to endeavor to get him forward, independent of the 9th corps, to make an isolated attack, an attack of his own, independent of the 9th corps. Owing to the obstacles presented—the fact that there was no proper *debouche* for our troops to that portion of the enemy's line, and the fact that the crater was overcrowded with men—General Ord, considering those obstacles insurmountable, confined his operations to sending forward, I think, only one brigade. But General Ord and his division commanders have made reports, which will be placed before you. I forgot to bring them with me to-day.

At about 9.45 a. m. the same orders were sent to General Ord as to General Burnside, with reference to the withdrawal of the troops. That finishes all that passed between General Ord and myself.

The other supporting column was under Major General Warren, on the left.

In the original order General Warren was directed to mass his available troops on the right of the line, and to make all his preparations to support General Burnside in the assault wherever he should be ordered.

At 4.40 a. m. the following despatch was sent to him.—(Document 25.)

At 5.50, one hour afterwards, and immediately after my receiving the information that General Burnside's corps occupied the crater, the following despatch was sent to him.—(Document 26.)

I wish to call the attention of the court to the fact that as early as 5.50 I authorized General Warren, if he saw any opportunity of doing anything with his corps, not only in support of General Burnside, but as an independent operation of his own, that he should take advantage of it and push forward his troops. His reply, dated 6 a. m., is as follows.—(Document 27.)

At 6.15 a. m. another despatch was received from him, as follows.—(Document 28.)

Then at 6.20 another despatch, No. 29, came from General Warren, in which he states that what we thought was a heavy line of the enemy behind the line occupied by Burnside's troops, as the sunlight comes out and the smoke clears away, proves to be our own troops in the enemy's position.

You will perceive that at 5.40 I authorized General Warren and directed him to make an attack without waiting for the support of General Burnside—that is, if circumstances would justify his making an attack; and that his replies here indicate that no such attack was practicable. Coming to that conclusion, and receiving information from the signal officers that the enemy had left their extreme right, which I presumed they would do, to mass on the centre to receive our attack, the following despatch was sent to General Warren at half past six o'clock.—(Document 30.)

General BURNSIDE asked for the reading of the despatch to General Wilson, commanding a cavalry division.

General MEADE replied that he did not have the despatch with him now, but would procure it for him. The order to General Wilson was written, he said, about the same time as the above despatch to General Warren—about half past six a. m.

General BURNSIDE wished to be informed whether or not the order to General Wilson was rescinded.

General MEADE replied that the order to the cavalry was rescinded when the infantry was ordered to withdraw.

General MEADE then resumed the reading of despatches, presenting Documents 31 and 32.

General BURNSIDE. I would like to know what that despatch to the cavalry was, and exactly what time it was rescinded.

General HANCOCK. If you will recollect the matter, we will have it called for subsequently.

General MEADE. Just make a memorandum of it, and I will have it sent. Indeed, I am not positive, but I think my despatches to General Sheridan, of the cavalry, are here. If they are, they will be read.

The next despatch in order is the following, dated 7.30 a. m., to General Warren.—(Document 33.)

General Ayres still remained on the right, and the orders still existed to do anything with him that could be done to advantage. At 7.50 a. m. we have the next despatch from General Warren.—(Document 34.)

Nothing further was received while we awaited developments from General Crawford until 8 a. m., when the following despatch was received from General Warren.—(Document 35.)

Notwithstanding that it was considered that General Warren's original order authorized him to take the batteries if it could be done, inasmuch as he was directed to move and attack with General Crawford, and as it was suggested that General Ayres might be required, it was thought proper to send him the following order at 8¾ a. m.—(Document 36.)

At 9.15 a. m. the following despatch was received from General Warren.—(Document 37.)

At this time the conclusion had been arrived at by the lieutenant general commanding and myself that the affair was over, and that nothing more could be done; and soon afterwards, orders similar to those which were sent to others were sent to General Warren, that he should not make any attempt to take the two-gun battery. The following despatches were sent to General Warren.—(Documents 38, 38½, 39, and 40.)

These are all the orders and communications that passed between General

Warren and myself. He was authorized to attack, if he could see a good chance to attack. When he reported no chance to attack, and was asked what force he had available, he reported that he had no force available except he moved Ayres. He was directed not to move Ayres until information was received from Crawford; only, if he could attack the two-gun battery in his front, he was ordered to attack it, and then the operations were subsequently suspended.

Now I have read you the communications that passed between myself and General Grant, myself and General Burnside, myself and General Ord, and myself and General Warren. It now remains for me to read the communications that passed between myself and General Hancock, and myself and General Mott.

The first was a communication sent 4.40 a. m. to General Mott.—(Document 41.)

At 4.50 a. m. the following despatch was sent to the telegraph operator at the headquarters of the 18th corps.—(Document 42.)

The following despatch, dated July 30, 6 a. m., was sent to General Hancock, after the mine was occupied.—(Document 43.)

The following despatches were sent and received.—(Documents 44, 45, 45½, 45¾, 46, 47, 48, 49, 50, 51, and 52.)

These include the despatches sent to the cavalry. I would explain that the separate orders to General Wilson were issued because General Sheridan, commanding the cavalry corps, was across the James river, at Deep Bottom, with two divisions, and I had to issue separate orders to General Wilson, so that he might be ready for the movement next day.

Here are some despatches which are of no particular consequence, but I will leave them here. They are despatches from the signal officers, indicating the movements of the enemy:

General BURNSIDE. I would suggest that all the despatches should be left.

General HANCOCK. General Meade is now giving his direct testimony, and only such despatches are numbered as he wishes to incorporate. The others will be left here and can be called for at any time.

General MEADE. Well, I will read these despatches, and you can number them and put them down.—(Documents 54, 55, 56, 57, and 58.)

It was on those reports of the signal officers that General Warren's orders were predicated.

The following is the report of the chief of engineers.—(Document 59.)

I believe I have now read every despatch that I have received, and the court are fully aware of all the information that I received on the ground.

General BURNSIDE said that before the court adjourned he would like to ask what latitude was allowed in the investigation.

General HANCOCK explained that the court had gone back to the orders from General Meade, the orders from General Grant, and to the first inception of the mine.

General MEADE. I would state that in the general orders issued on the night previous to the assault the cavalry was ordered to make this attack on the left. Two divisions of the cavalry corps were over at Deep Bottom. They could not cross the river until after the second corps had crossed, so that it was late in the day before they came up. Indeed, the head of the column did not appear before the offensive operations were suspended. As General Wilson had been ordered to be in readiness, however, and in view of the unavoidable delay of Sheridan, orders were sent to General Wilson not to wait for General Sheridan, but to push on himself to the Weldon railroad and make an assault upon the enemy. No report was received from General Sheridan. General Sheridan was sick. General Gregg reported in the evening that he had advanced his cavalry, and that they had found the enemy in force at Ream's Station, at Gurley's house, and at various other points along the railroad. There was no attack made by the cavalry except at Lee's mills, where General Gregg, encountering cavalry, drove them away to water his horses.

When it was known that our offensive operations were suspended, orders were sent to the cavalry that they should push on as far as possible and find out the enemy's position; but the original orders about going into town were modified, inasmuch as the operations in our immediate front were suspended.

I desire to say to the court that it has not been my disposition or intention to throw censure upon anybody for the unfortunate failure; that, indeed, I have not been furnished with the necessary information to enable me to do so. I have not yet received Major General Burnside's, or his subordinate commanders', official reports. I have very little knowledge of what actually transpired except from the despatches you have heard read here. I have been groping in the dark since the commencement of the attack. I did not wish to take any unpleasant measures, but I thought it my duty to suggest to the President of the United States that this matter should be investigated, and that the censure should be made to rest upon those who are entitled to it. What I have done has been to show that I tried to do all I could to insure success.

During the day General Burnside and some of his staff, Generals Potter and Ferrero of the 9th corps, were present.

The court adjourned, to meet at 10 o'clock a. m. on the 9th.

THIRD DAY.

Court Room, Headquarters Second Corps,
August 9, 1864.

The court met pursuant to adjournment.

Present: Major General Hancock, Brigadier Generals Ayres and Miles, and Colonel Schriver, judge advocate.

The reading of the record of the second day was proceeded with until suspended at page 30, document 25, by General Burnside's verbal application to have all the documents bearing date after 2 o'clock p. m. on the 30th July, and all evidence relating to events subsequent to that time, removed from the record, the reasons for which, by direction of the court, were reduced to writing, and presented as follows :

Headquarters Ninth Army Corps,
August 9, 1864.

Gentlemen: I beg to submit to the court that all testimony, whether by despatches or otherwise, relating to occurrences subsequent to 2 p. m. on 30th July last, at which time our troops had withdrawn from the enemy's line, and the assault was over, should be erased from the record, and no such evidence admitted in future.

The terms of the order appointing the court distinctly limit the action of the court to reporting the "facts and circumstances attending the unsuccessful assault on the enemy's position on the 30th July, 1864," and "their opinion whether any officer or officers are answerable for the want of success of said assault," and whatever events happened subsequent to the withdrawal have no relation to the success or want of success of the assault, and are not within the purview of the court.

Moreover, certain of these subsequent occurrences have been made the subject of charge against me by the major general commanding the army, and on which charges I am to be tried by another court. They, therefore, should not be investigated by this court.

I am, gentlemen, very respectfully, your obedient servant,
A. E. BURNSIDE, *Major General.*
Court of Inquiry,
Maj. Gen. Hancock, *President.*

The following paper was then submitted by Major General Meade :

"I respectfully submit to the court that the objection raised by Major General Burnside is not tenable. As I have before said, I consider my conduct the subject of the court's investigation. To show that I was not, and could not be, held responsible for the manner of the withdrawal, and the circumstances attending it, it is necessary for me to show that I was not furnished with any information; and furthermore, I claim the right to show in evidence that no effort on my part was omitted to obtain the necessary information.

"Independent of this personal consideration, and my rights as one whose conduct is under examination, I beg leave also to submit that the receiving of these official despatches in this case cannot, in any way, affect the case of General Burnside when on trial on the charges referred to by him. Those charges are disobedience of orders, and have no reference to his management of affairs on the 30th; because, even should it be proved to the satisfaction of the court (and I shall be glad to hear that it is) that General Burnside is in no way responsible for the lamentable failure on the 30th, it does not alter the facts of the case whether he obeyed or disobeyed my orders on that or any other occasion.

"This is a foreign matter, stands on its own merits, and has no connexion with the proceeding of this court, beyond the fact that these documents will be produced in both cases.

"Again, I respectfully submit, General Burnside's objections should have been made earlier in the proceedings, because among the charges preferred against him is one based on the very disrespectful despatch sent by him to me at light, a. m., July 30, and this despatch should be thrown out on the same ground, which would at once prevent me from stating my case in the manner in which I claim I have the right to.

"I beg leave to call the attention of the court to the hour of 2 o'clock being specified in General Burnside's objections, and ask the court to note that there is no evidence before them when the assault, if any, was made, or what occurred at 2 o'clock.

"I take it this court must modify the rules which would govern courts of inquiry when the conduct of only one individual is called in question. This court has to pass judgment on the conduct of numerous officers, and the relative rights of each should be considered.

"As I understand it, no one in particular is arraigned here, and, therefore, what occurs here can only be repeated elsewhere to the detriment of any of the parties concerned, and must be repeated.

"These are official documents, part of the archives of the army of the Potomac, and their production in my vindication will give no weight to their production against General Burnside, should he be tried on the charge of disobedience of orders. For these reasons I must respectfully insist on the court's receiving them."

General Burnside then submitted the following:

"In reply to General Meade's argument, I beg to say that there is no evidence on the record, and none furnished by the documents in question, that General Meade did in any way, by aide-de-camp or otherwise, use means to obtain any information in reference to the withdrawal, or anything that occurred after he left my headquarters, about 11 o'clock, until after 6 o'clock in the evening, instead of, as he states 'no effort being omitted on his part to obtain the necessary information.' Nor was such effort made, to my knowledge. General Meade himself states, in his argument, that the charges have no reference to the management of affairs on the 30th; and as these charges contain in full the documents to which I object, they therefore should be excluded here.

"A. E. BURNSIDE, *Major General.*"

The court was cleared. The court was opened, and the following decision of the court announced:

The proper time for objection to the reception of evidence is when it is offered and before accepted. Due notice was given to all persons who were supposed to be interested in the investigation (of which General Burnside was one) to be present if they so willed. The court, however, decides that the evidence, documentary and verbal, in question has a bearing on the conduct of individuals other than General Burnside. The court is ordered to examine into the "facts and circumstances attending the unsuccessful assault on the enemy's position on the 30th of July," and the authorities permit a court of inquiry to enter into such incidental examination of particular points as may become necessary to a full understanding of the matter at issue.

The court, therefore, considers it a duty to examine into all the circumstances of the assault, the subsequent withdrawal of the troops, and everything connected therewith.

The judge advocate continued the reading of the record of the second day, and, on completion, it was approved, several corrections having been made by the witness, whose meaning had not been fully understood.

The examination of Major General Meade was then resumed.

Question by judge advocate. When did Mott's division leave Deep Bottom, and arrive at the 18th corps to relieve it?

Answer. Orders were given in person to Major General Hancock about 5 or 6 o'clock on the evening of the 28th, requiring him to withdraw Mott's division, then in his line of battle, in the presence of the enemy, after dark, and send it to report to General Ord, commanding the 18th corps. Orders were subsequently given to General Ord, when the division came up, about daylight on the 29th, to mass it in the woods near the railroad, out of sight of the enemy, and at dark on the evening of the 29th to put it in his trenches to relieve his corps.

Adjourned till 10 o'clock a. m. on the 10th.

FOURTH DAY.

Court Room, Headquarters Second Corps,
August 10, 1864.

The court met pursuant to adjournment.

Present: Major General Hancock, Brigadier Generals Ayres and Miles, and Colonel Schriver, judge advocate.

There were also present Generals Ferrero, Potter, and Wilcox, of the 9th corps, General Mott, of the 2d, and General Carr, of the 18th.

The proceedings of the third day were read and approved.

Testimony of General Meade continued.

Questions by General Burnside:

Question. Where were your headquarters during the action of the 30th?

Answer. From four o'clock until about eleven—I am not exactly confident as to the time of leaving it—my headquarters, as announced in the order of battle on the day previous, were established at the headquarters of the 9th corps. At eleven o'clock, or about that time, as near as I can remember, I removed to the headquarters of the army of the Potomac, which are situated about three-quarters of a mile to the eastward of the headquarters of the 9th corps, and are in telegraphic communication with the same headquarters where I remained during the rest of the day.

Question. How far was that from the scene of action?

Answer. If by the scene of action is meant the crater of the mine and that portion of the enemy's line in front of it, so far as I have knowledge of the ground, derived from maps, I should suppose that the headquarters of the 9th corps were possibly a mile to the eastward of the crater, and my headquarters are three-quarters of a mile, as I stated, beyond that, still further to the east.

Question. Could anything of the action be seen from there?

Answer. Nothing could be seen from any of the points that I occupied.

Question. Did you go further to the front during the action? If so, where?

Answer. I did not leave the headquarters of the 9th corps during the active operations.

Question. Did you not know that there were several positions on our line where you could see the action for yourself, and yet be in as proper a place for you as in General Burnside's permanent camp, and also have full personal communications with Generals Burnside and Ord, and be much nearer to General Warren, and likewise have telegraphic communication with the rest of the army?

Answer. I undoubtedly was aware that there were points of the line where I could see more of the action than I could see at the position I occupied, but I was not aware that there was any point where I could see anything particularly, or on which I could base any orders. I adopted the position I did in consequence of its being a central one and in telegraphic communication with all parts of the line where officers were stationed with whom it was necessary to communicate; and having a large staff, and many communications to receive, and many persons to communicate with, and being there in telegraphic communication, I considered it more proper to remain where I announced to the army my headquarters would be, and where all information could be sent to me, than to make any change of position as intimated in the question. Besides which, I desire to say to this court that it has been a matter of policy with me to place myself in such position that my communications made, and the replies made thereto, should be made in such way as a record could be kept of them, and not be confined to verbal communications, which are often subject to misapprehension and to misconstruction. There undoubtedly was telegraphic communication from General Burnside's headquarters in the field—the fourteen-gun battery, as it was called—with the other headquarters in the army.

Question. Did you not have an aide-de camp with General Burnside during most of the action?

Answer. During a portion of the time I did have Captain Sanders, aide-de-camp, at the headquarters of General Burnside. I sent him there in consequence of not receiving any communication from General Burnside, in the hope that he would be enabled to send me some information.

Question. Was not Captain Sanders sent there before the mine exploded?

Answer. No, sir; he was sent there some considerable time after the mine exploded; that is, upon the duty that I now refer to. I have previously stated to the court that before the mine exploded I sent two officers to endeavor to explain the delay. One was Captain Jay, and one might have been Captain Sanders; but they returned before the explosion of the mine. After the explosion of the mine I sent Captain Sanders on the duty that I now refer to, which was to remain at General Burnside's headquarters and communicate to me anything which he could ascertain. I think it further proper to add to this answer to this question that, finding I did not get the information which I desired to have, or which I thought I could have, and fearing that my having sent an aide-de-camp—the object being to facilitate the transmission of information—might be used to deter responsible officers from communicating information to the commanding general, I withdrew Captain Sanders, before the action closed, by an order.

Question. For what purpose was he sent? Was it not to report to you the state and progress of affairs, and did he not so report?

Answer. I have already answered the first part of that question. As to his reports, all the despatches from him are on file in my evidence before the court. As to whether he reported all he should have reported, and all the information to be obtained, I presume the court will ascertain from him and from other evidence.

Question. Was there any information not furnished you by General Burnside, or through other sources, which, if received, would have influenced your conduct of the action? If so, what?

Answer. I have already informed the court that all the information I received has been placed before them in the shape of official documents. It is impossible for me to say what my action would have been if I had received any other information. I acted upon the information I received.

Question. What time did Captain Sanders leave General Burnside to return to you?

Answer. I should say it was about half past eight; between that and nine, as near as I can recollect. I have a copy of the order to him, which I can furnish if desired.

Question. You state that General Burnside's despatch of 9 a. m. was the first information you had received that any collision had taken place, or that there was any enemy in our front; had you not, before the receipt of this despatch, written to General Burnside in reference to General Griffin's attack and repulse; also, received a despatch from Captain Sanders speaking of captured colors; also, seen and examined rebel prisoners taken that morning?

Answer. In reply to that question, I would say that I am willing to assume that there is an apparent discrepancy in my testimony, which I am very glad to have an opportunity of explaining. I should suppose that any one cognizant of the circumstances that took place on that day, even of the most general nature, would know that I never meant to say that I did not know that there was no enemy anywhere. I was fully aware that when the crater was occupied a number of prisoners were taken. I was also aware that the enemy occupied their lines both on the right and on the left of the position occupied by General Burnside; and I did know that Captain Sanders had made a report of captured colors, and that an attack had been made in front of Griffin; but my whole attention was absorbed in the endeavor to have a charge made to the crest, and my thoughts were all upon that; and when I said this was the first intimation I had of there being any enemy in the front, I meant any enemy so situated as to prevent a direct assault upon the crest. Besides which, I must throw myself upon the consideration of the court, and say that the vast number of despatches, the frequency with which they were sent and received, was such that my memory may not serve me well, and the incidents may be, in a measure, not related in the exact order in which they occurred. I wish to call the attention of the court to a very important fact for the benefit of General Burnside, if it results to his benefit as well as to mine, and that is the difficulty of having the time of these despatches uniform. A despatch is sent to me marked with the time of the officer who sends it, but the time by his watch may be ten or fifteen minutes different from mine. But I do honestly and conscientiously say that that was the first positive information, when I received that despatch that the men of the 9th and 18th corps were returning, that I had that there was any such force or disposition of the enemy as to render it questionable that that assault could be made.

General Burnside here remarked, "I want the record in such a shape as to enable the casual reader and the revising officer to see that there was, before that time, an effort on my part, or on the part of some person near me, to give information, and not an effort to cast any imputation on General Meade, and I do not desire to invalidate his testimony, but simply to elaborate. I am confident that there is no disposition on the part of General Meade to make erroneous statements."

Question. Have you a note written me by you about two weeks before the assault as to the practicability of an assault in my front, my answer thereto, your second letter, and my reply, and will you be kind enough to furnish copies?

Answer. I presume that those documents, like all other official documents, are on file. I will have a search made for them, and as soon as they are discovered will very cheerfully furnish General Burnside or the court a copy of them.

[General Burnside explained that one of them was a semi-official letter, and General Meade being reminded of the purport of it, answered that he did not think he had it.]

By the court:

Question. What knowledge had you of the movements of the different divisions of the enemy on July 30?

Answer. I had very positive information from deserters, not only those who came within my own lines here, but those who came into the lines of General

Butler, and those who came into the lines of General Hancock, that there were but three divisions of the enemy in our front, consisting of Mahone's division of Hill's corps, and Johnson's and Hoke's divisions of Longstreet's corps; and that the other divisions of Lee's army were on the north side of the James river, confronting General Hancock and Sheridan, on the 29th. I also received the same information from prisoners taken that morning. During the operations I received information from the signal officer on the plank road that the enemy were moving troops from their right to their centre, which I anticipated, and upon receiving that information the orders were sent to General Warren to endeavor to turn the enemy's right by pushing forward General Crawford, and to General Wilson to push on without delay, without waiting for the arrival of General Sheridan, coming from Deep Bottom.

Question. Did the order to suspend operations (given about 9 a. m. July 30) originate with Lieutenant General Grant?

Answer. No, sir; the order, I think, originated with myself. Some time before the order was given, I informed Lieutenant General Grant that, as far as I could see, there was no prospect of our succeeding in the manner in which we had expected to do; that the time had passed for the coup-de-main to succeed; and I suggested to him that we should immediately withdraw the troops, to which he acceded. About that time a despatch was received from the signal officer of the 5th corps, stating that the colored troops had captured a brigade of the enemy, with four of their colors, to which, however, I did not attach much importance, not knowing how a signal officer could see an operation of that kind when it did not come to me from the officer in charge of the operations. We nevertheless suspended this order and held it in abeyance until the arrival of the despatch of General Burnside, informing me that some of the men of the 18th and 9th corps were retiring, and I think also that the Lieutenant General himself rode down to our trenches and made some personal examination, and had seen General Ord, and had some conversation with him. Upon his return, from what he had heard from General Ord, and subsequently an officer coming in and saying that the colored troops, instead of capturing a brigade and four colors, had themselves retired in great confusion, which information, I think, was given me by Major Fisher, the chief signal officer, I again referred the subject to the lieutenant general, and again gave him my opinion that, as it was then about 9.25, it was unnecessary to make any other efforts, and an unnecessary sacrifice of life; my idea being that they could be withdrawn without any difficulty then, or we should have difficulty later in the day in withdrawing them. To this he assented, and the order was given to withdraw them. Afterwards, when the information was received from General Burnside of the difficulty of retiring, then the order was modified.

Question. Were any instructions given for destroying the bridges in Petersburg in case the crest was gained?

Answer. There were not, for two reasons: and first, if we had succeeded, as I hoped we would, in overcoming the enemy, we should have driven them across the Appomattox, and should have wanted those bridges to follow them, but the contingency of their destroying those bridges was held in view, and it was to meet that contingency that the chief engineer was ordered to have a pontoon train brought up so that we could throw our own bridges. My expectation was, that if we had succeeded in the coup-de-main, these three divisions of the enemy would have gone out of our way, and we should be enabled to cross not only the Appomattox, but also Swift run, and open up communication with General Butler at Bermuda Hundred before General Lee could send any re-enforcements from the five divisions that he was known to have north of the James river.

BATTLE OF PETERSBURG. 141

Major General A. E. BURNSIDE, United States volunteers, duly sworn, says:

Soon after this army arrived before Petersburg I received a note from General Potter, stating that if it was desirable, the fort in front of his position could, in his opinion, be mined; and that he would, at my request, make a statement of the matter, or would come to my headquarters with Colonel Pleasants, of the 48th Pennsylvania, and lay the matter before me verbally.

I sent him word that I would be glad to take the matter into consideration; and accordingly he and Colonel Pleasants came to my headquarters, and laid before me a plan for running a mine to that position. In the course of the conversation Colonel Pleasants remarked to me that this thing had first been suggested by the men of his regiment, who, I think, were stationed in the advance line, and pretty much all of whom were miners, from Schuylkill county, Pennsylvania. The matter was fully discussed, and I authorized General Potter to commence the work—making the remark, if I remember right, that it could certainly do no harm to commence it, and it was probably better that the men should be occupied in that way, and I would lay the matter before General Meade at my earliest opportunity. We parted with that understanding, and the work was commenced.

Probably at the first interview that I had with General Meade I mentioned the matter to him. He said to me that he had no instructions in reference to siege operations in his front; that that was a matter for the lieutenant general to decide upon; that he could not authorize any work of that kind, but he would acquiesce in it—and I am inclined to think that I have upon record a letter to the same effect from General Meade. This work was started and progressed with the full knowledge of General Meade; in fact, I was in almost daily communication with him, and much conversation was had upon that subject.

When the gallery was first started there were many discouragements, in the way of prophecies as to its failure, which had to be overcome, and a great many suggestions as to the mode by which the work should proceed. I, however, left the matter entirely in the hands of General Potter, Colonel Pleasants and his regiment, feeling satisfied that these miners had experience in matters of that kind which would enable them to accomplish this work.

When it began to be demonstrated that we would probably reach a point under the enemy's fort, conversations were had with reference to the feasibility of an assault after the explosion had taken place. Feeling that the old troops of the 9th corps had experienced very hard service during the campaign, and had been in so many engagements that they were very much wearied, and their ranks thinned, I made up my mind, if I was called on to make an assault with the 9th corps, to place the fourth division, under General Ferrero, in the advance, inasmuch as that division had not suffered so severely—in fact, had not been in any general engagement during the campaign, but had frequently been very honorably engaged on the outposts of the army. General Ferrero himself, and all his officers, expressed to me their utmost confidence in his troops, and especially his confidence in their ability to make a charge, or, in other words, a dash. I accordingly instructed him to drill his troops with a view to leading the advance, in case the 9th corps was called upon to make the attack.

Soon after this, General Meade called upon me for a statement as to the practicability of making an assault in my front, which call seemed to have been general, or, rather, seemed to have been made upon all the generals commanding corps then on the advance line. I answered him, giving to him, as I conceived to be, under the circumstances, a proper opinion, stating that I thought the chances were fair that a successful assault could be made from my front, if it could be supported in a specific way, and I could have the discretion of determining when the supporting columns should be put in. General Meade answered me to the effect that he commanded this army, and that he could not give to any one the authority to determine as to the time that his troops should be put in action; that he would be glad to receive from me at all times such suggestions as I might make, but that he himself would take the responsibility of re-enforcing any force that he should see fit to order in action, or words to that effect. I at once wrote him a letter, stating that I had no disposition whatever to claim the right to put other troops than my own in action; that I had simply made this suggestion because I had given troops to other corps commanders to support their columns, which they themselves had used during the campaign, without any interference on my part, and I simply meant to ask what I had granted to others. That while I was certainly not anxious to put my own troops in action, the troops of any other corps could be called upon to make the assault; that I was fully willing to accord to General Meade more military skill than I possessed, and more ability to put troops in action, but that my troops had been given to corps commanders, both on my right and on my left, and placed in action by them; and, as I before said, I simply desired to have accorded to me what I had accorded to them.

It was decided, I believe, at that time, that no assault should be made; but I, notwithstanding, sent for General Ferrero, and directed him to go down to our advance line and select positions for concentrating his division, to look at the positions on the line over which he had to pass, and to reconnoitre the ground over which his division would have to pass in an assault upon Cemetery hill. I also directed him to send his brigade commanders down for the same purpose, and indicated to him exactly the position which I wanted him to take and the parts of the line over which I desired him to pass. I requested that he would present to me a plan for the manœuvring of his troops in case an assault of that kind were ordered.

In accordance with that General Ferrero presented me a plan, which is in substance laid down in my plan of attack and contained in the proceedings already before you.—(See document L.) I approved of this plan, especially that part of it which contemplated the movement of troops to the right and left of the breach which we might make in the line, in order to allow the other column to proceed to the front without any molestation from any of the enemy that might be left in the rifle-pits on the right and left of the breach. This must have been fifteen or twenty days, if not more, before the assault was made. I was afterwards informed by General Ferrero that his troops had been drilled for a movement of that kind, and was informed by a large number of his officers that it was their understanding that they were to make an attack with them; that, if I mistake not, they had passed over lines on intrenchments, performing the movement with a view to familiarizing their men with the movement, and they each and all expressed to me the greatest possible confidence in their ability to accomplish the work, which I considered a very material element in making the movement.

Nothing of importance occurred for a few days before the mine was sprung, except ordinary conversations with reference to the charge which was to be placed in the mine.

I, myself, from a long experience in experiments with gunpowder—having been a manufacturer of arms several years before the war commenced, and in constant practice with fire-arms—had a particular view with reference to the mode in which the mine should be charged, and the amount of charge to be placed in it. It was not in accordance with the methods laid down in scientific works upon the subject of military mining, but entirely in accordance with all experience in mining and blasting by civil engineers, within the last two or three years, since the method of heavy tamping had been abandoned. It is not worth while for me to enter here into an explanation of my theory, because I can present the report of the officer who built the mine, and that will explain the matter fully. It is sufficient to say that the mine was charged partially upon my theory and partially upon the theory of the old established plan of military mining. In the theory which I decided to be adopted large charges could be used without detriment, in my opinion, to persons in the immediate proximity of the mine; but persons who were not of my opinion felt that the effect of this mine at great distances, with the charge which I proposed to place in it, would be very great; and it became, from some cause or other, known to my troops, both officers and men, that a difference of opinion of that kind had arisen, and to such an extent that I have had general officers come to me and ask me if I did not think the charge I was putting in the mine was too large. I did not think the charge so large that there was danger of injuring our own men. This feeling among the men had a certain effect which I will leave for the court to decide, and, if they request it, I will send them the names of witnesses who have mentioned to me that impression on the subject long before the mine exploded, so that there can be no mistake as to the impression that prevailed at the time. I, myself, was satisfied, without knowing definitely, that the charge which I desired to place in the mine could be placed there with safety. I witnessed this anxiety among the troops with a good deal of concern. But that it did not prevail in the division which it was supposed would make the assault—it not being then upon our lines—was a source of gratification to me. This court will see, by looking at the documents which General Meade has presented, that I was directed to keep the amount of powder placed in the chambers within the limits of rules prescribed by military works upon that subject. I, however, in several verbal communications with General Meade, insisted upon the other method; and it was finally decided that we should place in the mine eight thousand pounds of powder instead of twelve thousand pounds. The ground that I took was this: that the depth of the mine, or rather the bottom of the chambers, was fixed; the greater the explosion the greater the crater-radius, and less inclination would be given the sides of the crater, and the greater breach on the right and left of the charges would be made, thereby giving a greater space for the troops to pass over and a less inclination for them to pass up and down in the line. It was, however, determined that eight thousand pounds of powder should be put in instead of twelve, and the mine was accordingly exploded with that charge. The decision in reference to the charge to be placed in the mine was given in ample time to let me make arrangements for that amount of powder.

The general facts and movements connected with this army, for the first three or four days previous to the fight, are so well known to the court that I will not delay them by any statement as to my correspondence and personal intercourse, or anything of that nature, up to Thursday before the fight.

On that day (Thursday, two days before the fight) I went to General Meade's headquarters. He spoke to me in this way:

"I have received information that it is impossible for General Hancock to advance beyond his present position; he has succeeded in inflicting upon the enemy a severe punishment, and captured some four pieces of cannon, but is not able to advance beyond that point," (or, at any rate, it was decided that he should not advance beyond that point.) "A large force of the enemy from this position has been attracted to that side of the river by this movement of General Hancock, and General Grant desires that an attack should be made here." (I think he made that last remark, but I will not be positive; he either said that General Grant desired, or he, himself, desired that an attack should be made.) He asked how long it would take to charge the mine. There was some correspondence before and after that time—I do not know if it is in your proceedings or not—in reference to the time necessary to charge the mine. I think it very likely that General Meade has placed all the documents before you. Previous to this he had written to me to present my *project* for this movement, which is now before you. During this conversation, on Thursday, he said to me: "I cannot approve of your placing the negro troops in the advance, as proposed in your project." I asked him why. He said: "Because I do not think they should be called upon to do as important a work as that which you propose to do, certainly not called upon to lead," or words to that effect. I, in a considerable conversation, urged upon General Meade the necessity for placing General Ferrero's division in the advance. I stated to him that the three white divisions had been on the advance line, and under fire from the moment of the establishment of the line, on the 18th or 19th of June, until that time; that they were very much wearied, had contracted a habit of covering themselves by every method within their reach, and that I was satisfied they were not in a condition to make anything like as much of a dash upon the enemy's line as General Ferrero's division, which had not been under any considerable fire from the time of its arrival at this place to that moment. I told him I considered my troops to be as good as they ever were, with the exception of this weariness and the habit—which had almost become a second nature—of protecting themselves from the fire of the enemy. In fact, upon this subject I was very, very urgent.

I will here present to the court some of the reasons for forming this opinion, which reasons were presented to General Meade. Take an intermediate date, say the 20th of July, and there were, for duty, nine thousand and twenty-three (9,023) muskets in the three old divisions of the ninth corps, which occupied the line. From the 20th of June, which was after the fight at this place, to the day before the fight on the 30th day of July, these divisions lost as follows:

Killed, 12 officers, 231 men; wounded, 44 officers, 851 men; missing, 12 men, making a total of 1,150 men; which is over twelve (12) per cent. of the command, without a single assault on the part of the enemy, or of our own troops. These casualties were caused from picket firing and shell firing, and extended pretty evenly over the whole line. I think that the whole of General Wilcox's division was on the line for thirty days, or more, without relief. General Potter's and General Ledlie's divisions had some small reliefs, enabling those gentlemen to draw some of their men off at intervals, for two or three days at a time, at certain intervals during this period.

A considerable portion of our line was so situated as to render it impossible to keep pickets to the front of them. It was, in fact, situated very much as a portion of the line occupied by the second corps, at Coal Harbor. As I stated before, I stated these facts to General Meade, except that I will not say that I gave him these exact figures; but the full substance of what I have stated here was given to him, together with the statement of the loss of officers and men, and the way in which the losses occurred. And, in fact, statements were made regularly to General Meade, so that these facts were in his possession, but were not made with the same particularity to him as I have made them here.

The ninth corps also lost in the fight of the 17th and 18th of June 2,903 men, and in the action of the 30th of July 3,828.

The following are the figures, more in detail:

June 17 and 18—killed, 29 officers, 348 men; wounded, 106 officers, 1,851 men; missing, 15 officers, 554 men. Total, 2,903.

July 30—killed, 52 officers, 376 men; wounded, 105 officers, 1,556 men; missing, 87 officers, 1,652 men. Total, 3,828.

General Meade said to me that he was going to see General Grant, and would submit the question to him as to whether the colored troops would be allowed to take the advance or not. This, as I said, was on Thursday—I think in the forenoon. He said to me that he would start at one o'clock, and would return that evening.

I parted with him, and on the next morning, not having heard anything from General Meade, and knowing, from information that I had received, that he had returned from City Point during the evening, I imagined that no further action was to be taken in the matter, and that I was to be allowed to place the fourth division in the advance.

On Friday forenoon General Wilcox and General Potter, two of my division commanders, came to my headquarters, and we talked over the matter of the fight which was to take place on Saturday morning. I said to one or both of them to this effect: that I had been very much worried and troubled the day before lest General Meade would overrule that part of my plan which contemplated the putting in of the colored troops; but that I hoped nothing further would be heard from it, because General Meade had gone to City Point the day before, and the matter was to be referred to General Grant; and that inasmuch as I had not heard from General Meade, I took it for granted that he had decided to allow the thing to remain as it was. This I must necessarily give in substance, because my conversations with my division commanders are not guarded. They can be called upon themselves to state what they know about the matter.

Soon after that, say eleven o'clock, Generals Meade and Ord came to my headquarters. I am under the impression that I broached the subject myself as to the colored division taking the advance, but whether I did or not, he informed me that General Grant coincided with him in opinion, and it was decided that I could not put that division in advance. I felt, and I suppose I expressed, and showed, very great disappointment at this announcement; and finally, in the conversation which occurred, and to which there are two witnesses here present, I asked General Meade if that decision could not be changed. He said: "No, general, it cannot; it is final, and you must put in your white troops." No doubt in the conversation I gave some of the reasons for not wishing to put the white troops in that I had given at his headquarters, but of that I am not certain.

This was the day before the fight. I said to General Meade that that would necessarily change my plan. Now, this conversation either occurred at that time, or it occurred at a later hour in the day, say one or two o'clock, when General Meade returned to my headquarters; because he went off with General Ord for an hour or two, say, and returned to my headquarters. It is not impossible that this conversation occurred in the afternoon, instead of in the forenoon of the 29th.

After some conversation with Generals Wilcox and Potter as to which troops should take the advance, one of them remarked to me that I had better send for General Ledlie, and we would talk the matter over as to which one of the divisions should take the advance. I sent for General Ledlie, and after some discussion of the matter, I decided that, taking everything into consideration, it should be but fair that these gentlemen should cast lots for the advance. General Wilcox was probably better situated as to position for the advance, as his troops then were, than either of the other divisions—certainly than General Ledlie; but his troops, as I stated before, had been constantly on the line, with the exception of an intermission of a day or two, which rendered it, if anything, desirable that General Ledlie's troops should lead instead of his. General Potter's troops had been, next to General Wilcox's, more constantly on the line, and I think he was, next to him, better situated for the advance; but, as I have indicated by previous remarks, General Ledlie's division was less fatigued, and in my opinion it was more just to call upon them to make the charge, and they had fought as gallantly as troops could fight on the 17th, and I therefore did not hesitate to call upon them in consequence of any lack of faith in their courage.

So I said, "It will be fair to cast lots," and so they did cast lots, and General Ledlie drew the advance. He at once left my headquarters in a very cheerful mood to make his arrangements for the advance, as no time could be lost in making the necessary arrangements, as it was then certainly three o'clock in the afternoon, and the assault was to be made next morning.

I directed him to take his brigade commanders and go to the front with Colonel Loring, my inspector general, who was entirely conversant with the ground, and I indicated to Colonel Loring about the position I desired General Ledlie to take, and I also stated verbally to General Wilcox and General Potter about the positions I desired them to take with their division; and the ground being familiar to all of us, enabled us to talk very understandingly and easily upon the subject. General Potter expressed some doubt as to finding room enough on the right of the covered way to place his troops, of which I was in doubt myself, the general instructions being for General Potter to mass all his troops, if possible, on the right of his covered way, General Wilcox to occupy his covered way and such portions of the railroad cut as was necessary, and room to be found between the two for General Ledlie, who had the assaulting column. At all events, there was, as far as I know, a distinct understanding between myself and my division commanders as to the positions to be occupied by the troops. Not that they did finally occupy exactly the positions which I indicated to them, because some of them were immaterially modified by correspondence, I think, between Generals Wilcox, Potter, and myself. It is sufficient to say that General Ledlie's troops were massed in about the same position as I had desired to mass General Ferrero. The arrangement which General Meade objected to, of sending troops down to the right and left to clear the way, was dispensed with; it having been understood before that that was a part of the plan or of the arrangements, the plan was made to accord with General Meade's views; in other words, in consequence of his objection, I did not give any instructions for troops to pass down to the right and left, but to make at once for the crest.

The commanding general had been urgent in his views, that in order to carry the crest—that is, Cemetery hill—a dash must be made at it without reference to formation; that there would be no time for manœuvring; that if we attempted to handle the troops as proposed in my plan, he was satisfied it would be a failure. If I mistake not, the amount of these views was expressed before General Potter and General Wilcox. Generals Meade and Ord called at my headquarters and had a conversation there in reference to my plans. General Ord went with General Meade to our signal station, and General Ord took a look at the position of the enemy. After returning to my headquarters, General Ord said he would send staff officers to me to report, in order that they also might reconnoitre the ground and pick out positions for troops. Instead of staff officers coming, I think that in almost every instance the general officers of General Ord's corps came themselves. I gave them facilities for reconnoitring the position of the enemy, and also gave them instructions as to where these troops were to mass in rear of our lines. I received General Meade's order, which is on your record. I sent him a copy of my order, which I have not here at present, but which I will procure and present at the end of my evidence. There were some details into which I did not enter in this order, in consequence of the verbal understanding which existed between myself and my division commanders; that fact, I believe, being noted in the order.

During that night our troops were concentrated in accordance with those orders, ready for the attack; and General Ord's troops were also concentrated as nearly as possible in accordance with my understanding with his officers. During the night some changes were necessarily made in the positions of General Ord's troops—changes which are always consequent upon the movement of as large a body of men as a corps in the night; but every effort, in my opinion, was made by his officers, and also by my own, to carry out to the letter the instructions given by General Meade and by myself. Inasmuch as you will have an opportunity of examining both of these orders at your leisure, it will not be necessary for me to enter into the details as to the movements that were directed.

The action was to commence with the explosion of the mine, which was ordered to take place at half past three o'clock. It may not be amiss to state here that the mine had been ready charged since the 23d. General Potter was ordered to see that Colonel Pleasants exploded the mine at the time indicated by General Meade.

My order for the movement of the 30th stated that I would make my headquarters at the fourteen-gun battery, which is not far from the centre of the line occupied by the 9th corps. Just before leaving my permanent headquarters, say at two o'clock in the morning, there came from General Meade a despatch stating that if I desired to delay the time for the explosion of the mine in consequence of the darkness, I could do so. I telegraphed him back that the mine would be exploded at the hour designated. I went to the place designated as my headquarters at the proper time, and, like every one else, awaited with great anxiety the explosion of the mine. I need not say to this court that my anxiety on the occasion was extreme, particularly as I did not know the reason of the delay. I waited for several minutes, and thinking that there was some miscalculation as to the time it would take the fuze to burn up to the charge, I sent an aide-de-camp to find out what was the reason of the delay. Soon after that I sent a second aide-de-camp. Soon after that time Major Van Buren arrived at my headquarters and told me the cause of the delay. In the mean time Captain Sanders, I think, or some other one of General Meade's staff, came to my headquarters to know the reason. I said to him that I had sent to ascertain the reason; that I could not tell him then. Another despatch, either written or verbal, came to know the reason, and I sent word again that I did not known the reason, but as soon as I could ascertain it I would give the general the reason. I then got another despatch from General Meade, that if the mine had failed I must make a charge independent of the explosion of the mine. Having almost made up my own mind that the mine had failed, or that something had occurred which we could not discover during that morning, and feeling the absolute necessity, as General Meade expressed in his despatch, of doing something very quickly, I was on the eve of sending an order for the command to be ready to move forward, as directed by General Meade; but I said again, "I will delay, to ascertain what is the reason of the non-explosion of the mine."

I had nothing that I could report up to the time that Major Van Buren came to my headquarters. I gave to those aids freely the statement that I did not know the reason of the non-explosion of the mine, but that as soon as I learnt it I would inform the commanding general. As I before stated, Major Van Buren came to my headquarters and told me that the fuze had gone out, and that a gallant soldier named Sergeant Reese, of the 48th Pennsylvania, had volunteered to go into the gallery to ascertain whether the fuze was really burning still and burning slowly, or whether it had failed. He discovered that it had failed, and refired it; and Major Van Buren further said that General Potter had told him that the mine was to explode at a certain minute. This was, I think, within eleven minutes of the time of the explosion. I am not sure that I did not receive a similar message from an aide-de-camp to General Potter. I think I did.

Within one minute of the time designated by Major Van Buren—and it was a fact which was cognizant to every one—I was not with the advance column of troops that was to make the charge. I understand that there was considerable anxiety among the men, after and before the explosion, as to the effect it might have upon them, and I have been informed by Colonel Loring, my inspector general, (who may be called before this court,) who was with the column, that it took probably five minutes to get the men in perfect condition to dash forward. After their ranks were re-established, they went forward, as far as I could see or know, or hear, in the most gallant possible style, until they arrived within the crater. Here, owing to the inequalities of the ground, and possibly other reasons, which will be matters of investigation in this court, there was a pause, the men to a considerable extent disorganized, and it was so reported to me. I will state here, though, that I have not been able to make up my mind that any set of troops of this army, or any other army, that had gone through the labor that these troops had gone through for the last thirty days, could be made to do better than they did upon that occasion.

I saw with me there, at my headquarters, Captain Sanders. I think I remarked to him that I was glad he was to be with me on that day, as he had been with me during the fight on the 18th, and had been the means of communication between General Meade and myself; and I was very much pleased that he was present with me on that morning, and I think I so expressed myself. At all events, my impression was—he did not tell me so—that he was to remain with me during the morning. The despatches I received from General Meade, which I hope the court will examine carefully, bore the marks of very great anxiety—such as I was at the time feeling—to learn the information which I was about the same time endeavoring to learn, and at the same time unable to give him; and I so stated to his aides-de-camp. I, of course, was glad that no movement was made by me (as General Meade must be) in accordance with the order to attack in case the mine had failed.

From that time until the time that the troops were withdrawn I endeavored to give at all important points—I do not mean in minutiæ—to General Meade by telegraph, and to Captain Sanders by word, all the information of which I was possessed. I, of course, was in a position in which I could examine the movements of the troops. For half an hour at a time I would be away from my headquarters. I went with General Warren once down the covered way to the front. The covered way was full of troops, and there was no way of going on horseback or of carrying any number of staff officers; and from the positions we were to reconnoitre, it would not have been advisable to carry any number of officers to that point. The despatches that I sent to General Meade are, I think, on record; and I think, if carefully examined without reference to the numerous despatches I received from him, it will be ascertained that at every important epoch correct and definite information was sent to him, either by Captain Sanders or myself, up to the receipt of a despatch which was misunderstood by me, and which appears upon your record, and bears the positive certainty of insubordination, for which I must be responsible and must necessarily suffer. I will state the circumstances under which the despatch was given me. It was handed to me by Captain Jay, who came up to me and said, "General Meade desires me to say that this is for you personally," or words to that effect, no doubt meaning that it was for my personal attention. I misunderstood the tenor of it, no doubt; read it and put in my answer, which is also on record before you.

The orders that I gave from time to time to my division commanders were principally verbal orders given through my aides-de-camp. I had with each division a responsible aide-de-camp, who was in constant communication with me, and, if I mistake not, I did not receive from Generals Ferrero or Ledlie a single written despatch, and but one or two each from Generals Potter and Wilcox; but at the same time, I received verbally frequent information of all that was going on in order to enable me to direct the movements of my troops.

After giving orders for all the white troops to be shoved in, and sending additional orders forward, which were also reiterated by division commanders, for the troops to advance and move upon the crest in accordance with the understanding and plan of the night before, which were plain and distinct, I received from General Meade an order to put in my whole force and move for the crest at once. I had not done this because I was satisfied that there was very great difficulty attending the formation of the troops in the crater, in consequence of the great number there.

I have since learned that considerable progress had been made in the formation at that time; indeed, the troops were progressing to the right and left, and, to my knowledge, had driven the enemy; General Potter to the right, and General Wilcox to the left.

A despatch, which was intended for me, from Colonel Loring, went to my old headquarters, and was read by General Meade. I was cognizant of that fact, and I knew that General Meade was aware of the circumstances which surrounded the troops at that place, because General Meade sent an orderly with a message stating that he had read the despatch himself. It was therefore not necessary for me to re-communicate the information I had received from Colonel Loring. After my three divisions had been put into the position they occupied in the works, I hesitated to put in this colored division.

I remember having told General Meade that in case the colored division should falter in the advance, I did not think it would affect our old white divisions—certainly as to holding their position; that if the white divisions were to falter in the advance, it would be impossible to get the black division to pass them. I am not sure but I told him this the very day before the battle, in my tent. I received from General Meade an order to put in my whole force, which I did. I sent an order to General Ferrero to go to the top of the crest with his division. One of my aids was there at the time, Colonel Loring, and took the responsibilty of saying that that should be stopped, because he was satisfied that I had not received his despatch. He came to me, and I said my orders were peremptory to put in my whole command, and he himself told General Ferrero to put in his division at once, and go to the top of the crest if possible. The colored division was put in, and, from what I can learn, no officers or men behaved with greater gallantry than they did. After passing the white troops and attempting something like a formation they were driven back by the enemy, and driven through the white troops, the white troops, or the principal portion of them, still maintaining their position, fighting as gallantly as three divisions ever fought.

I witnessed this repulse myself, and at the same time saw that the enemy had been repulsed by our own white troops, the black troops coming to the rear to a very considerable extent.

There is one point to which I wish to call the attention of the court. I sent to General Meade a despatch at 6.20, stating that if General Warren's reserve force could be concentrated at that time, I thought it would be well, or something to that effect, and I would designate to him when that force should be put in. To that despatch you have the answer.

Not far from that time General Warren came himself to my headquarters, if not exactly at that time. I then said to him, "General, let us look at this position," having in view answering the question which General Meade desired me to answer. General Warren and I went down to the front, leaving my headquarters, and going down a covered way until we got to a position on the left-hand side of General Potter's covered way beyond. We got on a mound of earth, and reconnoitred the enemy's position until we were satisfied. I said to General Warren, "I think your plan would be to strike across by the fort which enfiladed our line," or something to that effect. At any rate, whatever opinion I expressed to General Warren, it is sufficient to say that he told me that he should go back and explain to General Meade the circumstances, and, if possible, to get him to come to the front and look for himself. That, of course, satisfied me with reference to that point of General Meade's inquiry.

Although this narrative is very disconnected, I believe I have stated in it all the material points.

I do not know of a single order of mine that was not carried out by my di vision commanders. I do not know of any lack of energy on their part in carrying out my views, and the views of the commanding general, except, possibly, in the case of General Ledlie, who was quite sick on that day, and who, I thought afterwards, ought to have gone to the crater the moment his men were in. But I understood that he was very sick, and could hardly have walked that far under the oppressive heat. He was within one hundred and twenty (120) yards of his brigades, I should say.

Between half past nine and ten o'clock I received two despatches from General Meade with reference to withdrawal. They are marked numbers 12 and 15 in the record before you. I was very much concerned in reference to the matter, because, although we had met with some reverses, I could not help feeling myself that we could hold the position which we occupied, if we could not gain more ground. In fact I was under the impression at the time that we were gaining ground in the direction of the enemy's rifle-pits to the right and left, and I felt that if troops were put in on our left flank, that then we would have been enabled to establish ourselves on the enemy's line, which, of course, would have made our position secure. However, that is simply a matter of opinion, upon which the commanding general had to decide. I also felt that if we could gain no more ground, we could run out lines at an angle to the crater, and establish a salient upon the enemy's lines, which would be of material advantage to us in future operations, particularly in making him vacate that part of the line which is now opposite my front, and in fact, as I had not given up all hopes of carrying the crest even, if a positive and decided effort were made by all the troops. But feeling disinclined to withdraw the troops, I got on my horse and rode over to General Meade's headquarters, which were at my permanent headquarters. He and General Grant were there together. General Ord and I entered the tent, and General Meade questioned General Ord as to the practicability of the troops being withdrawn. I made the remark that none of General Ord's troops were in the enemy's line, and he would have no trouble in withdrawing; that none but the troops of the ninth corps were in the line, and I thought that my opinion on that subject would probably be a proper one to be received, and I stated that I did not think that we had fought long enough that day; that I felt that the crest could still be carried if a decided effort were made to carry it. To that I received the reply that the order was final, or something to that effect.

General Meade, in his evidence, states that I gave no reasons why I thought the crest could be carried; and it will not be amiss for me to say that no reasons were asked, and that he simply stated that the order was final. I was then satisfied that the best time to withdraw those troops would be after nightfall; that it would be best to retain possession of the place till after nightfall. I thought, from reports which I had received from my aides-de-camp and division commanders, that we could then withdraw the troops. I had myself witnessed a very handsome repulse of the enemy by our troops just before leaving to go to General Meade's headquarters.

[At this point the court took a recess. After recess, General Burnside resumed his testimony, saying:]

I will supply one or two omissions in this disjointed narrative now. Some time before I received the order from General Meade to put in my whole force, I received a verbal message from General Wilcox, by one of his aids, Captain Brackett, that it was useless to send more troops up that line at that point; that all the troops were there that could be handled or could be used, or words to that effect; and that an immediate attack should be made, both upon our right and left. That is as far as I can remember of the message. I am under the impression I immediately transmitted this message to General Meade, either by a staff officer of my own, or by one of his. I also said that, in several conversations with General Meade, I stated to him that I was satisfied that the explosion of the mine in our front, and the advance of our troops, would enable a strong skirmish line to carry everything on the left. I am of the impression that I expressed that opinion to General Meade the day before the fight, in the presence of General Potter and General Wilcox. I know that I expressed it to him a half dozen times. After it had been decided by General Meade, finally, that the troops were to be withdrawn, I was necessarily very much exercised as to the best method of withdrawal. I had directed General White, who was acting on that day as chief of staff, to remain on the line until he heard from me, and that I would send him the result of my interview with General Meade. I wish to read here the despatch I sent him, and the accompanying note written by General White:

UNITED STATES MILITARY TELEGRAPH,
Headquarters Ninth Army Corps, July 30, 1864.

I have no discretion in the matter. The order is peremptory to withdraw. It may be best to intrench where we are for the present; but we must withdraw as soon as practicable and prudent.

A. E. BURNSIDE,
Major General.

Brigadier General WHITE,
Chief of Staff.

Division commanders will instruct in accordance with the within despatch; the officers on the line to consult and determine the time of evacuation.
By order of Major General Burnside:

J. WHITE,
Brigadier General and Chief of Staff.

Official:

EDWARD M. NIEL,
Assistant Adjutant General.

I sent for my division commanders after sending that despatch. Feeling confident, from the reports I had received, that our people would be able to hold the position which they then occupied, until night certainly, and feeling that, if they were not, one time for evacuation was about as good as another, I thought it best to have perfect understanding as to the method of withdrawal. They came to my headquarters, and it was decided that we should dig a trench or trenches from our main line to the crater, and thereby enable them to withdraw without serious loss. It will be remembered that this distance is but a little over one hundred yards, and taking into consideration the radius of the crater, it is probably less than that distance. General Wilcox had already given instructions, as he informed me, and as I know, to dig a trench connecting our advance line with the crater, and I am not sure that the other division commanders had not commenced like operations. I remember the fact being stated, at the conversation at my headquarters, that the work was going on; and that was decided upon as the best method of withdrawal. The despatch which I sent to General White, and which I have just handed to the court, was received by him in time to be read by two of the division commanders before they left the front for my headquarters, and was forwarded by them to the general officers in the crater.

One of those general officers was taken prisoner, and the other two are available as witnesses before this court. Their names are Generals Hartranft and Griffin. As to the effect of this despatch, I will leave it for the persons present to give evidence of, particularly as an important despatch from myself to General Meade, here, contains my opinion of it.

Adjourned till August 11.

FIFTH DAY.

Court Room, Headquarters Second Corps,
August 11, 1864.

The court met pursuant to adjournment.

Present: Major General Hancock, Brigadier Generals Ayres and Miles, and Colonel Schriver, judge advocate.

The proceedings of the 4th day were read (General Burnside's testimony first) and approved, after various corrections by General Burnside.

Generals Ferrero, Wilcox, and Potter were present also.

General Burnside's testimony continued:

In concluding my testimony, I simply desire to call the attention of the court to the fact that important evidence before them would indicate that I had not given proper information of what was going on in my front during the action on the 30th, and to say to them that, up to the time the mine was exploded, there was nothing possible for me to report, because I could not answer questions which General Meade propounded to me by one or two different despatches, except by saying that I did not know the reason for the delay, and as soon as I learnt it I would inform him of it, which I think I did by verbal communications, either by Captain Sanders or Captain Jay. As soon as I ascertained the cause of the delay, I requested Major Van Buren, who informed me of it, to state to Captain Jay, fully, the causes, and he will be able to state to you whether he did so or not.

The explosion of the mine, as I before said, was a fact evident to every one along the line, and each and every command there had its orders to do a certain work, which were so explicit as to enable them to move at once to that work: first, orders to corps commanders under General Meade; next, orders from corps commanders to their division commanders, and so on.

I reported to General Meade by despatch when we made a breach in the enemy's works, as will be seen by your record. I also reported to him soon after, in answer to probably frequent anxious despatches, that we were endeavoring to advance—that it was hard work, but that we hoped to succeed; which was the full extent of the knowledge then in my possession, and all that I could learn from personal observation of the contest in the neighborhood of the breach. Soon after he received the report of my inspector general, stating the condition of the troops in the crater, and in the rifle-pits to the right and left of it. This report was intended for me, but was opened by General Meade and sent to me by him. The obligation resting upon me to send him a copy was therefore removed, inasmuch as I knew that he had already seen its contents, from his own statement. I reported to him a short time after that, or just before, that I thought it was the proper time to concentrate General Warren's troops, and that I would indicate to him the time when I thought they ought to go in, for there was hardly room at that time for them to go in on our front. I received an answer from him stating the object of his despatch, and that he desired to know if it was practicable for General Warren's force to be put in upon our left. At about that time, certainly before I could determine the fact, I came into contact with General Warren personally at my headquarters, and he and I made the personal reconnoissance that has been before alluded to. I parted with General Warren with the distinct understanding that he was to report to General Meade the condition of affairs in his front, and, as I before said, with the statement that he would endeavor to get General Meade to come to the front himself, which I considered to be sufficient answer to General Meade's despatch, particularly as General Warren went directly from me to the telegraph office. It is possible that in this I made a mistake.

At another juncture I reported to him that I thought that was the time for General Warren to be put in promptly. Soon after that time, and before it would have been possible for me to have sent any other intelligent report, I received orders to withdraw the troops to our own intrenchments.

During the engagement General Meade also received from Captain Sanders, his aide-de-camp, who was at my headquarters, certainly three written despatches and one verbal despatch, which he acknowledges, independent of the verbal despatch which I speak of giving to him before the explosion of the mine. I desire to say that Captain Sanders was near me constantly; knows that I never failed to give an aide-de-camp, situated as he is, every possible information; heard all my conversations with my aides-de-camp, and I think had free access to every despatch and report that reached me from the front or from my division commanders. I learned personally, in presence of General Humphreys's chief of staff of the army of the Potomac, that that was the understanding of Captain Sanders.

There were some papers which I desired to have removed from the record of this court in consequence of certain conditions which surrounded them, and which this court has made a very proper decision upon; but as they form a portion of the record, it becomes necessary for me also to state some of the circumstances which surround one of these papers, which was a despatch sent by me to General Meade containing an objectionable remark, which will be recognized on the record by all the members of the court. In conversation with two mutual friends of General Meade and myself, I became satisfied that I had misunderstood the note which he had sent me from the front on that morning. I obtained permission to go to City Point to see General Grant, and I stated to him the circumstances of the case, among other things upon which we conversed. I left him with the understanding that I should return and withdraw the letter which I had written to General Meade. General Wilson, of the cavalry, was present at this interview. I returned to my headquarters and found upon my table charges preferred against me, and a request that I should be relieved from command in this army, against neither of which have I any complaint to make, but simply make this explanation to remove any responsibility from the shoulders of General Meade which might possibly attach to the letter which he wrote to me, and which I imagined at the time indicated a belief on his part that I was not disposed to tell him the truth on the day of the action.

When I went to my headquarters at my permanent camp, and learned from General Meade himself that the order to withdraw was final, I at the same time learned that offensive operations had ceased on both the flanks of the line which we had occupied, and to which we were ordered to withdraw.

I have stated to the court, as well as I knew how, the means taken by me to effect that withdrawal securely, with one exception, I think, which is, that I started General Ferrero off at once with definite instructions to put all the force that he could get to work to dig a trench or trenches from our old line to the crater, in order that our men might come out, and that he started off on the moment. What followed that will no doubt be inquired into by the court.

Soon after I learned that offensive operations were to cease on our flanks, it became evident that all the operations of this corps were to be independent. General Meade left my headquarters, making no request of me for information. I received no despatch from him until the evening of the day after which the troops were driven out of the crater, and to a certain extent were re-established in our own lines. The negligence on my part to report after that time I will not attempt to justify myself for, by any reasons, before this court, inasmuch as it will probably become the subject of charges pertaining to things that took place long after the troops had come inside of our own lines.

I should not dwell so fully upon my rule of conduct in matters of this kind, but for the fact that matters of a like nature have been elaborated upon in evidence which now lies before this court. I can readily conceive General Meade's anxiety, which would induce him to write frequent despatches; but in my rule of conduct with my officers I have rather cultivated the idea that frequent despatches, unless they are well authenticated, are not desirable—particularly despatches with reference to the condition of the troops and calls for re-enforcements.

I endeavored during my movements on that day to obey every order that was given to me. I put every single man of the 9th corps in action. I was not called upon to fight a field fight. There was no opportunity to manœuvre troops. There was no discretion about looking out for flanks beyond that which fell upon commanders managing their troops in action; there was simply an obligation on my part to rush these troops through the crater and gain the top of the crest, without reference to formation; and I put three divisions on as promptly as I knew how. And when I received the order to put my whole force in, I threw the fourth division in, with the most positive and distinct orders to my division commanders, given in the evidence before this court. I had no possible chance to push batteries forward to protect the flanks, or of moving troops forward to protect them; I simply had to gain the crest. I obeyed every order to the best of my ability, and did everything that I could do to place my troops in that position.

I have not elaborated as much as to the features of the ground in my front at the mine as I might have done, and I will not delay the court with it now. I will endeavor to make that as distinct as possible in my official report, which will probably be prepared by to-morrow morning, and will probably be laid before this court, together with the reports of the division and brigade commanders of my command.

I desire now to insert certain papers here, which relate to the evidence that I have given before you. The battle-order of General Meade is already before you. The document I now hand you is the circular containing the battle-order to my corps—(Document 60.) I sent a copy of this to General Ord, General Warren, and to the headquarters of the army, and I should have sent a copy to General Hancock had he been here at that time.

I present now the order for the siege, dated July 9, directing operations on this line, and desire to state, as the reason for presenting it, that the works on my front had been conducted with the understanding that there would be an attempt made to capture the position of the enemy by military operations, conducted under the chief engineer of this army and the chief of artillery, together with the corps commanders.—(Document 61.)

I now desire to present a copy of a correspondence between General Meade and myself early in July. The first is an answer of mine to a circular sent to corps commanders with a view to ascertaining what were the chances of the success of an assault in their fronts, and is as follows.—(Document 62.)

I beg to say here that this is specifically an answer in reference to an assault in my front, which was the only opinion I was required to give. The second document is General Meade's answer to my letter, and is as follows.—(Document 63.)

My reason for stating that my answer to General Meade was semi-official, and that the whole correspondence was of that nature, was the fact that it is marked at the top "confidential." The despatches sent by General Meade to me were marked likewise, but in this copy that is omitted. The envelopes, at least, were marked "confidential."—(Document 64.)

Questions by the judge advocate:

Question. Were you in a position to see all the operations of the assault before Petersburg, or how much of them?

Answer. I was in a position, at different times, to see every particle of the assault before Petersburg—at one time in one position, at another in another. Not that I desire to convey the impression that I was all the time looking to the front; but that, at proper intervals of time, I could see all that was desirable to see.

Question. What was the distance from the fourteen-gun battery to the crater?

Answer. I should say six hundred or six hundred and fifty yards. I wish to state that, whilst at my headquarters, in order to get a look at what was going on on certain portions of the front, we placed ourselves upon the magazine of the fort, or upon the high ground just in rear of the fort, or upon the high ground just to the right or left of the fort. I was, however, frequently to a considerable extent in advance of the fort, as was the case when General Warren and myself made our reconnoissance; and I also visited a commanding position on the opposite side of General Potter's covered way during the engagement, from which other parts of the line could be seen. The fort I refer to is the fourteen-gun battery, which is established immediately in rear of the old brick wall and chimneys, and is essentially on our main line, say fifty yards to the rear. The advance line is about one hundred and fifteen yards from the crater; the main line is about four hundred yards from that, and then the battery is a short distance, say fifty yards, in rear of the main line. But the position from which most of the movements could be seen was in advance of the main line, between the two lines.

Question. What preparations were made for the passage of the attacking columns from the breastworks, as directed by General Meade's order?

Answer. All the preparations were directed to be made that were possible, such as removing *abatis*, and so forth, as directed by General Meade's order; but it was not expected by any one that any considerable success could attend any work of that kind without serious loss to the command, and discovery on the part of the enemy. The *abatis* in front, which was the only serious obstruction, was very much cut up by the enemy's fire, and did not present as serious an obstacle to the movement of troops as it would be supposed by a person hearing that the *abatis* still remained in front of the line. I have never ascertained from any one that the troops were at all obstructed in passing over, and I am therefore free to say I made no special inquiry upon that subject. If I remember right, it is the first time it has occurred to me since the reading of General Meade's order; but I do remember that not much was expected to be done, in view of our close proximity to the enemy. This refers to the front, over which the troops had to pass. I will state definitely that there was no expectation on my part that that portion of the order could be carried out without discovery, and without very great harm to the troops that would have to prepare this work, and in my order I placed no clause of that nature; but it was distinctly understood that the troops were to be provided with pioneer tools and other means of clearing away such obstructions as might be in the way—understood between myself and the division commanders.

Question. Did you intend that the obstructions should not be removed until the pioneers advanced with the columns, or did you intend that they were to be removed by the division commanders the night before, and what division commanders were charged with the execution of that order?

Answer. I did not intend any of my division commanders to do any work in the way of removing obstructions on that night, because I did not expect that they could do it; and, besides, I was ordered to be relieved on the line by General Ord's troops, and to concentrate my troops for the assault. But I will state again that there was an understanding between the division commanders and myself that anything that could be done in that direction would be done. I did not expect them to do anything; there was no order to that effect from me, unless it was contained in my verbal orders to the division commanders. My remarks now apply to work on the advance line, where I did not suppose any work could be done without discovery by the enemy, in consequence of its close proximity to the enemy's line to the front of the main line. There were covered ways cut both to General Wilcox's and to General Potter's front.

Question. What time elapsed from the springing of the mine to the forward movement of the assaulting columns, and how long was it before the crater was reached by the storming party?

Answer. At the risk of involving the same difference in time as in similar matters, I will state that it was about five minutes until the advance column moved forward, and say ten minutes before the leading column reached the crater. This delay occurred in consequence of the hesitation which has been already alluded to in my evidence, but not personally known to me, and it is not impossible that I may be mistaken as to the time. There was only one column started to move to the crater, because the divisions were ordered to go in succession, the first division, General Ledlie commanding, leading, in consequence of the probability that a breach would not be made sufficiently broad in the enemy's line to admit more than one column, my intention up to the day of the attack being to make the assault by my plan, which you have before you.

Question. To what did you attribute the halting of the troops in the crater instead of proceeding to the crest immediately as by the order?

Answer. To the breaking up of the column in consequence of the inequality of the ground, and to the continual habit of the men for the last thirty or forty days of protecting themselves by almost every obstruction they came in contact with.

Question. In what order and tactical formation were your divisions ordered to to go in?

Answer. I ordered the division commanders to use their discretion in carrying their divisions in, giving them my general views on the subject, my general directions being to carry them in if possible in column by regiments; but the regiments being so unequal—some being not more than one hundred strong, and some six or seven hundred—it was thought best for them to go in in such formation as to be able to deploy rapidly in two lines as soon as they gained the crest, General Ledlie taking the centre, General Potter taking the line perpendicular to the main line of works, and General Wilcox the line parallel to the Jerusalem plank road.

Question. Were these movements of the divisions successive or simultaneous?
Answer. They were successive.
Question. What was the interval between them?

Answer. General Ledlie was to move first; General Wilcox was to follow General Ledlie as soon as possible after General Ledlie had cleared the breach; then General Potter was to follow General Wilcox. As soon as I ascertained that General Ledlie had made a halt, I sent orders at once to General Wilcox and to General Potter to proceed, without reference to General Ledlie, in the order in which they had been directed to move. I ordered them to go in at once without reference to going through the breach, and proceed at once, as before directed, without reference to General Ledlie, thinking that if they could find room to get through to the right and left, and could move forward, it would enable General Ledlie also to move forward with his troops. And, finally, General Ferrero was moved, upon the last order from General Meade to put in my whole force. I think that the troops were moved forward as rapidly as they could be moved forward under the circumstances, and I know that they did not pass by the flanks of General Ledlie to go to the crest; but it was in consequence of obstacles produced by the firing of the enemy and the rough ground in the crater of the enemy's works. But they did go to the right and left, driving away a considerable portion of the enemy from those lines, and made several distinct attempts to charge to the front. My own opinion is, that the principal obstacle was the presence of the enemy to our right and left, which enabled them, the moment our troops attempted to advance to the top of the crest, to give them a fire in the rear.

Question. For what distance on each side of the crater were the enemy's works abandoned immediately after the explosion of the mine?

Answer. I should say one hundred and fifty yards, or more, on each side.

Question. To your own personal knowledge did any of your troops get beyond the crater, and how far towards the crest?

Answer. As far as I could see, there were lines formed beyond the crater, and attempts made to charge, but the lines were repulsed; but to say how far, I would not be willing to express an opinion.

Question. Can you tell how far it was from the crater to the crest?

Answer. From the crater to the crest, I should say was five hundred yards.

Question. How long did your troops remain in the crater before the order was given to retire?

Answer. The order was given to retire, I think, about half past nine. When the order was given to retire, I went to General Meade's headquarters, consulted with him, ascertained that it was final, and decided that our best method of retiring was to hold the crater until dark, and then retire by trenches.

(The question was repeated, and the witness requested to give a more specific answer.)

Question. How long did your troops remain in the crater before the order was given to retire?

Answer. They remained there until about two o'clock. I think the order reached them about 11.40. They remained there about four hours before the order was given to me to retire.

Question. Did Generals Wilcox's and Potter's divisions attack the crest, or did they proceed perpendicularly along the enemy's intrenchments to the right and to the left?

Answer. The principal part of their movements was in that direction, with all possible directions to move to the front as fast as possible.

Question. Had you authority to put in the supports, (of other corps,) or had any one else who was present and could see what was going on?

Answer. Although I can designate no order upon which I had a right to put in supports, yet I am satisfied that any support which I called upon General Ord for would have been given me; and it is almost impossible that there was such an order. At all events, he expressed every willingness to give me all the support possible, no matter what the movements of his troops were, and consulted freely with me, and asked me at what points I thought he ought to put his corps in. I told him I thought it could move off to our right, and make a very considerable diversion in our favor, or something to that effect, and he told me that he had issued an order to that effect. He spoke of the ground being broken in that direction, and wanted to know if I thought he could go over my line of works. I told him I thought he could; that it is the same ground that Generals Wilcox and Potter fought over on the 18th, and that a portion of his column could move forward in that direction, the balance moving down the covered way.

Question. Were you the senior officer present, and did you regard yourself responsible for putting in at the proper time the troops designated as supports in orders?

Answer. I was the senior officer present in front of my own corps; but I never dreamed of having any authority whatever to order in the troops of any other corps. I might have had authority to call upon other troops, but I had no authority to order any in that I know of.

Question. You don't consider yourself responsible for anything further than your own corps?

Answer. No, sir, except as to making such suggestions as I thought were proper. I did not think that I had any general command that day. In fact, I had no authority to order in any other troops than my own corps, General Meade having specially reserved that right to himself in the correspondence before you.

The court then adjourned to meet at 10 o'clock a. m. on the 12th instant.

SIXTH DAY.

COURT ROOM, HEADQUARTERS SECOND CORPS,
August 12, 1864.

The court met pursuant to adjournment.

Present: Major General Hancock, Brigadier Generals Ayres and Miles, and Colonel Schriver, judge advocate.

The proceedings of the fifth day were read and approved.

The testimony of Major General Burnside was resumed.

Questions by the judge advocate:

Question. What brigade commanders were in and about the crater near the enemy's line?

Answer. All the brigade commanders of the corps, I think.

Question. What division commanders?

Answer. I do not know positively that any division commander was in the crater, unless possibly General Potter. Their headquarters were upon the advance line, something over one hundred yards from the crater.

Question. Please describe the covered ways through which the troops passed from the rear up to your line, how long they were, and their direction with reference to your line of works.

Answer. Both the covered ways were, in general direction, perpendicular to the advance line, particularly just before approaching it. There were advantages taken of the depression of the ground in rear that made certain portions of them at angles to the line—some obtuse and some acute. The covered ways were built so as to enable columns to move under comparatively good shelter entirely up to our advance line, or, in other words, to the low ground just in rear of our advance line, and were capable of allowing regiments to pass by twos if not by fours. The commencement of all the covered ways was in the depressed ground in rear of the main line, or, in other words, in rear of the fourteen-gun battery; and I should think that they would average, including the zigzag, a thousand yards.

Question. In what formation did the colored troops move to the assault?

Answer. The colored troops moved from their position in rear of our advance line by flank up to the position we had carried in the enemy's line, and from there endeavored to move in line to the front.

Question. Could General Ord's troops get into action at any other point than at the crater?

Answer. I received positive information from General Potter that his troops were not in the way, and that General Ord's could have moved to the right, and I distinctly understood from General Ord that he had given orders for his troops to move to the right of the ground that we occupied. As to how many obstacles they would have met in that movement I am not here prepared to say. I am satisfied of one thing, that General Ord gave the necessary orders for an advance in that direction. As to the efforts that were made, I am not personally cognizant. General Potter, who held the right of our line, is a more intelligent witness upon that point than I am.

Question. Did any officer report to you that his troops could not be got forward?

Answer. No, sir. I received a report from Colonel Loring, which General Meade opened, stating to me that there was great difficulty in getting the troops to move from that crater, or something to that effect. That paper is lost, as far as I can find. I have ordered it to be looked for. But Colonel Loring was not a commander of troops; he was an aide-de-camp of mine. But no commander of troops reported to me that his troops could not be brought forward.

Question. Please state what were the obstacles, *abatis* or other obstacles, in front of the enemy's line in the neighborhood of the crater. Were they a serious opposition to the passage of troops?

Answer. On the right and left of the crater, beyond the parts that had been effected by the explosion, there were both *abatis* and *chevaux-de-frise*, principally the latter, constructed by placing rails in the parapet, sharpening the points, and, I suppose, tying them back, or putting in sticks, to hold them in their positions; but of that I cannot say, because I was not close enough to determine that fact. Considerable *abatis* was in one portion of the line, lying upon these rails, which the enemy had not been able to place in consequence of the constant fire from our troops in the front line. I do not think the obstacle was remarkably formidable, but it was a sufficient obstacle to stop the progress of troops. There would have been a necessity for their removal by pioneers before troops could have passed over.

Question. How much of the enemy's breastworks were blown up by the springing of the mine? How much of the *abatis* destroyed?

Answer. The report of Colonel Pleasants will be before you, and he will give you that exactly. I should place it at from one hundred and forty-five to one hundred and fifty feet—say one hundred and fifty feet. There was not as much of their line disturbed as I expected. I supposed that for a considerable distance on the right and left of the line the earth would have been so much disturbed as to cause *chevaux-de-frise* to fall from the parapet.

Question. Was the ground around the crater commanded by the ground held by the enemy?

Answer. Yes, sir, to a very great extent.

Question. What was your opinion at the time of the force of the enemy resisting your advance on the 30th of July?

Answer. From data received by me, and especially from a despatch received very soon before the order to withdraw came, I judged there was about a division and a half, certainly not to exceed two divisions. This force consisted of troops that were in the line when the mine was exploded, and troops that were moved from the enemy's right. No troops were reported to me as having moved from the enemy's left. There was a signal station in front of my line from which, I think, any important movement of troops from the enemy's left could have been discovered. They certainly could not have approached our line from the enemy's left without being observed. I received a despatch from my signal officer, Captain Paine, stating that the enemy's right was very much weakened. This was not communicated to me direct, inasmuch as I had left my headquarters to visit General Potter's, and it did not reach me in time to communicate the substance of it to General Meade before the orders to withdraw came.

Question. What was the nature of the enemy's fire concentrated on the crater, immediately after the explosion of the mine—how much artillery fire? Please explain that, if you know.

Answer. The artillery fire was very light indeed, and had the advance troops been in condition to assault, and made the kind of an assault that they could have made, or that they had made in the beginning of the campaign, there is no doubt in my mind but they could have gained the crest. For a long time, comparatively speaking, the fire, both of musketry and artillery, was very light. What I mean by a long time is fifteen minutes, say.

Question. Why did not your troops remain, as you wished, to hold the crater, and for what purpose did you propose to hold it?

Answer. I received a positive order to withdraw to our intrenchments. I left my chief of staff with a view to getting that order rescinded. Finding that it was final, I telegraphed to him to that effect, and he communicated to the general officers in the crater that the order was final. In fact, he sent a copy of my telegram to them. My reason for desiring to hold the crater was, that if we could have connected it with diagonal lines reaching from a point, say one hundred and fifty yards to the right, to General Potter's extreme left, and another line extending to it from our old line one hundred and fifty yards from General Wilcox's extreme right, we would have a salient which would have been quite as easy to hold, if not more easy, than the one we now hold, and would have given us, I think, command of a considerable portion of the enemy's line both on our right and left, forcing him, I think, even if we had made no further attempt to carry the crest, to move his whole line back to that position.

Question. You have said somewhere in the testimony that 3,828 was the 9th corps's loss. At what phase of the action did the loss chiefly occur?

Answer. I have already given a detailed account of the killed, wounded, and prisoners. A large proportion of the prisoners were lost after the order to withdraw had been received, and I think a considerable portion of the killed and wounded. I will not venture to say now that so great a proportion occurred after that time as was indicated in the despatch sent by me to General Meade, and which is now before the court; but that was not far wrong, in my opinion.

Question. Why were the men withdrawn at the time they were?

Answer. The despatch stating that there was a final order to withdraw had reached the crater, and it was known to both officers and men that such a despatch was in existence. At the last assault of the enemy, General Hartrauft gave the order to his command to withdraw, and sent word down the line that he had given this order; and such portion of the command as could get out of the crater and the enemy's lines returned to our own lines. General Hartrauft was not, in fact, authorized to make such a movement; but I have not the slightest doubt in my own mind but he thought he was carrying out the spirit of the order. It was one of those misunderstandings which are so likely to happen at so critical a time. He had before reported that they would be able to hold their position, which report was made previous to any knowledge on his part of the fact that we were ordered peremptorily to withdraw.

Question. Did any troops, to your knowledge, misbehave, fail to go forward when ordered, or disobey orders in any way or at any time during the action? If so, name them.

Answer. A considerable portion of the troops failed to go forward after repeated orders from their officers and extreme efforts to cause them to advance; but I do not believe that, under the circumstance, any of the troops can be counted guilty of misbehavior. It is a fact that the black troops broke and ran to the rear in considerable of a panic, which indicates misbehavior; but they went in late, found in the enemy's works quite a mass of our own troops unable to advance, and during their formation, and, in fact, during their advance between the two lines, they were subjected to probably the hottest fire that any troops had been subjected to during the day; and I do not know that it is reasonable to suppose that after the loss of so great a portion of their officers they could have been expected to maintain their position. They certainly moved forward as gallantly under the first fire, and until their ranks were broken, as any troops I ever saw in action.

Question. Who conducted the retirement of the troops from the crater?

Answer. That question is entirely answered by the answer to the question previously put, but I will reiterate it. General Hartrauft, unexpectedly to me and to the division commanders, made a move with his brigade in consequence of the receipt of the despatch to which I have referred, and the word was passed along the line to retire, upon which all the troops came back to our lines that could get back.

Question. Where were the division commanders while the troops were in the crater?

Answer. The division commanders were at their headquarters on our old advance line, say one hundred and fifteen yards from the crater, moving at intervals from one point to another at that line, until it was decided that the order to withdraw was final, when I sent for the division commanders to come to my headquarters to arrange for the withdrawal; soon after which I sent General Ferrero to make arrangements for digging trenches. In fact, preparations had already been made for that purpose before the division commanders came to my headquarters. Before this work could be done the troops were driven from the crater in the manner in which I have designated.

By the court:

Question. How did all your troops cross from the advance line of works to the assault—by the flank or in line?

Answer. Generals Ledlie and Wilcox crossed in line; Generals Potter and Ferrero by flank.

Question. Could the troops of the different divisions have been formed, the night previous to the assault, in lines parallel to the advance line, and near it?

Answer. They were formed in that position as nearly as possible, all of the advanced division being formed exactly in that way.

Question. Was the mine placed under charge of the engineer department of the army of the Potomac?

Answer. No, sir, it was not. In fact, two of the young engineers who reported for duty at my headquarters stated expressly that they were instructed that they had nothing to do with the mine.

Question. Were there working parties detailed to follow the assaulting troops, carrying tools, gabions, and so forth, to crown the crest when gained?

Answer. Yes, sir. There was an engineer regiment detailed to follow each division of white troops, with all the necessary tools; and all necessary preparations were made for pioneers in the division of colored troops. There were no instructions to carry gabions, but all these engineer regiments were fully equipped with necessary tools for intrenching, if we had been successful in crowning the crest.

Question. Why did not the division commanders go to the front, particularly when the troops ceased to advance?

Answer. I do not know.

Question. Was General Hartrauft in command in the crater?

Answer. He was not in command in the crater.

Question. Had you been permitted to put your corps into action according to your own views—that is, the colored division in advance—do you think the result would have been different?

Answer. For reasons already given, and given before the fight, and from observations on that day, I am forced to believe that the fourth division (the colored division) would have made a more impetuous and successful assault than the leading division.

The receipt of orders requiring the presence elsewhere of two members of the court caused its adjournment until it should be reconvened by the President, or some other proper authority.

11

SEVENTH DAY.

HEADQUARTERS SECOND CORPS,
Jones House, August 29, 1864.

The court met, pursuant to the orders from the President, at ten o'clock a. m. Present: Major General Hancock, Brigadier Generals Ayres and Miles, and Colonel Schriver, judge advocate.

The proceedings of the sixth day were read and approved.

The judge advocate submitted a letter which he received from Major General Burnside, respecting his testimony, as follows:

"COLEMAN'S EUTAW HOUSE,
"*Baltimore, August* 15, 1864.

"COLONEL: You will remember that, in answering the last question put to me as to the reason none of my division commanders went into the crater, I made some explanation after saying 'I don't know;' but it was finally decided to let the answer be, 'I don't know.'

"Lest it may be understood to be a censure upon those officers, I beg to add to the answer the following: I think General Potter was in the crater, and I am satisfied that the others felt that they were in the best position to command, except General Ledlie, who, I understood, was sick. The court can determine.

"Please lay this before the court, and believe me yours, very truly,
"A. E. BURNSIDE, *Major General.*

"These officers, with the exception of General Ledlie, have served with me long and gallantly, and I do not desire to do aught to injure their well-earned reputation.

"COLONEL SCHRIVER,
"*Inspector General, Army of the Potomac, Judge Advocate, &c.*"

Record of the court of inquiry instituted by Special Order No. 258, 1864, *War Department.*

	Page.
Testimony of Major I. C. Duane, United States Engineers	128
" Brigadier General R. B. Ayres, United States Volunteers	133
" Major General G. K. Warren, United States Volunteers	137
" Lieutenant General U. S. Grant, United States Army	148
" Lieutenant Colonel C. B. Comstock, Aide-de-Camp	150
" Major General E. O. C. Ord, United States Volunteers	153
" Brigadier General R. B. Potter, United States Volunteers	167
" Brigadier General E. Ferrero, United States Volunteers	179
" Brigadier General O. B. Wilcox, United States Volunteers	185
" Major General A. A. Humphreys, United States Volunteers	188
" Brigadier General H. I. Hunt, United States Volunteers	191
" Lieutenant W. H. Beuyaurd, United States Engineers	194

Major I. C. DUANE, engineer corps, sworn, says to questions by the judge advocate:

Question. Were you present at the assault of the 30th of July, and in what capacity did you serve?

Answer. It was on the 5th corps front, assisting in directing the artillery fire.

Question. Can you produce maps showing the lines then occupied by the armies?

Answer. Yes, sir. I here produce two maps, showing the general positions of the armies, and the position of the 9th corps in detail. These maps are marked Nos. 65 and 66, appendix.

Question. What, in your opinion, were some of the causes of failure on that occasion?

Answer. One cause was, that the troops, instead of moving up by division front, (column of division,) moved up by the flank. Another was, that they stopped in the crater, instead of pushing immediately forward. The points between which they could have taken on the ridge are the points on the map between Clark's house and Cemetery hill. Those being taken Petersburg, was in our possession. I have no doubt the enemy had guns in that position, but I do not know that he had any works; if there were any works there, they were screened by the trees. No guns were opened immediately after the assault. The distance from the crater to the crest is about five hundred yards.

Question. Could the troops have gone forward by division front?
Answer. I think they could if proper working parties had been sent to remove the abatis.

Question. Were there any working parties with them?
Answer. I do not know. I was directed not to interfere with General Burnside in his operations. I had no control over the operations in that part of the line.

Question. Were there engineer officers to lead or direct the assaulting columns?
Answer. Lieutenant Beuyaurd, of the engineers, was on duty on that front, and was available in case the general commanding that corps wished to make use of an engineer. Captain Farquhar was also on duty with the 18th corps, and was present, but not under my orders.

Question. What arrangements were made for facilitating the debouch of the troops from our lines and passage over the enemy's parapets?
Answer. I do not know.

Question. Were the obstructions at the enemy's line formidable? Of what did they consist?
Answer. They consisted of a strong rifle-pit, with a good abatis in front. Such obstructions are formidable, in case there are troops behind the parapets to defend them. In this instance there did not appear to be sufficient force behind the parapet to prevent these works being carried.

Question. How was our artillery fire as to effectiveness on that occasion?
Answer. It completely silenced the batteries of the enemy that were in position, and had been in position previous to this day, on the 5th corps front. I had nothing to do with the right, which was on the 18th corps line.

Question. In your opinion, was the point of attack a judicious one?
Answer. I did not consider it so, although there was a chance of success The point of attack was on a re-entrant on the line, which exposed an attacking column to a fire on both flanks and front.

Question. Did you at any time make that known to the authorities?
Answer. I did, two or three days previous to the attack.

Question. In written or verbal communications?
Answer. I had frequently made it known verbally; two days previous to the attack, in writing, to the general commanding the army of the Potomac.

Question. Can you produce that report?
Answer. I can; and I will hand it to the judge advocate. (It is marked 67.)

Question. What is your opinion of the mine as a means of assault?
Answer. It is a very unusual way of attacking field fortifications. I do not think that there was any reasonable chance of success by such an attack.

Question. Had the engineer department anything to do with it?
Answer. It had not.

Question. Please to state what advantage would have resulted from holding the crater simply?
Answer. No advantage.

By the court:

Question. Did you see this explosion and assault?
Answer. I saw the explosion. I did not see the assault distinctly; I was too far to the left.

Question. You could not see how far to the right or left the enemy's parapet was abandoned from any fire that came from it?
Answer. No, sir.
Question. What artillery of the enemy did you see open and play upon that assaulting column within the first fifteen minutes after the explosion?
Answer. I did not see any. They opened on our batteries, but I did not see them open on the column. I did not see them open on the column, and do not think they did. They opened with 30-pounders on us.
Question. Although you did not think the mine, as a means of assault, promised much success, do you believe, from the circumstances that transpired, it would have been a success had the troops gone to the top of the crest?
Answer. I believe it would.
Question. Do you believe that there was any difficulty in the way of the troops going to the crest during the first fifteen minutes?
Answer. I do not think there was the slightest difficulty.
Question. Do you think that, immediately after the explosion, had there been proper working parties at work, the parapet of the enemy could have been cleared of sufficient of the obstructions and abatis within the first fifteen minutes to have allowed a brigade front to have passed over?
Answer. Yes; I think there could.
Question. There was no other difficulty in crawling over the parapet except the fire?
Answer. No, sir; and the abatis was a loose abatis of limbs pitched over the parapet. In some places it was a rail abatis—rails inclined forward.
Question. What should the storming party have done when they reached the crest, had they reached it? what should have been their first operation—to have proceeded to Petersburg or intrenched themselves?
Answer. I think they should have intrenched on the crest. I do not think they could have stayed in Petersburg, as it was commanded.
Question. Had you ever been called upon for any gabions or any materials for making a parapet upon the enemy's intrenchments?
Answer. No, sir.
Question. Were any gabions prepared in this army except by the engineer department for those works?
Answer. None.
Question. Nor any other material of that kind—facines, and so forth—to assist in making a parapet?
Answer. No.

Brigadier General R. B. AYRES, United States volunteers, sworn by the judge advocate:

Question. General, were you present at the assault on the 30th of July, and had you facilities for seeing the progress of affairs on that day?
Answer. My division was a part of the command of the 5th corps, massed upon the right of the 5th corps, and upon the left of the 9th, in the railroad cut, for purposes indicated in the order of assault. I was directed by General Warren to make my headquarters with his at the five-gun battery, in the corner of the woods in front of the Avery house. I was in that position when the mine was sprung and the assaulting columns went forward. The general directions of those columns as they marched forward were visible from this position. As the troops filed out we could see them distinctly. After quite a large force filed out there, they seemed to have formed a line of battle at one time along, in, or near the enemy's rifle-pits, adjacent to the mine. A body of troops also filed behind that line to the left, as we looked at them, apparently to march around

the line and advance to the crest, which was the object to be gained—Cemetery hill. After a time I saw those troops go back again towards the right, coming in still behind that line of battle standing. Directly after this I was requested by General Warren to ride to the 15-gun battery, to see what chance offered me to put my division in on the left of the troops still standing, as I described. I went there, made an examination, turned to General Warren and stated to him that as the troops were massed in our old line in rear of the mine in great crowds it would be very difficult to march my division through there unless they made a way for me; but if a way was made I could march my division by the flank, face it to the left, sweep down to the left, carry a certain battery there was firing across, and clean out the rifle-pits they occupied. General Warren rode with me a second time there, immediately after this. First, my division was ordered to be closed up as soon as possible, to be in readiness; then we rode together to the 15-gun battery. As we crossed the field between this 5-gun battery and the 15-gun battery I saw the negro troops coming back to the rear like a sand-slide. By the time we got to the corner of the 15-gun battery numbers of them were sweeping through that—sweeping around from different quarters; some one side and some another, some into the covered ways and some into the field between. A close observation assured me that that line of battle which I first described was replaced by the enemy in the rifle-pits on the right of the mine. I saw their battle-flags, and their bullets fell around us. Some one then proposed that General Warren should immediately put in the 5th corps at that moment. General Warren and myself concluded that the time was passed; they had lost what they had, excepting those men who were left in the crater. And immediately after that we rode to our position at the 5-gun battery, and I received notice that the movement was suspended, and a few moments after orders to send my division to its camp.

Question. Please to relate some of the chief causes of failure on that occasion.

Answer. Firstly, those troops that went to make their attack seemed to be going out simply by the right flank from two covered ways; therefore, the heads of regiments arrived at the crater in that condition, when there should have been a line of battle arriving there. These men rushed into the crater, and a considerable amount of time was lost in endeavoring to get troops in some formation to advance properly in line of battle. Arrangements should have been made, that when that mine was sprung the troops which were to make the assault to carry the crest, which looked down upon the city, should advance in line of battle, so that they would have been in hand and subject to the command of their officers. That, in my judgment, was the principal cause of the failure. The commencement of the assault, in my judgment, was the cause of its entire failure. If those dispositions had been made, and those troops had advanced in line of battle instead of in columns of regiments, I believe they would have taken that crest. There was a great deal of work which should have been done along our old line nearest to the crater and to the south of the line of the gallery, so that troops could have really marched forward at least in two regiments abreast. That being done, and those troops advanced as I described, I believe they would have taken that crest readily, and I believe that then, if the supports had been thrown in promptly, that crest would have been held and success would have crowned the operation. After it was clear that the thing had failed I think that prompt orders should have been given to withdraw, in one rapid movement, all the troops left in the crater, to bring them out in one body rapidly back to their lines.

Major General G. K. WARREN, United States volunteers, being duly sworn, says:

By the judge advocate:

Question. General, were you present at the assault on the 30th July, the day the mine was sprung, near this place; and if so, in what capacity?

Answer. I was there in command of the 5th corps.

Question. Will you please to state what, in your opinion, were some of the chief causes of that failure?

Answer. To mention them all at once, I never saw sufficient good reasons why it should succeed. I never had confidence in its success. The position was taken in reverse by batteries, and we must, as a matter of course, have expected a heavy fire of artillery when we gained the crest, though we did not get near enough to develop what that would be. I never should have planned it, I think.

Question. As it was planned, had you an opportunity of seeing whether the plan was carried out in the best manner—the plan having been adopted?

Answer. I can mention some faults. There was a great defect, I think, in the preparation for the movement of the assaulting column. I judge so from the way the column moved, as I did not visit the exact point. And second, I think the first force, instead of moving straight on the hill, should have cleared the intrenchments right and left of the crater, so as not to have exposed the advancing column to a flank fire. I tried to make a similar assault there on the 18th of June, and that very same battery that operated on the left flank of Burnside's force that day was in operation on the previous occasion, and stopped all my efforts.

Question. Could you mention that battery particularly by showing it on the map, or designating it in some way?

Answer. It is the first battery on the south side of the mine.

Question. Was our artillery fire effective on that occasion?

Answer. As much so as it could be. I heard Colonel Abbot complain that a group of trees in front of one of his large batteries was left standing, and it was his desire to have it cleared away.

Question. Did he say whose business it was to clear it away? Did he find fault with any one? In whose front was it?

Answer. In General Burnside's front. I remember he said General Burnside had told him that he was afraid clearing it away might disclose his intention; but I do not think that he said whose fault it was that it was not done, or whether it was a fault, except in interfering with his battery.

By the court:

Question. Aside from any general principle with reference to the matter upon which you predicated the chances of success, do you think that after the mine exploded there really was a chance of success?

Answer. There are so many ifs in it. If we could have carried that first line of rifle-pits, and then maintained ourselves after we got to the crest, we would have had success; but I do not believe any troops will stand on an open plain with artillery, covered by redoubts, playing upon them; and I think that is what the enemy had then, or ought to have had, if they did not. If they have been there all this time without that preparation, they are much more unprepared than I think they are.

Question. Did they open much artillery fire for the first fifteen minutes or half hour after the explosion?

Answer. I should say not a great deal, not where I was; only a very little. There was no particular danger in my vicinity for a group of horsemen standng right out in plain sight, as we did all the time. Their batteries were mainly placed for enfilading any line attacking, and probably reserved their fire until that line approached.

Question. Aside from that operation of the 9th corps, if the 5th corps, supported by another, could have been thrown round on the enemy's right, occupying those two railroads and turning his right, what was the chance of success in that direction?

Answer. It would be impossible for me to say. I do not know what the nature of their defences was in that direction. I believe, from what I have heard, that the very brigade which repulsed General Burnside was located there in the morning, and my corps at that time had no force in reserve, except General Ayres's division and a brigade of General Crawford's and a brigade of General Cutler's.

Question. Was there any force of the enemy there strong enough to resist the number of troops we had disposable, had they been put in properly after the first assault had failed?

Answer. I can answer that question and cover a little more. When we attacked, in the first operation on Petersburg, we had more force than on this occasion, and the enemy had about the same, I think; and I don't believe that the blowing up of the mine made up for the difference in the increased strength of the earthworks, as they were on the 18th of June and the 30th of July; and if the operation of the 18th of June decided anything, I think it decided that the operation of the 30th of July would have met with the same result.

Question. Did you feel the want of any person on the field who could see for himself and give commands on the spot? Had that any effect upon the result? Or do you think that any person ought to have been present who should have had command of the storming party and all the troops ready to take part in the operation?

Answer. I think some one should have been present to have directed my command as well as General Burnside's and General Ord's—some one person; but whether that would have affected the result or not I am not prepared to say.

Question. Did you experience any uncertainties and doubts for the want of such a person's presence there?

Answer. Yes.

Question. Were there moments when such a person's presence was necessary in order to decide at once what should be done?

Answer. I think it was necessary that some one should have been there. If you have my official report it will show you that I was in doubt whether to move to the left or move to the right to help General Burnside, and that I had to await the transmission of despatches and corresponding answers—my report shows how much; but I do not know that that would have affected the main result at all. My report is a complete answer to your question. Sometimes, in these badly planned or badly inaugurated assaults, the longer and better they are pressed the worse we are off—great losses being sustained after the time and chance of success are gone.

The court adjourned, to meet at 10 o'clock a. m. on 30th August.

EIGHTH DAY.

HEADQUARTERS SECOND CORPS,
Jones House, August 30, 1864.

The court met pursuant to adjournment.

Present: Major General Hancock, Brigadier Generals Ayres and Miles, and Colonel Schriver, judge advocate.

The proceedings of the seventh day were read and approved.

By General Meade:

Question. What did you mean by saying "some one should have been present to have directed my command, together with the commands of Generals Ord and Burnside?" Were you not aware that the commanding general of the army of the Potomac was in the field, and in telegraphic communication with yourself and the other officers alluded to?

Answer. I saw from my position, which was, I suppose, about four hundred yards from General Burnside's, as well as could be seen in the morning in the smoke, that the assault was not going on very rapidly, and that no effort had been made to do what I thought was the first essential—to take that battery on the left of the mine. I then went to General Burnside's, which was as close to the scene of operations as a man could be and see well. There I found Generals Burnside and Ord engaged in conversation. I suggested to General Burnside that that battery should be taken at once; he asked me to go down the line and take a look at it from another point, and I did so. Upon returning, I saw I was confirmed in my first opinion, and he asked me if my troops could not take it. At that time all the approaches leading down to where the mine was were filled with his troops, still slowly moving down, and there was no chance for me to get at the battery, except to go over an open field. I, however, determined to put in General Ayres's division at once, and try to take it, and went back for that purpose, when I got a despatch from General Meade, the exact language of which I do not remember, to the effect that I would await information from some operations which had been directed or that were then going on on the left; and then it was that I wrote one of the despatches in which I said that I thought some one should be there to direct whether I should attempt to take that battery or go with my division round to the left, as General Crawford reported that he was unable to do anything, with what force he had there, on the plank road. I will qualify what I said about the loss of time. I lost considerable time talking to General Burnside; I lost some time in going to see the battery with him; I lost some time in writing despatches and awaiting answers; and, in an operation of that kind, every moment was of vital importance, for before I got the order to go in and take the battery, the enemy had driven nearly all of General Burnside's line out of the intrenchments he had taken.

If General Burnside had given me any orders, as I was there for the purpose of supporting him, I would have obeyed them; but he seemed to act as if what we did was to be done after consultation, and, therefore, I thought that some one should have been right there to have directed at once, without a moment's loss of time, what should be done and what should not.

Those despatches show the extent of the loss of time. But, as I said in my testimony yesterday, I do not know that it affected the result at all. But, in reply to the direct question, if I thought there should have been some one there to give promptly positive orders what to do, I gave my first answer.

Question. How much time was occupied in these consultations, reconnoissances, and other matters referred to by you? and would not the commanding general, had he been at the point referred to by you, have been compelled to consume the same time?

Answer. I do not remember how much time was lost, and cannot tell exactly, unless I can have my official report, or a copy of it, or some records of that kind to refer to. But it was a point of observation at which I should have consulted with nobody.

Everything was plainly to be seen.

Different persons might look at it differently, but it was a position where any one man could see the whole. In my opinion, the most important time was lost before I went to that point.

Question. Why did you consume the time which you acknowledge to have been lost, and why did you not at once telegraph the commanding general about what you saw and what you thought could or should be done?

Answer. The time that I speak of was consumed by General Burnside. In my instructions I was directed to support him; and I informed him where my headquarters were, as stated, not far from him. I waited there for his directions. I thought that my being with him, under orders to support him, the time lost was lost by him and not by me. I did keep the commanding general as promptly informed of everything as I possibly could. Even if I had chosen to have acted independently, according to my own discretion, subject to the approval of the commanding general, all the approaches to the point were occupied by General Burnside's troops. I could not have moved mine without getting them mixed up with his.

By the court:

Question. Did you not mean, in your previous answers, that it was your belief that if the commanding general had been on that field there would have been a pressure brought to bear to push those troops of the 9th corps that occupied those trenches forward faster than they went?

Answer. I think that the controlling power should have been there, and nowhere else, so that there should have been no reference to anywhere else.

Question. When you replied to the last question put to you yesterday, did you consider that the commander of the army of the Potomac should have been present in person, or that some one should have been invested with the command of all the troops engaged in the assault as supports, reserves, &c., if said command was not there?

Answer. I meant that some one person, having general command, should have been there to have seen and directed all at once.

Lieutenant General U. S. GRANT, United States army, being sworn and examined by the judge advocate, says:

Question. Will you please to state what, in your judgment, caused the failure of the attack on the enemy's lines on the 30th of July?

Answer. It seemed to me that it was perfectly practicable for the men, if they had been properly led, to have gone straight through the breach which was caused by the explosion of the mine, and to have gone to the top of Cemetery hill. It looked to me, from what I could see and hear, that it was perfectly practicable to take the men through; but whether it was because the men themselves would not go, or whether it was because they were not led, I was not far enough to the front to be qualified to say.

Question. What orders which you issued were not executed, if any?

Answer. I could send you copies of all the despatches that I wrote. The orders for the assault were issued by General Meade, in obedience to general instructions from me. I saw the detailed order of General Meade before the mine was exploded, and I thought that the execution of that order was practicable. That order, I presume, you have before you. My order was to General Meade, and then General Meade made his order from what I directed him to do, and sent me a copy of it; and I thought it was all that could be required. I recollect that, failing on the north bank of the river to surprise the enemy, as we expected or hoped to do, but instead of that drew a large part of his force to the north side, I telegraphed to General Meade that we would now take advantage of the absence of that force of the enemy to explode the mine and make an assault on Petersburg.

By the court:

Question. From your information, how many of the enemy were in Petersburg at the time of this assault?

Answer. My information was, that three divisions were left in Petersburg, with one brigade absent from those divisions—Johnson's. From the best evidence, none of the enemy's troops crossed the James river until 2 o'clock of the 30th of July, on their way back. Then they had fully sixteen miles to travel to get back, with, however, the advantage of a railroad near them to carry many of the men. The distance I guess at, when I say sixteen miles.

Lieutenant Colonel C. B. COMSTOCK, aide-de-camp, being duly sworn and examined by the judge advocate, says:

Question. Were you at or near the scene of the assault on the 30th of July; by whose orders, and in what capacity?

Answer. I was at General Burnside's headquarters, as aide-de-camp to Lieutenant General Grant, and afterward at General Warren's headquarters by General Grant's orders.

Question. Did you see General Burnside in person; and had you conversation with him?

Answer. I had some conversation with him.

Question. Relate the conversation in brief.

Answer. I went from General Burnside's headquarters, to the position he had in the front, to ascertain how things stood; I suppose the time was about an hour after the explosion of the mine. He told me that his troops were forming then for an assault to carry the crest of the hill. That was the only important point in the conversation.

Question. Did he give you any information to communicate to General Grant?

Answer. I do not recollect that he did.

Question. Had you an opportunity of forming an opinion as to the cause or causes of the failure on that day?

Answer. I had not, from anything that I saw myself.

By the court:

Question. Were you so situated that you could see this assault?

Answer. I could not until I went to General Warren's headquarters, which was about 7 o'clock. I could not see the details.

Question. Had you made such an examination prior to the assault that would enable you to give a professional opinion as to the chances of success in attempting to take Cemetery hill by assault, considering the explosion of the mine as the basis of the assault?

Answer. I had.

Question. I wish you would state to the court what the chances of success were, using this mine as a means of inaugurating the assault.

Answer. I thought it entirely impracticable when the mine was made, if the enemy's line should be held in full force. This opinion was formed a week or ten days prior to the assault. Afterwards, with the knowledge I had of the movement of the enemy's troops from the south to the north side of the river, I thought an assault was entirely practicable.

Question. What do you suppose would have been the best plan for the assaulting troops to have followed after having reached Cemetery hill—made a lodgement on and fortified that place, or proceeded immediately into the town of Petersburg?

Answer. I suppose the first step should have been to have made a lodgement on Cemetery hill, and then to have pushed up troops to hold it at all hazards. The disposition of the troops would depend upon the nature of the ground.

Question. From your knowledge of the nature of the intrenchments, our own and the enemy's, do you think that immediately after the explosion of the mine, if proper working parties had been arranged, there would have been any difficulty in removing sufficient obstructions to have enabled our troops to have moved against those intrenchments in line of battle?

Answer. I do not think there would have been any difficulty.

Major General E. O. C. ORD, United States volunteers, being duly sworn and examined by the judge advocate, says:

Question. Please state what was your command at the assault on the 30th of July.

Answer. My command was composed of two divisions to aid in the assault, one of which belonged to the 10th corps, and was under General Turner, and the other to the 18th corps, under General Ames. The divisions numbered, General Ames's about 3,500 and General Turner's 4,000 available muskets, or probably a little less.

Question. What were your troops ordered to do?

Answer. My troops were ordered to a position in the rear of General Burnside's corps, with a view to supporting it. The positions were selected by General Burnside.

Question. Did your troops experience any interference from the 9th corps moving into position on that occasion?

Answer. After General Burnside's troops had made the assault and pushed forward, probably about an hour or a little more after the explosion of the mine, he said to me, "Now you can move your troops forward." I sent orders immediately to the leading division to move forward rapidly, according to the programme, following the division that was in front of it, which was the rear division of General Burnside's corps. In the course of twenty minutes after the order was sent out by a staff officer, General Turner reported to me that he found the way blocked, that the approach to the place of debouch was occupied by the divisions in front, and that he had found himself in front of General Potter's troops.

This was the report made by him. General Potter's troops, according to the programme, were to precede his.

Question. Were any arrangements made for the passage of troops through the abatis, and over the parapets, to go to the front on that day?

Answer. When I went to the front I found the troops debouching by a single opening. The parapet had been thrown down, and the abatis had been removed, and the troops were moved out by that opening.

Question. Please state the dimensions of that opening; would it admit of the passage of troops in column, or line, or how?

Answer. I cannot give the exact dimensions, because my attention was occupied principally in watching what was going on in front of this place; but my impression is that the opening was large enough for a column of a company front to go out over pretty rough ground. I do not know whether there was more than one opening; I only saw that one.

Question. That was the one your troops passed through?

Answer. No, my troops did not all pass through that way; I directed a portion of my troops to go over the parapet.

Question. Did you direct them to go over the parapet because, in your judgment, the opening was inadequate?

Answer. I gave those directions because the ground in front of this place of exit was occupied by other troops, and there was no room after they got out for them to be of service without moving for a considerable distance by the flank, to the right and left.

Question. How were the troops that debouched to the assault formed to advance?

Answer. When I went to the front, I saw white troops moving out by the flank into the crater and the trenches near; I say by the flank, but I will explain that they passed along by twos and threes, and sometimes fours, along this space, which was pretty well swept by the fire of the enemy—the space between our trenches and the crater formed by the explosion of the mine. These white troops were followed afterwards by some colored troops, who also moved out, as it were, by flank, though the appearance of moving by flank may have been caused by the columns being somewhat disordered and hesitating in the move, so that a few moving forward first, and others following them, would diminish the width of a column, and give the troops the appearance of moving by flank.

Question. In your opinion, was this movement by flank judicious, or was it unavoidable?

Answer. I would not suppose it was a judicious move, under the circumstances, if it could have been avoided; I rather think, if intended to be a movement with a front of one or more companies, then the kind of formation I saw was caused by the hesitation of the troops in the rear, and the natural disposition of those men who are more or less timid in following those in front to string themselves out in almost single file.

Question. What, in your opinion, were some of the causes of failure on that occasion?

Answer. I think the first cause was that the troops were not well disciplined; they probably had not had time to become soldiers. The next cause may have been that they passed out of the trenches by one place of exit, and through the covered way to a considerable extent, which necessarily impeded the progress of troops going out, especially as troops began coming in by the same covered way.

Question. Were the obstacles met by our troops, in your opinion, formidable?

Answer. I did not go to the front until difficulties were reported in the way of carrying out the order received from General Meade, to move my division out to the right, independent of the troops in my front, and endeavor to reach the crest of the hill; it was reported by the division commanders that the nature of the ground was such that they could not get out that way. I went down to inspect the ground myself, and I derived the impression that there were difficulties in the way of getting out from the position occupied by my men at that time, except in one place. They were in the long covered way—the way leading to the angle from which the troops debouched; the ground was swampy, covered with more or less undergrowth and trees, and appeared to run obliquely in front of the enemy's trenches. If the troops should get into that swamp and undergrowth it would have been difficult to have kept them in order, and the enemy would have had them at a greater disadvantage, raking them if they occupied the trenches. The covered way was a pretty deep one, and I supposed from the fact of its being there, leading to the place of exit, it was swept by a very heavy fire from the enemy's batteries. It was reported that the stream running through the marsh was bridged in one place by a narrow bridge where we crossed it, and that it was a difficult place for troops to pass over; when I got there I saw that it was very muddy, that delays would be occasioned, and that it was a difficult place to attempt to take the enemy's intrenchments, and we would have got on the ground just under the enemy's works, and probably been exposed to a very severe fire.

Question. Did any troops, to your knowledge, misbehave or disobey orders?

Answer. None that I know of, except after, when an assault was made by some colored troops, followed by a brigade of the 10th corps, which assault was made about 8 o'clock, while I was in the front line of our trenches and within less than one hundred yards of the crater, and what I would call the movement of assault; the men were repulsed by a very heavy concentrated fire which enveloped that point of exit—the enemy having massed forces on the right and front, and some fire coming from the left.

Question. In your opinion, had the first troops that went forward not hesitated nor halted in the crater, could they not have got to the desirable point—that is, Cemetery hill?

Answer. I know nothing about their halting, or the facilities that they had for getting forward, except through what I heard from others, I not having been present at that time.

Question. How was our artillery firing, as far as you observed—effective or otherwise?

Answer. The artillery fired very rapidly and for a long time; and, judging from the reports in the enemy's newspapers which I have seen since, we must have done considerable damage by our artillery upon their columns moving across to the place of attack.

Question. Were the obstructions north and south of the crater removed sufficiently to admit the passage of troops in line of battle—say brigade front?

Answer. I did not see that any obstructions made by the enemy's trenches had been removed when I was there, except what had been removed by the explosion of the mine at the crater. Their ditch still remained, and I counted the regimental flags of our troops in my front occupying the trench. I do not know whether there was a strong abatis before the attack, so that I refer only to the ditch and the parapet.

By the court:

Question. Do you think the assault would have been successful there, had the best dispositions been made that you are conversant with?

Answer. From what I learned afterwards of the behavior of the troops after the explosion, when the enemy was most alarmed, I think that the assault, if it had been made with no more vigor, would have failed, no matter what the disposition. If the troops had behaved properly elsewhere, I think the probability of success would have been increased by having more openings, a simultaneous assault, and increased material; but if the troops would have behaved as improperly as they are reported to have done in front, not going forward when ordered, I think the assault would have failed, no matter what the disposition.

Question. In your opinion, was there any necessity for an officer of rank being present who should have had a more general command than the commander of the troops making the assault and the commanders of the supports and reserves? should there have been an officer present to have combined the whole command nearer than the commander of the army, who was only in telegraphic communication with the different commanders of troops on the field? should there have been one single person there invested with authority to direct the whole operation? and would the result have been different if such had been the case?

Answer. The only commands referred to as present there—the assembling corps and the reserves—were under General Burnside and myself; and upon reporting to General Burnside, I accompanied him to the trenches, and told him I would obey any instructions he gave me; so that the whole of the operations were under his orders, until the orders came from higher authority to make the change referred to, and to discontinue the assault. General Burnside being the senior officer, I considered that he had a right to give me orders. He directed me to place my troops in the rear until after his troops should have made the assault, and until he learned when they would be necessary, and where, which I did. General Burnside was to give me word when to move my troops, and where to move them. I told him I considered myself bound to obey any instructions that he might give me, and that any instructions that he would give would be obeyed with alacrity; so that, so far as concerns the movements directed by him, I do not think the presence of any other officer in those two corps would have made any change in moving forward.

Question. Could your troops, when they were called into action, have advanced to the front over the enemy's parapet, and have gotten through in line of battle in any front greater than that of two regiments, at the time you were sent in, on each side of the crater?

Answer. I think it probable that my troops might have gotten in on the left of the crater at that time, if they had advanced through the opening by fronts of regiments, or even companies, gotten into the enemy's trenches; but my answer must be understood to convey only a knowledge of what I saw. I do not know what force the enemy had on the left. I only know that the resistance on the right was very great, and they appeared to have a severe fire upon the troops on the right of where we advanced to the crater. My troops were directed to support General Burnside on the right.

Question. Were you present when the mine exploded? Do you consider that the troops might have advanced to the top of Cemetery hill on that ridge, had they been properly led forward, or the troops behaved properly?

Answer. I do not consider I was present when the mine exploded.

By General Meade:

Question. Where was your general position on the field during the operation of the morning?

Answer. When the mine exploded, and probably for an hour and a half or two hours afterwards, I was with General Burnside in the trenches in rear of one of the batteries about one-third or a half mile from the point of assault; after that for half an hour I was up to the front as far as I could get without going into the crater, or outside our line of intrenchments as far as the head of my advanced division was. I then returned, and General Burnside and myself occupied the same place in the rear of this battery for probably an hour, except that I rode to the rear where General Meade was, and passed around a little, trying to rally some troops who were going from the front. This took me till between 9 and 10 o'clock, when General Burnside and myself both rode to the rear to learn something about an order that was issued in regard to our future movements.

Question. Could anything be seen from this point with sufficient distinctness to have enabled the commanding general to give orders other than he did from the point occupied?

Answer. Immediately after the explosion, the fire from both our batteries and the enemy's came very heavily, and the cloud of smoke prevented us from seeing anything that was going on there. We were ignorant of the condition of things except from the information staff officers brought us, or from the nature of the firing we heard, up to the time that I informed myself by going to the front.

Question. Did you hear any staff officer report to General Burnside that the troops could not be got to advance from the crater? If so, how many officers so reported, and do you know their names?

Answer. The first two or three reports that were brought to General Burnside were brought by officers whose names I do not know, and not until some considerable time had expired after the explosion; and although I did not hear the reports distinctly enough to repeat them, they were not satisfactory, and indicated that the troops could not be moved readily forward.

Question. Did you not report to the commanding general that the troops were overcrowded in the crater, and the enemy's works adjacent, and that in your judgment there was no probability of the crest of Cemetery hill being carried—this somewhere between 9 and 10 a. m., at the headquarters of the commanding general in the field?

Answer. I did. I would say, in addition to my answer, that General Burnside and myself were present at the time, and the question was, whether we could carry it at that time; and my answer intended to convey whether *we*—General Burnside and myself, with our forces—could have done so, had they let us; and after the troops were disorganized and driven back, those who made the attack later and those who made the attack earlier were packed in the trenches adjacent; that, under the circumstances, we could not carry it with all our troops at that point of attack.

Question. Did General Burnside, about 10 a. m., when at his commanding general's headquarters on the field, say that he could maintain his lodgement in the crater, and that he could take Cemetery hill before night, if so permitted?

Answer. General Burnside disagreed with me, when I said I did not think we could take it. I supposed he meant that he could take it with the force he had, consisting of his own corps and my reserves, though he said something about it was time then for the 5th corps to move up. The remark was made by General Burnside, with a view to persisting in the attack which he commenced, and it had been my opinion, ever since I was near enough to see what was going on in the crater, that the sooner we withdrew our troops, when we got into such a bad position, the better, and any persistence in the attack at that point I looked upon as very improper.

Question. Was it not understood at this time that offensive operations should cease, but that the crater should be held till the troops could be securely withdrawn, and that this would probably be till night?

Answer. I think such was General Burnside's understanding, and I know he received such orders. My troops were all inside the intrenchments, except those who had run into the enemy's trenches to avoid the tremendous fire which they met when they went out.

By General Warren:

Question. Do you remember seeing General Warren at the battery at General Burnside's station?

Answer. I do.

Question. Was not the whole field at that time sufficiently clear from smoke to be visible, and had been so for some time previously at that point?

Answer. I do not know whether it was after my return from the vicinity of the crater or before that I saw General Warren. My impression is that each time I looked from the parapet before I left the trenches—which was two or three times that I rose to look to the front—the smoke obscured the view, so that I, at least, could form no definite idea of what was going on at the front. After the firing from the batteries on our side had ceased, which was probably an hour from the time of the assault, the atmosphere was clearer; but even then I could make out really little of what was going on in front, from the distance, the peculiar position of the point of attack, and from the fact, too, that I do not see very well, because I am near-sighted.

Brigadier General R. B. POTTER, United States volunteers, being sworn and examined by the judge advocate, says:

Question. Were you in a position to see the operations of the assault before Petersburg on the 30th of July, and in what capacity?

Answer. I was commanding the 2d division 9th army corps.

Question. Do you regard it as a failure or otherwise?

Answer. I regard it as a failure.

Question. To what cause or causes do you attribute this?

Answer. Firstly, to the failure of the troops who had the advance on that day to carry out the orders to advance through the enemy's line and seize the hill. Secondly, that when it was evident that this part of the plan had failed no attempt was made at a diversion, at any other part of the line, to enable the troops, which were thrown into confusion at this point, to be re-formed. I would further state that I do not think the preliminary arrangements were very perfect.

Question. What preparations were made, or what orders were given for the same, to pass troops through the abatis and over the parapet in front of the 9th corps? Did you receive any orders yourself?

Answer. I received no orders whatever in relation to that matter, except what are contained in the general order from the headquarters of the army of the Potomac. I was furnished a copy of that order, but no other order.

Question. But what preparations were made, or what orders were given for the same, to pass troops through the abatis and over the parapet in front of the 9th corps?

Answer. The general order of General Burnside—I suppose it might be called the order of attack—was the only order given in writing. Verbal instructions were given to have the pioneers of the different regiments, and a sort of pioneer regiment that we call the engineer regiment, in each division, prepared with their tools, &c., to prepare the breastworks for the passage of field batteries, in case we were successful in moving forward. My regiment was immediately in the neighborhood of the breastwork, ready to carry out these instructions, and my pioneers were also prepared. I had orders not to disturb anything immediately in the vicinity of the mine, so as not to attract the attention of the enemy to that point. I was told to withdraw everything from that part of the line for a space of two or three hundred yards, except a thin line of skirmishers, and not to attract the enemy's attention there, if I could help it.

Question. How were the 9th corps troops formed for the assault—your own division for instance?

Answer. My own division was to have been formed left in front, to move forward by the flank, so that when my troops had passed the line of the enemy's intrenchments, by fronting their front would be to the right, my division being intended to cover the right of the advance. One brigade of my division was massed between the railroad and the advance line of works on the right-hand side of my covered way, and south of the mine. I had orders not to allow any troops on the left of the covered way. The other brigade was partially in the trenches, and about to be relieved by some of the troops of the 18th corps. Two or three regiments, which I was ordered not to put in the assault, were not in the trenches.

Question. What time elapsed from the springing of the mine till the forward movement of the assaulting columns?

Answer. I do not know, sir; I did not see the movement of the first division. The first of my regiments commenced to move, I should think, about eight or ten minutes after the mine exploded. My division was to move third in order, but I took the liberty of altering the programme a little. After I received the order of Major General Burnside—I received the order about nine o'clock at night—after thinking the matter over, it occurred to me that it would be a very long time before my division would have an opportunity to get forward, as the divisions of Generals Ledlie and Wilcox were to precede me. I therefore commanded General Griffin, who had the lead in my division, to deploy a line of skirmishers to the right of this crater, and in case the assault seemed to be successful and General Ledlie moved forward, he should advance his skirmishers to the right, and if he did not find so much serious opposition as to detain him there, he should push his troops forward to the right and move forward nearly parallel with General Ledlie. I gave him these orders about twelve o'clock at night, and I do not think that I communicated to General Burnside that I had made this change. Therefore my troops commenced moving as soon as General Griffin found that General Ledlie's column had started.

This leading division commenced moving and passed into the right of the crater and turned down to the right.

Question. Did the troops halt in the crater?

Answer. Yes, sir.

Question. Why?

Answer. No reason at all that I know of.

Question. What was the nature of the obstructions in the enemy's line, formidable or otherwise?

Answer. To the right of the crater there was an ordinary line of rifle-pits, with a sort of *chevaux-de-frise* in front of it, made by pointed stakes being driven into the ground. Immediately in rear of this, and to the right of it, there were two covered ways. One seemed to be a covered way, and one, perhaps, a place dug to carry something out of the fort. There were transverse lines of rifle-pits, and some coverings thrown up by the men to protect themselves—one running in these angles between the advance line and this covered way, which runs off towards Petersburg, and another running on the bank of the ravine which runs up through the enemy's line to the right of the mine, about the line I was ordered to take.

Question. What was the degree of artillery firing on that point—the point of assault?

Answer. Immediately after the assault, very light; afterwards the fire was very severe indeed—as severe as I ever saw.

Question. What time elapsed, as near as you can tell, from the time of the assault till the time this severe fire commenced?

Answer. I should think fully half an hour.

Question. Was the ground around the crater commanded by the ground held by the enemy?

Answer. Yes, sir; that is, immediately in rear of the enemy's line which we had pierced the ground commanded it, and the ground to the right on the other side of the ravine commanded it. In speaking of the right, I mean our right. The ground to the left I did not notice so well, because I had no business there.

Question. For what distance on each side of the crater were the enemy's works abandoned after the explosion of the mine?

Answer. To the right of the crater the front line was abandoned for a space of two hundred and fifty or three hundred yards I should think; that is, the enemy's troops rushed out of this line back to these covered ways, and so forth. From the hasty glance I gave to the left, there did not seem to be anybody within three hundred yards. Perhaps it would be better to say that the line was only partially abandoned; they did not all go—some went and some did not.

Question. Could the troops have proceeded to the crest immediately after reaching the crater?

Answer. I do not know any reasons why they could not.

Question. Did any troops that you know of advance from the crater to the crest?

Answer. Some of my troops advanced from the right of the crater towards the crest; I suppose they went upwards of two hundred yards, and they were driven back.

Question. Why, do you suppose, were they driven back?

Answer. At that time they were driven back by the fire. They were too weak to advance further.

Question. By the fire of artillery or of infantry?

Answer. Both.

Question. At what hour was that?

Answer. That must have been about half or three-quarters of an hour after the mine exploded.

Question. Do you think that if your men had been adequately supported, they could have gone forward to the crest notwithstanding the obstacles that presented themselves, firing, and so forth, at that hour?

Answer. I think that if I had had my whole division together at that time, if the ground had been such that I could have had my whole division together and made that charge, I could have gone to the crest.

Question. When these troops fell back where did they go?

Answer. They fell back partially into this covered way leading from the fort to the right, and a few were driven into the crater of the mine.

Question. How long was it after they got in before they were ordered to retire; how long were you in that place, or wherever they were?

Answer. Until the general order came to withdraw the troops.

Question. How long would you estimate that time to be?

Answer. It must have been five or six hours. It seems to me we did not get that order till about 11 o'clock. General Burnside sent for me, I should think, about 10 o'clock in the morning, and stated that he had received an order to withdraw, and asked me if I thought we could hold the position. I told him I thought we could hold the position, but unless something was going to be done there was no use in it. He said it was an important point, or something of that sort, and I asked him if I would make arrangements to withdraw, and he told me no; that he was going to see General Meade, and that I should wait until he should have consulted with him. Half or three-quarters of an hour afterwards I received a copy of a telegram to General White, who was acting as his chief of staff, with an indorsement on the back of the despatch to the effect that it should be submitted to the officers in the crater, or something to that effect, for their opinion as to how they should withdraw. Subsequently I started to go into the crater to consult with them, and I received an order from an aide-de-camp of General Burnside to report in person at his headquarters.

Question. Was the time a fit one to withdraw, in your opinion?

Answer. The troops were not withdrawn at all. They were driven out by the enemy.

Question. When did the chief loss of men occur?

Answer. The chief loss in my division occurred between half past six and ten o'clock in the morning. The heaviest loss was at the time that some of the troops of the 4th division (the colored division) met with a check and were repulsed.

Question. Was it in the act of retiring from the crater?

Answer. More than half the prisoners I lost were lost in the crater. I should explain that I had very few men in the crater; that seeing how it was overcrowded, and that one or two regiments that attempted to pass through were lost among the other troops, I endeavored to get my troops out of there; but when some of the other troops gave way, and the operation of General Ferrero's troops was unsuccessful and they gave way, I had some stragglers forced into the crater. I suppose I had not more than two hundred men in there. My troops were holding the line to the right of that mostly.

Question. By whom was this removal of the troops conducted?

Answer. It was not conducted at all, sir. The circumstances were these: After we had received this order General Burnside directed me to report at his headquarters. I went to his headquarters, met there the other division commanders, and we consulted upon the best plan which should be adopted to withdraw the troops. I had previously sent out orders to connect my right with the crater by an intrenchment, if possible. While we were returning from this consultation an assault was made upon the crater, and the enemy recovered possession of it. Then all the troops were forced back to our line except two regiments that I had sent beyond the ravine to silence a battery, and these I withdrew about four o'clock in the afternoon.

Question. Do you know whether any troops misbehaved or disobeyed orders in any way, or at any time, during the action?

Answer. I do not know that I can answer that exactly. I know by the reports of my staff officers, and so forth. But I saw troops lying there when they had been ordered to go forward. Immediately after the mine exploded, probably within ten minutes, Colonel Pleasants, who had charge of the explosion, and whose regiment, having built the mine, being relieved from duty on that day, except as a sort of provost guard with orders from the 9th army corps, had volunteered as an aid on my staff, and as soon as the mine was exploded he rushed forward into the crater, and the troops were moving up; and he reported to me that the troops could not be made to move forward; that was, the troops of the 1st division. He showed me his hand, which was blistered in driving them up. It was Marshall's brigade of Ledlie's division.

By the court:

Question. What tools were the engineer regiments supplied with?

Answer. Axes, spades, and picks. The engineer regiment, I think, was supplied particularly with axes to cut down the abatis.

Question. Did they move forward?

Answer. Yes, sir.

Question. Did they destroy the abatis?

Answer. The *chevaux-de-frise* on the enemy's lines for two or three hundred yards was broken down.

Question. Was there any difficulty in passing a brigade or regimental front over our intrenchments and on either side of that crater to the front?

Answer. It might have been done on the left, but not on the right.

Question. What was the difficulty on the right?

Answer. The difficulty on the right was that where you would have to form your troops you would have to pass through a wooded ravine and swamp. A heavy regiment which charged through in regimental front, I think, got very badly broken up. They would have succeeded better further to the right.

Question. Where did you stay during the attack?

Answer. Most of the time I stayed on the hill on this side of the railroad—a point where you can see the ground.

Question. Did all of your troops go into action?

Answer. My troops all went into action except my engineer regiment, which had just moved up to the front.

Question. Did they all get as far as the crater?

Answer. All except one regiment got beyond the crater.

Question. Did you ever go to the crater?

Answer. I never went to the crater myself. I was within about eighty yards of it—just off to the right of it.

Question. At the time your skirmish line was ordered up the hill did any individual members of your division get to the top of the crest?

Answer. I do not think there did. It was reported to me that some did; but having investigated it since, I am satisfied that they did not.

The court adjourned, to meet at ten o'clock on the 31st of August.

NINTH DAY.

HEADQUARTERS SECOND CORPS,
August 31, 1864.

The court met pursuant to adjournment.

Present: Major General Hancock, Brigadier Generals Ayres and Miles, and Colonel Schriver, judge advocate.

The proceedings of the eighth day were read and approved.

Brigadier General EDWARD FERRERO, United States volunteers, being duly sworn, to questions by judge advocate says:

Question. Were you at the assault on the 30th of July, and what was your command?

Answer. I was; commanding the 4th division of the 9th army corps, (colored troops.)

Question. What was their formation for the attack?

Answer. There was no formation, further than moving down in rear of the third division, as directed in the orders, by the flank in the covered way.

Question. Was this the most judicious?

Answer. It was the only formation that could be adopted under the circumstances.

Question. Please to state the circumstances.

Answer. There being no position to mass the troops.

Question. Why was there no position?

Answer. On account of there being three other divisions in advance of mine, which would occupy all the available ground where my troops could have been formed.

Question. What orders had you to prepare the parapet for the debouch of troops?

Answer. I had no orders whatever.

Question. State some of the causes of the failure, if you regard it so.

Answer. I do regard it as a failure.

Question. State some of the causes, briefly.

Answer. The failure of the 1st division to go forward immediately after the explosion.

Question. Do you attribute their halting and not going forward to misbehavior on their part?

Answer. Not being present there, that I could not say. In my opinion, there is no reason that I know of why they should not have gone forward.

Question. State the reasons why you arrived at that conclusion.

Answer. I would state that there could have been no obstructions whatever at that time, from the fact that the crater was crowded with troops, in and about it, when my division went through and passed over the obstacles, not only the obstacles occasioned by the explosion, but also the mass of troops in the crater. They went through and passed beyond those troops at a time when there was heavy firing; whereas those troops that had gone forward on the lead could have gone forward with a very slight loss, in my opinion. I would state that, in my opinion, the order of battle for the movements of troops on that day was extremely faulty. If I understand it right, the object to be attained was to gain the crest on Cemetery hill; and to take advantage of the momentary paralyzation of the troops in and about the crater, caused by the explosion of the mine, it was necessary that the troops that made the assault should move with the utmost rapidity to gain that crest. I contend that the point of the assault was not properly selected to carry out that object; that the obstructions which the explosion of the mine would naturally create would disorganize the troops and prevent them moving forward with the rapidity that was desired. Furthermore, I would state that the manner in which the troops went in would not lead them to attain the object that was desired. The two divisions that followed the leading division were to have protected the flanks of the same. Now, how could they protect the flank when the leading division, the head of that column, would hardly have reached the crest before the 2d division would have reached the crater, subjecting the 1st division to flank fires, and to be taken in reverse? And even had the 3d division, which had the second position in column, have gotten through, it would have taken a long time before the 2d division, which was the third in column, could have reached its proper point to protect the right flank of the 1st division. I mean to convey the idea, that either other movements should have been made on the flank of the leading division, or that division should have been deployed to the right and left, engaging the enemy on the flank, so as to give the assaulting column an opportunity to advance rapidly to the crest of the hill.

By the court:

Question. How long was it after the explosion of the mine before the assaulting column moved forward?

Answer. I was not with the leading division; therefore I cannot give you the exact time, but it was very shortly after.

By the judge advocate:

Question. State to the court how the 4th division, (colored troops,) your own command, conducted themselves on the occasion.

Answer. I would state that the troops went in in the most gallant manner; that they went in without hesitation, moved right straight forward, passed through the crater that was filled with troops, and all but one regiment of my division passed beyond the crater; the leading brigade engaged the enemy at a short distance in rear of the crater, where they captured some two hundred odd prisoners and a stand of colors, and recaptured a stand of colors belonging to a white regiment of our corps. Here, after they had taken those prisoners, the troops became somewhat disorganized, and it was some little time before they could get them organized again to make a second attempt to charge the crest of the hill. About half an hour after that they made the attempt and were repulsed by a very severe and galling fire, and, I must say, they retreated in great disorder and confusion back to our first line of troops, where they were rallied, and there they remained during the rest of the day and behaved very well. I would add that my troops are raw new troops, and never had been drilled two weeks from the day they entered the service till that day.

Question. If your division had been the leading one in the assault, would they have succeeded in taking Cemetery hill?

Answer. I have not the slightest doubt, from the manner in which they went in under very heavy fire, that had they gone in in the first instance when the fire was comparatively light, they would have carried the crest of Cemetery hill beyond a doubt.

By the court:

Question. Did you go forward with your division?

Answer. I went to our first line of works, and there remained to see my command go through. I would state, that I deemed it more necessary that I should see that they all went in than that I should go in myself, as there was no hesitation in their going forward whatever. I was at no time at a further distance than eighty or ninety yards from my division.

Question. Where were you after they had all passed the crater, and were, as you say, at one time half an hour in reorganizing?

Answer. I was immediately in front of the crater on our front line of works. I would also state that one regiment was checked between the crater and our front line, unable to get through; and I was at that time making every effort to get that regiment through, with the intention of passing through myself as soon as they got past, but it was impossible for me to do so from the crowded state of the troops that were there.

Question. Were the obstructions in front of the first line of works of a character to admit the passage of a horseman or a piece of artillery, after the whole corps had passed?

Answer. They would not admit of the passage of either, because the parapet of the rifle-pit had never been dug away. I was compelled to remove *abatis* on our own front, under fire, to get my command through by the flank.

Brigadier General O. B. WILCOX, United States volunteers, being duly sworn, says to questions by judge advocate:

Question. Were you in a position to see the operation of the assault before Petersburg on the 30th of July, and in what capacity?

Answer. I commanded the 3d division of the 9th army corps. At the time of the explosion of the mine I was at Romer's battery, just in rear of my second brigade, and in good position to observe the assault.

Question. Do you regard the attack as a failure?

Answer. I do.

Question. State some of the causes of it.

Answer. The first and most obvious cause was the failure of the 1st division to go forward when there was no firing, for the fire of the enemy was suspended for fifteen to twenty minutes. In the next place, I think that the troops that went in support of the leading division should have gone in almost simultaneously with it, and should have gone to the right and left, avoiding the crater, but going near it, and then bearing down the enemy's works to the right and left, so as to have prevented the enemy bringing flank and reverse fires to bear on the advancing columns. The order of attack stated that my division should wait until the 1st division had cleared the enemy's works. For that reason, of course, the three divisions could not have gone in simultaneously. It was the published order that prevented it in part. The attention of the enemy was not attracted to any other point than the crater. I consider that the third reason. Almost as soon as the enemy's first astonishment was over they concentrated an almost circular fire around the crater. Their field batteries came out in position on different points on the Jerusalem plank road and on Cemetery hill. They kept up a flank and reverse fire; and a battery in the grove of trees on our right was so situated, the line of the rebel works taking a direction a little re-entering, that almost as soon as they opened fire at all, they began to fire nearly in rear of the crater. I would say, that at the meeting in General Burnside's tent, when Generals Ord and Meade were present, I supposed it was intended that the two divisions following the leading division should move to the right and left, and that the duty of the 9th corps was to clear the ground to enable the 18th corps to move forward. If that plan had been carried out, I think it would have been successful; but I do not think that the temporary occupation of Cemetery hill by a small force would have insured the success of that attack. I think that ultimately they would have been driven out, unless we had a large force, two corps at least, to fight a battle at those works. Now, to go back to the interview which General Burnside had with his division commanders, where General Meade was present, it was a well-understood thing there that this was intended to be a surprise, and it was thought by all the generals, including General Meade himself, that, unless it should be a complete surprise, it would be a failure; and the written order which was published to the commanders did not fully, in fact did not substantially, give the order of attack as it was understood at this interview. I mean General Burnside's order of attack. At the time the matter was talked over I certainly understood that I was to move down and clear the enemy's works on the left, and then move up towards the Jerusalem plank road. The order stated that I would bear to the left and take a position on the Jerusalem plank road.

Question. What preparations were made, and what orders were given, to pass troops over the parapet and through the enemy's works?

Answer. None but the written orders before the court. The *abatis*, what was left of it when my division passed over, was no obstacle whatever.

Major General A. A. HUMPHREYS, United States volunteers, chief of staff, being duly sworn, says to questions by the judge advocate:

Question. Were you with General Meade during the assault on the 30th of July?

Answer. I was.

Question. What was the substance or language of a despatch which he received from Lieutenant Colonel Loring, assistant inspector general of the 9th corps, but addressed to General Burnside, about 5.45 a. m. of that day?

Answer. The substance of the despatch was, that some of the troops there, I think Ledlie's division, were in the crater, and would not go forward, and asking that some other division or some other troops should be sent to go forward to the crest. The main point with me, however, was, that his troops were in the crater, and were not going forward as they ought to have done.

Question. Relate what passed at the interviews between General Burnside and Generals Grant and Meade after the former had been directed to withdraw the troops from the crater, and prior to the withdrawal of the troops.

Answer. I recollect the directions to General Burnside, which were, that if he could not withdraw his troops with security during the day they should be withdrawn at night; that the best time for the withdrawal of the troops he himself should be the judge of. My impression is that General Burnside did not wish to withdraw them. He certainly so expressed himself to me after General Meade left, for I did not leave the headquarters of General Burnside the same time as General Meade, but remained there a short time. I do not know whether he so expressed himself to General Meade and General Grant or not. I thought I understood the conditions that existed there, and there was no question in my mind as to the necessity of withdrawing them.

Question. Did you understand it to be his wish to maintain his position in the crater?

Answer. I did not pay much attention to what he said to General Meade and General Grant, but he so expressed himself to me afterwards; but inasmuch as he stated no facts which put a different aspect on the condition of things, I did not consider that he gave very good reasons for his wish. He certainly differed from General Ord.

Question. Did you hear General Ord give any opinion as to the probable success of carrying the crest if persisted in for a certain time; and if so, what was it?

Answer. I heard him then or before express the opinion that the time was past. He was averse to it. I did not pay so much attention to what was said at that time, for the reason that the facts were well known, and the conclusions come to in regard to them.

Question. Were you at the fourteen-gun battery, near which General Burnside had his temporary headquarters, on that day?

Answer. Yes, I rode out there; I think it was between 10 and 11 o'clock when I rode out there. I had been there before, and am somewhat familiar with the ground.

Question. Could anything be seen from there with sufficient distinctness to have enabled the commanding general to give orders other than he did, from the point occupied by him?

Answer. I think not. I do not think it made any difference whether he was there, or whether he was at the point he occupied. In the gratification of a personal wish to see simply, he might have seen something more, but it would not have made any difference in the conclusions arrived at; he would have understood matters as thoroughly where he was as if he had seen them.

Question. Ought the assault on that day to have been successful?

Answer. I think so; I was confident that it would have been successful.

Brigadier General H. I. HUNT, United States volunteers, chief of artillery, army of the Potomac, being duly sworn, says, in answer to questions by judge advocate:

Question. Please to state in what capacity you were serving during the assault on the enemy's lines on the 30th July, and days preceding it.

Answer. I am chief of artillery of the army of the Potomac, and had charge of the siege operations on this side of the Appomattox.

Question. Relate briefly what arrangements were made for opposing the enemy's artillery fire on that occasion, and if they were successfully carried out.

Answer. Batteries that had been constructed several weeks preceding the assault had armaments placed in them, from the plank road to the Hare house; there were eighteen siege guns in the line, eighteen large mortars, and twenty-eight cohorns along in the lines in front, and some eighty field-pieces. The object was to silence the fire of the enemy's batteries in the redoubt which formed their salient on the plank road, and especially all of their guns which bore upon the ground in front of the mine. The fire was opened immediately upon the explosion of the mine, and was very successful in keeping down the enemy's fire.

Question. Was the enemy's artillery fire formidable, and particularly directed to the point of our assault, after the explosion of the mine?

Answer. The fire did not become very formidable; it was almost entirely silenced soon after it opened, with the exception of one gun in a battery next to the mine, and a battery on the crest beyond the mine, and a few guns that were used by the enemy on our right of the mine, towards the railroad. The gun that was in the work next the mine was so placed that it was protected from all direct fire, and a sufficient number of mortars could not be brought to bear upon it to stop it. No large mortars had been placed to control that battery, as, according to the plan of assault, that work might reasonably be supposed to fall into our hands within ten or fifteen minutes after the explosion; all the guns in that battery were silenced, however, excepting that one. The battery on the crest of the hill directly in front of the mine was almost shut up after firing two or three rounds, as we had some heavy guns bearing on it, and a number of field guns. I was not where I could see the fire from our right of the mine. I had Colonel Monroe in charge there, and he reported that the fire was pretty well kept down. On the left they occasionally fired a shot.

Question. Under the circumstances, then, ought not the assault have succeeded?

Answer. I think so; that is, so far as it depended upon us. I do not know what the enemy had behind the crest; the object was to take the crest.

Question. Have you formed any opinion as to the causes of the failure of the assault on that occasion?

Answer. I do not know what other causes might have existed, but I attributed the failure to the want of promptitude in pushing forward assaulting columns immediately on the explosion of the mine. I believed, from the first, that if that were not done promptly the attack would probably fail.

Question. Was the enemy's fire directed upon the point of attack very formidable at any time, so as to prevent reasonably resolute troops from pushing onward?

Answer. I think not; certainly not within the period within which their advance should have taken place.

Lieutenant W. H. BEUYAURD, United States engineers, being duly sworn, says to questions by judge advocate:

Question. Were you present at the assault on the rebel lines on the 30th July, and in what capacity?

Answer. I was with General Burnside on that morning. I was sent by Major Duane to report to him for duty as an engineer.

Question. Were you in a situation then to see the progress of events on that day?

Answer. Not all the time; a portion of the time I was with General Burnside at his headquarters, and then, afterwards, I was at different points along the front. I was not in such a position that I could see everything that was going on.

Question. Were there working parties for the assaulting columns, and engineer officers to lead them?

Answer. Not that I know of.

Question. No arrangements had been made with you by General Burnside for anything of that sort?

Answer. No, sir; not previous to the assault.

Question. Do you know if any arrangements were made for the debouch of our troops from our lines, and their passage over the enemy's?

Answer. No, sir; General Burnside did not give me any instructions in regard to taking away the abatis or the rifle-pit on the front line.

Question. Were the obstructions on the enemy's line formidable, and of what did they consist?

Answer. They had a pretty strong abatis in front of their rifle-pits.

Question. Could they have been removed by working parties that usually accompany assaulting columns?

Answer. I did not go near enough to the crater along that line to judge of that, although it appeared to be merely the usual abatis placed in front of works, and placed in the usual position.

Question. Did you see the explosion of the mine?

Answer. Yes, sir.

Question. Was its effect to clear for any distance, and if so how much, the enemy's parapets?

Answer. Only a portion of the parapet was blown down; a portion of it remained standing. I suppose the crater that was formed might have been forty or fifty yards long, and perhaps twenty wide.

Question. Was the breach sufficient and practicable for the passage of troops in line?

Answer. I did not go in to look at the crater, and consequently I could not say whether they could go in without further work being done or not. I could not tell how deep it was.

Question. As an engineer would you criticise that point of attack?

Answer. I had been there working on that front before, and I had frequently expressed the opinion that the enemy could bring a flank fire all along there. That is, their line formed a kind of re-entering there.

Question. Did you ever chance to hear why that point was selected, or do you know?

Answer. I did hear that that mine was made because that hollow in front was a good position to run a mine from.

Question. State briefly some of the causes, in your opinion, of the failure of the assault.

Answer. I think one cause was the way in which the troops were taken in by the flank, passed down these covered ways, one on the right and the other on the left, on which General Ferrero's troops went down. I understand that only a portion of our parapet was taken away, and the troops had to go through by the flank instead of advancing in line. The portion of the ground south of the covered way was the way along which the troops could have advanced in line, the railroad cut being only six feet high in one place. The troops could easily have advanced through that. The troops were not in their proper positions at the time of the assault; that is, a portion of the troops were away back beyond the edge of those woods, when they should have been in the hollow.

By the court:
Question. Had you been placed in charge of a proper working party, suitably equipped, could you not, immediately after the explosion of the mine, have levelled the enemy's parapets, so as to have allowed troops in line of battle to have passed through?
Answer. I think I could. When the enemy afterwards had a flank fire between the enemy's line and ours, I offered to General Burnside to run a covered way from our line to the enemy's line on the right and left of the crater. (Lines marked on map 66 a and a'.)

By the judge advocate:
Question. Would any advantage have ensued from simply holding the crater, without advancing further?
Answer. No, sir; I do not think so.

By the court:
Question. Were there any preparations made in the way of collecting gabions, and so forth, so that, if the troops had been successful, we could have crowned the crest?
Answer. No, sir, not that I know of.
Question. Were tools collected or used, picks, shovels, axes, &c.?
Answer. I did not see any.

The court adjourned, to meet at ten o'clock on the 1st of September.

Record of the court of inquiry instituted by Special Orders No. 258, 1864, War Department.

		Page.
Testimony of	Brigadier General O. B. Wilcox, (recalled,) U. S. Vols	199
"	Brigadier General S. G. Griffin, U. S. Vols	200
"	Brigadier General J. F. Hartrauft, U. S. Vols	205
"	Surgeon O. P. Chubb, 20th Michigan Vols	210
"	Colonel H. G. Thomas, U. S. Colored Troops	216
"	Colonel C. S. Russell, 28th U. S. Colored Troops	223
"	Brigadier General A. Ames, U. S. Vols	227
"	Colonel H. L. Abbott, 1st Connecticut Artillery	234
"	Brigadier General G. Mott, U. S. Vols	237
"	Major J. C. Duane, (recalled,) U. S. Engineers	240
"	Lieutenant Colonel J. H. Barnes, 29th Massachusetts Vols	241
"	Lieutenant Colonel G. B. Robinson, 3d Maryland Battery	245
"	Major G. M. Randall, 14th New York Heavy Artillery	248
"	Lieutenant Colonel J. A. Monroe, 1st Rhode Island Artillery	251
"	Captain T. Gregg, 45th Pennsylvania Vols	253
"	Surgeon H. S. Smith, 27th Michigan Vols	256
"	Brigadier General J. C. Carr, U. S. Vols	260
"	Captain F. N. Farquhar, U. S. Engineers	265
"	Lieutenant A. A. Shedd, 43d U. S. Colored Troops	274
"	Captain E. T. Raymond, 36th Massachusetts Vols	275

TENTH DAY.

HEADQUARTERS SECOND CORPS,
September 1, 1864.

The court met pursuant to adjournment.
Present: Major General Hancock, Brigadier Generals Ayres and Miles, and Colonel Schriver, judge advocate.
The proceedings of the ninth day were read and approved.

General Wilcox recalled.

By the judge advocate:

Question. In your testimony yesterday you stated that, at the time of the explosion of the mine, you were at Romer's battery. Where were you the rest of the time?

Answer. Immediately after the explosion I started for the head of my column, which was on the left, and in the rear of the first division. I arrived at the front line of works nearest the crater before the whole of the first division had crossed. The head of my column had already commenced moving for the crater, and was then occupying the left portion of the enemy's works.

By the court:

Question. You stated that General Burnside's order directed that your division should bear to the left, and take up a position on the Jerusalem plank road. What was the cause of the failure to execute this manœuvre?

Answer. The first division was to move on Cemetery hill. I would state that Cemetery hill bore rather to the right of my front, so that it was necessary that Cemetery hill should be occupied before any ground beyond it could be occupied. In pursuance of my original expectation, I had given orders that the leading regiment should turn down to the left in the line of works, and the 27th Michigan started down that line. As soon as General Burnside perceived that the first division was not moving forward, he sent me orders to move forward my division direct upon Cemetery hill. My idea was to carry out the spirit of what was understood the day before, and my plan was to throw the whole division on the left into line, so that the right would rest on the Jerusalem plank road; and that would have completely protected the flank of the first division. This movement was begun, but the commanding officer of the 27th Michigan was shot, and the way the first division moved forward by division created more or less confusion; and by the time I received the order to advance on Cemetery hill, or before that in fact, the enemy had concentrated such a fire that we could not advance any further.

Brigadier General S G. GRIFFIN, United States volunteers, being duly sworn, says to questions by judge advocate:

Question. Were you at the assault on the 30th of July, and what was your command?

Answer. I was at the assault; my command was the second brigade, second division, (General Potter's,) 9th army corps.

Question. Did you regard that assault as a failure?

Answer. Yes, sir, I think I should, because we did not hold the ground.

Question. State some of the causes that you attribute this to.

Answer. In the first place, I should say that the troops in the front did not advance exactly as they should nor as far as they should. Probably the best ground was not selected. Then the cause of our not holding the ground was the piling in of so many troops in certain parts of the ground, where there was no room for them, and a panic having seized those troops, caused the disaster.

The enemy concentrated all their fire upon that point as soon as we attacked, which was another great reason, no doubt. We received their fire at that point from all directions, and very soon after we first arrived there it was a very sharp fire.

Question. Why were all the troops directed to that point?
Answer. I do not know.
Question. Do you think that arrangement was faulty?
Answer. The execution of the plan seemed to be faulty.
Question. Were any arrangements made for passing the troops through the abatis of our line, and over the parapet in front of the enemy's?
Answer. For my part, in my brigade I had a pioneer corps and skirmishers to clear the way for them.
Question. Did your command go beyond the crater?
Answer. It did.
Question. About how far?
Answer. I should judge two hundred yards. It might be more, or it might be less. It could not have been much less, however; that is, as near as I can judge.
Question. Why did you retire?
Answer. My troops were driven back from that point. They afterwards retired from the crater under orders. They were driven back from the advanced position at the time the panic seized the negroes, which more or less affected all our troops, and the negroes rushing through them as they did, carried them back. The rebels made a very desperate attack at the same time.
Question. If the enemy's parapets had been levelled on each side of the crater, or made practicable for the passage of troops, what would have been the probable result?
Answer. I am not sure that I can tell what the result would have been. Probably the troops might have advanced more readily and with more force, but it was not a thing easy to do.
Question. Do you know anything that prevented the troops, having attained the crater, from going forward immediately to the crest of Cemetery hill?
Answer. Nothing more than the sharp fire from the enemy.
Question. What kind of fire?
Answer. All kinds. I would state here that there is another reason why my troops could not go forward. The ground where they were was broken up with covered ways and numerous rifle-pits of the rebels. We had just driven the rebels out, and my troops occupied their places; therefore, in that position, disconnected as many of them were, it was difficult and almost impossible to form them to make a direct charge; but if a column had moved further to the left, I did not see any reason why they should not have gone in.
Question. Suppose you had had working parties to level the works, those working parties being supplied with facines and other necessary preparations to render a passage practicable, could you not have gone forward then?
Answer. I do not think there was time for that work. It would have taken hours. I think the time to go forward was at the first, because, very soon after we went there, the enemy concentrated their troops and poured into us at that point a terrible fire from every quarter.
Question. The great mistake, then, was the halting of the troops in the crater?
Answer. Yes, sir.
Question. Whose troops were they?
Answer. General Ledlie's division.
Question. Could the troops have gone over the enemy's parapets on the left of the crater in line of battle immediately after the explosion of the mine?
Answer. I think they could, but I could not say positively, because my attention was directed more particularly to the right of the crater.

Question. Could they have done it on the right?

Answer. No, sir, on account of those numerous cross-lines and pits and covered ways, which were full of the enemy's troops even after we arrived there; and others kept pouring in in addition to those that were already there.

Question. When the troops retired from the crater, was it compulsory from the enemy's operations, or by orders from your commander?

Answer. Partly both. We retired because we had orders. At the same time a column of troops came up to attack the crater, and we retired instead of stopping to fight. This force of the enemy came out of a ravine, and we did not see them till they appeared on the rising ground immediately in front of us.

Question. Where was your position during the contest?

Answer. I went up with my brigade, and while we were there I was most of the time in the crater, or near it, with my troops all the time.

Question. What was the force that came out to attack you—the force that was exposed in the open?

Answer. Five or six hundred men were all that we could see. I did not see either the right or left of the line. I saw the centre of the line as it appeared to me. It was a good line of battle. Probably, if we had not been under orders to evacuate, we should have fought them and tried to hold our position; but, according to the orders, we withdrew.

Brigadier General J. F. HARTRAUFT, United States volunteers, being duly sworn, says to questions by judge advocate:

Question. Were you at the assault on the 30th of July, and what was your command?

Answer. I was there; my command was the first brigade of the third division (General Wilcox's) of the 9th corps.

Question. Did you regard the attack as a failure?
Answer. I did.

Question. What, in your opinion, were some of the causes of that failure?

Answer. The massing of the troops in the crater, where they could not be used with any effect. I think that the troops, instead of being sent to the crater, should have been sent to the right and left, so as to have moved in line of battle, when they could have advanced in some kind of shape; but after they came into the crater, in the confusion they were in, other troops being brought up only increased the confusion, and by that time the enfilading fire of the enemy's artillery and infantry had become very annoying, which also made it very difficult to rally and form the troops.

Question. Do you know any reasons why the troops did not go to the right and left of the crater? Were there any physical obstacles to prevent them?

Answer. No, I think troops could have been sent there. The second brigade of my division was sent to the left of the crater. They took a portion of the pits. If a vigorous attack had been made on the right and left of the crater, I think the enemy's pits could have been taken without any difficulty, and the line occupied.

Question. What was the formation of your command in moving forward?

Answer. I formed my command, which was immediately in rear of the first division, (which was the assaulting division,) in one or two regiments front. I put two small regiments together; and my instructions were, after I passed through the crater with my advance, to form to the left of the first division, protecting its left flank while they were advancing, and form my line as the regiments would come up, so as to form a line of battle on the left of the first division.

Question. If the troops that first went into the crater had not delayed there, could they not, considering the consternation that the explosion of the mine made in the enemy's camp, have got forward to the crest of Cemetery hill?

Answer. I think they could have moved up to that crest immediately, if they had made no halt at all, under the consternation of the enemy. I think they would have had to re-enforce them speedily in order to hold that hill.

Question. The re-enforcements were there, were they not?

Answer. Yes, sir.

Question. And there was nothing to prevent that result?

Answer. I have thought, sometimes, that it would have been difficult to have sent troops through the crater in sufficient force to sustain the first division in advance on that hill; that the troops would have had, after all, to have been sent to the right and left of the crater, because very soon after I was in the crater myself the enemy were seen on the hill about the position we were to take, and was moving troops to the right. A dozen rebels were seen in the corn-field. My brigade moved right on after the first division, and after my fourth regiment had gone forward I went forward myself to the crater. The fifth regiment was then ordered forward, and was going up.

Question. Did you remain till the troops retired?

Answer. Yes, sir.

Question. Did they retire in confusion?

Answer. Yes, sir.

Question. Driven out?

Answer. They were driven out at the same time that I had passed the word to retire. It was a simultaneous thing. When they saw the assaulting column within probably one hundred feet of the works, I passed the word as well as it could be passed, for everybody to retire, and I left myself at that time. General Griffin and myself were together at that time. The order to retire we had indorsed to the effect that we thought we could not withdraw the troops that were there on account of the enfilading fire over the ground between our rifle-pits and the crater without losing a great portion of them, that ground being enfiladed with artillery and infantry fire. They had at that time brought their infantry down along their pits on both sides of the crater, so that their sharp-shooters had good range, and were in good position. Accordingly we requested that our lines should open with artillery and infantry, bearing on the right and left of the crater, under which fire we would be able to withdraw a greater portion of the troops, and, in fact, every one that could get away. While we were waiting for the approval of that indorsement, and the opening of the fire, this assaulting column of the enemy came up, and we concluded—General Griffin and myself—that there was no use in holding it any longer, and so we retired

By the court:

Question. What was the fault owing to—owing to the orders that were given, or to the execution of those orders? Was it that the plan was bad, or that the troops or their commanders behaved badly?

Answer. Not being familiar with all the orders and arrangements, I could not say. So far as my own command was concerned, we did all that we could do.

Question. Could you have been ordered to have done it in a better way?

Answer. I think if they had gone forward in line of battle it would have been successful. I consulted with General Bartlett and General Griffin and Colonel Humphreys, and we were all of the opinion that no more troops should be sent to the crater. After that the colored division passed right through the crater while we were in it.

Question. How did those colored troops behave?

Answer. They passed to the front just as well as any troops; but they were certainly not in very good condition to resist an attack, because in passing through the crater they got confused; their regimental and company organization was completely gone.

Question. What general officers were in or about the crater on the enemy's line during all this time?

Answer. General Griffin, General Bartlett and myself, of the 9th corps, and the general commanding the division of the 10th corps that was there, (General Turner.) I did not see any others, although there might have been others there.

Surgeon O. P. CHUBB, 20th Michigan volunteers, 9th corps, being duly sworn, says to questions by judge advocate:

Question. Were you at the assault on the 30th of July?
Answer. I was.
Question. State what you did there.

Answer. I accompanied the 2d brigade, of the 3d division of the 9th corps, across the ravine, and up to within about ten rods of our breastworks, at the point where the troops passed through immediately after the explosion of the mine. I took position in a bomb-proof, which had been used as some regimental headquarters, and remained there for the purpose of dressing wounded. This bomb-proof is located at a point about ten rods in rear of our line. Shortly after I took up that position, Generals Ledlie, of the 1st division, and Ferrero, of the 4th, came up to the front of the bomb-proof, and shortly afterward came in and took seats. This was in the morning, about half an hour after the explosion of the mine. That was some time before the colored troops came up. The 3d division (General Wilcox's) was then lying in a little dip of the ground—lying flat upon the ground to avoid shelling at that point, and General Ledlie's troops, of the 1st division, had crossed over our breastworks and gone over to the fort immediately after the explosion. I saw them go up. I was where I could see the explosion and the movement of the troops as they passed over the space between our works and the fort. Our division and our brigade of that division remained in that position for some time. General Ledlie came there and sat down in front of the place where I was; remained there some little time, and afterwards went inside and sat down—I could not tell how long, but not a great length of time after, because General Ferrero came in. His troops were then lying in the covered way and on the flat. They had not yet come up to go into action. While things were in that position, our 3d division made a move, charged over the works, some of them went to the fort, and some, I believe, came back. Then General Ferrero had brought his division up to that point, and seemed to be waiting for some orders or movement. General Ledlie received orders in my hearing to move his troops forward from where they were then lying. The order came something like this, as near as I can recollect: "The general wishes you to move your troops forward to the crest of the hill, and hold it." To the best of my recollection, that was the meaning of the order at least, and, I think, very near the words. I do not know whom the order came from. It was brought by an officer, and I supposed that "the general" meant General Burnside. General Ledlie despatched an aid or some other officer to order that done. Then, shortly afterwards, came an order to General Ferrero to move his division through, and charge down to the city. He replied that he would do so "as soon as those troops were out of the way." He did not designate what troops, so that I understood "those troops" meant the troops that were already there. But this order came two or three times, and the last time it came the order was peremptory "to move his troops forward at once." His answer to the order always was, that he would do so as soon as "those troops" were out of the way; and whenever General Ferrero made that answer, General Ledlie sent an aid to order the troops out of the way, and see that it was done, so that it became my impression that it was his troops that were in the way. These two general officers were in the bomb-proof with me. General Ledlie's troops were in the crater, and General Ferrero's were in the rear. After General Ferrero received this last peremptory order he went out; General Ledlie went out with him, and the colored troops commenced moving past the door of the bomb-proof—as it was in the track that troops took—and moved up; and I stepped out, and saw them go over our works just in front of where General Ledlie's division passed over. Then they passed out of sight of where I was standing; but in a very short time I heard they were coming back; and sure enough, they poured down all along in that vicinity, with a good many white troops mixed with them. About that time General Ferrero returned. I am not positive whether General Ledlie returned or not; and in answer to somebody who asked him how the battle was going, General Ferrero said we had lost everything, or something to that effect; that we were repulsed. He said it was nonsense to send a single body of troops, colored or white, forward at one single place, in front of lines held by us, to throw them in the face of a re-enforced enemy, or an enemy who had opportunities to bring other forces to bear. General Ferrero said he thought his division was needlessly slaughtered.

By the court:
Question. Did you see General Ledlie when his division advanced?
Answer. No, sir, I did not. Our division was lying in the covered way at the point in our first line of works about opposite the fourteen-gun battery, as it is called, and I had passed up the line of the hill to the crest, where I looked over the breastwork and saw those troops move forward, but I could not see everything distinctly, because there was considerable distance across the ravine or hollow to his division.
Question. Was there any conversation between those generals and yourself, while they were in the bomb-proof, bearing on this subject?
Answer. I asked General Ledlie, soon after he came in, if his division had been properly supported. The reason of my asking it was that I thought I heard some remark of his that led me to think it had not been, and, besides, I myself was entirely in the dark in regard to the delay; and so I asked him if his division had been properly supported as it was intended, and he said it had.
Question. Did you hear him give any reason for the division halting?
Answer. No, sir. From the efforts he made to have them ordered forward somewhere, I judged that it was contrary to his expectation that they did halt. He frequently sent up aids to have them moved forward somewhere, and from the order that came to him I supposed it was to the crest of the hill. The aid who brought the order said: "The general wishes you to move forward to the crest of the hill."
Question. Do you know any reason why he was not with his troops himself?
Answer. No, sir. But during almost the last moments of his stay there he sent an aid to ascertain how things were going on, and remarked that he could not go himself, as he had been hurt in the side by a spent ball. I cannot state positively when this occurred; it seemed to be after I first saw him; but I recollect his having mentioned that fact quite late in the forenoon, nearly noon, for the first time. I have a strong impression that he came back there after General Ferrero's troops moved forward, but I could not say so positively.

Colonel H. G. THOMAS, 19th United States colored troops, being duly sworn, says to questions by judge advocate:
Question. Were you at the assault on the 30th of July, and what was your command?
Answer. I was at the assault on the 30th of July, and commanded the second brigade, fourth division, 9th corps, (colored troops.)
Question. What was the formation of your troops in going to the assault?

Answer. The formation was by file left in front, which brought us faced by the rear rank when we made the charge.
Question. The head of your troops struck the enemy's line where?
Answer. I forced my brigade around the right of the crater, contrary to orders, because the crater was so full that no man could get through; that is, I left two staff officers to force them through. I went straight to the front and filed to the right, and went into these rifle-pits in the enemy's line as far as the head of the first brigade of our division, which I was ordered to support.
Question. Did you get beyond the line of the crater with your troops?
Answer. I did, sir.
Question. How far?
Answer. I should say about between three and four hundred yards to the right of the crater, and in front of it. I was ordered to support the first brigade when it made its charge.
Question. Did you get beyond the enemy's line?
Answer. I did, sir; I led a charge which was not successful. The moment I reached the head of the first brigade I started out the 31st colored regiment, which was in front, but it lost its three ranking officers in getting in position, and did not go out well.
Question. What, in your opinion, were some of the causes of the failure of the general assault on that day?
Answer. So far as I can judge from my own stand-point, my utter inability to make a decent charge with my own brigade was the fact that the pits, into which we were sent, were entirely occupied by dead and dying rebel troops, and our own from the first division of our corps, General Ledlie's. There was no room for us to move up. We were delayed, I should think, an hour and a half, in the covered way through which we moved, from the fact, so far as I can learn, that the first division did not make the charge. We were to occupy the pits after they made the charge.
Question. Do you know why the first division did not go forward?
Answer. I do not, sir.
Question. Did you see any of the appliances for overcoming obstacles that usually accompany troops—working parties with tools?
Answer. I saw no such preparations to remove obstacles in the enemy's line. I had no such assistance.
Question. Do you think the mode of marching up your command was a judicious one—the form, I mean?
Answer. No, sir; it was injudicious, for two reasons: First, we moved up by the flank; that I consider injudicious. And, secondly, we were ordered up left in front, which made us face by the rank rear, which was not a satisfactory way of manœuvring.
Question. Was it a verbal or a written order; and by whom was it issued?
Answer. It was a verbal order, issued by General Ferrero about eleven o'clock on the night before. The order to me that night was to go up by division, follow the first brigade, and to move left in front. But early in the morning I learned from a staff officer, whom I sent out to tell me when the first brigade moved, that it was filing along the covered way. My instructions were to follow the first brigade. I was detained at least an hour and a half in the covered way by the troops in front, and by the order of the assistant inspector general of the corps. He finding the pits into which we were to go full of troops, suspended the other order until he could see General Burnside.
Question. How did your particular command retire from the front?
Answer. In confusion.
Question. Driven?
Answer. Driven back by a charge of the enemy.
Question. And not by any orders?

Answer. No, sir; they received no orders. They were ordered to stop by myself and all my staff, who were in the pits. When I got into this position on the right of the crater, the fire was very severe; there was also a very severe enfilading fire from the right. I attempted one charge, without success, the moment I reached there. I could not get more than fifty men out. I sent word to General Burnside by Major Van Buren, of his staff—as he was the only staff officer I saw in the pits except my own—that unless a movement was made to the right, to stop the enfilading fire, not a man could live to reach the crest; but that I should try another charge in ten minutes, and hoped I would be supported. In about eight minutes I received a written order from General Ferrero in pretty near these words: "Colonels Seigfried and Thomas, commanding first and second brigades: If you have not already done so, you will immediately proceed to take the crest in your front." It was signed in the ordinary official manner: "By order of General Ferrero: George A. Hicks, captain and assistant adjutant general." I cannot produce that order because I destroyed it when I was captured in Petersburg. Colonel Seigfried had, I think, already received it, as he was in the crater. I sent word to Colonel Seigfried's brigade on my right, where I supposed the colonel to be, that I was about to charge; that we should go over with a yell, and that I hoped to be supported. I went over with two regiments and part of a third, but I was driven back. The moment they came back the white troops in the pits all left, and they after them. I was not supported at all in my charge.

Question. Where was the division commander all this time?

Answer. I do not know. When I went up with my brigade he was in a bomb-proof on the left, with the commanding officer of the first division. Generals Wilcox, Ledlie, and Ferrero were in the bomb-proof on the left.

Question. Was the bomb-proof a good place to see what was going on?

Answer. No, sir; there were places near there where something could be seen, but the earth about the crater prevented almost anything being seen immediately to the left of it. The dirt was thrown up very high. There were, I think, however, places near there where a view could be got.

Question. From what you know of affairs that day, is it your opinion that the assault ought to have been successful if the troops engaged in it had performed their duty?

Answer. Going up so late as I did, I am not a good judge, but I think from what I could see at the late hour at which I got in, that if the division that went in first had gone ahead, there is no question of our taking the crest on that ridge, Cemetery hill, hardly with the loss of a man. We waited in the covered way over an hour, with almost no musketry on our right. We were detained; there we could not get up.

By the court:

Question. Did you ever go over that ground afterwards?
Answer. I did, sir.
Question. Under what circumstances?
Answer. I went over it two days afterwards, the 1st of August, when the flag of truce was out.
Question. Did you see anything in the nature of the enemy's defences that would change the opinion you formed on the day of the assault?
Answer. No, sir.
Question. Did you see any obstacles in the nature of the ground?
Answer. No, sir.
Question. Did you have an opportunity of seeing what the enemy had on the top of Cemetery hill?
Answer. No, sir; I did not have an opportunity of seeing just what they might have had there.

Question. Did you see any works there?
Answer. No, sir; I do not think there were any.
Question. How did the colored troops behave?
Answer. They went up as well as I ever saw troops go up—well closed, perfectly enthusiastic. They came back very badly. They came back on a run, every man for himself. It is but justice to the line officers to say, that more than two-thirds of them were shot; and to the colored troops, that the white troops were running back just ahead of them.

Colonel CHARLES S. RUSSELL, 28th United States colored troops, being duly sworn, says to questions by the judge advocate:

Question. Were you at the assault on the 30th?
Answer. Yes, sir.
Question. And what was your command?
Answer. I was a lieutenant colonel, commanding six companies of the 28th United States colored troops, Thomas's brigade, of Ferrero's division.
Question. Did your command participate in the assault?
Answer. Yes, sir. We left the covered way to make the assault before eight o'clock, and ten minutes after eight part of my regiment with two others went over the outside of the enemy's line into what seemed to be a covered way beyond, to go to Cemetery hill. Mine was to have been third in order, but it became second,
Question. How far in advance did you get toward Cemetery hill?
Answer. Not exceeding fifty yards. We were driven back.
Question. By what?
Answer. I should judge by about from two to four hundred men, infantry, which rose up from a little ravine and charged us. Being all mixed up and in confusion, and new troops, we had to come back.
Question. Do you think you could have maintained yourself in that position if you had been supported by troops that were known to have been in the crater at that time?
Answer. No, sir; I do not think we could, considering our condition. There were no two companies together; the officers were shot down, and the troops were very much dispirited. They were all in there just as thick as they could possibly stick. The orders were to advance and take the crest of that hill at once, and I went right over with all the men I could gather, supposing that all the rest would follow. Not more than 150 or 200 men out of the three regiments went outside.
Question. Did your troops sustain a good deal of loss in that affair?
Answer. Yes, sir; I lost nearly half, and seven officers out of eleven.

By the court:

Question. Do you think that if you had advanced on the right or left of the crater, where the ground was more practicable, you would have done better?
Answer. Yes, sir; I think that if we had gone up there an hour before we could have carried the crest, for there was but little musketry fire at that time.
Question. Where were you during that interval?
Answer. In the covered way, in rear of a battery of $4\frac{1}{2}$-inch guns.
Question. Was the division cammander around there?
Answer. The division commander was at the head of the division. I saw him when we went into the crater. I passed him and spoke to him. He was then on the left of the first line of rifle-pits built by our people. I mean the most advanced line of rifle-pits.
Question. What did Colonel Siegfried's brigade do.

Answer. That brigade, instead of going into the crater, as near as I can tell, seemed to file to the right; at least that was my impression.

Question. Did they go over the enemy's breastworks?

Answer. I do not know, sir. My impression is that they did not.

Question. I mean the breastworks of which the crater was a continuation.

Answer. No, sir; I do not think they did.

By the judge advocate:

Question. Did you form any opinion as to the cause of that failure?

Answer. Yes, sir.

Question. What was it?

Answer. Delay. It was Lieutenant General Grant who moved us up, about 5 o'clock, for we had not started from our bivouac in those woods at 5 o'clock. General Grant rode up and asked what brigade that was, and what it was doing there. That was some time after the explosion of the mine and the cannonading had commenced. General Grant told us to move on. The order was not given to me directly; it was given to Colonel Thomas. Then we moved into the covered way and remained there till 8 o'clock.

The court adjourned to meet at 11 o'clock on the 2d September.

ELEVENTH DAY.

SEPTEMBER 2, 1864.

The court met pursuant to adjournment.

Present: Major General Hancock, Brigadiers General Ayres and Miles, and Colonel Schriver, judge advocate.

The proceedings of the 10th day were read and approved.

Brigadier General A. AMES, United States volunteers, being sworn, says in answer to questions by judge advocate:

Question. Were you present at the assault on the 30th day of July, and what was your command?

Answer. Yes, sir; I was present where I could see the last part of it. I had a division of the 18th army corps.

Question. Did your troops experience any interference from the 9th corps in moving into position in rear on that occasion?

Answer. Not directly. My division was a support. I understood from the commanding officer of the corps that my troops were held in reserve for any emergency that might arise, or a battle that might be fought after we had taken possession of the heights, and at no time were my troops further advanced than the woods in rear of our own works. At one time I was ordered to take my division in to support General Turner's. The idea was that he was to advance, and I was to carry my division in on his right, being careful not to get in in advance of him, so as to have his left flank interfered with. Upon receiving the order I understood that I was expected to move to the front through the covered way, but I found that there was still a brigade of General Turner's division in reserve, and as I passed through the covered way I saw that it was blocked up by one of General Turner's brigades. As it was intended that I should go to the front with my troops, I first went to see what kind of ground I was to pass over, and found that the covered way was blocked up by troops, as well as in some places by wounded coming to the rear, and in others by men carrying ammunition to the front. When I got to our most advanced position beyond the creek or bottom, I found that General Turner had a brigade massed there, and that there were evidently more troops in front than could be well handled. I had a conversation with General Turner, and the state of affairs was such that we thought it desirable that General Ord, from whom we received our orders, should know that it was impossible for us to move to the front at once, going down through the covered way, as he intended that we should. I immediately wrote a note to General Ord, requesting him to come down to the front and see the state of affairs for himself, otherwise his orders would probably not be obeyed. I went to the rear and found him, and came down to the front with him; and he then decided that our troops, at least that my division, should not move forward.

Question. Were the arrangements that were made for the passage of troops through the abatis near the parapet to go to the front adequate?

Answer. I think not. I did not examine it in particular, but I was down there when part of General Turner's command went to the front, and having nothing else to do, I drove some of his men over the parapet, and I found that they experienced great difficulty in getting through the abatis. The place that I refer to was at our right of the mine.

Question. State some of the causes for the failure of the assault on that occasion, in your opinion.

Answer. I then formed the opinion, and I have not seen any cause to change it, that at the time I was there a clear head, where it could see what was going on, and see the difficulties at the front, might have corrected a great many of the faults that then existed. I think the trouble was, no one person at the front was responsible, in consequence of which there was no unity of action. It took a long time for commanders in the front to communicate with those in the vicinity of the 14-gun battery in the rear, on the top of the high hill. My idea is that everybody appeared to be acting for himself, with no particular determination to go any further than he was compelled to. So far as I could see, when I arrived there, that appeared to be the state of the case.

Question. Will you, as far as your observation goes, remark upon the formation of the troops as they went forward, and also as to their preparation with all things needful for passing over the enemy's line of works and establishing themselves on the further side?

Answer. I remained in the rear with my troops until I was ordered to advance, and at this time part of the 10th corps had already advanced to our most advanced work, and the rest, as I stated, were in the covered way; and I did not see any of the 9th corps—the white troops of it—make any movements whatever. They had all moved forward and occupied the crater before I had gone to the front, so that I am ignorant of their formation. I know that the colored troops went down the covered way before the division of the 10th corps. It was my opinion, the case being as it was, that the division of the 10th corps should not have passed down the covered way; that they might have passed down the hill to the bottom, then passed over our works, and then up over the open ground towards the enemy's. I think all the troops should have gone that way. The massing of our troops at our most extreme advanced position, and then, crowded as they were, forming them for an advance, created more or less confusion. It would be likely to do so among the best of troops, and certainly it did in the 9th corps. I was going to remark that it was my opinion that, instead of waiting to have moved down the covered way, it would have been proper for me to have avoided the covered way and moved over the open ground. There was very little fire upon that ground, and the enemy could have probably brought but little there at best; and I think the division could have been moved down the hill and up over the open ground without serious loss—no more than might be expected; and then the troops would have been already in position to have acted with some considerable vigor, and with a reasonable hope of adequate results.

Question. Do you know of, or did you see, anything like fascines, gabions, or such things as are generally used, and considered necessary, indeed, for an affair of that kind, on the ground?

Answer. No, sir. When I saw the difficulty in passing our troops from our most advanced work to the crater, and saw that there was a little depression where the ground rose on each side of it—not much, to be sure, but almost enough to cover the troops—I recommended to my superiors, General Ord, and also his staff, that men with shovels should go out and throw up—certainly on the left of the crater, on a little rising ground—a rifle-pit or breastwork to cover our men, so that they could pass from our line of works to the crater without danger; but I learned that there were no tools there for any such work; but it was concluded that these tools should be obtained, and afterwards Captain Farquhar, of the engineers, told me that he had sent for the tools, and that they would go to work and make this covered way. But before anything could be accomplished, the troops were running back.

Question. Do you think the plan for the assault was one that, with ordinary diligence and skill, ought to have been successful?

Answer. I don't see how ordinary troops, with good commanders, and one head to direct, could have possibly failed under the circumstances. It was necessary that some one person should be present to direct the various movements and make them one operation. If there had been, perhaps the result would have been different.

Question. Do you think it would have been any benefit to our arms to have held the crater simply?

Answer. That, I think, would depend upon our ultimate object. I think it would have been no use to have held the crater if we had remained inactive, or on the defensive, as we have done since. If it was our intention to work up to the crest by mining, it would have been so many hundred yards to our advantage.

Question. Would it not have been difficult to hold the place in consequence of the fire that could have been brought to bear upon it? Is not that the re-entrant point in the line?

Answer. Yes, sir. The enemy's fire, at least as I saw it, was at least a semicircle. That is, a continuation of the line of fire from one side in the direction of the crater would strike the enemy's works on the other, making the line of fire a semicircle.

Question. You regard the order to withdraw the troops at the time it was given a judicious one, do you?

Answer. I think so, under the circumstances. I understood that the troops in the crater did not move forward; and that being the case, the sooner they went back the better.

Colonel H. L. ABBOT, 1st Connecticut artillery, being duly sworn, says to questions by judge advocate:

Question. Did you participate in the assault on the 30th July, and what was your command, and what were your particular duties at that time?

Answer. I did participate in the assault. I was in command of all the heavy guns and mortars, 81 in all. I remained most of the time on the left, in charge of the mortar batteries especially. We expected fire from the enemy's salient, and I had sixteen mortars to keep it down, and I remained chiefly there and by Van Ried's battery.

Question. Do you regard the artillery fire on that occasion as very effective; and was it what it ought to have been, and what it was meant to be?

Answer. I do, sir. I think it accomplished all we hoped to do.

Question. Were there at any point obstacles to the fire of the artillery which ought to have been removed?

Answer. Yes, sir; in front of what we call the 14-gun battery.

Question. Please to state what they were.

Answer. This battery is nearly in front of the mine, and some trees were growing a little to its left, which masked the fire of the guns upon the next rebel battery to our left of the mine. These trees it was our wish to have removed. They had not been when the battery was first established, because we did not wish to show the enemy what we were doing. As soon as the six $4\frac{1}{2}$-inch guns were in position, I was anxious to have them cleared away.

Question. What measures did you take to effect that?

Answer. I had, on several occasions, conversation with General Burnside on the subject, in which I referred to the necessity of their being cleared away before we could use the battery to advantage. On the night of the 27th, working parties were ordered by him to cut the trees, but they were driven off after accomplishing very little. On the night of the 28th I represented the matter to General Hunt, chief of artillery, at the headquarters of the army of the Potomac. I went with him to the telegraph office, when he telegraphed General Burnside, I should think about seven o'clock in the evening, urging him to have the trees removed. One of my captains, Captain Pratt, who commanded the battery, was so desirous of having his field of fire clear, that he took some of his own company and cut partially that night, no working parties coming. On the night of the 29th, the matter was again raised—by whom I do not know—but General Burnside declined to have any trees cut on that night, lest it might give the rebels an idea of the attack. But a party was formed which did begin to cut as soon as the mine exploded. It partially but not entirely cleared away the trees, and the guns were enabled to do some service, but they could not see one flanking gun which did us a good deal of harm. I could not see myself, from where I was, exactly what that gun was doing. I received orders from General Hunt—I should think about half past seven o'clock, but I cannot be sure as to the exact time—to try to turn some of my mortars upon it, as it was making trouble. I did so, and made some good shots in that direction, but I do not think the fire of the gun was stopped. The battery was too far of. The trees that were removed were removed partly by my men and partly by the negroes.

Question. Were you in a situation to tell the court whether the artillery fire of the enemy was at all effective, and how soon after the explosion of the mine?

Answer. It would be very difficult to state positively on account of the smoke and the noise of our own guns. I do not think that they fired any guns for nearly an hour. I could not detect any, although I was watching carefully at Van Reid's battery, so as to make any alteration in our fire that might be necessary. I am sure they did not fire from the place we expected it most, in front of the 5th corps. I do not think they fired during the day from here to do any damage. They fired a few shots, however. They fired from a 30-pounder at our battery, which, of course, did not amount to anything. This gun was on the plank road. Over on the right I could not form any exact idea of what they were doing, but I could see that there was certainly no heavy firing. There were only a few straggling shots in that direction. Where we most feared the fire, we did not get any at all. The firing that they did, according to the reports I have received, was from a light battery on the crest, and it was once moved from its position by our mortar batteries on our right, near the left of the 18th corps. We expected fire from the two flanks, and we had a heavy fire of mortars to stop both fires.

Brigadier General B. MOTT, United States volunteers, being duly sworn, says, to questions by judge advocate:

Question. Will you state to the court what time and under what circumstances you relieved the 18th corps, previous to the assault on Petersburg?

Answer. I left across the James river on the night of the 28th July. I crossed the river at 9 o'clock, and one of General Ord's aids met me and put me in position before daylight next morning. As soon as it was dark, on the night of the 29th, I relieved the 18th corps and one division of the 10th, in the intrenchments, and completed the operation about eleven o'clock.

Question. What did General Ord say to you as to the practicability of making an assault in your front in connexion with the operation of the mine?

Answer. He wished me to say to General Hancock, and he said that he had also telegraphed to General Meade, that it was not practicable to make an assault there on account of a good abatis being in front of the enemy's work, and on account of their being well wired, so that it was impossible for the men to get through.

Question. During the assault of General Burnside through the crater and subsequent to that time, did you make any examination to see whether the enemy had left your front or not?

Answer. Yes, sir.

Question. What was the result?

Answer. I sent a staff officer to each brigade commander to instruct them to make a demonstration to see if the enemy had left. General De Trobriand, commanding the 1st brigade, attempted to advance his pickets which he had out. In doing so he had one officer and fifteen men killed. Colonel Madill, commanding the 2d brigade, said he had a position from which he could see if any one left his front, and not a man left since daylight. Colonel McAlister commanding the 3d brigade, made a demonstration by sounding the bugle for a charge, and snapped some caps, and he immediately received a volley from the enemy's works. He had no pickets out in the daytime.

Question. What time was this?

Answer. I think it was about 7 o'clock, about the time I got a despatch, when General Burnside reported that the enemy had left his front.

The court then adjourned, to meet at 10 o'clock on the 3d of September.

TWELFTH DAY.

SEPTEMBER 3, 1864.

The court met pursuant to adjournment.

Present: Major General Hancock, Brigadier Generals Ayres and Miles, and Colonel Schriver, judge advocate.

After taking testimony of all the witnesses present on this day, the proceedings of the eleventh day were read and approved.

Major DUANE recalled.

Question. Were there pontoon trains, sand-bags, &c., in readiness at convenient points near the place of assault on the 30th of July, as ordered by Major General Meade?

Answer. There were.

Question. Were engineer officers detailed for each corps?

Answer. There were.

Question. You stated in your former testimony that you were near the 5th corps at the time of the assault. Were there arrangements made for passing the field artillery through the works in front of that corps?

Answer. I think not. I did not understand that it was part of the plan that the troops of the 5th corps should advance through that part of their front. They were to have advanced on the 9th corps front. I understood it was intended that they should pass through the enemy's lines opposite the left of the 9th corps. I had no conversation with General Meade on that subject. I merely inferred it from what I had heard.

Question. Were the pioneers equipped for destroying the enemy's abatis, and were intrenching tools in readiness for use when required for the 5th corps in their progress against the rebel line?

Answer. I do not know. The pioneers were not under my orders.

Question. Why did not the engineer department take charge of the engineering operations and be responsible for their execution?

Answer. General Burnside took charge of the operations, and I was directed by General Meade not to interfere with them. I had once or twice attempted to send officers to direct the operations, and General Burnside would not allow them to do so.

Lieutenant Colonel JOSEPH H. BARNES, 29th Massachusetts volunteers being duly sworn, says to questions by judge advocate:

Question. Were you in the crater at the assault on the 30th of July, and what was your command?

Answer. No, sir; I was not in the crater.

Question. Were you near it?

Answer. I was near it on the outside.

Question. In what formation did your command go forward?

Answer. It will be necessary to state that I did not go forward with my command proper. On the night previous I was in command of the division picket, and on the picket being relieved, in accordance with orders I had received, I followed my command, but did not reach my command proper until after they had moved forward to the assault. I went forward to the crater at the head of the troops of the fourth division, (colored troops.)

Question. What was the condition of things in or about the crater when you arrived there?

Answer. When I arrived at the crater the negro troops were pouring through the opening down into the crater. I hesitated about going in there with them, there was so much confusion at the bottom of the crater, and I remained outside with a captain, who had been brigade officer of the day, who was with me. We remained outside the crater until all the negro troops had passed in; then, my orders being to join my command, and seeing a color in the earthworks about one hundred yards to the right of the crater, I moved to the right, supposing it might be my color, keeping all the time about one hundred yards from the ditch. Arriving at that point I found it was not my regimental color; but meeting the commanding officer of the 13th Indiana regiment of the 10th corps, I stopped to converse with him. There were in front of me at this time, lying outside the earthworks, negro troops in two lines—that is to say, four deep. They were lying on their faces in line of battle immediately on the outside of the ditch. Directly in front of them was another line of negro troops in the ditch, mingled with the white troops of the first division. I did not go into the crater, because I was desirous, if possible, of learning where my regiment was before getting in. In justice to myself I might say, that it was a much more exposed position outside the ditch than it was inside; but, as I said before, I desired to find my regiment first; but being unable to do so, I had determined to go in and look for it in the ditch. Just as I was about to step forward about half a dozen officers of the negro troops rose up and attempted to get their commands out of the work—for the purpose of advancing, I should judge, although I knew nothing of what the movements were to be, and therefore only judged so from their actions. About 200 men, white and black, rose right in my front, their officers attempting, as I understood, to advance them, but they immediately fell back; and thereupon the two lines of negro troops that had been lying in front of me near the ditch rose to their feet and went back to the rear, marching over the 13th Indiana regiment, which remained in its position. This was about one hundred yards on the right of the crater.

Question. The white troops in the crater belonged to what division?
Answer. They belonged to the first division, (General Ledlie's.)
Question. State to the court, if you know, or give your opinion as to why they hesitated or stopped in the crater and did not go forward.
Answer. Of my own knowledge I do not know.
Question. Did any of the troops of the first division get beyond the crater towards the enemy?
Answer. I do not know.
Question. In your opinion, how did this hesitation or rest in the crater affect the result of the action?
Answer. In my opinion, it affected it in this manner: The hesitation and the length of time consumed in reorganizing or rearranging the men for moving forward enabled the enemy immediately in front to be prepared, not only for our advance, which they were, but to advance against us, which they did.
Question. Do you know whether the division and brigade commanders were present when the troops halted in the crater?
Answer. No, sir; I do not know of my own knowledge.

By the court:

Question. How many troops were there in those two lines which lay just along the enemy's rifle-pit?
Answer. The number from the crater to a short distance to my right was, I should judge, six or seven hundred, possibly more. I could not say how many more there might be, because of the nature of the ground, there being a descent in the ground, beyond which I could not see.
Question. Did they at any time charge up the slope towards Cemetery hill?
Answer. They did not to my knowledge.
Question. When they rose up and went to the rear, in what order did they go?
Answer. In disorder.
Question. Were those troops again brought forward that day?
Answer. Not to my knowledge; some of them were rallied in rear of the next line in the rear.

Lieutenant Colonel GILBERT P. ROBERTSON, third Maryland battalion, being duly sworn, says to questions by judge advocate:
Question. Were you in the crater at the assault on the 30th of July, and what was your command on that occasion?
Answer. I was in the crater at the assault, and I formed part of the third line making the assault; the brigade was in three lines; I belonged to the second brigade of the first division.
Question. In what formation did your command go forward?
Answer. In column of battalions.
Question. Did any of your troops get beyond the crater?
Answer. Yes, sir; some of them did. My brigade went to the right of the crater to the breastwork in front of the battery, which was in accordance with the orders from Colonel Marshall the night before.
Question. Did the mass of the troops of the first division halt in the crater and about it, or did they go forward towards the crest?
Answer. I did not see any of them go forward towards the crest. A majority of them went through the crater perpendicular to our front. I kept to the right.
Question. You know the fact that those troops halted there?
Answer. Yes, sir.
Question. Do you know why they halted?
Answer. I could not positively say why, without it was in consequence of the ground being so small and so many of them getting together in the crater. There was great confusion in the crater.

Question. Was not there plenty of ground in front; why did they not go?

Answer. Yes, sir. I cannot answer what transpired on the left. I went to the right and kept up a fire, and advanced as far as I could, until I got to an angle in the works, which was held by the rebels. I used the Spencer rifle upon them. The battalion numbered only fifty-six men.

Question. Was there confusion at that point of attack, or were the troops in any order?

Answer. I could not see any order at all. There was nothing but confusion in the crater. What was in the covered way beyond the crater towards Petersburg I could not say.

Question. Did you have an opportunity of observing whether efforts were made by division and brigade officers to relieve the troops from this disorder?

Answer. Yes, sir; every effort that could be made was made by Colonel Marshall and myself, for he had given orders that I should be obeyed, as I was next in command. I saw no division commander in the crater at the time.

Question. What was the cause of this confusion that you say existed in the crater?

Answer. I cannot assign any reason for the confusion if it was not, as I said, the ground being so much torn up and the place being so small. And when they got in there the fire was pretty strong.

Question. What was the nature of the enemy's fire at that time, heavy or otherwise?

Answer. When we got there the fire was not so strong as it was half an hour afterwards.

Question. What kind of fire was it, artillery or musketry?

Answer. Both. I would call it a moderate fire. I do not think the heavy fire commenced until after 8 o'clock. I think we had fire there from their mortar batteries.

Major GEORGE M. RANDALL, 14th New York heavy artillery, being duly sworn, says to questions by judge advocate:

Question. Were you in or about the crater on the 30th July, and what was your command?

Answer. I was in the crater, and was acting aid to General Ledlie.

Question. In what formation did your division go forward?

Answer. It went forward, as I should judge, by the flank. They did not go forward in solid column, as we expected they would do.

Question. Do you know any reason why they did not?

Answer. No, sir.

Question. Were you near the head of the column? Or were you among the first that got into the crater?

Answer. I was about the second line. I was ordered by General Ledlie to go forward with the advancing column.

Question. Had you an opportunity of observing why the troops halted in the crater?

Answer. Yes, sir. I saw the 14th New York and 2d Pennsylvania heavy artillery pass through the crater and occupy traverses in rear of the fort, and there they remained.

Question. Were efforts made to urge them forward, according to the plan?

Answer. Yes, sir.

Question. And at a time, too, when they were not in disorder?

Answer. They were very much in disorder when they arrived at the crater. That was just the difficulty. If the regiments had been in their proper places when they arrived at the crater we would have taken the crest of the hill. But they were scattered, and it was impossible to get any of the regiments together. Colonel Robinson and myself attempted to get them forward, but could not do so.

Question. While this was going on, was there a fire of any account from the enemy?

Answer. No, sir; there was not much when we first advanced in there.

Question. Please to state, in your opinion, what it arose from.

Answer. I cannot tell exactly. I suppose it was because, when the mine exploded, they were so much excited; for when the mine exploded, they hardly knew what they were doing. It appeared to be the opinion of all who were there that immediately after the explosion one good regiment in solid column could have gone forward without any difficulty. But we were in there only a short time when the enemy opened on our right and left.

Question. Was the division commander present during this confusion?

Answer. Not in the crater.

Question. Is it your opinion that this hesitation affected the result of the action?

Answer. Yes, sir.

Question. Do know whether there were any pioneers with tools or engineer troops with fascines or gabions ready to come forward to crown the crest in the event of your getting up on Cemetery hill?

Answer. I think I saw the 25th Massachusetts, first division, with shovels and spades; I cannot positively say, but I think I saw them there somewhere.

By the court:

Question. To all appearances were the rebels awake and vigilant before and up to the time of the springing of the mine, or were they apparently asleep and unprepared?

Answer. They appeared to be awake. When I was on the first line, the line that General Wilcox's division occupied, shots were continually fired by the enemy from the fort before the mine exploded. They came from the right or left; at least from the immediate vicinity of the fort.

Question. Are you certain they came from the enemy?

Answer. Yes, sir, I am positive of it.

Question. Where was the division commander during the assault?

Answer. He was in rear of the first line, the line occupied by General Wilcox's troops. I carried orders to him, and found him always in rear of the first line, sitting down behind the parapet.

Question. Do you know any reason why General Ledlie was not with his division in front?

Answer. No, sir.

Colonel J. A. MONROE, 1st Rhode Island artillery, being duly sworn, says to questions by judge advocate:

Question. Were you at the assault on the 30th July, and in what capacity did you serve?

Answer. I was there as chief of artillery of the 9th army corps.

Question. What preparations were made, such as making openings for passing field artillery through our line of works, when it should become necessary in the front?

Answer. No such preparations were made to my knowledge.

Question. What preparations were made for unmasking our artillery, such as cutting down the trees and obstructions that were in front?

Answer. No preparations had been made immediately before the explosion. Some had been made weeks before. The trees in front of what is known as the "heavy work" were left standing until the morning of the 30th, directly after the explosion of the mine, when a few of the trees were cut down.

Question. Do you understand that some of the batteries were masked by those trees?

Answer. They were not exactly masked, but the trees obstructed the fire of the batteries.

Question. Were you aware that the 5th corps' artillery was to find its way to the front through openings that were to be made in the 9th corps's front?

Answer. No, sir.

Question. What have you to say about the fire of the enemy's artillery, as to its commencement and its formidableness on that day?

Answer. It was not severe at all at first. Half or three-quarters of an hour after—it might have possibly been an hour—they had a battery firing which enfiladed our line on the right. That fire came apparently from one or two guns on Cemetery hill.

By the court:

Question. What troops occupied that line?

Answer. I think it was the first division of the 9th corps, which had endeavored to move up towards the crest of Cemetery hill by the way of the Chimneys, where there is another battery. The fire of the enemy's battery on Cemetery hill was not formidable, because the heavy battery of ours kept it almost completely silenced.

Question. Had those trees been removed, could our batteries have played on the enemy's guns on our right of the crater, which were firing across the plain, over which our troops were to charge?

Answer. Yes, sir. They could also have fired upon a battery in the edge of the woods, almost in front of the crater, that was enfilading our line.

Question. What is the reason the trees were not cut down?

Answer. I called General Burnside's attention to it three weeks before. I went to the general the night before the explosion of the mine, and tried to get a large party to cut those trees down, and he said no trees should be cut down until the mine should have exploded. I asked him for a detail, and he gave me eighty men, which were to be set at work immediately after the explosion of the mine. I put them to work, two men to a large tree and one man to a small one' and they commenced cutting, but only a few trees were cut down, the party was so small.

Captain THEODORE GREGG, 45th Pennsylvania volunteers, (9th corps,) being duly sworn, says to questions by judge advocate:

Question. Were you at the assault on the 30th July, and what was your command?

Answer. I was at the assault on the 30th July; my command was the 45th Pennsylvania veteran volunteers, first brigade, second division, 9th army corps.

Question. State briefly what you observed about the operations on that day.

Answer. My regiment was in the intrenchments opposite the rebel fort that was blown up. About half past three o'clock, on the morning of the assault, I received orders from Captain Raymond, aid to Colonel Bliss, commanding the brigade, to leave part of the regiment, deployed as skirmishers, and go back with the remainder to the edge of the woodlands and form on the right of the 4th Rode Island, and remain there until further orders. When the explosion took place I was ordered by Captain Peckham, who was also an aid to Colonel Bliss, to follow the 4th Rhode Island. We marched by the flank, left in front, through the covered way. On arriving at our front line of the works opposite the crater the order was given to double-quick across the open plain. On arriving in front of the rebel works we found several regiments lying down on the ground, and a great many men killed and wounded. I then received orders to charge across the crater. I gave the command "Face by the right flank," in order to march in line of battle, and on arriving at the edge of the crater I faced again by the left flank, and marched in single file around and in rear of the crater. The crater was filled with the troops of the first and second divisions of the 9th army corps. General Bartlett, commanding the first brigade, first division, General Griffin, commanding the second brigade, second division, and General Hartrauft, were in the crater. They appeared to be endeavoring to rally the troops for the purpose of charging forward to some buildings, about four hundred yards in the rear of the crater, towards Petersburg, and, I believe, on Cemetery hill. I was ordered by General Bartlett to charge across the plain and secure those buildings, so that we could use them to operate as sharpshooters against the enemy's artillery. At the same time Captain Peckham ordered me to form in line of battle and then charge down in the rear of the enemy's line of rifle-pits on the right—that is, to face by the rear rank and charge the enemy in the rifle-pits on the right. As soon as they should see the colors of the 45th, other regiments of the first brigade, of the second division, were to charge forward. As soon as I had the regiment formed in line I received an order from General Griffin and other officers to charge to the left of the crater, in order to create a diversion in favor of other regiments of the second brigade. The crater was filled with troops.

Question. What troops were they?

Answer. I knew them to be troops of the first and second divisions by seeing General S. G. Griffin and other officers, as well as men whom I had known before. They were very much mixed up, and could not be got forward by their officers. Some officers attempted to rally them and some did not.

Question. Was there any firing at this time?

Answer. There was. The enemy's fire could not reach the men in the crater, but there was heavy firing at this time in front of the crater from field-pieces about those buildings. The enemy also had an enfilading fire of artillery from the fort situated on our left, and from another battery on our left, and at a deep cut in the railroad. I received so many orders from so many different commanders at that time that I did not know which to obey.

Question. Where was your division commander?

Answer. I do not know where he was. I did not see the division commander there at any time during the action. I understood that he was on the ground. He might have been there, and, in the confusion, I not have seen him. Neither did I see our brigade commander. General Potter was our division commander and Colonel Bliss our brigade commander.

Surgeon H. E. SMITH, 27th Michigan volunteers, (9th corps,) being duly sworn, says to questions by judge advocate:

Question. Were you at the assault on the 30th July, and in what capacity?

Answer. I was in charge of the surgeons on the field of the third division, to see that the wounded were attended to and taken to the rear.

Question. Had you an opportunity, on that occasion, of observing any of the military movements?

Answer. Nothing more than seeing our troops advance over our breastworks. I was there when the colored troops were ordered to advance, and heard General Burnside's aid give repeated orders to General Ferrero to take his troops up and charge towards Petersburg. I think he gave the order three times. The third order General Burnside sent to General Ferrero was an imperative order to advance. To the previous orders General Ferrero would make the answer, that the other troops were in his way, and he could not possibly advance while they were there, and if they would be taken out of the way he would go ahead.

Question. General Ferrero was present?

Answer. Yes, sir.

Question. Any other generals?

Answer. General Ledlie was present. Those were the only generals I saw.

Question. Did General Ledlie make any reply, that you heard, when this order was given to General Ferrero?

Answer. I did not hear him make any reply or any statement on the subject of that order from General Burnside.

Question. What troops did you understand General Ferrero to allude to as being in the way?

Answer. I did not understand. I supposed they were those troops that had made the charge. The general was in front of a bomb-proof which had been used as a regimental headquarters, and was situated about 10 or 12 rods, as near as I could judge, in rear of the work. This bomb-proof was fronting to the rear.

Question. Did General Ferrero leave that place and accompany his troops to the front when they left?

Answer. He did. General Ledlie, I think, left the bomb-proof for a very short time. That was about the time of the stampede of the darkeys. Then, I think, both General Ledlie and General Ferrero returned about that time. I am not positive, however, for I was busy seeing that the wounded were being attended to. General Ledlie asked me for stimulants, and said he had the malaria, and was struck with a spent ball. He inquired for General Bartlett, as he wanted to turn the command over to him and go to the rear. It was one of General Bartlett's aids, I believe, who replied that he was in the crater.

Question. You say that during the stampede Generals Ferrero and Ledlie returned to the bomb-proof. How long did they remain there?

Answer. General Ferrero remained a very short time. He was exhausted. I think he came in for the purpose of getting some stimulant, too, and, I think, he went out immediately after I gave him the stimulants. General Ledlie remained some time longer, probably half an hour, I should judge.

Question. You mention stimulants. What were they, hartshorn, materia medica, or what?

Answer. It was rum, I think. I had rum and whiskey there, and I think I gave them rum.

Question. How often did you administer stimulants to those two officers during that day?

Answer. I think that once was the only time. I was not in the bomb-proof all the while that they were there. It was perfectly safe in there, but it might not have been outside. I had to go out to look after the wounded.

Question. Were there any brigade or regimental commanders in the bomb-proof, any commanding officers besides those whom you have named?

Answer. Yes, sir.

Question. Name them.

Answer. There was a colonel commanding a brigade of colored troops, Colonel Siegfried, I believe. He came there after the stampede quieted down a little, after the troops stopped going to the rear. Also Lieutenant Colonel Cutchin, of the 20th Michigan. He came in from the crater, about the middle of the day, to see General Wilcox, to learn if anything could be done to relieve the troops in the crater, as they were suffering very much for water, and also from the artillery fire of the enemy.

Question. What was the reply?

Answer. General Wilcox was not there, sir.

Question. How long did the colonel stay there?

Answer. Half an hour, at least. He was very much exhausted in running over. He said he had come through a very heavy fire, and it was almost certain death to come from the crater to that place.

Brigadier General J. C. CARR, United States volunteers, being duly sworn, says to questions by judge advocate:

Question. Were you at the assault on the 30th of July, and what was your command?

Answer. Yes, sir, I was at the assault. My command was the first division of the 18th army corps and a portion of a colored division of the one known as Hinck's division of colored troops. I had one brigade of that division.

Question. Had you opportunities of observing the progress of events on that day; were you in a situation to see things?

Answer. Nothing but my own command. I took position in the trenches with my own command. I relieved the troops of General Burnside's command, the 9th army corps, on the evening before, with the exception that I had one brigade, which I did not put in the front line. I kept that in reserve to fill the vacancy left in our line at the point where the assaulting column was to debouche from our intrenchments.

Question. Could you see the formation of the assaulting column?

Answer. Yes, sir; I saw it before it made the assault.

Question. What was the formation?

Answer. I should judge it was in column of battalions.

Question. Was that the first division?

Answer. I think it was, sir. It was very dark, not yet daylight in the morning. I left General Burnside's headquarters at twenty minutes after three o'clock, and as I passed going down I could see the column on my left in column of battalions, I should judge. The position I had did not afford me a good opportunity for observing anything but my own immediate command, as I was in the trenches during the engagement, and remained there until 12 o'clock that day.

At about half past 8 o'clock General Turner, of the 10th corps, was ordered to form his division in rear of the intrenchments, and in doing so he found that it would crowd too much on the troops in his front, and that there was no room to get his division in there. He immediately sent for General Ord to come down—I think it was General Ames who called upon General Ord to come down—and see the position of the troops for himself, and he went down to see the position of the troops in the trenches. As General Turner was forming his command, an attempt was made by the troops on my right to charge the rifle-pits. I saw a vacancy, a gap that I thought about four regiments would fill, and assist that line of battle that was going over our breastworks to take those rifle-pits. I immediately took command of part of Turner's division, and ordered them over the line to join the line of troops then advancing, and told them to charge the rifle-pits in their front, which they did. That was about two hundred yards on the right of the crater. After putting those troops in, I stepped back from the intrenchments some ten or fifteen yards towards the covered way, and I had scarcely got back to the lower end of the covered way when the stampede began, and I suppose two thousand troops came back, and I was lifted from my feet by the rushing mass, and carried along with it ten or fifteen yards in the covered way. What staff I had with me assisted me in stopping the crowd in the covered way, and in putting some of them in position in the second line: some were in the first line. I left General Potter in the covered way.

Question. Was there any good reason that you know of for this retirement of the troops?

Answer. No, sir.

Question. Did you notice any arrangements that were made for the passage of troops over the parapet and through the abatis of our lines?

Answer. No, sir. There was no abatis in the front where I was, at least I did not notice any abatis. There was abatis to the right of it.

Question. If you had moved your troops to the front how would you have got through our lines? what mode would you have taken to get them through? what formation would you have adopted?

Answer. I should have formed a column of divisions.

Question. Were there intervals made in our line for the passage of such a column?

Answer. I could not say, sir; all I know is what was in my immediate front. I saw that there were no obstructions to prevent troops passing over our intrenchments to the enemy's works. The rifle-pit I speak of was an advanced work of the enemy where they had a thin line of skirmishers; the main line was behind it.

Question. Did the enemy fire from the main line upon your party that took the pits?

Answer. Yes, sir; briskly with musketry. I do not know the exact hour, but I think that it was about half past 8 a. m.

Question. How did those troops of the 10th corps that you took forward pass over the parapet of our line?

Answer. They went over by a flank movement.

Question. How long did those troops of the 10th corps hold the pits that they took?

Answer. Just as long as I was walking about thirty paces. I had just got into the mouth of the covered way when they came back. I saw officers waving their swords on the pits, but they did not stay a great while.

The court then adjourned, to meet at ten o'clock on the 5th of September.

THIRTEENTH DAY.

HEADQUARTERS SECOND CORPS,
Jones's House, September 5, 1864.

The court met pursuant to adjournment.

Present: Major General Hancock, president; Brigadier Generals Ayres and Miles, and Colonel Schriver, judge advocate.

Captain F. U. FARQUHAR, United States engineers, being duly sworn, says to questions by judge advocate:

Question. Were you at the assault on the 30th of July, and in what capacity?

Answer. I was present, and was chief engineer on the staff of General Ord-commanding the 18th corps.

Question. Were you in a situation to observe the operations on that day?

Answer. I was a portion of the time, after the smoke cleared away.

Question. Did you witness the explosion of the mine?

Answer. Yes, sir; I saw the explosion of the mine.

Question. Relate what you saw done unusual on such occasions—occasions of assault; state some of the omissions, if any, and the principal causes which conduced to the failure of the assault.

Answer. At or near fifteen minutes before 5 a. m. the explosion of the mine took place. Immediately on the explosion the artillery opened, and, I should judge, three or five minutes afterwards we heard the cheer of the assaulting party. Nothing could be seen from the time of the opening of the artillery for twenty-five minutes or half an hour, when the smoke commenced to clear away. At the time of the explosion of the mine the general officers in command were in the covered way, in rear of the 14-gun battery, near what are known as "Thomas's Chimneys," I believe. Between half and three-quarters of an hour after the explosion Lieutenant Colonel Loring, of General Burnside's staff, came from the front, and reported that the troops that were in the crater were lying there, and could not be pushed forward or gotten out of it. It was fully three quarters of an hour after the explosion of the mine before the enemy opened any

14

artillery, and then not at all severe. At the time of the explosion, Turner's division of the 10th corps, which was under General Ord's command, was lying at or near the mouth of, or entrance to, the covered way on the right of the 14 gun battery. Ames's division of the 18th corps was in rear of that strip of woods which is in rear of the 14-gun battery. Both the covered ways on the right and left of this 14-gun battery were filled with troops of the 9th corps—the negro division being in the left covered way. There seemed to be an unaccountable delay in the advance of the supports to the first assaulting column. I cannot tell the exact time. I did not see the second one go up, but I heard the cheer some time after—how long I cannot recollect. Somewhere between half past six and seven o'clock I went to the front line, to which the assaulting columns had started. The ground immediately in front of our salient from which our forces started was favorable for charging over, as the troops were partially protected pretty near all the way up from the left flanking fire by a very small ridge; the men could have passed over easily, and there were very few dead or wounded lying on that space between our line and the crater. The men seemed to be lying in the crater, and on our side of the crater, but no movements seemed to be taking place. I saw General Turner at that time going to the crater. There seemed to be a lack of enthusiasm or spirit in both officers and men. The negro division filed over our parapet and went into the crater by the flank, exposing their whole line as they passed over from our line to the enemy's to the fire from both sides of the crater. At between nine and ten o'clock the cross-fire of the enemy in front of the salient had become so severe that hardly a man could pass from our salient to the crater without being hit. At this front line that I went to there seemed to be no person of any authority to meet any emergency that might arise, and in that, in my opinion, lies one of the chief causes of the disaster. The chief causes of failure are, in the first place, that the mine was in the wrong place, because it was in a re-entrant; and in the second, that there was no officer present to make any new dispositions or movements to meet any emergency that might arise. It seemed to me, so far as I could see, that the troops were not ready to move. They were in the covered ways, and so situated that you could not follow the assaulting columns up with the necessary supports. As it was, the assaulting column, if it had gone forward, would be a mile ahead before the supports could get up. I was present when General Turner sent back a note to General Ord, saying that he could not get his troops forward on account of General Burnside's troops being in the way. General Ord then sat down and wrote a letter to General Meade—I believe it was General Meade— telling him that he would advance Turner's division as soon as General Burnside's troops were out of the way. He showed it to General Burnside, who asked him not to send it, for he would have his troops out of the way immediately; but whether he ever sent it or not, I do not know. General Ord then went to the front himself at the time that General Turner said he could not get his troops forward, and found the same state of things existing—that the covered way was filled up with General Burnside's troops going to the front, and that the wounded were being brought to the rear in the same covered way that the troops going forward to fight were going forward in. There was no reason why the troops should move through the covered way at all. From the position of the assaulting columns and the troops fighting, the enemy could not notice troops passing down the slope of the hill without going through the covered way. The colored troops seemed to be well led, and followed their officers with as much enthusiasm as any other troops that day. They seemed to go about two hundred or two hundred and fifty yards to the right of the crater, going towards the enemy's intrenchments. Then there came a halt, and by that time General Turner had got one of his brigades to the front, and he ordered an assault with his brigade. Instead of passing along the edge of the crater as the other troops had done, which gave them a temptation to lie down, he charged to the right of the crater. It was just then that the negroes came back, and his men were carried back with them. I went to the front immediately after this affair, when I saw General Turner, and he seemed to be very much distressed about it.

Question. State if there were any means taken for crowning the crest if gained—working parties with fascines, gabions, intrenching tools, &c.

Answer. I can speak only with reference to myself. I had my sappers and miners equipped with tools, ready to move with the 18th corps when it should move.

Question. With the ordinary performance of their duties by officers and men, on such occasions, ought not the assault to have been successful?

Answer. It was successful, for the line was carried. It only wanted some person present to tell them what to do afterwards. I think that, had there been any person of authority at the place, even at our own front line, at the salient, to have given directions at the proper time, we had ninety-nine chances in a hundred of being successful in the object expected to be gained. From my own experience I know that it would take you at least three minutes to get to the front through the covered way, because it was so crowded, and three minutes to get back again to where the general was, and then count your time for observation besides; and at that time, when the opposing forces were so close to each other, ten minutes would make a great deal of difference. I think that, with the exception of a lack of enthusiasm, the troops behaved as well as ever troops behaved. What they wanted was handling. Just in front of the crater, in rear of the enemy's line, there was a sort of a redoubt or earthwork upon the hill, from which not a shot was fired. There was not a soul between the crater and that position, and I believe that position was the objective point of the assault. And I think, had the troops been pushed forward properly, the columns following as one column should have followed another, there would have been no difficulty in the place being carried.

Question. Then there were no physical obstacles in the way of our success?
Answer. No, sir.

Question. Is it your opinion that, if we had not had the mine, we would have been more successful?

Answer. No, sir. The mine of itself was a success. The consternation of the enemy in consequence of the explosion of the mine more than compensated for the flanking fire which they opened upon us. But it was three-quarters of an hour before they opened fire.

Question. Were adequate preparations made for the passage of our troops over our parapets and through the abatis?

Answer. There seemed to be room enough at our salient to pass over certainly in regimental front.

Question. Could artillery have passed through?

Answer. No, sir. I saw no place where artillery could have passed through at any point within two hundred or two hundred and fifty feet of the salient. I do not know how practicable it was further to the right or left. Leading up from the hollow to the front, the covered ways were very narrow, not at all adequate to the necessities of the occasion for conveying troops to the front. And there was room enough in that hollow to have massed all the troops under cover of the darkness. Had that been done, as it was not light when the mine should have exploded, they would all have been in the enemy's lines before they could have been much hurt.

Question. Who gave you orders for preparing the fascines, gabions, and intrenching tools, and working parties, in the 18th corps?

Answer. I got them from General Ord. All I had were shovels, spades, picks, and sand-bags.

Question. Did you see General Burnside on that occasion?

Answer. Yes, sir; I saw him quite frequently.
Question. Any of his division and brigade commanders?
Answer. I only noticed one division commander.
Question. Name him.
Answer. General Potter. If the others were there I did not happen to see them.

There being no more witnesses in attendance the court adjourned, to meet at 10 o'clock on 6th September.

FOURTEENTH DAY.

HEADQUARTERS SECOND CORPS,
Jones's House, September 6, 1864.

The court met pursuant to adjournment.

Present: Major General Hancock, president; Brigadier Generals Ayres and Miles; and Colonel Schriver, judge advocate.

The proceedings of the 12th and 13th days were read and approved.

There being no more witnesses* present, the court was cleared.

The record of evidence was referred to, and discussions took place; after which the court adjourned, to meet at 10 o'clock a. m. on the 7th September.

FIFTEENTH DAY.

HEADQUARTERS SECOND CORPS,
September 7, 1864.

The court met pursuant to adjournment.

Present: Major General Hancock, president; Brigadier Generals Ayres and Miles; and Colonel Schriver, judge advocate.

Discussion was resumed; and the court then adjourned till 10 o'clock on the 8th September.

SIXTEENTH DAY.

HEADQUARTERS SECOND CORPS,
September 8, 1864.

The court met pursuant to adjournment.

Present: Major General Hancock, president; Brigadier Generals Ayres and Miles; and Colonel Schriver, judge advocate.

Lieutenant A. A. SHEDD, 43d United States colored troops, being duly sworn, says, to judge advocate's

Question. Were you at the assault on the 30th July, and in what capacity?
Answer. As aide-de-camp to Colonel Siegfried, commanding 1st brigade, 4th division, 9th corps.
Question. Were you in the crater at any time?
Answer. I was.
Question. Were any of your troops there?
Answer. They were; they went in under Colonel Siegfried; they were not all in.
Question. If they halted there, why did they so?
Answer. There were so many troops in before they came; that is one reason.
Question. What efforts were made to push them forward beyond the crater?

---

* The following named officers, on account of sickness or absence, did not appear as witnesses before the court: Brigadier Generals Ledlie, Turner, and Burnham; Colonel Siegfried; and Lieutenant Colonels Loring and Pleasants.

Answer. The colonel (Bates) of the 30th regiment colored troops led his through; that is the only one I saw go through the crater.

Question. Was Colonel Siegfried present with his troops in the front all the time?

Answer. He was; he came out when the troops did, about 10 to 11 o'clock.

Captain E. T. RAYMOND, 36th Massachusetts volunteers, duly sworn, says, to judge advocate's

Question. Were you at the assault on the 30th July, and in what capacity?

Answer. I was, as brigade inspector, 1st brigade, 2d division, 9th corps.

Question. What was your general position on the field on that occasion?

Answer. In the crater a portion of the time; part near the right of our brigade, in our works.

Question. Under whose immediate orders were you serving?

Answer. Colonel Z. R. Bliss, 7th Rhode Island volunteers, commanding the brigade.

Question. Was he with his troops all the time?

Answer. He was. At 7 o'clock we moved down the covered way, from in rear of our batteries, in front of our reserve camp. Three regiments went into the crater; the remainder of the brigade stopped in the works. About 8 o'clock I was sent into the crater by Colonel Bliss, to ascertain why the three regiments in front did not charge—he remaining in the works, with four regiments of the brigade. I went, and found the three regiments were formed in the covered way beyond the crater, towards Cemetery hill.

Question. Where did the covered way strike the enemy's pits to the left of the crater?

Answer. Facing their front, it led a little to our right of the crater, tending off a little to the right of Cemetery hill.

Question. What efforts were made to bring up the regiments which were left in the works by their commanders?

Answer. The three regiments which went forward were first to charge before the rear regiments were to move forward.

Question. With what part of the brigade was Colonel Bliss?

Answer. With the portion that was left behind. He remained with the last regiment, and did not go forward at all to my knowledge.

The court, after discussion with closed doors, adjourned, to meet at 10 o'clock on the 9th September.

SEVENTEENTH DAY.

HEADQUARTERS SECOND CORPS,
September 9, 1864.

The court met pursuant to adjournment.

Present: Major General Hancock, president; Brigadier Generals Ayres and Miles; and Colonel Schriver, judge advocate.

The proceedings of the 14th, 15th, and 16th days were read and approved.

The court, with closed doors, then resumed the discussion of the testimony; and decided on the following finding and opinion:

FINDING.

After mature deliberation on the testimony adduced, the court find the following facts and circumstances attending the unsuccessful assault on the 30th July.

The *mine*, quite an important feature in the attack, was commenced by Major General Burnside soon after the occupation of his present lines, without any directions obtained from the headquarters of the army of the Potomac. Although its location—and in this the engineers of the army concur—was not considered by Major General Meade a proper one, it being commanded from both flanks and reverse, the continuance of the work was sanctioned.

It was not the intention of the lieutenant general commanding, or of the major general commanding the army of the Potomac, it is believed, to use the mine in the operations against Petersburg, until it became known that the enemy had withdrawn a large part of his forces to the north side of the James river, when it was thought advantage might be taken of it in an assault. All the Union troops sent north of the James had been recalled in time to participate in the assault, so that the whole of the forces operating in front of Petersburg were disposable.

The mine was ordered to be exploded at 3.30 a. m., but, owing to a defective fuze, it did not take place till 4.45.

The detailed order or plan of operations issued by Major General Meade is in accordance with General Grant's instructions, and was seen and approved by the latter previous to its publication. It is marked K in the appendix.

It is the concurrent testimony that, had the order been carried out, success would have attended the attack. Also, it is in evidence that General Meade met General Burnside and three of his division commanders the day before the assault, and impressed upon them that the operation was one of *time;* that unless prompt advantage were taken of the explosion of the mine to gain the crest, it would be impossible to get it, or the troops to remain outside of their lines.

That order directed that General Burnside should "form his troops (the 9th corps) for assaulting," and that General Ord, commanding the 18th corps, and General Warren, commanding the 5th corps, should support the assault on the right and left respectively.

Major General Burnside's order (No. 60, appendix) directed Brigadier General Ledlie's division, immediately on the explosion of the mine, to be moved forward and crown the crest known as Cemetery hill. Brigadier General Wilcox was to move his division forward as soon as possible after General Ledlie's, bearing off to the left, and Brigadier General Potter was to follow and go to the right. Brigadier General Ferrero was to move his (colored) division next, and pass over the same ground that General Ledlie's did.

Five minutes after the explosion of the mine General Ledlie's division went forward, and it was followed by those of Generals Wilcox and Potter, though it is in evidence that the latter did not move in the prescribed order, and that they were not formed in a manner to do the duty assigned them.

General Ledlie's division, instead of complying with the order, halted in the crater made by the explosion of the mine, and remained there about an hour, when Major General Meade received the first intimation of the fact through a despatch from Lieutenant Colonel Loring, assistant inspector general of the 9th corps, intended for General Burnside, in which he expressed the fear that the men could not be induced to advance.

This crater was on the enemy's line of works, and was fifty to sixty yards long, twenty yards wide, and twenty to twenty-five feet deep. It was about five hundred yards from the Cemetery crest.

General Burnside was then (5.40 a. m.) ordered to push forward to the crest all his own troops, and to call on General Ord to move forward his troops at once. It is in evidence, that when the order was communicated to General Ferrero, commanding the colored division, he said he could not put in his troops until the troops already in front should be moved out of the way. They did go forward, however, after some delay, but only to be driven back, and in their flight to rush impetuously against other troops, destroying their formation, and producing disorder.

At 6.10 a. m., inquiry being made of General Burnside if it would be an advantage for Warren's supporting force to go in at once on the left, the answer was, "There is scarcely room for it in our immediate front." The importance of the utmost promptness, and the securing of the crest at once, at all hazards, were urged upon him at 6.50 a. m.

At 7.20 a. m. General Burnside reported to General Meade that he was doing all in his power to push forward the troops, and if possible carry the crest, and also that the main body of General Potter's division was beyond the crater. It does not appear in evidence, however, that they ever got any considerable distance, not exceeding two hundred yards, beyond the crater towards the crest, whence they were driven back immediately. This was also the fate of the few colored troops who got over the enemy's line for a moment.

At 9 o'clock a. m. General Burnside reported many of the 9th and 18th corps were retiring before the enemy, and then was the time to put in the 5th corps. It having just been reported, however, by two staff officers (not General Burnside's) that the attack on the right of the mine had been repulsed, and that none of the Union troops were beyond the line of the crater, the commanding general thought differently; and the lieutenant general concurring, General Burnside was directed at 9.50 a. m. to withdraw to his own intrenchments immediately or at a later period, but not to hold the enemy's line any longer than was required to withdraw safely his men. This order brought General Burnside to General Meade's headquarters, where he remonstrated against it, saying by nightfall he could carry the crest. No other officer who was present, and who has testified before the court, concurred in this opinion. The troops in the crater were then ordered to retire; but before it could be effected they were driven out with great loss, at two o'clock p. m. These troops, however, were making preparations to retire, and but for that would probably not have been driven out at that time.

The 5th corps did not participate at all in the assault, and General Ord's command only partially, because the condition of affairs at no time admitted of their co-operation, as was contemplated by the plan of assault.

The causes of failure are—

1. The injudicious formation of the troops in going forward, the movement being mainly by flank instead of extended front. General Meade's order indicated that columns of assault should be employed to take Cemetery hill, and that proper passages should be prepared for those columns. It is the opinion of the court that there were no proper columns of assault. The troops should have been formed in the open ground in front of the point of attack, parallel to the line of the enemy's works. The evidence shows that one or more columns might have passed over at and to the left of the crater, without any previous preparation of the ground.

2. The halting of the troops in the crater instead of going forward to the crest, when there was no fire of any consequence from the enemy.

3. No proper employment of engineer officers and working parties, and of materials and tools for their use, in the 9th corps.

4. That some parts of the assaulting columns were not properly led.

5. The want of a competent common head at the scene of the assault, to direct affairs as occurrences should demand.

Had not failure ensued from the above causes, and the crest been gained, the success might have been jeoparded by the failure to have prepared in season proper and adequate debouches through the 9th corps lines for troops, and especially for field artillery, as ordered by Major General Meade.

The reasons why the attack ought to have been successful are:

1. The evident surprise of the enemy at the time of the explosion of the mine, and for some time after.

2. The comparatively small force in the enemy's works.

3. The ineffective fire of the enemy's artillery and musketry, there being scarcely any for about thirty minutes after the explosion, and our artillery being just the reverse as to time and power.

4. The fact that some of our troops were able to get two hundred yards beyond the crater towards the crest, but could not remain there or proceed further for want of supports or because they were not properly formed or led.

OPINION.

The court having given a brief narrative of the assault, and "the facts and circumstances attending it," it remains to report that the following named officers engaged therein appear, from the evidence, to be "answerable for the want of success" which should have resulted:

I. Major General *A. E. Burnside*, United States volunteers, he having failed to obey the orders of the commanding general—

1. In not giving such formation to his assaulting column as to insure a reasonable prospect of success.

2. In not preparing his parapets and abatis for the passage of the columns of assault.

3. In not employing engineer officers who reported to him to lead the assaulting columns with working parties, and not causing to be provided proper materials necessary for crowning the crest when the assaulting columns should arrive there:

4. In neglecting to execute Major General Meade's orders respecting the prompt advance of General Ledlie's troops from the crater to the crest; or, in default of accomplishing that, not causing those troops to fall back and give place to other troops more willing and equal to the task, instead of delaying until the opportunity passed away, thus affording time for the enemy to recover from his surprise, concentrate his fire, and bring his troops to operate against the Union troops assembled uselessly in the crater.

Notwithstanding the failure to comply with orders, and to apply proper military principles, ascribed to General Burnside, the court is satisfied he believed that the measures taken by him would insure success.

II. Brigadier General *J. H. Ledlie*, United States volunteers, he having failed to push forward his division promptly according to orders, and thereby blocking up the avenue which was designed for the passage of troops ordered to follow and support his in the assault. It is in evidence that no commander reported to General Burnside that his troops could not be got forward, which the court regard as a neglect of duty on the part of General Ledlie, inasmuch as a timely report of the misbehavior might have enabled General Burnside, commanding the assault, to have made other arrangements for prosecuting it before it became too late. Instead of being with his division during this difficulty in the crater, and by his personal efforts endeavoring to lead his troops forward, he was most of the time in a bomb-proof, ten rods in rear of the main line of the 9th corps works, where it was impossible for him to see anything of the movements of troops that were going on.

III. Brigadier General *Edward Ferrero*, United States volunteers—

1. For not having all his troops found ready for the attack at the prescribed time.

2. Not going forward with them to the attack.

3. Being in a bomb-proof habitually, where he could not see the operation of his troops, showing by his own order issued, while there, that he did not know the position of two brigades of his division, or whether they had taken Cemetery hill or not.

IV. Colonel Z. R. *Bliss*, 7th Rhode Island volunteers, commanding 1st brigade, 2d division, 9th corps—

In this: that he remained behind with the only regiment of his brigade which did not go forward according to the orders, and occupied a position where he could not properly command a brigade which formed a portion of an assaulting column, and where he could not see what was going on.

V. Brigadier General O. B. *Wilcox*, United States volunteers.

The court are not satisfied that General Wilcox's division made efforts commensurate with the occasion to carry out General Burnside's order to advance to Cemetery hill, and they think that more energy might have been exercised by Brigadier General Wilcox to cause his troops to go forward to that point.

Without intending to convey the impression that there was any disinclination on the part of the commanders of the supports to heartily co-operate in the attack on the 30th day of July, the court express their opinion that explicit orders should have been given assigning one officer to the command of all the troops intended to engage in the assault when the commanding general was not present in person to witness the operations.

WINFIELD S. HANCOCK, *Major General U. S. Vols.,*
President of Court.

EDWARD SCHRIVER, *Inspector General U. S. A.,*
Judge Advocate.

The court then adjourned *sine die.*

WINFIELD S. HANCOCK, *Major General U. S. Vols.,*
President of Court.

EDWARD SCHRIVER, *Inspector General U. S. A.,*
Judge Advocate.

APPENDIX TO THE RECORD OF THE COURT OF INQUIRY.

APPENDIX A.

Despatches from Major General Meade to Lieutenant General Grant, July 24, 26, and 28, 1864, and from General Grant to General Meade, July 24, 26, 28, 29, and August 1, 1864.

A.

"HEADQUARTERS ARMIES OF THE UNITED STATES,
"*City Point, Virginia, July 24,* 1864.

"GENERAL: The engineer officers who made a survey of the front from Bermuda Hundred report against the probability of success from an attack there; the chances they think will be better on Burnside's front. If this is attempted, it will be necessary to concentrate all the force possible at the point in the enemy's line we expect to penetrate. All officers should be fully impressed of the absolute necessity of pushing entirely beyond the enemy's present line, if they should succeed in penetrating it, and of getting back to their present line promptly if they should not succeed in breaking through.

"To the right and left of the point of assault all the artillery possible should be brought, to play upon the enemy in front during the assault. Thin lines would be sufficient for the support of the artillery, and all the reserves could be brought on the flank of their commands nearest to the point of assault, ready to follow in if successful. The field artillery and infantry, held in the lines during the first assault, should be in readiness to move at a moment's notice, either to their front or to follow the main assault, as they should receive orders. One thing, however, should be impressed on corps commanders; if they see the enemy giving way in their front, or moving from it to re-enforce a heavily assaulted position of their line, they should take advantage of such knowledge, and act promptly without waiting for orders from their army commander.

"General Ord can co-operate with his corps in this movement, and about five thousand troops from Bermuda Hundred can be sent to re-enforce you, or can be used to threaten an assault between the Appomattox and James rivers, as may be deemed best.

"This should be done by Tuesday morning, if done at all. If not attempted, we will then start at the date indicated to destroy the railroad as far as Hicksford, at least, and to Weldon if possible.

"Please give me your views on this matter, and I will order at once. In this I have said nothing of the part to be taken by the cavalry, in case the enemy's lines are assaulted. The best disposition to be made of them probably would be to place them on the extreme left, with instructions to skirmish with the enemy, and drive him back, if possible, following up any success gained in that way according to the judgment of the commander, or orders he may receive.

"Whether we send an expedition on the railroad, or assault at Petersburg, Burnside's mine will be blown up.

"As it is impossible to hide preparations from our own officers and men, and consequently from the enemy, it will be well to have it understood as far as possible that just the reverse of what we intend is in contemplation.

"I am, general, very respectfully, &c.,

"U. S. GRANT, *Lieutenant General*.

"Maj. Gen. GEORGE G. MEADE, *Commanding Army of the Potomac*.

"Official copy:

"S. WILLIAMS, *A. A. G.*"

B.

"HEADQUARTERS ARMY OF THE POTOMAC,
"*July* 24, 1864.

"GENERAL: I have received your letter per Lieutenant Colonel Comstock. In reply thereto I have to state that yesterday I made in person a close and careful reconnoissance of the enemy's position in my front. Although I could not detect any positive indication of a second line, yet, from certain appearances at various points, I became satisfied that a second line does exist on the crest of the ridge, just in rear of the position of Burnside's mine. I have no doubt of the successful explosion of the mine, and of our ability to crown the crater, effect a lodgement, and compel the evacuation of the enemy's present occupied line, but from their redoubt on the Jerusalem plank road, and from their position in front of the Hare House, their artillery fire would render our lodgement untenable, and compel our advance or withdrawal.

"The advance, of course, should be made, but its success would depend on the question whether the enemy have a line on the crest of the ridge. If they have, with the artillery fire they can bring to bear on the approaches to this second hill, I do not deem it practicable to carry the line by assault, and from my examination, together with the evident necessity of their having such a line, I am forced to believe we shall find one there.

"I cannot, therefore, advise the attempt being made, but should it be deemed expedient to take the risks, and there is certainly room for doubt, I would like a little more time than is given in your note in order to place in position the maximum amount of artillery to bear upon the lines not assaulted. In reference to the assaulting force, it will be composed of the 9th and 2d corps.

"The 5th corps will have to remain in their present position, and be prepared to meet any attempt of the enemy to turn our left flank, which is not altogether unlikely, particularly if we should fail in our assault, and be compelled to withdraw.

"I am fully impressed with the importance of taking some immediate action, and am satisfied that, excepting regular approaches, the springing of Burnside's mine and subsequent assault is the most practicable, and I am not prepared to say the attempt would be *hopeless*. I am, however, of the opinion, so far as I can judge, that the chances of its success are not such as to make it expedient to attempt it.

"Very respectfully, yours,

"GEORGE G. MEADE,
"*Major General, Commanding*.

"Lieutenant General U. S. GRANT.

"P. S.—I enclose you a report of Major Duane, which confirms my views; if Wright is soon to return, and we can extend our lines to the Weldon railroad, we could then advance against the salient on the Jerusalem plank road, and make an attempt to carry them at the same time we assaulted in Burnside's front.

"This was my idea some time ago, and we have been preparing the necessary siege works for this purpose. Under your instructions, however, none of the heavy guns and material have been brought to the front, and it would take, perhaps, two days to get them up.

"GEORGE G. MEADE.

"Official copy:

"S. WILLIAMS, *A. A. G.*"

B 2.

"HEADQUARTERS ARMY OF THE POTOMAC,
"*Office of Chief Engineer, July* 24, 1864.

"GENERAL: In reply to your communication of this date, I have the honor to state that the line of the enemy's works in front of General Burnside is not situated on the crest of the ridge separating us from Petersburg; that the enemy have undoubtedly occupied this ridge as a second line.

"Should General Burnside succeed in exploding his mine, he would probably be able to take the enemy's first line, which is about one hundred yards in advance of his approach. Beyond this I do not think he could advance until the works in front of the 5th corps are carried, as the 9th corps column would be taken in flank by a heavy artillery fire from works in front of the centre of the 5th corps, and in front by fire from the works on the crest near the Cemetery hill. I do not believe that the works in front of the 5th corps can be carried until our lines can be extended to the left so as to envelop the enemy's line.

"Very respectfully, your obedient servant,

"J. C. DUANE,
"*Major Engineers, United States Army.*

"Major General MEADE, *Commanding Army of the Potomac.*

"Official copy:

"S. WILLIAMS, *A. A. G.*"

C.

"HEADQUARTERS ARMIES OF THE UNITED STATES,
"*City Point, July* 24, 1864.

"GENERAL: Your note, brought by Colonel Comstock, is received. It will be necessary to act without expecting Wright. He is now in Washington; but it is not fully assured yet that Early has left the valley, and if Wright was to start back no doubt the Maryland raid would be repeated. I am not willing to attempt a movement so hazardous as the one against intrenched lines, against the judgment of yourself and your engineer officers, and arrived at after a more careful survey of the grounds than I have given it. I will let you know, however, in the morning what determination I come to.

"Very respectfully, your obedient servant,

"U. S. GRANT, *Lieutenant General.*

"Major General MEADE,
"*Commanding Army of the Potomac.*

"Official copy:

"S. WILLIAMS,
"*Assistant Adjutant General.*"

D.

"HEADQUARTERS ARMY OF THE POTOMAC,
"*July* 26, 1864—12 m.

"Lieutenant General GRANT:

"More critical examinations from a new signal station would lead to the conclusion that the enemy have detached works on the ridge in front of Burnside, but they have no connected line. This fact increases the chances of a successful assault, taken in connexion with the fact that General Burnside does not now think the enemy have discovered his mine; on the contrary, believes they are laying the platform for a battery right over it.

"I have suspended the orders to load and discharge it to-morrow, as it may yet be useful in connexion with further operations.

"I am afraid the appearance of McLaws's division, together with Wilcox's, previously reported, will prevent any chance of a surprise on the part of our people to-morrow. Yesterday's Richmond Examiner also says your strategic movements are known, and preparations made to meet them, referring, I presume, to Foster's operations.

"There was considerable shelling by the enemy yesterday afternoon all along our lines, brought on, I think, by Burnside discovering a camp he had not before seen and ordering it shelled. No serious casualties were produced on our side, but the 5th corps working parties were very much annoyed and interrupted. With this exception, all was quiet.

"GEO. G. MEADE, *Major General.*

"Official copy:

"S. WILLIAMS, *A. A. G.*"

E.

[Cipher.]

"UNITED STATES MILITARY TELEGRAPH,
"*By telegraph from City Point*, 3 *p. m.*, dated *July* 26, 1864.

"Major General MEADE:

"The information you have just sent, and all information received on the subject, indicates a probability that the enemy are looking for a formidable attack either from General Burnside or north of the James river, and that they will detach from Petersburg heavily to prevent its success. This will make your remaining two corps, with the 18th, relatively stronger against the enemy at Petersburg than we have been since the first day. It will be well, therefore, to prepare for an assault in General Burnside's front, only to be made if further development justifies it. If made, it would be necessary to abandon most of the front now held by the 5th corps.

"U. S. GRANT, *Lieutenant General.*

"Official copy:

"S. WILLIAMS, *A. A. G.*"

F.

"HEADQUARTERS ARMY OF THE POTOMAC,
"5.30 *p. m., July* 26, 1864.

"Lieutenant General U. S. GRANT:

"Telegram 3 p. m. received. The only preparation that can be made is the loading of Burnside's mine. I cannot advise an assault with the 2d corps absent, for some force must be left to hold our lines and protect our batteries.

"The withdrawal of the 5th corps would prevent any attempt on our part to silence the fire of the enemy's guns in front of the 5th corps, and unless these guns are silenced no advance can be made across the open ground in front of the 9th corps.

"It is not the numbers of the enemy which oppose our taking Petersburg; it is their artillery and their works, which can be held by reduced numbers against direct assault.

"I have just sent you a despatch indicating an attack on my left flank by the enemy. This is my weak point, and a formidable attack turning my flank would require all my force to meet successfully.

"GEO. G. MEADE, *Major General.*

"Official:

"S. WILLIAMS, *A. A. G.*"

G.

"UNITED STATES MILITARY TELEGRAPH,
"*By Telegraph from City Point*, 12.20 *p. m.*, dated *July* 28, 1864.

"Major General MEADE:

"Your despatch of 12 m. received. Unless something turns up north of the James between this and night that I do not expect, you may withdraw Hancock, to be followed by Sheridan, and make arrangements for assault as soon as it can be made. We can determine by the movements of the enemy before the time comes whether it will be advisable to go on with the assault. I will put in the 18th corps, or not, as you deem best.

"U. S. GRANT, *Lieutenant General.*"

"Official:

"S. WILLIAMS, *A. A. G.*"

H.

"HEADQUARTERS ARMY POTOMAC, 1 *p. m., July* 28, 1864.

"Lieutenant General GRANT:

"Your despatch of 12.20 received. On reflection, I think daylight of the 30th is the earliest time it would be advisable to make the assault. Besides the time required to get up heavy guns and mortars, we require the night to make certain preliminary arrangements, such as massing troops, removing abatis from the debouch of the assaulting column, &c. I shall make the assault with the 9th corps, supported by the 2d. The reserves of the 18th should be held in readiness to take part, and, if developments justify it, all of Ord's and Warren's commands can be put in.

"GEO. G. MEADE, *Major General.*

"Official:

"S. WILLIAMS, *A. A. G.*"

I.

"Headquarters Armies of the United States,
"City Point, Va., July 29, 1864.

"General: I have directed General Butler to order General Ord to report to you for the attack on Petersburg. The details for the assault I leave to you to make out.

"I directed General Sheridan, whilst we were at Deep Bottom last evening, to move his command immediately to the left of Warren from Deep Bottom. It will be well to direct the cavalry to endeavor to get round the enemy's right flank; whilst they will not probably succeed in turning the enemy, they will detain a large force to prevent it. I will go out this evening to see you; will be at your headquarters about 4 p. m.

"Very respectfully, your obedient servant,
"U. S. GRANT, *Lieutenant General.*

"Major General Geo. G. Meade,
"*Commanding Army of the Potomac.*

"P. S.—If you want to be at any place on the line at the hour indicated, inform me by telegraph, and I will meet you wherever you may be.
"U. S. G.

"Official:
"S. WILLIAMS, *A. A. G.*"

J.

[Cipher—received 11.40 a. m.]
By telegraph from City Point, 9.30 *a. m., dated August* 1, 1864.

"Major General Meade:

"Have you any estimate of our losses in the miserable failure of Saturday? I think there will have to be an investigation of the matter. So fair an opportunity will probably never occur again for carrying fortifications; preparations were good, orders ample, and everything, so far as I could see subsequent to the explosion of the mine, shows that almost without loss the crest beyond the mine could have been carried; this would have given us Petersburg with all its artillery, and a large part of the garrison beyond doubt. An intercepted despatch states that the enemy recaptured their line with General Bartlett and staff, seventy-five commissioned officers, and nine hundred rank and file, and recaptured five hundred of their men.

"U. S. GRANT, *Lieutenant General.*
"Official:
"S. WILLIAMS, *A. A. G.*"

Appendix B.

Order of the Major General commanding, for the movement against the enemy's position, July 30, 1864.

K.

"Orders.]   "Headquarters Army Potomac, *July* 29, 1864.

"The following instructions are issued for the guidance of all concerned:

"1. As soon as it is dark, Major General Burnside, commanding 9th corps, will withdraw his two brigades under General White, occupying the intrenchments between the Plank and Norfolk roads, and bring them to his front. Care will be taken not to interfere with the troops of the 18th corps moving into their position in rear of the 9th corps. General Burnside will form his troops for assaulting the enemy's works at daylight of the 30th, prepare his parapets and abatis for the passage of the columns, and have the pioneers equipped for work in opening passages for artillery, destroying enemy's abatis, &c., and the intrenching tools distributed for effecting lodgements, &c.

"2. Major General Warren, commanding 5th corps, will reduce the number of his troops holding the intrenchments of his front to the minimum, and concentrate all his available forces on his right, and hold them prepared to support the assault of Major General Burnside.

The preparations in respect to pioneers, intrenching tools, &c., enjoined upon the 9th corps, will also be made by the 5th corps.

"3. As soon as it is dark, Major General Ord, commanding 18th corps, will relieve his troops in the trenches by General Mott's division of the 2d corps, and form his corps in rear of the 9th corps, and be prepared to support the assault of Major General Burnside.

"4. Every preparation will be made for moving forward the field artillery of each corps.

"5. At dark, Major General Hancock, commanding 2d corps, will move from Deep Bottom, to the rear of the intrenchments now held by the 18th corps, resume the command of Mott's division, and be prepared at daylight to follow up the assaulting and supporting columns, or for such other operations as may be found necessary.

"6. Major General Sheridan, commanding cavalry corps, will proceed at dark from the vicinity of Deep Bottom to Lee's Mill, and at daylight will move with his whole corps, including Wilson's division, against the enemy's troops defending Petersburg on their right by the roads leading to that town from the southward and westward.

"7. Major Duane, acting chief engineer, will have the pontoon trains parked at convenient points in the rear, prepared to move. He will see that supplies of sand-bags, gabions, fascines, &c., are in depot near the lines, ready for use.

"He will detail engineer officers for each corps.

"8. At half past three in the morning of the 30th Major General Burnside will spring his mine, and his assaulting columns will immediately move rapidly upon the breach, seize the crest in the rear, and effect a lodgement there. He will be followed by Major General Ord, who will support him on the right, directing his movement to the crest indicated, and by Major General Warren, who will support him on the left.

"Upon the explosion of the mine, the artillery of all kinds in battery will open upon those points of the enemy's works whose fire covers the ground over which our columns must move, care being taken to avoid impeding the progress of our troops.

"Special instructions respecting the direction of fire will be issued through the chief of artillery.

"9. Corps commanders will report to the commanding general when their preparations are complete, and will advise him of every step in the progress of the operations, and of everything of importance that occurs.

"10. Promptitude, rapidity of execution, and cordial co-operation are essential to success, and the commanding general is confident that this indication of his expectations will insure the hearty efforts of the commanders and troops.

"11. Headquarters during the operations will be at the headquarters of the 9th corps.

"By command of Major General Meade.

"S. WILLIAMS, *Assistant Adjutant General.*

"Official:

"S. WILLIAMS, *A. A. G.*"

Appendix C.

Despatches from Major General Meade to Major General Burnside, commanding 9th army corps, and from Major General Burnside to Major General Meade, July 26, 29, 30, and 31, 1864; also despatches from General Meade to Captain Sanders, A. D. C., and from Captain Sanders to General Meade, July 30, 1864; also despatches from Lieutenant Colonel Comstock, A. D. C., to Lieutenant General Grant, July 30, 1864.

L.

"HEADQUARTERS NINTH ARMY CORPS, *July* 26, 1864.

"GENERAL: I have the honor to acknowledge the receipt of your notes of this morning by Captains Jay and Bache; also a telegram from the commanding general relating to the same subject.

"It is altogether probable that the enemy are cognizant of the fact that we are mining, because it has been mentioned in their newspapers, and they have been heard to work in what are supposed to be shafts in close proximity to our galleries; but the rain of night before last no doubt filled their shafts and much retarded their work. We have heard no sounds of work in them either yesterday or to-day, and nothing is heard by us in the mine but the usual sounds of work on the surface above. This morning we had some apprehensions that the left lateral gallery was in danger of caving in from the weight of the batteries above it and the shock of their firing; but all possible precautions have been taken to strengthen it, and we hope to preserve it intact. The placing of the charges in the mine will not involve the necessity of making a noise. It is therefore probable that we will escape discovery, if the mine is to be used within two or three days. It is nevertheless highly important, in my opinion, that the mine should be exploded at the earliest possible moment consistent with the general interests of the campaign. I state to you the facts as nearly as I can; and, in the absence of any knowledge as to the meditated movement of the army, I must leave you to judge the proper time to make use of the mine; but it may not be improper for me to say, that the advantages to be reaped from the work would be but small if it were exploded without any co-operative movements.

"My plan would be to explode the mine just before daylight in the morning, or about five o'clock in the afternoon; mass the two brigades of the colored division in rear of my line in column of divisions—double column closed in mass; the head of each brigade resting on the front line, and as soon as the explosion has taken place move them forward, with instructions for the divisions to take half-distance; and as soon as the leading regiments of the two brigades pass through the gap in the enemy's line, the leading regiment of the right brigade to come into line perpendicular to the enemy's line by the right companies on the right into line wheel, the left companies on the left into line,' and proceed at once down the line of the enemy's work as rapidly as possible; the leading regiment of the left brigade to execute the reverse movement to the left, moving up the enemy's line; the remainder of the two columns to move directly towards the crest in front as rapidly as possible, diverging in such a way as to enable them to deploy into columns of regiments, the right column making as nearly as may be for Cemetery hill; these columns to be followed by the other divisions of this corps as soon as they can be thrown in; this would involve the necessity of relieving these divisions by other troops before the movement, and of holding columns of other troops in readiness to take our place on the crest, in case we gain it and sweep down it. It would be advisable, in my opinion, if we succeed in gaining the crest, to throw the colored division right into the town. There is a necessity for the co-operation, at least in the way of artillery, of the troops on my right and left; of the extent of this you will necessarily be the judge. I think our chances of success in a plan of this kind are more than even. The main gallery of the mine is five hundred and twenty-two (522) feet in length; the side galleries about forty feet each. My suggestion is, that eight magazines be placed in the lateral galleries—two at each end, say a few feet apart, in branches at right angles to the side galleries; and two more in each of the side galleries, similarly placed, situated by pairs, equidistant from each other and the end of the galleries, thus:

[See diagram, page 17.]

"Tamping beginning at the termination of the main gallery for, say, one hundred feet, leaving all the air space in the side galleries. Run out some five or six fuzes and two wires, to render the ignition of the charge certain. I propose to put in each of the eight magazines from twelve to fourteen hundred pounds of powder, the magazines to be connected by a trough of powder instead of a fuze.

"I beg to enclose a copy of a statement from General Potter on the subject. I would suggest that the powder train be parked in a wood near our ammunition train, about a mile in rear of this place. Lieutenant Colonel Pierce, chief quartermaster, will furnish Captain Strang with a guide to the place.

"I beg also to request that General Benham be instructed to send us, at once, eight thousand (8,000) sand-bags, to be used for tamping and other purposes.

"I have the honor to be, general. very respectfully, your obedient servant,

"A. E. BURNSIDE, *Major General, Commanding.*

"Major General HUMPHREYS, *Chief of Staff.*

"Official:

"S. WILLIAMS, *Assistant Adjutant General.*"

M.

"HEADQUARTERS ARMY OF THE POTOMAC,
"10¼ *a. m., July* 29, 1864.

"Major General BURNSIDE, *Commanding 9th Corps:*

"I am instructed to say that the major general commanding submitted to the lieutenant general commanding the armies your proposition to form the leading columns of assault of the black troops, and that he, as well as the major general commanding, does not approve the proposition, but directs that these columns be formed of the white troops.

"A. A. HUMPHREYS, *Major General, Chief of Staff.*

"Official:

"S. WILLIAMS, *A. A. G.*"

M 1.

"HEADQUARTERS ARMY OF THE POTOMAC,
"*July* 26, 12 m., 1864.

"Major General BURNSIDE:
"I wish you would submit in writing your project for the explosion of your mine, with the amount of powder required, that the preliminary question may be definitely settled. You had better also look for some secure place in the woods, where the powder required can be brought in wagons, and kept under guard; thus saving the time it will take to unload it from the vessels and haul it to your camp. Whenever you report as above, and designate a point, I will order the powder brought up.
"GEORGE G. MEADE, *Major General.*

"Official:
"S. WILLIAMS,
"*Assistant Adjutant General.*"

M 2.

"HEADQUARTERS ARMY OF THE POTOMAC,
"*July* 26, 1864

"Major General BURNSIDE, *Commanding 9th Corps:*
"GENERAL: The major general commanding directs me to inquire whether anything has transpired connected with your mine that leads you to believe it is in danger from countermining. If it is your conviction that it is so endangered, then the commanding general authorizes you to make every preparation for springing it; but directs that you do not explode it earlier than to-morrow afternoon, Wednesday, the 27th, say at four o'clock, if not otherwise ordered. The commanding general further directs me to say that the charge of the mine should be determined by the usual rules governing such subjects. It is not intended by the commanding general to follow the explosion of the mine by an assault or other operations. If, therefore, the mine can be preserved for use at some early future day, when circumstances will admit of its being used in connexion with other operations, the commanding general desires that you take no steps for exploding it as herein prescribed.
"A. A. HUMPHREYS,
"*Major General and Chief of Staff.*

"Official:
"S. WILLIAMS,
"*Assistant Adjutant General.*"

N.

"HEADQUARTERS ARMY OF THE POTOMAC,
"*July* 29—9¾ *p. m.*, 1864.

"Major General BURNSIDE, *Commanding 9th Corps:*
"A despatch from General Ord refers to the late hour at which his troops will relieve yours in the trenches. The commanding general has informed General Ord that it is not necessary for you to wait for your troops to be relieved in the trenches by General Ord before forming them for the assault. They should be formed for the assault at the hour you deem best, without any reference to General Ord's troops, who will enter the vacated trenches as soon as they can.
"A. A. HUMPHREYS,
"*Major General and Chief of Staff.*

"Official:
"S. WILLIAMS. *A. A. G*"

O.

"HEADQUARTERS ARMY OF THE POTOMAC,
"*July* 30, 1864—3.20 a. m.

"Major General BURNSIDE:
"As it is still so dark, the commanding general says you can postpone firing the mine if you think proper.
"A. A. HUMPHREYS,
"*Major General and Chief of Staff.*

"Official:
"S. WILLIAMS, *A. A. G.*"

P.

"By Telegraph from Ninth Army Corps,
"Dated July 30, 1864—3.20 a. m.

"Major General HUMPHREYS:
"The mine will be fired at the time designated. My headquarters will be at the 14-gun battery.

"A. E. BURNSIDE, *Major General.*

"Official:

"S. WILLIAMS, *A. A. G.*"

Q.

"Headquarters Army of the Potomac,
"*July* 30, 1864—4.15 a. m.

"Major General BURNSIDE:
"Is there any difficulty in exploding the mine? It is now three-quarters of an hour later than the time fixed upon for exploding it.

"A. A. HUMPHREYS,
"*Major General and Chief of Staff.*

"Official:

"S. WILLIAMS, *A. A. G.*"

R.

"Headquarters Army of the Potomac, *July* 30, 1864.
"OPERATOR at General Burnside's field headquarters:
"Is General Burnside at his headquarters? The commanding general is anxious to learn what is the cause of delay.

"A. A. HUMPHREYS,
"*Major General and Chief of Staff.*

"Official:

"S. WILLIAMS, *A. A. G.*"

S.

"Headquarters Army of the Potomac,
"*July* 30, 1864—4.29 a. m.

"Major General BURNSIDE:
"If the mine cannot be exploded, something else must be done, and at once. The commanding general is awaiting to hear from you before determining.

"A. A. HUMPHREYS,
"*Major General and Chief of Staff.*

'Official:

"S. WILLIAMS, *A. A. G.*"

T.

"Headquarters Army of the Potomac,
"*July* 30, 1864—4.35 a. m.

"Major General BURNSIDE, *Commanding 9th Corps:*
"The commanding general directs that, if your mine has failed, you make an assault at once, opening your batteries.

"A. A. HUMPHREYS,
"*Major General and Chief of Staff.*

"Official:

"S. WILLIAMS, *A. A. G.*"

U.

"Headquarters Army of the Potomac,
"*July* 30, 1864—5.40 a. m.

"Major General BURNSIDE:
"What news from your assaulting column? Please report frequently.

"GEO. G. MEADE, *Major General.*

"Official:
"S. WILLIAMS, *Assistant Adj. General.*"

V.

"By Telegraph from Battery Morton,
"5.40 *a. m., dated July* 30, 1864.

"General MEADE:
"We have the enemy's first line and occupy the breach. I shall endeavor to push forward to the crest as rapidly as possible.

"A. E. BURNSIDE, *Major General.*

"P. S.—There is a large fire in Petersburg.

"W. W. SANDERS, *Captain and A. D. C.*

"Official:
"S. WILLIAMS, *Assistant Adj. General.*"

W.

"Headquarters Army of the Potomac,
"*July* 30, 1864—5.40 a. m.

"Major General BURNSIDE, *Commanding 9th Corps:*
"The commanding general learns that your troops are halting at the works where the mine exploded. He directs that all your troops be pushed forward to the crest at once. Call on General Ord to move forward his troops at once.

"A. A. HUMPHREYS, *Major Gen. and Chief of Staff.*

"Official:
"S. WILLIAMS, *Assistant Adj. General.*"

X.

"By Telegraph from Headquarters, 14-Gun Battery,
"*July* 30, 1864—5.50 a. m.

"Major General MEADE:
"The 18th corps has just been ordered to push forward to the crest. The loss does not appear to be heavy. Prisoners coming in.

"W. W. SANDERS, *Captain and C. M.*

"Official:
"S. WILLIAMS, *Assistant Adj. General.*"

Y.

"Headquarters Army of the Potomac,
"*July* 30, 1864—6 a. m.

"Major General BURNSIDE:
"Prisoners taken say there is no line in their rear, and that their men were falling back when ours advanced; that none of their troops have returned from the James. Our chance is now. Push your men forward at all hazards—white and black—and don't lose time in making formations, but rush for the crest.

"GEO. G. MEADE, *Major Gen., Commanding.*

"Official:
"S. WILLIAMS, *Assistant Adj. General.*"

Z.

"BY TELEGRAPH FROM HEADQUARTERS 14-GUN BATTERY,
"*July* 30, 1864—6.10 a. m.

"General MEADE:

"General Burnside says that he has given orders to all his division commanders to push everything in at once.

"W. W. SANDERS, *Captain and C. M.*

"Official:
"S. WILLIAMS,
"*Assistant Adjutant General.*"

No. 1.

"HEADQUARTERS ARMY OF THE POTOMAC,
"*July* 30—6.05 *a. m.*, 1864.

"Major General BURNSIDE, *Commanding 9th Corps:*

"The commanding general wishes to know what is going on on your left, and whether it would be an advantage for Warren's supporting force to go in at once.

"A. A. HUMPHREYS,
"*Major General and Chief of Staff.*

"Official:
"S. WILLIAMS,
"*Assistant Adjutant General.*"

No. 2.

"[Telegraph from headquarters 9th corps.]
"*Dated July* 30—6.20 *a. m.*, 1864.

"Major General MEADE:

"If General Warren's supporting force can be concentrated just now, ready to go in at the proper time, it would be well. I will designate to you when it ought to move. There is scarcely room for it now in our immediate front.

"A. E. BURNSIDE, *Major General.*

"Official:
"S. WILLIAMS,
"*Assistant Adjutant General.*"

No. 3.

"HEADQUARTERS ARMY POTOMAC,
"*July* 30—6.50 *a. m.*, 1864.

"Major General BURNSIDE:

"Warren's force has been concentrated and ready to move since 3.30 a. m. My object in inquiring was to ascertain if you could judge of the practicability of his advancing without waiting for your column. What is the delay in your column moving? Every minute is most precious, as the enemy undoubtedly are concentrating to meet you on the crest, and, if you give them time enough, you cannot expect to succeed. There is no object to be gained in occupying the enemy's line. It cannot be held under their artillery fire without much labor in turning it. The great point is to secure the crest at once and at all hazards.

"GEO. G. MEADE, *Major General.*

"Official:
"S. WILLIAMS,
"*Assistant Adjutant General.*"

No. 4.

"[By telegraph from 5th army corps.]
"JULY 30—7 *a. m.*, 1864.

"Lieutenant General GRANT:

"Several regiments of Burnside's men are lying in front of the crater, apparently, of the mine. In their rear is to be seen a line of battle of a brigade or more, under cover, and I think between the enemy's line and ours. The volley firing half ($\frac{1}{2}$) hour ago was from the enemy's works in Warren's front.

"C. B. COMSTOCK, *Lieut. Colonel.*

"Official:
"S. WILLIAMS,
"*Assistant Adjutant General.*"

No. 5.

"[Telegraph from headquarters 9th corps.]

"Received about 7.20 a. m., July 30, 1864.
"General MEADE:
"I am doing all in my power to push the troops forward, and, if possible, we will carry the crest. It is hard work, but we hope to accomplish it. I am fully alive to the importance of it.
"A. E. BURNSIDE, *Major General.*
"Official:
"S. WILLIAMS,
"*Assistant Adjutant General.*"

No. 6.

"HEADQUARTERS ARMY OF THE POTOMAC,
"7.30 a. m., July 30, 1864.
"Major General BURNSIDE:
"What do you mean by hard work to take the crest? I understand not a man has advanced beyond the enemy's line which you occupied immediately after exploding the mine. Do you mean to say your officers and men will not obey your orders to advance; if not, what is the obstacle? I wish to know the truth, and desire an immediate answer.
"GEO. G. MEADE, *Major General.*
"Official:
"S. WILLIAMS, *Assistant Adjutant General.*"

No. 7.

"HEADQUARTERS ARMY OF THE POTOMAC,
"*July* 30—8 *a. m.*, 1864.
"To Major General BURNSIDE:
"Since writing by Captain Jay, Captain Sanders has come in and reported condition of affairs. He says Griffin has advanced and been checked; this modifies my despatch. Still I should like to know the exact morale of your corps. Ord reports he cannot move till you get out of the way. Can't you let him pass out on your right, and let him try what he can do?
"GEO. G. MEADE, *Major General.*
"Official:
"S. WILLIAMS, *Assistant Adjutant General.*"

No. 8.

"HEADQUARTERS 9TH CORPS, BATTERY MORTON,
"*About* 7.35 *a. m.*, *July* 30, 1864.
"General MEADE:
"Your despatch by Captain Jay received. The main body of General Potter's division is beyond the crater. I do not mean to say that my officers and men will not obey my orders to advance; I mean to say that it is very hard to advance to the crest.
"I have never in any report said anything different from what I conceived to be the truth; were it not insubordinate, I would say that the latter remark of your note was ungentlemanly.
"Respectfully, yours,
"A. E. BURNSIDE, *Major General.*
"Official:
"S. WILLIAMS, *Assistant Adjutant General.*"

No. 9.

"[By telegraph from 5th army corps.]
"HEADQUARTERS ARMY OF THE POTOMAC,
"8 a. m., July 30, 1864.

"To Lieutenant General GRANT:

"About a brigade more of our men has moved up to the crater, and then filed off to the right along the enemy's line; they are still moving to the right.

"C. B. COMSTOCK,
"*Lieutenant Colonel and Aide-de-Camp.*

"Official:

"S. WILLIAMS, *Assistant Adjutant General.*"

No. 10.

"[By telegraph from headquarters 9th army corps.]
"8.45 a. m., July 30, 1864.

"To General MEADE:

"One gun has just been taken out of the mine, and is now being put in position. Have not heard anything from the attack made from the left of mine. One (1) set of colors just sent in, captured by the negroes.

"W. W. SANDERS, *Captain and C. M.*

"Official:

"S. WILLIAMS, *Assistant Adjutant General.*"

No. 11.

"[By telegraph from headquarters 9th army corps.]
"9 a. m., July 30, 1864.

"General MEADE:

"Many of the ninth (9th) and eighteenth (18th) corps are retiring before the enemy. I think now is the time to put in the fifth (5th) corps promptly.

"A. E. BURNSIDE, *Major General.*

"Official:

"S. WILLIAMS, *Assistant Adjutant General.*"

No. 12.

"HEADQUARTERS ARMY OF THE POTOMAC,
"*July* 30, 1864—9.30 a. m.

"Major General BURNSIDE, *Commanding 9th Corps:*

"The major general commanding has heard that the result of your attack has been a repulse, and directs that if, in your judgment, nothing further can be effected, that you withdraw to your own line, taking every precaution to get the men back safely.

"A. A. HUMPHREYS,
"*Major General and Chief of Staff.*

"General Ord will do the same.

"A. A. HUMPHREYS,
"*Major General and Chief of Staff.*

"Official:

"S. WILLIAMS, *Assistant Adjutant General.*"

No. 13.

"[By telegraph from headquarters 9th army corps.]
"9 a. m., July 30, 1864.

"To Major General MEADE:

"The attack made on right of the mine has been repulsed. A great many men are coming to the rear.

"W. W. SANDERS, *Captain and C. M.*

"Official:

"S. WILLIAMS,
"*Assistant Adjutant General.*"

No. 14.

"[By telegraph.]

"HEADQUARTERS 5TH ARMY CORPS,
"*July* 30, 1864—9.35 a. m.

"To Lieutenant General GRANT:

"I cannot see that we have advanced beyond the enemy's line in the vicinity of the mine. From here, it looks as if the enemy were holding a line between that point and the crest.

"C. B. COMSTOCK,
"*Lieutenant Colonel and Aide-de-Camp.*

"Official: "S. WILLIAMS,
"*Assistant Adjutant General.*"

No. 15.

"HEADQUARTERS ARMY OF THE POTOMAC,
"*July* 30, 9¾ a. m., 1864.

"To Major General BURNSIDE, *Commanding 9th Corps*:

"The major general commanding directs that you withdraw to your own intrenchments.

"A. A. HUMPHREYS,
"*Major General, Chief of Staff.*

Official: "S. WILLIAMS,
"*Assistant Adjutant General.*"

No. 16.

"HEADQUARTERS ARMY OF THE POTOMAC,
"*July* 30, 10 a. m., 1864.

"Major Generals BURNSIDE and ORD:

"You can exercise your discretion in withdrawing your troops now or at a later period; say to-night. It is not intended to hold the enemy's line which you now occupy any longer than is required to withdraw safely your men.

"GEO. G. MEADE, *Major General.*

"Official: "S. WILLIAMS,
"*Assistant Adjutant General.*"

No. 17.

"HEADQUARTERS ARMY OF THE POTOMAC,
"*July* 30, 1864—7.40 p. m.

"Major GENERAL BURNSIDE, *Commanding 9th Corps:*

"The major general commanding desires to know whether you still hold the crater; and if so, whether you will be able to withdraw your troops from it safely to-night, and also to bring off the wounded. The commanding general wishes to know how many wounded are probably lying there. It will be recollected that on a former occasion General Beauregard declined to enter into any arrangement for the succor of the wounded and the burial of the dead lying under both fires; hence the necessity of immediate and active efforts for their removal in the present case.

"A. A. HUMPHREYS,
"*Major General and Chief of Staff.*

"Official: "S. WILLIAMS,
"*Assistant Adjutant General.*"

No. 18.

"HEADQUARTERS ARMY OF THE POTOMAC,
"*July* 30, 1864—10.35 p. m.
"Major General BURNSIDE, *Commanding 9th Corps:*
"The major general commanding desires to know whether you have any wounded left on the field; and directs me to say that he is awaiting your reply to the despatch of 7.40 p. m.
"A. A. HUMPHREYS,
"*Major General and Chief of Staff.*
"Official:

"S. WILLIAMS,
"*Assistant Adjutant General.*"

No. 18¼.

"HEADQUARTERS ARMY OF THE POTOMAC,
"*July* 31, 1864—8.40 a. m.
"To Major General BURNSIDE, *Commanding 9th Corps:*
"The major general commanding directs me to call your attention to the fact that you have made no report to him upon the condition of affairs in your front since he left your headquarters yesterday, and that you have made no reply to the two special communications upon the subject sent you last night at 7.40 p. m., and at 10.40 p. m.
"I am also directed to inquire as to the cause of these omissions.
"A. A. HUMPHREYS,
"*Major General and Chief of Staff.*
"Official:

"S. WILLIAMS,
"*Assistant Adjutant General.*"

No. 18½.

"BY TELEGRAPH FROM HEADQUARTERS 9TH CORPS,
"*July* 31, 1864—9 a. m.
"Major General HUMPHREYS:
"Your despatch was received just as I was making out a report of our casualties. I have used every means to get something like accurate reports, but it has been difficult.
"The rumors are very numerous and exaggerated. I will send report by messenger. The order to retreat caused great confusion, and we have lost largely in prisoners.
"General Ord's men on our lines were not relieved.
"A. E. BURNSIDE, *Major General.*
"Official:

"S. WILLIAMS,
"*Assistant Adjutant General.*"

No. 18¾.

"BY TELEGRAPH FROM HEADQUARTERS 9TH CORPS,
"*July* 31, 1864—6.40 p. m.
"Major General HUMPHREYS:
"The loss in this corps in the engagement of yesterday amounts to about 4,500; the great proportion of which was made after the brigade commanders in the crater were made aware of the order to withdraw.
"A. E. BURNSIDE, *Major General.*
'Official:

"S. WILLIAMS,
"*Assistant Adjutant General.*"

No. 19.

"HEADQUARTERS ARMY OF THE POTOMAC,
"*July* 31, 1864—7.20 p. m.
"Major General BURNSIDE, *Commanding 9th Corps:*
"Your despatch relative to the loss in your corps yesterday is received.
"The commanding general requests that you will explain the meaning of the latter part of your despatch, and again reminds you that he has received no report whatever from you of what occurred after 11 a. m. yesterday.

"A. A. HUMPHREYS,
"*Major General and Chief of Staff.*

"Official:

"S WILLIAMS,
"*Assistant Adjutant General.*

No. 19¼.

"BY TELEGRAPH FROM 9TH CORPS,
"*July* 31, 1864—9.10 p. m.
"Major General HUMPHREYS, *Chief of Staff:*
"Your despatch of 7.20 p. m. received. Just before the order for withdrawal was sent in to the brigade commanders in the crater, the enemy made an attack upon our forces there and were repulsed with very severe loss to the assaulting column. The order for withdrawal, leaving the time and manner of the execution thereof to the brigade commanders on the spot, was then sent in, and while they were making arrangements to carry out the order the enemy advanced another column of attack. The officers, knowing they were not to be supported by other troops, and that a withdrawal was determined, ordered the men to retire at once to our old line. It was in this withdrawal, and consequent upon it, that our chief loss was made. In view of the want of confidence in their situation, and the certainty of no support, consequent upon the receipt of such an order, of which moral effects the general commanding cannot be ignorant, I am at a loss to know why the latter part of my despatch requires explanation.

"A. E. BURNSIDE, *Major General.*

"Official:

"S. WILLIAMS,
"*Assistant Adjutant General.*

No. 20.

"HEADQUARTERS ARMY OF THE POTOMAC,
"*July* 31, 1864—9¼ p. m.
"Major General BURNSIDE, *Commanding 9th Corps:*
"Your despatch explanatory of that in relation to the loss in your corps yesterday is received.
"The major general commanding directs me to say that the order for withdrawal did not authorize or justify its being done in the manner in which, judging from your brief report, it appears to have been executed, and that the matter shall be inquired into by a court.
"The major general commanding notices that the time and manner of withdrawal was left to the brigade commanders on the spot. He desires to know why there was not a division commander present where several brigades were engaged, and by whom the withdrawal could have been conducted.

"A. A. HUMPHREYS,
"*Major General and Chief of Staff.*

"Official:

"S. WILLIAMS,
"*Assistant Adjutant General.*"

Appendix D.

Despatches from Major General Meade to Major General Ord, commanding 18th army corps, and from Major General Ord to Major General Meade, July 29 and 30, 1864.

No. 21.

"HEADQUARTERS ARMY OF THE POTOMAC,
"*July* 29, 9¾ *p. m.*, 1864.

"Major General ORD, *Commanding* 18th *Corps:*

"Your despatch of 9.25 p. m. is received. The commanding general does not consider it necessary for General Burnside to wait for your troops to relieve his in the trenches. General Burnside can form his troops for the assault without reference to yours, and your troops can file into the trenches at any time after they are vacated. General Burnside is telegraphed to that effect.

"A. A. HUMPHREYS,
"*Major General, Chief of Staff.*

"Official copy:

"S. WILLIAMS, *Assistant Adjutant General.*"

No. 22.

"HEADQUARTERS ARMY OF THE POTOMAC,
"*July* 30, 4.50 *a. m.*, 1864.

"Major General ORD, *Commanding* 18th *Corps:*

"General Burnside is ordered, if his mine has failed, to open all his batteries and assault at once. You will consider the orders the same as if the mine had exploded and the assault made in consequence.

"A. A. HUMPHREYS,
"*Major General, Chief of Staff.*

"(Just before this was finished the mine exploded and the batteries opened. It was not sent.—A. A. H.)

"Official copy:

"S. WILLIAMS, *Assistant Adjutant General.*"

No. 23.

"HEADQUARTERS ARMY OF THE POTOMAC,
"*July* 30, 6 *a. m.*, 1864.

"Major General ORD, *Commanding* 18th *Corps:*

"The major general commanding directs that you at once move forward your corps rapidly to the crest of the hill, independently of General Burnside's troops, and make a lodgement there, reporting the result as soon as attained.

"A. A. HUMPHREYS,
"*Major General, Chief of Staff.*

"Official copy:

"S. WILLIAMS, *Assistant Adjutant General.*"

No. 23¼.

"[By telegraph from headquarters 9th army corps.]

"JULY 30, 8 *a. m.*, 1864.

"To General MEADE:

"General Turner in my front reports that the only place I can get out of the line is opposite the crater. It is already full of men who cannot develop. I shall put in my column as soon as I can. It is impossible, by reason of the topography, to charge in the manner you indicate. I must go in by head of column and develop to the right. This is reply to orders from General Meade to push for crest of hill regardless of General Burnside's troops. General Ames makes similar reports.

"E. O. C. ORD, *Major General.*

"Official copy:

"S. WILLIAMS, *Assistant Adjutant General.*"

No. 23½.

"HEADQUARTERS ARMY OF THE POTOMAC,
"*July* 30, 9¾ *a. m.*, 1864.
"Major General ORD, *Commanding* 18*th Corps :*
"The major general commanding directs that you withdraw your corps to the rear of the 9th corps, in some secure place.
"A. A. HUMPHREYS,
"*Major General, Chief of Staff.*
"Official copy:
"S. WILLIAMS, *Assistant Adjutant General.*

No. 24.

"HEADQUARTERS ARMY OF THE POTOMAC,
"*July* 30, 10 *a. m.*, 1864.
"Major Generals BURNSIDE and ORD:
"You can exercise your discretion in withdrawing your troops now or at a later period, say to-night.
"It is not intended to hold the enemy's line which you now occupy any longer than is required to withdraw safely your men.
"GEORGE G. MEADE, *Major General.*
"Official copy:
"S. WILLIAMS, *Assistant Adjutant General.*"

APPENDIX E.

Despatches from Major General Meade to Major General Warren, commanding 5th army corps, and from Major General Warren to Major General Meade, July 30, 1864.

No. 25.

"HEADQUARTERS ARMY OF THE POTOMAC,
"*July* 30, 4.40 *a. m.*, 1864.
"Major General WARREN, *Commanding* 5*th Corps :*
"General Burnside is directed, if his mine has failed, to open all his batteries and assault. Upon hearing his batteries open you will open all in your front.
"A. A. HUMPHREYS,
"*Major General and Chief of Staff.*
"Official:
"S. WILLIAMS, *Assistant Adjutant General.*

No. 26.

"HEADQUARTERS ARMY OF THE POTOMAC,
"*July* 30, 5.50 *a. m.*, 1864.
"Major General WARREN, *Commanding* 5*th Corps :*
"General Burnside is occupying the crater with some of his troops. He reports that no enemy is seen in their line. How is it in your front? Are the enemy in force there or weak?
"If there is apparently an opportunity to carry their works, take advantage of it and push forward your troops.
"A. A. HUMPHREYS,
"*Major General and Chief of Staff.*
"Official:
"S. WILLIAMS, *Assistant Adjutant General.*"

No. 27.

"[By telegraph from 5th army corps.]

"JULY 30, 6 a. m., 1864.

"To Major General HUMPHREYS:

"Your despatch just received. It is difficult to say how strong the enemy may be in my front. He has batteries along the whole of it. I will watch for the first opportunity. I can see the whole line well where I am. The enemy has been running from his first line in front of General Burnside's right for some minutes, but there seems to be a very heavy line of troops just behind it in high breastwork. There is a battery in front of General Burnside's left which fires towards the river, the same as it did on the 18th of June, and which our artillery fire has but very little effect on.

"G. K. WARREN, *Major General.*

"Official copy:

"S. WILLIAMS, *Assistant Adjutant General.*"

No. 28.

"[By telegraph from headquarters 5th army corps.]

"JULY 30, 6.15 a. m., 1864.

"To Major General HUMPHREYS:

"I have just received a report from my line on the centre and left. The enemy opened with musketry when our firing commenced, but our own fire kept it down, and also that of all their artillery except in the second line on the main ridge, from which they fire a little. Major Fitzhugh, of the artillery, is badly wounded by a musket ball in the thigh. None of the enemy have left my front, that we can see.

"G. K. WARREN, *Major General.*

"Official copy:

"S. WILLIAMS, *Assistant Adjutant General.*"

No. 29.

"[By telegraph from 5th army corps.]

"JULY 30, 6.20 a. m., 1864.

"To Major General HUMPHREYS:

"What we thought was the heavy line of the enemy behind the line occupied by General Burnside's troops proves, as the sunlight comes out and the smoke clears away, to be our own troops in the enemy's position.

"G. K. WARREN, *Major General.*

"Official copy:

"S. WILLIAMS, *Assistant Adjutant General.*"

No. 30.

"HEADQUARTERS ARMY OF THE POTOMAC, *July* 30, 6.30 a. m., 1864.

"Major General WARREN, *Commanding 5th Corps:*

"The signal officer reports that none of the enemy's troops are visible in their works near the lead works. The commanding general wishes, if it is practicable, that you make an attack in that direction. Prisoners say there are but three divisions in the works, and but one line of intrenchments, thinly filled with their troops.

"A. A. HUMPHREYS, *Major General and Chief of Staff.*"

"A despatch just going to Wilson to make a lodgement on the Weldon railroad and move up along it to the enemy's right flank.

"Official copy:

"S. WILLIAMS, *Assistant Adjutant General.*"

No. 31.

"HEADQUARTERS FIFTH ARMY CORPS, *July* 30, 6.40 *a. m.*, 1864.

"General HUMPHREYS:

"I have all my troops on my right except General Crawford's. I have sent him your despatch, with directions to do whatever he can on the left with Baxter's brigade and half of Ledlie's.

"Do you mean for me to move Ayres in that direction? The enemy have a 30-pounder battery on the main ridge in my front, behind their first line. We cannot make out what his second line is.

"Respectfully,

"G. K. WARREN, *Major General.*

"Official copy:

"S. WILLIAMS, *Assistant Adjutant General.*"

No. 32.

"HEADQUARTERS ARMY OF THE POTOMAC, *July* 30, 7 *a. m.*, 1864.

"Major General WARREN, *Commanding 5th Corps:*

"What about attacking the enemy's right flank near the lead works with that part of your force nearest to it?

"A. A. HUMPHREYS, *Major General, Chief of Staff.*"

"Official:

"S. WILLIAMS, *Assistant Adjutant General.*"

No. 33.

"HEADQUARTERS ARMY OF THE POTOMAC, *July* 30, 7½ *a. m.*, 1864.

"Major General WARREN, *Commanding 5th Corps:*

"Your despatch respecting attacking the enemy's extreme right received. The general commanding will await General Crawford's reconnoissance before determining whether you should send Ayres also in that direction.

"A. A. HUMPHREYS, *Major General, Chief of Staff.*

"Official:

"S. WILLIAMS, *Assistant Adjutant General.*"

No. 34.

"HEADQUARTERS FIFTH ARMY CORPS, *July* 30—7.50 *a. m.*

"Major General HUMPHREYS:

"I have just returned from the scene of General Burnside's operations. In my opinion, the battery of one or two guns to the left of General Burnside's should be taken before attempting to seize the crest. It seems to me it can be done, as we shall take the infantry fire quite obliquely. This done, the advance upon the main hill will not be difficult. I think it would pay you to go to General Burnside's position. You can see in a moment, and it is as easy to communicate with me as by telegraph.

"It will be some time before we can hear from Crawford.

"Respectfully,

"G. K. WARREN, *Major General.*

"Official copy:

"S. WILLIAMS, *Assistant Adjutant General.*"

No. 35.

"BY TELEGRAPH FROM HEADQUARTERS 5TH ARMY CORPS,

"*July* 30, 1864—8 *a. m.*

"Major General HUMPHREYS:

"I sent your despatch to General Crawford with directions to do what he could. He says the lead works are over a mile from the angle of my picket line. I do not think an attack upon the enemy's works at or near that point at all practicable. With the force I can spare, I can make a demonstration if it is desired; the cavalry are moving and I will have my left uncovered. He sent word he will await further orders. He is so far off that I do not think it well to wait for anything more he can do, and I renew my suggestion that you take a look at things from General Burnside's headquarters and direct me either to go in with Burnside or go around to my left with Ayres's division and I do the other thing.

"Official copy:
"G. K. WARREN, *Major General.*

"S. WILLIAMS,
"*Assistant Adjutant General.*"

No. 36.

"HEADQUARTERS ARMY OF THE POTOMAC,
"*July 30, 1864—8¾ a. m.*

"Major General WARREN, *Commanding 5th Corps:*

"Your despatch is received. The major general commanding directs that you go in with Burnside, taking the two-gun battery. The movement on the left need not be carried further than reconnoissance to see in what force the enemy is holding his right. The cavalry are ordered to move up on your left and to keep up connexion.

"A. A. HUMPHREYS,
"*Major General, Chief of Staff.*

"Official copy:

"S. WILLIAMS
"*Assistant Adjutant General.*"

No. 37.

"BY TELEGRAPH FROM HEADQUARTERS 5TH ARMY CORPS,
"*July 30, 1864—9.15 a. m.*

"Major General HUMPHREYS:

"Just before receiving your despatch to assault the battery on the left of the crater occupied by General Burnside, the enemy drove his troops out of the place and I think now hold it. I can find no one who knows for certainty or seems willing to admit, but I think I saw a rebel battle-flag in it just now and shots coming from it this way. I am therefore, if this is true, no more able to take the battery now than I was this time yesterday. All our advantages are lost. I await further instructions, and am trying to get at the condition of affairs for certainty.

"Official copy:
"G. K. WARREN, *Major General.*

"S. WILLIAMS,
"*Assistant Adjutant General.*"

No. 38.

"HEADQUARTERS ARMY OF THE POTOMAC,
"*July 30, 1864—9.25 a. m.*

"Major General WARREN:

"The attack ordered on the two-gun battery is suspended.

"GEO. G. MEADE, *Major General.*

"Official copy:

"S. WILLIAMS,
"*Assistant Adjutant General.*"

No. 38½.

"BY TELEGRAPH FROM HEADQUARTERS 5TH CORPS,
"*July 30, 1864—9.45 a. m.*

"Major General HUMPHREYS, *Chief of Staff:*

"GENERAL: I find that the flag I saw was the enemy's, and that they have reoccupied all the line we drove them from, except a little around the crater which a small force of ours still hold.

"Respectfully,
"G. K. WARREN, *Major General.*

"Official copy:

"S. WILLIAMS,
"*Assistant Adjutant General.*"

No. 39.

"HEADQUARTERS ARMY OF THE POTOMAC,
"*July* 30, 1864—9.45 a. m.
"General WARREN, *at 9th Corps Headquarters:*
"A despatch has been sent to your headquarters, rescinding order to attack; all offensive operations are suspended. You can resume your original position with your command.
"GEORGE G. MEADE.
"Official:
"S. WILLIAMS,
"*Assistant Adjutant General.*"

No. 40.

"HEADQUARTERS ARMY OF THE POTOMAC,
"*July* 30, 1864—5 p. m.
"Major Generals WARREN and BURNSIDE:
"Signal officers report the enemy returning rapidly from the north side of the James. Every preparation should be made to strengthen the line of works where any obstacles have to-day been removed. The lines should be held strongly with infantry and artillery, posted wherever practicable—available reserves held in hand ready for movement in case it becomes necessary. I anticipate offensive movements on the part of the enemy, and expect it will be by a movable column, turning our left and threatening our rear.
"GEORGE G. MEADE,
"*Major General, Commanding.*

"Major General Hancock will, to-night, resume his former position, and General Ord his also.

"Official copy:
"S. WILLIAMS, *Assistant Adjutant General.*"

APPENDIX F.

Despatches from Major General Meade to Brigadier General Mott, commanding division, 2d army corps, and to Major General Hancock, commanding 2d army corps; also despatches from Major General Hancock to Major General Meade, July 30, 1864.

No. 41.

"HEADQUARTERS ARMY OF THE POTOMAC,
"*July* 30, 1864—4.40 a. m.
"Brigadier General MOTT, *Commanding Division in intrenchments of 18th Corps, Old Headquarters of 18th Corps:*
"General Burnside is ordered, if his mine has failed, to open all the batteries on his front and assault at once.
"Upon hearing his batteries open, have all the batteries of the 18th corps opened.
"A. A. HUMPHREYS, *Major General, Chief of Staff.*
"Official:
"S. WILLIAMS, *Assistant Adjutant General.*"

No. 42.

"HEADQUARTERS ARMY OF THE POTOMAC, *July* 30, 1864—4.50 a. m.
"OPERATOR *at Headquarters 18th Corps:*
"Send the following message by orderly to General Hancock:
"Major General HANCOCK, *Commanding 2d Corps:*
"The commanding general wishes you to be about the headquarters of the 18th corps, so that he can communicate with you at any time.
"A. A. HUMPHREYS, *Major General, Chief of Staff.*
"Official:
"S. WILLIAMS, *Assistant Adjutant General.*"

No. 43.

"HEADQUARTERS ARMY OF THE POTOMAC,
"July 30, 1864—6 a m.

"Major General HANCOCK, *Commanding 2d Corps:*

"The major general commanding directs me to say that General Burnside reports the enemy's line in his front abandoned, and the prisoners taken say that there is no second line. The commanding general may call on you to move forward at any moment, and wishes you to have your troops well up to the front prepared to move. Do the enemy's lines in front of Mott's division appear to be thinly occupied, and is there any chance to push forward there?

"A. A. HUMPHREYS, *Major General, Chief of Staff.*

"Official copy:

"S. WILLIAMS, *Assistant Adjutant General.*"

No. 44.

"BY TELEGRAPH FROM HEADQUARTERS 2D ARMY CORPS,
"July 30, 1864—6 a. m.

"Major General HUMPHREYS:

"It is not possible to say about the line in front of General Mott, as both parties keep down, firing whenever a head is shown. General Ord left word for me by General Mott that there was no place to assault here, as the line was not only protected by abatis, but by wire. This was the decision of himself and his division commanders, and he requested General Mott so to inform me. I know nothing more about it. I will be prepared for your orders.

"W. S. HANCOCK, M. G.

"Official copy:

"S. WILLIAMS, *Assistant Adjutant General.*"

No. 45.

"BY TELEGRAPH FROM HEADQUARTERS 2D CORPS,
"July 30, 1864—6.20 a. m.

"Major General HUMPHREYS, *Chief of Staff:*

"I have sent out to have General Mott's line examined as far as practicable, to see how strong the enemy appear to hold their line in General Mott's front.

"W. S. HANCOCK, M. G.

"Official copy:

"S. WILLIAMS, *Assistant Adjutant General.*"

No. 45½.

"BY TELEGRAPH FROM HEADQUARTERS 2D CORPS,
"July 30, 1864—6.30 a. m.

"Major General HUMPHREYS:

"I have directed General Mott to advance a skirmish line to see whether the enemy hold a strong line in his front.

"W. S. HANCOCK, *Major General.*

"Official copy:

"S. WILLIAMS, *Assistant Adjutant General.*"

No. 45¾.

"BY TELEGRAPH FROM HEADQUARTERS 2D CORPS,
"July 30, 1864—6.50 a. m.

"General GEO. G. MEADE:

"The brigade next to General Burnside's attempted an advance of a skirmish line just now and lost the officer in command of the line and several men in getting over the parapet. The enemy's mortars are at work, but they cannot fire much artillery other than this. The other brigades have not yet been heard from. Your despatch is just received. I will continue to watch the enemy in my front.

"W. S. HANCOCK, *Major General.*

"Official copy:

"S. WILLIAMS, *Asst. Adj't General.*"

No. 46.

"HEADQUARTERS ARMY OF THE POTOMAC,
"*July* 30, 1864—7 a. m.

"Major General HANCOCK:
 The report from prisoners would indicate weakness in the enemy's line, and that a considerable portion has been vacated.
 "If Burnside and Ord gain the crest, the enemy cannot hold in your front, for they will be open to attack from front and rear. It was to take advantage of this contingency that I wanted you to have your troops in hand.
 "The orders to Mott are all right. If the enemy are in force and prepared, you will have o await developments; but if you have reason to believe their condition is such that an effort to dislodge them would be successful, I would like to have it made. Burnside now occupies their line, but has not pushed up to the crest, though he reports he is about doing so.
"GEO. G. MEADE.
 Official:
"S. WILLIAMS, *Asst. Adj't General.*"

No. 47.

"BY TELEGRAPH FROM HEADQUARTERS 2D CORPS,
"*July* 30, 1864—7 a. m.

"General HUMPHREYS, *Chief of Staff:*
 "Report from 2d brigade of General Mott's division shows that the enemy are there in some strength, having two batteries which they fire seldom, owing to the close proximity of our riflemen. The commanding officer of the brigade says he can see every man who leaves his front to their right, and none have left since daylight. He is using mortars effectively. I will report any change of troops.
"W. S. HANCOCK, *Major General.*
 "Official copy:
"S. WILLIAMS, *Asst. Adj't General.*"

No. 48.

"BY TELEGRAPH FROM HEADQUARTERS 2D ARMY CORPS,
"*July* 30, 1864—9 a. m.

"Major General HUMPHREYS:
 "General Mott's remaining brigade deceived the enemy in their front by putting their hats on rammers above the parapet, which elicited quite a spirited volley.
"W. S. HANCOCK, *Major General.*
 "Official copy:
"S. WILLIAMS, *Asst. Adj't General.*"

No. 49.

"HEADQUARTERS ARMY OF THE POTOMAC,
"*July* 30, 1864—9.25 a. m.

'Major General HANCOCK:
 "Offensive operations have been suspended. You will for the present hold in force the lines held by the 18th corps. Make your dispositions accordingly.
"GEO. G. MEADE, *Major General, Commanding.*
 "Official:
"S. WILLIAMS, *Asst. Adj't General.*"

APPENDIX G.

Miscellaneous papers.

 Despatches from Major General Humphreys to Major General Sheridan and Brigadier General Wilson, July 29, 1864.
 Despatches from Major General Humphreys, chief of staff, to Brigadier General White, temporarily commanding 4th division 9th corps, July 29, 1864.

Despatches from Major General Humphreys, chief of staff, to Colonel Wainwright, chief of artillery, 5th corps, July 30, 1864.
Despatches from signal officers, July 30, 1864.
Report of Major Duane, acting chief engineer of operations, July 30, 1864.

No. 50.

"HEADQUARTERS ARMY OF THE POTOMAC,
"*July 29, 1864*—10 p. m.
"Major General SHERIDAN, *Commanding Cavalry Corps:*
"The commanding general directs that you keep up connexion with our left, in the operations of to-morrow.
"A. A. HUMPHREYS,
"*Major General and Chief of Staff.*

"Official copy:
"S. WILLIAMS,
"*Assistant Adjutant General.*"

No. 51.

"HEADQUARTERS ARMY OF THE POTOMAC,
"*July 29, 1864*—10 a. m.
"Brigadier General WILSON, *Com'dg 3d Division Cavalry:*
"The major general commanding directs that you concentrate your division on the left, somewhere near the plank road, and hold its available force ready for prompt movement.
"The guard left with trains should be merely sufficient to protect them against any small irregular parties of the enemy. The dismounted enemy should form this guard. Please report your location as soon as established.
"Very respectfully, your obedient servant,
"A. A. HUMPHREYS,
"*Major General and Chief of Staff.*

"P. S.—The patrols and pickets on the north side of the Blackwater should be reduced to the minimum consistent with watching the main avenues of approach.
"Official copy:
"S. WILLIAMS, *Asst. Adj't General.*"

No. 52.

"HEADQUARTERS ARMY OF THE POTOMAC,
"*July 29, 1864*—2¼ p. m.
"Brigadier General WILSON,
"*Com'dg Cavalry Division, Jordan's Point:*
"The commanding general considers that not more than one regiment should remain north of the Blackwater, and that be so posted as to be brought in rapidly to-morrow morning.
"A. A. HUMPHREYS,
"*Major General and Chief of Staff.*

"Official copy:
"S. WILLIAMS, *Asst. Adj't General.*"

No. 53.

"HEADQUARTERS ARMY OF THE POTOMAC,
"*July 29, 1864*—3¼ p. m.
"Brigadier General WILSON, *Commanding 3d Division Cavalry Corps:*
"GENERAL: Major General Sheridan is ordered to move at dark to Lee's mill, and at daylight against the enemy's troops defending Petersburg on their right, by the roads leading to that town from the southward and westward.
"Your division will accompany him, and the commanding general directs that you be prepared to call in your patrols and pickets early to-morrow morning and move with the cavalry corps. You will send a staff officer to meet General Sheridan and receive his instructions.
"A. A. HUMPHREYS,
"*Major General and Chief of Staff.*

"Official copy:
"S. WILLIAMS,
"*Assistant Adjutant General.*"

No. 54.

"HEADQUARTERS ARMY OF THE POTOMAC,
"*July* 29, 1864—3 p. m.
"Brigadier General WHITE,
"*Commanding (temporary) Division,* 9*th Corps:*
"The major general commanding directs that, as soon as it is dark, you withdraw your command from the intrenchments you are now holding, and move to the position of the 9th corps, and report to your corps commander. You will call in your pickets upon moving.
"You will at once report to Major General Burnside, and receive his instructions as to the route you will take.
"Very respectfully, your obedient servant,
"A. A. HUMPHREYS,
"*Major General and Chief of Staff.*
"Official:
"S. WILLIAMS,
"*Assistant Adjutant General.*"

No. 55.

"HEADQUARTERS ARMY OF THE POTOMAC,
" *July* 30, 1864—4.34 a. m.
"Colonel WAINWRIGHT, *Chief of Artillery,* 5*th Corps:*
"General Burnside is directed, if his mine has failed, to open all the batteries on his front and assault at once. Upon hearing his batteries open, those of the 5th corps will open also.
"A. A. HUMPHREYS,
"*Major General and Chief of Staff.*
"Official:
"S. WILLIAMS,
"*Assistant Adjutant General.*"

No. 56.

"PLANK ROAD SIGNAL STATION,
"*July* 30, 1864—5 a. m.
"Major B. F. FISHER:
"There are no tents or the sign of any force on the right of the enemy's line near lead works.
"The two batteries directly in front of station, which opened heavily this morning, have ceased firing.
"A large building is burning in the city.
"I have seen no movement of the enemy's troops.
"J. B. DUFF,
"*Lieutenant, Signal Officer.*
"Official:
"S. WILLIAMS,
"*Assistant Adjutant General.*"

No. 57.

"[By telegraph from Plank Road Signal Station.]
"HEADQUARTERS ARMY OF THE POTOMAC,
"*July* 30, 1864—6.20 a. m
"Major FISHER:
"The enemy's infantry has been passing to our right for twenty minutes; first noticed them at a point due west of the station marching in rear of their line; they came out in plain view at a point northwest from station. The column was at least a strong brigade; all the camps, one-quarter mile of lead works, have been broken up; the largest visible from station has just been broken up and the troops moved to our right.
"J. B. DUFF, *Signal Officer.*
"Official:
"S. WILLIAMS,
"*Assistant Adjutant General.*"

No. 58.

"[By telegraph from 5th corps.]
"JULY 30, 1864.
"Major FISHER:
"The enemy are wholly concealed along the line in view of this station. Not one has been seen; only three guns, and those in redoubts, at Gregor House. Reply to us.
"Copy sent to General Warren.
"S. LYON, *Lieutenant.*
"Official:
"S. WILLIAMS,
"*Assistant Adjutant General.*"

No. 59.

"HEADQUARTERS ARMY OF THE POTOMAC,
"*Office of Chief Engineer, August 5,* 1864.

"SIR: In compliance with directions received from you to-day, I have the honor to make the following report of the duty performed by the engineer officers during the assault of July 30.
"In compliance with directions from the chief of staff, I detailed an officer of engineers for duty with each corps that was ordered to take part in the attack on the 30th of July.
"Major Michler, who was charged with selecting the position of the column on the right, after having reconnoitred the position, reported to General Ord, and was informed that his subordinate generals had already examined the position, were thoroughly acquainted with the ground, and required no further assistance. They had already determined to take the same position indicated by Major Michler. Two engineer officers belonging to the 18th corps accompanied the movement.
"Lieutenant Benyaurd, engineer, who has been on duty on the 9th corps front, reported to General Burnside, and remained with him during the whole affair.
"After having consulted with the commanding general of the 5th corps as to the direction his column would take, I proceeded to the batteries in front of that corps and assisted Colonel Abbott in directing their fire so as to silence that of the enemy against the assaulting column. I then repaired to the right of his line. By this time, however, the attack had been abandoned and my services were no longer required.
"Very respectfully,
"J. C. DUANE, *Major Engineers.*
"Official:
"S. WILLIAMS, *A. A. G.*"

No. 60.

CIRCULAR.]   HEADQUARTERS NINTH ARMY CORPS,
                                                                    July 29, 1864.

I. The mine will be exploded to-morrow morning at half past three by Colonel Pleasants. General Potter will issue the necessary orders to the colonel for the explosion.
II. General Ledlie will, immediately upon the explosion of the mine, move his division forward as directed by verbal orders this day, and if possible crown the crest at the point known as Cemetery hill, occupying, if possible, the cemetery.
III. General Wilcox will move his division forward as soon as possible after General Ledlie has passed through the first line of the enemy's works, bearing off to the left so as to effectually protect the left flank of General Ledlie's column, and make a lodgement, if possible, on the Jerusalem plank road, to the left of General Ledlie's division.
IV. General Potter will move his division forward to the right of General Ledlie's division as soon as it is apparent that he will not interfere with the movements of General Wilcox's division, and will, as near as possible, protect the right flank of General Ledlie from any attack on that quarter, and establish a line on the crest of a ravine which seems to run from the Cemetery hill nearly at right angles to the enemy's main line, directly in our front.
V. General Ferrero will move his division immediately after General Wilcox's until he reaches our present advance line, where he will remain until the ground in his front is entirely cleared by the other three divisions, when he will move forward over the same ground

that General Ledlie moved over, will pass through our line, and, if possible, move down and occupy the village to the right.

VI. The formations and movements of all these divisions, together with their places of rendezvous, will be as near as possible in accordance with the understanding during the personal interviews with the division commanders.

The headquarters of the corps during the movement will be at the fourteen-gun battery, in rear of the Taylor house. If further instructions are desired by the division commanders, they will please ask for them at once.

By order of Major General Burnside.

W. H. HARRIS, *Captain Ordnance, U. S. A.*

Official:

J. L. VAN BUREN, *Major and A. D. C.*

No. 61.

ORDERS.]   HEADQUARTERS ARMY OF THE POTOMAC,
July 9, 1864.

1. The operations of this army against the intrenched position of the enemy defending Petersburg will be by regular approaches on the front opposed to General Burnside's and General Warren's corps.

2. The siege works will be constructed under the direction of the acting chief engineer of the army, Major J. C. Duane, corps of engineers, upon plans prepared by him and approved by the commanding general. Those plans that relate to the employment of the artillery will be prepared jointly by the acting chief engineer and the chief of artillery of the army, Brigadier General H. J. Hunt, United States volunteers. Duplicates of the plan of siege will be furnished the commanders of the 9th and 5th corps.

3. The engineer officers and troops of the army will receive their orders from the chief engineer, who will regulate the hours at which they will go on duty.

4. The siege artillery will be served under the direction of the chief of artillery of the army, who will prescribe the hours at which artillery officers and troops go on duty.

5. A general of the trenches will be detailed daily for each of the two fronts designated where the siege operations are carried on by the commanders of the 9th and 5th corps respectively.

Guards of the trenches will in like manner be detailed daily from those corps. The strength of the guard will be determined by the commander of the corps furnishing it.

The general of the trenches is responsible for the security of the siege operations and the police and discipline of the trenches, and will dispose the guard so as to protect the working parties and repel sorties. For armed purposes, as well as for police and discipline, he commands all in the trenches.

He will report for instructions at the headquarters of his corps on the day previous to going on duty, and will confer with the officers of engineers and artillery in charge of the trenches and batteries, and visit the localities of the siege works, so as to make himself familiar with the ground, and determine upon the best disposition of the guard.

He will go on duty at 8 a. m., and, upon being relieved, will turn over to his successor all orders and instructions and information that he is possessed of pertaining to the duties specified.

The commander of the guard of the trenches will report to him for instructions at 8 a. m.

The guard of the trenches will go on duty at dark. Previous to the commencement of his tour of service, the commander will report for instructions to the general of the trenches.

The commander of the guard will report hourly to the general of the trenches what is transpiring in front, and immediately everything of importance.

The general of the trenches will make similar reports to the corps commander, who will transmit anything important to the commander of the army.

Upon being relieved, the general of the trenches will make a written report to his corps commander of the operations carried on during his tour, which will be forwarded to the commanding general of the army.

6. For the work of the trenches, details from the two corps named will be made upon the requisitions of the chiefs of engineers and artillery. These requisitions will specify the character and locality of the work to be performed.

An officer of high rank will be detailed daily to take charge of the working parties of each corps. He will be responsible for the faithful and energetic performance of duty by the working parties, and will see that they conform to the directions of the engineer and artillery officers in charge of the works.

In the event of an attack, he will command the working parties under the orders of the general of the trenches, and as soon after the commencement of his tour of duty as practicable he will report to that officer the manner in which the working parties are distributed.

He will report for instructions at the headquarters of his corps on the day before he goes on duty, and will confer with the engineer and artillery officers in charge of the trenches, and receive information from them as to the manner of performing the work, and visit the localities before dark, so as to make himself familiar with the same. He will go on duty at 8 a. m.

Upon being relieved, he will turn over to his successor all orders, instructions, and information pertaining to the duty that he may be possessed of.

Working parties will go on duty just before daylight. They will be equipped for action.

Upon being relieved, he will make a written report to his corps commander of the work executed by the working parties under his charge, which will be forwarded to the major general commanding the army.

7. Materials for the siege will be prepared by working parties detailed from the corps not in the trenches, upon requisitions of the acting chief engineer and chief of artillery.

8. The corps will relieve each other in the duties of the trenches should it be found necessary.

9. The acting chief engineer and chief of artillery will report every twelve hours to the commanding general the progress made in the operations.

The morning report will include a statement of the work proposed to be executed in the next twenty-four (24) hours following the tour of working duty then going on. These reports will be accompanied by drawings exhibiting the same.

Duplicates of these reports will be furnished to the commanders of the corps on whose front the operations are conducted.

By command of Major General Meade:
S. WILLIAMS, *Assistant Adjutant General.*

Official:
EDWARD M. NEILL, *Assistant Adjutant General.*

No. 62.

"HEADQUARTERS NINTH ARMY CORPS,
"*July* 3, 1864.

"I have delayed answering your despatch until I could get the opinion of my division commanders, and have another reconnoissance of the lines made by one of my staff. If my opinion is required as to whether now is the best time to make an assault, it being understood that if not made the siege is to continue, I should unhesitatingly say, wait until the mine is finished.

"If the question is between making the assault now and a change of plan looking to operations in other quarters, I should unhesitatingly say, assault now. If the assault be delayed until the completion of the mine, I think we should have a more than even chance of success. If the assault be made now, I think we have a fair chance of success, provided my corps can make the attack, and it is left to me to say when and how the other two corps shall come in to my support.

"I have the honor to be, general, very respectfully, your obedient servant,
"A. E. BURNSIDE,
"*Major General, Commanding 9th Army Corps.*

"Major General MEADE,
"*Commanding Army of the Potomac.*

"Official:
"S. WILLIAMS, *Assistant Adjutant General.*"

No. 63.

"HEADQUARTERS ARMY OF THE POTOMAC,
"*July* 3, 1864.

"GENERAL: Your note by Major Leydig has been received. As you are of the opinion there is a reasonable degree of probability of success from an assault on your front, I shall so report to the lieutenant general commanding, and await his instructions.

"The recent operations in your front, as you are aware, though sanctioned by me, did not originate in any orders from these headquarters. Should it, however, be determined to employ the army under my command in offensive operations on your front, I shall exercise the prerogative of my position to control and direct the same, receiving gladly at all times such suggestions as you may think proper to make. I consider these remarks necessary in consequence of certain conditions which you have thought proper to attach to your opinion, acceding to which in advance would not, in my judgment, be consistent with my position as commanding general of this army. I have accordingly directed Major Duane, chief engineer, and Brigadier General Hunt, chief of artillery, to make an examination of your lines and to confer with you as to the operations to be carried on, the running of the mine now in progress, and the posting of artillery. It is desirable as many guns as possible bearing on the point to be assaulted should be placed in position.

I agree with you in opinion that the assault should be deferred till the mine is completed, provided that can be done in a reasonably short period—say a week. Roads should be opened to the rear to facilitate the movements of the other corps sent to take part in the action, and all the preliminary arrangements possible should be made. Upon the reports of my engineer and artillery officers the necessary orders will be given.

Respectfully, yours,
GEO. G. MEADE,
Major General, Commanding.

Major General BURNSIDE,
Commanding 9th Army Corps.

Official:
S. WILLIAMS, *Assistant Adjutant General.*

No. 64.

[Confidential.]

HEADQUARTERS 9TH ARMY CORPS, *July 4,* 1864.

GENERAL: I have the honor to acknowledge the receipt of your letter of last evening, and am very sorry that I should have been so unfortunate in expressing myself in my letter. It was written in haste, just after receiving the necessary data upon which to strengthen an opinion already pretty well formed. I assure you, in all candor, that I never dreamed of implying any lack of confidence in your ability to do all that is necessary in any grand movement which may be undertaken by your army. Were you to personally direct an attack from my front I would feel the utmost confidence; and were I called upon to support an attack from the front of the 2d or 6th corps, directed by yourself, or by either of the commanders of those corps, I would do it with confidence and cheerfulness.

It is hardly necessary for me to say that I have had the utmost faith in your ability to handle troops ever since my acquaintance with you in the army of the Potomac, and certainly accord to you a much higher position in the art of war than I possess; and I at the same time entertain the greatest respect for the skill of the two gentlemen commanding the 2d and 6th army corps; so that my duty to the country, to you, and to myself, forbids that I should for a moment assume to embarrass you, or them, by an assumption of position or authority. I simply desired to ask the privilege of calling upon them for support at such times, and at such points, as I thought advisable. I would gladly accord to either of them the same support, and would be glad to have either of them lead the attack; but it would have been obviously improper for me to have suggested that any other corps than my own should make the attack in my front. What I asked, in reference to calling upon the other corps for support, is only what I have been called upon to do, and have cheerfully done myself, in regard to other corps commanders.

If a copy of my letter has been forwarded to the general-in-chief, which I take for granted has been done, that he may possess my full opinion, it may make the same impression upon him as upon yourself, and I beg that you will correct it; in fact, I beg that such impression may be, as far as possible, removed wherever it has made a lodgement. My desire is to support you, and in doing that I am serving the country.

With ordinary good fortune we can pretty safely promise to finish the mine in a week; I hope in less time.

I have the honor to be, general, very respectfully, your obedient servant,
A. E. BURNSIDE,
Major General, Commanding 9th Army Corps.

Major General MEADE,
Commanding Army of the Potomac.

Official copy:
S. WILLIAMS, *Assistant Adjutant General.*

HEADQUARTERS ARMY OF THE POTOMAC,
July 24, 1864.

MAJOR: Please give me, with as little de.ay as practicable, your views on the expediency of an assault on the enemy's works after a successful springing of General Burnside's mine, and particularly your views as to the subsequent operations after carrying the enemy's first line, and following up a lodgement on the crater of the mine.
Respectfully yours,
GEORGE G. MEADE,
Major General, Commanding.

Major J. C. DUANE,
Acting Chief Engineer, Army of Potomac.

HEADQUARTERS ARMY OF THE POTOMAC,
Office of Chief Engineer, July 24, 1864.

GENERAL: In reply to your communication of this date, I have the honor to state that the line of the enemy's works in front of General Burnside is not situated on the crest of the ridge separating us from Petersburg—that the enemy have undoubtedly occupied this ridge as a second line. Should General Burnside succeed in exploding his mine, he would probably be able to take the enemy's first line, which is about one hundred yards in advance of his approach. Beyond this I do not think he could advance until the works in front of the 5th corps are carried, as the 9th corps columns would be taken in flank by a *heavy artillery fire* from works in front of the centre of the 5th corps, and in front by fire from the works on the crest near the Cemetery hill.

I do not believe that the works in front of the 5th corps can be carried until our lines can be extended to the left so as to envelop the enemy's line.

Very respectfully, your obedient servant,
J. C. DUANE, *Major of Engineers.*

Major General MEADE,
Commanding Army of Potomac.